JOURNAL FOR THE STUDY OF THE NEW TESTAMENT SUPPLEMENT SERIES
101

JSOT Press
Sheffield

Neglected Endings

The Significance
of the Pauline Letter Closings

Jeffrey A.D. Weima

Journal for the Study of the New Testament
Supplement Series 101

Copyright © 1994 Sheffield Academic Press

Published by JSOT Press
JSOT Press is an imprint of
Sheffield Academic Press Ltd
343 Fulwood Road
Sheffield S10 3BP
England

Typeset by Sheffield Academic Press
and
Printed on acid-free paper in Great Britain
by Bookcraft
Midsomer Norton, Somerset

British Library Cataloguing in Publication Data

A catalogue record for this book is available
from the British Library

ISBN 1-85075-488-8

CONTENTS

ACKNOWLEDGMENTS

The writing of a PhD thesis is a daunting task, full of uncertainty, frustration, even fear. It is a task that one cannot complete without the spiritual, academic and emotional support of others. I wish to acknowledge, therefore, those who have been instrumental in the completion of this writing project.

First and foremost, I give thanks to God for answering my prayers and equipping me with the insight and perseverance needed to complete the task. Second, I wish to acknowledge the help of my supervisor, Dr Richard N. Longenecker, whose combination of academic ability and Christ-like disposition resulted not only in greatly improving the quality of the thesis but in setting an example of truly Christian scholarship that I can only hope to emulate in the years to come. Finally, I want to give thanks to my dear wife, Bernice. In a ten-year span of marriage that involved the birth of five children and the death of one, as well as the experience of moving fourteen times, she was and continues to be a source of constant encouragement and love. It is to her that this work is dedicated.

LIST OF TABLES

ABBREVIATIONS

Aeg	*Aegyptus*
AJP	*American Journal of Philology*
AsSeign	*Assemblées de Seigneur*
ATR	*Anglican Theological Review*
AusBR	*Australian Biblical Review*
AUSS	*Andrews University Seminary Studies*
BA	*Biblical Archaeologist*
BASOR	*Bulletin of the American Schools of Oriental Research*
Bib	*Biblica*
BibLeb	*Bibel und Leben*
BJRL	*Bulletin of the John Rylands University Library of Manchester*
BSac	*Bibliotheca Sacra*
BT	*The Bible Translator*
BZ	*Biblische Zeitschrift*
BZNW	Beihefte zur ZNW
CBQ	*Catholic Biblical Quarterly*
CTJ	*Calvin Theological Journal*
CurTM	*Currents in Theology and Mission*
EvQ	*Evangelical Quarterly*
EvT	*Evangelische Theologie*
ExpTim	*Expository Times*
GRBS	*Greek, Roman, and Byzantine Studies*
HNT	*Handbuch zum Neuen Testament*
HTR	*Harvard Theological Review*
IBS	*Irish Biblical Studies*
IDB	G.A. Buttrick (ed.), *Interpreter's Dictionary of the Bible*
IDBSup	*IDB*, Supplement Volume
IEJ	*Israel Exploration Journal*
Int	*Interpretation*
ITQ	*Irish Theological Quarterly*
JAC	*Jahrbuch für Antike und Christentum*
JAOS	*Journal of the American Oriental Society*
JBL	*Journal of Biblical Literature*
JETS	*Journal of the Evangelical Theological Society*
JJS	*Journal of Jewish Studies*
JNES	*Journal of Near Eastern Studies*

JR	*Journal of Religion*
JSNT	*Journal for the Study of the New Testament*
JSS	*Journal of Semitic Studies*
JTS	*Journal of Theological Studies*
Judaica	*Judaica: Beiträge zum Verständnis...*
KD	*Kerygma und Dogma*
Leš	*Lešonénu*
LSJ	Liddell–Scott–Jones, *Greek–English Lexicon*
MGWJ	*Monatsschrift für Geschichte und Wissenschaft des Judentums*
NIDNTT	C. Brown (ed.), *The New International Dictionary of New Testament Theology*
NovT	*Novum Testamentum*
NTS	*New Testament Studies*
RAC	*Reallexikon für Antike und Christentum*
RB	*Revue biblique*
RBén	*Revue bénédictine*
RevQ	*Revue de Qumran*
RHPR	*Revue d'histoire et de philosophie religieuses*
RSR	*Recherches de science religieuse*
RTP	*Revue de théologie et de philosophie*
RTR	*Reformed Theological Review*
ScEs	*Science et esprit*
SEÅ	*Svensk exegetisk årsbok*
ST	*Studia theologica*
TDNT	G. Kittel and G. Friedrich (eds.), *Theological Dictionary of the New Testament*
TJT	*Toronto Journal of Theology*
TLZ	*Theologische Literaturzeitung*
TRu	*Theologische Rundschau*
TSK	*Theologische Studien und Kritiken*
TynBul	*Tyndale Bulletin*
TZ	*Theologische Zeitschrift*
VTSup	*Vetus Testamentum*, Supplements
WTJ	*Westminster Theological Journal*
WW	*Word and World*
ZAW	*Zeitschrift für die alttestamentliche Wissenschaft*
ZNW	*Zeitschrift für die neutestamentliche Wissenschaft*

Chapter 1

INTRODUCTION

The examination and interpretation of any Pauline letter must take as its starting-point an analysis of the letter's epistolary structure. As Robert Funk observes: 'The first order of business [in the study of Paul's letters] is to learn to read the letter as a letter. This means above all to learn to read its structure.'[1]

Biblical scholars have been somewhat slow to recognize the importance of letter structure (epistolary analysis) for understanding Paul's writings. Of late, however, much work has been done in developing a clearer picture of the form of his correspondence. It is now widely acknowledged that the form of the Pauline letters consists of four major sections: (1) the Opening (sender, recipient, salutation); (2) the Thanksgiving; (3) the Body (transitional formulae, autobiographical statements, concluding paraenesis, apostolic parousia); and (4) the Closing (peace benediction, hortatory section, greeting, autograph, grace benediction).[2]

A great deal of scholarly attention has been given to the first three epistolary sections and, in particular, how formal variations within these

1.   R.W. Funk, 'The Form and Function of the Pauline Letter', *SBL Seminar Papers* (Missoula, MT: Scholars, 1970), p. 8.
2.   Note, however, J.L. White's insistence that the thanksgiving section ought to be viewed as part of the opening section, so that Paul's letters consist of three major units rather than four: e.g., 'Saint Paul and the Apostolic Letter Tradition', *CBQ* 45 (1983), pp. 438-39; 'Ancient Greek Letters', in *Greco-Roman Literature and the New Testament* (ed. D.E. Aune; Atlanta: Scholars, 1988), pp. 96-99. White's assertion has merit in light of the similarity between the Pauline thanksgiving and a thanks-offering phrase to a deity often found in the opening of Hellenistic letters. Nevertheless, since the Pauline thanksgiving differs in significant ways, both formally and functionally, from its counterpart in Greco-Roman letters, most scholars view the thanksgiving as a major unit within Paul's letters, distinct from the opening, body, and closing sections.

sections aid our understanding of Paul's letters. By comparison, however, the fourth section has been all but completely ignored. In order to demonstrate the need for a comprehensive, detailed study of the closing conventions in the Pauline letters and to highlight the hermeneutical value of such an inquiry, I will begin with a survey of the attention given in the past to epistolary analysis and its implications for biblical interpretation.

1. *Epistolary Analysis: A Historical Survey*

Epistolary research, particularly as it relates to biblical studies, has been, until recently, a scattered and fragmentary field of inquiry. It is necessary, therefore, to set out a brief overview of significant non-biblical studies and then move on to a survey of those works involving an epistolary analysis of the biblical text.

a. *Non-Biblical Studies*

Although some work on ancient letters was done during the last half of the nineteenth century,[1] the discipline of epistolary analysis as it pertains to letter writing in the Greco-Roman world really took off in the early twentieth century with the discovery in Egypt of thousands of papyrus documents, the majority of them being letters dating from approximately the second century BC to the second century AD.[2] These dramatic finds resulted in a flurry of studies on ancient Greco-Roman letters. Of these, the most significant formal analyses were done by Ferdinandus Ziemann[3] and Francis Exler,[4] each of whom examined epistolary conventions in the openings and closings of letters. Other studies of note

1. E.g., A. Westermann, *De epistularum scriptoribus Graecis I–VIII. Progr.* (Lipsiae: Staritz, 1851–1854); W. Roberts, *The History of Letter Writing from the Earliest Period to the Fifth Century* (London: Pickering, 1853); V. Martin, *Essai sur les lettres de St. Basil le grand* (Rennes, 1865); P. Albert, *Le genre épistolaire chez les anciens* (Paris: Hachette, 1869); R. Hercher, 'Zu dem griechischen Epistolographen', *Hermes* 4 (1870).
2. For a captivating and thorough account of the major discoveries, see E.G. Turner, *Greek Papyri. An Introduction* (Princeton: Princeton University Press, 1968), pp. 17-41.
3. F. Ziemann, *De Epistularum Graecarum Formulis Sollemnibus Quaestiones Selectae* (Berlin: Haas, 1912).
4. F.X.J. Exler, *The Form of the Ancient Greek Letter: A Study in Greek Epistolography* (Washington: Catholic University of America, 1923).

include Johannes Sykutris' summary of ancient letter theory and categorization of ancient letters by literary and functional types,[1] Bradford Welles' collection and analysis of seventy-five Hellenistic royal letters,[2] Clinton Keyes' examination of ancient Greek letters of recommendation,[3] and Henry Steen's treatment of those phrases ('clichés') of an ancient letter-body that serve to soften or intensify epistolary imperatives.[4]

The work of Heikki Koskenniemi[5] deserves special mention because it goes beyond a mere examination of form to a study of the nature or 'idea' of ancient letters in relation to their form or 'phraseology'. Koskenniemi identified three characteristic functions of a Greco-Roman letter: (1) it serves as a means of expressing a friendly relationship (φιλοφροσύνη); (2) it functions as a substitute for the author's presence (παρουσία); and (3) it continues a dialogic conversation in writing (ὁμιλία).[6]

Koskenniemi's ground-breaking insights were extended by later epistolographers, who emphasized the twofold purpose of a letter to be that of maintaining personal contact and conveying information, and who connected these purposes to the structure of an ancient letter. Thus the opening and closing parts of a letter came to be viewed as the means by which personal contact was maintained, while the body served to impart information.[7] This development is of significance for the present study, since it partially accounts for the lack of attention given to the Pauline letter closings. Many epistolographers, in fact, assume that a letter closing merely serves to maintain contact between Paul and his

1.   J. Sykutris, 'Epistolographie', in *Realencyklopädie der klassischen Altertumswissenschaft*, Supplement 5 (ed. A. Pauly, G. Wissowa, and W. Kroll [1931]), pp. 186-220.

2.   C.B. Welles, *Royal Correspondence in the Hellenistic Period* (New Haven: Yale University Press, 1934).

3.   C.W. Keyes, 'The Greek Letter of Introduction', *AJP* 56 (1935), pp. 28-44.

4.   H.A. Steen, 'Les Clichés épistolaries dans les lettres sur Papyrus Grecques', *Classica et Mediaevalia* 1, 2 (1938), pp. 119-76.

5.   H. Koskenniemi, *Studien zur Idee und Phraseologie des griechischen Briefes bis 400 n. Chr.* (Helsinki: Akateeminen Kirjakauppa, 1956).

6.   Koskenniemi, *Des griechischen Briefes*, pp. 34-47. The latter half of the book involves a detailed analysis of these three characteristics in the papyrus letters.

7.   E.g., J.L. White, 'The Structural Analysis of Philemon: A Point of Departure in the Formal Analysis of the Pauline Letter', *SBL Seminar Papers*, 1 (Missoula, MT: Scholars, 1971), pp. 11-12; 'Saint Paul and the Apostolic Letter Tradition', p. 435; 'Ancient Greek Letters,' p. 96.

readers, without being in any meaningful way related to the issues addressed in the body of the letter.

In the decades following Koskenniemi's seminal work, a number of studies of nonbiblical, ancient letters have appeared on the scene. The following are the most significant of these studies. William Doty's doctoral dissertation traced the development and form of the letter within Hellenism and early Christianity.[1] Klaus Thraede's study of the ancient Greek letter is similar in focus to Koskenniemi's monograph except that it concentrates more on the literary letter tradition in the analysis of actual letters.[2] Chan-Hie Kim examined the familiar letter of recommendation,[3] while John White focused his attention on the body of the Greek letter[4] and on the official petition.[5] White also collaborated with Keith Kensinger in an attempt to categorize Hellenistic letters according to their specific function (e.g., letters of request, information, order, or instruction).[6] Martin Stirewalt examined the form and function of the Greek 'letter-essay'.[7] Abraham Malherbe assembled an extensive collection of comments about the idea of a letter by ancient epistolary theorists.[8] Stanley Stowers proposed a catalogue of six epistolary types of Greco-Roman letters based largely on ancient epistolary theory.[9] And White's most recent monograph contains a collection of one hundred

1. W.G. Doty, 'The Epistle in Late Hellenism and Early Christianity: Developments, Influences and Literary Form' (unpublished PhD dissertation; Madison, NJ: Drew University, 1966).
2. K. Thraede, *Grundzüge griechisch-römischer Brieftopik* (Munich: Beck, 1970).
3. C.-H. Kim, *The Familiar Letter of Recommendation* (Missoula, MT: Scholars, 1972).
4. J.L. White, *The Body of the Greek Letter* (Missoula, MT: Scholars, 1972).
5. J.L. White, *The Form and Structure of the Official Petition* (Missoula, MT: Scholars, 1972).
6. J.L. White and K. Kensinger, 'Categories of Greek Papyrus Letters', in *SBL Seminar Papers* (ed. G. MacRae; Missoula, MT: Scholars, 1976), pp. 79-92.
7. M.L. Stirewalt, Jr, 'The Form and Function of the Greek Letter-Essay', in *The Romans Debate: Revised and Expanded Edition* (ed. K.P. Donfried; Peabody: Hendrickson, 1977, 1991), pp. 147-71.
8. A.J. Malherbe, 'Ancient Epistolary Theorists', *Ohio Journal of Religious Studies* 5 (1977), pp. 3-77. This essay was later published as a monograph under the same title in the SBL Sources for Biblical Study 19 (Atlanta: Scholars, 1988).
9. S.K. Stowers, *Letter Writing in Greco-Roman Antiquity* (Philadelphia: Westminster, 1986).

and seventeen documentary letters from Greco-Roman Egypt, along with a discussion of Greek letter writing.[1]

Surveying the history of epistolary analysis over the past century, it becomes apparent that—with the exception of the early works of Ziemann and Exler[2]—the closing section of an ancient letter has not been treated in any detail. Modern epistolographers, it seems, are little different than the ancient epistolary theorists who likewise paid scant attention in their discussions to closing (and opening) formulae. Still, letter writers of the ancient world were clearly aware that variations in closing formulae were significant. In the fictitious letter of Dionysius, for example, the writer comments about the greeting formula that he employs:

> I use 'Do well' in greeting you, if indeed it is better than 'Joy to you' (which it is not). But it is better than 'Have pleasure,' which Lasthenia and Speusippus use.[3]

Here the writer recognizes that the type of greeting formula used is significant in indirectly conveying information from the sender to the recipient.

b. *Biblical Studies*

The discovery of the non-literary papyrus letters from the Fayum district of Egypt quickly captured the attention of biblical scholars, who saw in them great potential for shedding light on the interpretation of the NT letters. The leading figure during this period in the application of papyrology to biblical studies was unquestionably Adolf Deissmann. It was Deissmann who popularized the study of the papyri as he repeatedly brought forth from these non-literary papyrus letters illustrations of NT language and usage, as well as of contemporary customs and legal procedures. Deissmann's high optimism as to the significance of these papyri for understanding Paul's letters is evident, for example, in the following confession:

---

1.   J.L. White, *Light from Ancient Letters* (Philadelphia: Fortress, 1986).

2.   Some general comments about the closings of ancient letters can be found in a few of the works cited above. See also two additional articles by J.L. White: 'Epistolary Formulas and Clichés in Greek Papyrus Letters', in *SBL Seminar Papers*, 2 (Missoula, MT: Scholars, 1978), pp. 289-319; 'Ancient Greek Letters', pp. 85-106.

3.   A.J. Malherbe (ed.), *The Cynic Epistles* (Missoula, MT: Scholars, 1977), p. 305. This example is also cited by Stowers, *Letter Writing*, pp. 20-21.

> These poor scraps of papyrus, or potsherds inscribed with fragments of
> letters from unknown Egyptians, have taught me to understand the true
> nature of St. Paul's Epistles and, ultimately, the course by which primitive
> Christianity developed on the literary side.[1]

But while Deissmann highlighted the significance of the newly
discovered papyri for understanding much regarding both the form and
content of Paul's letters, he simultaneously curtailed any impetus for a
detailed epistolary analysis of the apostle's letters themselves. He did this
by identifying Paul's letters completely with the non-literary Egyptian
papyri and by characterizing the apostle as one who, amidst the hectic
pace of travel, preaching, and dealing with conflicts, wrote his letters
'without any careful arrangement, unconstrainedly passing from one
thing to the other, often indeed jumping'.[2] Deissmann argued that Paul
'was not a literary man', that he 'wrote with absolute abandon', and
that his thoughts in the letters 'were dashed down under the influence
of a hundred various impressions, and were never calculated for
systematic presentation'.[3]

Deissmann's portrayal of Paul's letters as documents haphazardly
thrown together has largely controlled the thinking of the present century, with the result that it has severely impeded any formal, epistolary
analysis of the apostle's writings. Thus while the early decades of the
twentieth century witnessed a phenomenal growth of form-critical studies
on the Synoptic Gospels, the same period, paradoxically, saw almost no
research on the form of Paul's letters and on the ways in which epistolary analysis contributes to a better understanding of his writings.

An early objection to this state of affairs within biblical studies was
raised in 1931 by Martin Dibelius, who outlined the need for a form-
critical examination of the NT letters, in general, as well as a form-critical
study of the book of Acts.[4] A few other studies of Paul also addressed

---

1. A. Deissmann, *Light from the Ancient East* (trans. L.R.M. Strachan; London:
Hodder & Stoughton, 1910), p. 143.

2. A. Deissmann, *Paul: A Study in Social and Religious History* (trans.
W.E. Wilson; London: Hodder & Stoughton, 1912), p. 14.

3. Deissmann, *Light from the Ancient East*, pp. 240-41. See also his extended
discussion in *Bible Studies* (trans. A. Grieve; Edinburgh: T. & T. Clark, 1901), pp. 3-
59.

4. M. Dibelius, 'Zur Formgeschichte des Neuen Testament (ausserhalb der
Evangelien)', *TRu* 3 (1931), pp. 207-42. See also his *From Tradition to Gospel*
(trans. B.L. Wolfe; New York: Charles Scribner's Sons, 1935), pp. 238-40.

this concern. These included the works of Paul Wendland,[1] George Boobyer,[2] and Leonard Champion,[3] as well as those of Joseph B. Lightfoot and George Milligan, who paid attention to epistolary features in their commentaries on the various Pauline letters.[4] A notable exception to the general state of affairs in this period is the massive monograph of Otto Roller.[5] For although primarily concerned with establishing the authenticity of Paul's letters, Roller's investigation involved a detailed form-critical analysis of both ancient Greek letters and the letters of Paul. And particularly in connection with the concerns of this thesis, it need be observed that Roller saw the nature of the closing formulae as being influenced or determined by the character of the opening formulae.

With the exception of the few works mentioned above, however, studies on the form of the Pauline letters have remained during most of the twentieth century an endangered species. In 1939, after surveying Pauline research since the turn of the century, Paul Schubert referred to the 'apathy so noticeable in the study of the form of the Pauline letters'.[6] He contended that biblical scholars throughout history have been too influenced by one assumption about Paul:

> There is basically very little difference of bias or objective between the work of Marcion, Augustine, Luther, F.C. Baur, Pfleiderer, Wrede, Schweitzer, Karl Barth, Lohmeyer, and Loisy. They all share the basic but unwarranted assumption that Paul was essentially or primarily a theologian; that his system of theology constitutes the essential content of his letters; and that his theology was a marvel of logical consistency. A correlate of this assumption is that a study of the form of the Pauline letters is a waste of time, as far as the understanding of these letters is concerned.[7]

1. P. Wendland, 'Die urchristlichen Literaturformen', in *HNT* 1: Teil 3 (Tübingen: Mohr, 1912), pp. 191-357.
2. G.H. Boobyer, *'Thanksgiving' and the 'Glory of God' in Paul* (Leipzig: Noske, 1929).
3. L.G. Champion, *Benedictions and Doxologies in the Epistles of Paul* (Oxford: Kemp Hall, 1934).
4. J.B. Lightfoot, *Notes on the Epistles of St. Paul* (London: Macmillan, 1895); G. Milligan, *St. Paul's Epistles to the Thessalonians* (London: Macmillan, 1908).
5. O. Roller, *Das Formular der Paulinischen Briefe: Ein Beitrag zur Lehre vom antiken Briefe* (Stuttgart: Kohlhammer, 1933).
6. P. Schubert, 'The Form and Function of the Pauline Letters', *JR* 19 (1939), p. 370.
7. Schubert, 'Form and Function of the Pauline Letters', p. 374.

Schubert's challenge, however, went virtually unheeded for another thirty years or so. For as late as 1972, John White could still with justification express the following complaint:

> Unfortunately, the letter form has not been brought sufficiently into view as a whole, in either the common letter tradition or in the New Testament letters. Though roughly three-quarters of a century has elapsed since the first major papyri finds...little has been done by the way of thorough literary analysis.[1]

The call for an analysis of the form of Paul's letters, first raised by Dibelius and later by Schubert, was revived once again by Robert Funk[2] and, to a lesser degree, by Béda Rigaux.[3] This time, however, the appeal to examine the Pauline letters first of all as letters fell on more receptive ears, and a new period of interest in epistolary analysis began. This shift of interest is most clearly seen in the existence from 1970 to 1975 of the Pauline research group within the Society of Biblical Literature (SBL) that dealt with 'The Form and Function of the Pauline Letters'. In addition, from 1975 to 1979 the 'Ancient Epistolography Group' within the SBL studied not only Hellenistic and Pauline letters but Akkadian, Assyrian, Hebrew and Aramaic letters as well.[4] The plethora of articles, monographs and commentaries that have appeared in the past two decades that involve some kind of formal analysis of Paul's letters also testifies to the growing recognition among biblical scholars of the importance of epistolary analysis for interpretation.

When one examines the increasing number of form-critical studies of Paul's letters, it quickly becomes evident that scholarly attention has been mostly directed to the thanksgiving and body sections of the letters, with somewhat less attention paid to the opening sections. By comparison, however, the closing sections of Paul's letters have been

---

1.   White, *Body of the Greek Letter*, pp. 1-2. For a similar assessment, see R. Russell, 'Pauline Letter Structure in Philippians', *JETS* 25 (1982), p. 295.

2.   R.W. Funk, 'The Letter: Form and Style', in *idem, Language, Hermeneutic, and Word of God* (New York: Harper & Row, 1966), pp. 250-74. A similar challenge was issued earlier in Funk's address to the 1964 annual meeting of the American Academy of Religion, entitled 'Form Criticism, Literary Criticism, and the Phenomenology of Language: Towards the Future of New Testament Studies'.

3.   B. Rigaux, 'Form-Criticism and the Letters', in *idem, Letters of St. Paul* (trans. C. Ynoick; New York: Herder & Herder, 1968; English trans. of *Saint Paul et ses lettres* [Paris: Desclee, 1962]), pp. 115-46.

4.   For an overview of the group's activities, see J.L. White, 'The Ancient Epistolography Group in Retrospect', *Semeia* 22 (1981), pp. 1-14.

virtually ignored. Although a few scattered articles on individual formulae or epistolary conventions found within letter closings have appeared,[1] comprehensive treatments of this final section of the Pauline letter are almost non-existent.

One exception is Harry Gamble's study of the literary and textual unity of Paul's letter to the Romans.[2] Yet while Gamble provides a good beginning comparison between closing conventions in Hellenistic letters and those found in the Pauline letters, his examination of this issue is overly brief.[3] Gamble's concern is not so much with the letter closings themselves but with whether the final chapter of Romans fits the general pattern of Paul's other letter closings and so can be considered part of the original letter.

A second exception is the recent work of Franz Schnider and Werner Stenger on NT letter formulae.[4] Their treatment of closing conventions involves a more detailed analysis than Gamble's study. Nevertheless, it fails to deal with *all* the epistolary conventions found in Paul's letter closings.[5] More important, however, is the fact that Schnider and Stenger, like Gamble before them, fail to demonstrate how the Pauline letter closings relate in any significant way to the major concerns previously dealt with in the bodies of their respective letters.

The lack of attention given to the closings of Paul's letters is somewhat surprising, particularly since several scholars have pointed out the potential value of these final sections for understanding the major issues

1. E.g., G.J. Bahr, 'The Subscriptions in the Pauline Letters', *JBL* 87 (1968), pp. 27-41; R. Jewett, 'The Form and Function of the Homiletic Benediction', *ATR* 51 (1969), pp. 13-34; T.Y. Mullins, 'Greeting as a New Testament Form', *JBL* 88 (1968), pp. 418-26; *idem*, 'Benediction as a New Testament Form', *AUSS* 15 (1977), pp. 59-64.

2. H. Gamble, Jr, *The Textual History of the Letter to the Romans* (Grand Rapids: Eerdmans, 1977).

3. Gamble's study of closing conventions in ancient Hellenistic letters is dealt with in only nine pages (*Textual History*, pp. 57-65) while closing conventions in the Pauline letters take up nineteen pages (pp. 65-83). He does, however, have more detailed comments about the letter closing of Romans.

4. F. Schnider and W. Stenger, *Studien zum Neutestamentlichen Briefformular* (Leiden: Brill, 1987).

5. Most of the discussion is centred on the greetings and the closing autograph. Little or no discussion occurs regarding the final grace benediction, the peace benediction, the doxology, or other epistolary conventions belonging to the letter closing. See, 'Das Postskript', pp. 108-167.

addressed earlier in their respective letters. Almost a century ago Adolf Deissmann stated: 'More attention ought to be paid to the concluding words of the letters generally; they are of the highest importance if we are ever to understand the Apostle.'[1] Gordon Wiles, in his study of Paul's prayers, observes that the prayers for peace (usually identified as the 'peace benedictions') in the Thessalonian letters 'reflect more immediately the exhortations and warnings which have preceded it in the epistle' so that such prayers can be said 'to summarize and place the spotlight on the central message of the letter'.[2] Robert Jewett similarly comments that the closing peace benediction of 1 Thess. 5.23-24 'serves, in fact, to summarize and climax the entire epistle'.[3] And Paul-Émile Langevin concludes his study of this same closing passage by also noting that 'this benediction echoes several themes or major preoccupations of the letter. It even provides a certain synthesis.'[4]

Calvin Roetzel bemoans the fact that the Pauline letter closing has received scant attention, since there can be 'discovered in it important clues to the viewpoint of the letter as a whole'.[5] In regard to the closing of Paul's letter to the Galatians, Hans Dieter Betz states that 6.11-18 'becomes most important for the interpretation of Galatians. It contains the interpretive clues to the understanding of Paul's major concerns in the letter as a whole and should be employed as the hermeneutical key to the intentions of the Apostle'.[6] In the same vein, Richard Longenecker comments: 'So 6.11-18 must be seen as something of a prism that reflects the major thrusts of what has been said earlier in the letter, or a paradigm set at the end of the letter that gives guidance in understanding what has been said before.'[7]

Despite, however, such suggestive observations, the epistolary form

---

1. Deissmann, *Bible Studies*, p. 347.
2. G. Wiles, *Paul's Intercessory Prayers* (Cambridge: Cambridge University Press, 1974), pp. 65-66.
3. Jewett, 'Form and Function of the Homiletic Benediction', p. 24.
4. P.-É. Langevin, 'L'intervention de Dieu, selon 1 Thes 5,23-24. Déjà le salut par grâce', *ScEs* 41 (1989), p. 90 (trans. mine).
5. C.J. Roetzel, *The Letters of Paul* (Atlanta: John Knox, 1975), p. 36. See also his observations in 'I Thess. 5.12-28: A Case Study', *SBL Seminar Papers*, 2 (ed. L.C. McGaughy; Missoula, MT: Scholars, 1972), pp. 367-83.
6. H.D. Betz, *Galatians* (Philadelphia: Fortress, 1979), p. 313. Betz, however, makes this statement from the perspective of rhetorical criticism rather than epistolary analysis.
7. R.N. Longenecker, *Galatians* (Dallas: Word Books, 1990), pp. 288-89.

and function of the Pauline letter closings has remained a largely ignored subject. Biblical commentaries generally treat this material in a cursory manner, and are typically at a loss to explain how a particular closing relates to its respective letter as a whole. There are at least three reasons which may account for this scholarly neglect of the Pauline letter closing.

First, the lack of attention given to the closing sections may be partially due to a natural tendency to focus on the perceived 'weightier' sections of Paul's letters: the thanksgivings and the bodies. The closing (and opening) sections, however, are not without significance. As Ann Jervis notes: 'The opening and closing sections are where Paul (re)establishes his relationship with his readers and where the function of each of his letters is most evident.'[1] Thus, rather than being insignificant, the letter closings serve an important function in the overall argument of the letter. For Paul skillfully uses these final sections to place himself and his readers in such a relationship to one another that his purposes in the letter are furthered.

Second, the widespread disinterest in the closing sections may also be attributable to a belief that the body of a letter contains the particular topic of concern whereas the closing (and opening) are primarily conventional in nature and serve only to establish or maintain contact. Illustrative of this assumption is the following statement of John White:

> Whereas the body conveys the specific, situational occasion of the letter, the opening and closing tend to convey the ongoing and general, aspect of the correspondents' relationship. Whereas the opening and closing enhance the maintenance of contact, the 'keeping-in-touch' function of the letter writing, the body expresses the specific reason(s) for writing.[2]

Although White is speaking here only of ancient Hellenistic letters,[3] such thinking appears to control the way most scholars view the closings in Paul's letters as well. Yet as Paul Schubert insisted some time ago, the

---

1. L.A. Jervis, *The Purpose of Romans: A Comparative Letter Structure Investigation* (Sheffield: JSOT Press, 1991), p. 42. See also G. Lyons, who notes that in a speech or written discourse the opening and closing are where the speaker makes his purpose explicit (*Pauline Autobiography: Toward a New Understanding* [Atlanta: Scholars Press, 1985], pp. 26-27).

2. White, 'Ancient Epistolography Group', p. 7. See also White, *Body of the Greek Letter*, p. 63.

3. White, however, makes a similar statement about the openings and closings of Paul's letters in his 'Structural Analysis of Philemon', p. 27.

epistolary situation modifies *every* item in a letter.[1] There is, therefore, good reason to believe that epistolary closings are to be seen as being intimately related to the concerns addressed in the bodies of their respective letters.

Third, the Pauline letter closings may also have been ignored out of a belief that the diverse formulae found within these final sections have been largely borrowed from the liturgical practices of the early Christian church, and so any particular letter closing is assumed to be unrelated to the rest of the letter. An example of such a viewpoint can be seen in Leonard Champion's monograph on the benedictions and doxologies that occur primarily in the final section of Paul's letters:

> This examination of the benedictions and doxologies in the epistles of Paul has shown quite clearly then that they are not essential to the thought of the epistles and that they can be separated quite easily from their context.[2]

But even if there was a liturgical origin for many (or all) of Paul's benedictions and doxologies, this does not preclude the possibility that these stereotyped formulae have been adapted by the apostle in such a way as to make them intimately connected to the concerns addressed in their respective letters.

The purpose of this present study, then, is to rectify the imbalance that has existed in the history of epistolary analysis and to provide a comprehensive, detailed study of the closing conventions in Paul's letters. A Pauline letter closing, I hope to demonstrate, is not a mere formal abstraction, simply designed to maintain contact with the addressees (although that goal is surely part of its intended purpose). Rather, it is a carefully constructed unit, shaped and adapted in such a way as to relate it directly to the major concerns of the letter as a whole, and so it provides important clues to understanding the key issues addressed in the body of the letter. Thus the letter closing functions a lot like the thanksgiving, but in reverse. For as the thanksgiving foreshadows and points ahead to the major concerns to be addressed in the body of the letter,[3] so the closing serves to highlight and encapsulate the main points previously taken up in the body.

---

1.   Schubert, 'Form and Function of the Pauline Letters', p. 377.
2.   Champion, *Benedictions and Doxologies*, p. 34.
3.   See P. Schubert, *Form and Function of the Pauline Thanksgivings* (Berlin: Töpelmann, 1939); P.T. O'Brien, *Introductory Thanksgivings in the Letters of Paul* (Leiden: Brill, 1977).

This study, therefore, has a twofold purpose: (1) to determine the extent
to which the closing conventions in Paul's letters echo and recapitulate
the main points previously taken up in their respective bodies; and (2) to
demonstrate how the letter closings provide interpretive clues for a
richer understanding of their respective letters.

2. *Epistolary Analysis: Its Relationship to Rhetorical Criticism*

Although the past two decades have witnessed an increasing awareness
of letter structure and the important role it plays in the interpretation of
Paul's letters, epistolary analysis as a methodological approach has been
somewhat overshadowed during this same period by rhetorical criticism.
It has, in fact, become more in vogue to examine Paul's letters vis-à-vis
the categories developed by the ancient Greek and Latin rhetoricians.

A rhetorical approach to the study of NT letters is by no means new.
One can trace rhetorical readings from Augustine[1] through the Middle
Ages and the Reformation,[2] and right up to the close of the nineteenth
century.[3] But interest in rhetorical analysis of the biblical text waned
dramatically at the turn of the century. It became, in fact, virtually
non-existent in the first half of the twentieth century. Its resurrection is
commonly dated to the 1969 presidential address of James Muilenburg
to the Society of Biblical Literature.[4] In the period since then, however,
the discipline of rhetorical criticism has moved from obscurity to the
forefront of biblical studies.[5] It is appropriate, therefore, to address briefly
the relationship between epistolary analysis and rhetorical criticism.

Generally speaking, there is little contact or discussion between those

1. See Book Four of Augustine's *On Christian Doctrine* (trans.
D.W. Robertson, Jr; Indianapolis: Bobbs Merrill, 1958) which uses works by Cicero
to analyze the rhetorical style of the biblical writers, especially Paul.
2. See, for example, the works of Martin Bucer and Heinrich Bollinger, who
simply assumed that Paul should be read through the eyes of Quintilian.
3. See G.A. Kennedy, *Classical Rhetoric and Its Christian and Secular
Tradition from Ancient to Modern Times* (Chapel Hill: University of North Carolina
Press, 1980).
4. J. Muilenburg, 'Form Criticism and Beyond', *JBL* 88 (1969), pp. 1-18.
5. For a historical survey of the dramatic rise in the use of rhetorical criticism by
biblical scholars, see D.F. Watson, *Invention, Arrangement, and Style: Rhetorical
Criticism of Jude and 2 Peter* (Atlanta: Scholars, 1988), pp. 1-8; F.W. Hughes, *Early
Christian Rhetoric and 2 Thessalonians* (Sheffield: JSOT, 1989), pp. 19-30;
B.L. Mack, *Rhetoric and the New Testament* (Minneapolis: Fortress, 1990), pp. 9-24.

who belong to the 'epistolary camp' (e.g., Robert Funk, William Doty, John White, Chan-Hie Kim, Terence Mullins, Stanley Stowers) and those of the 'rhetorical camp' (e.g., George Kennedy, James Muilenburg, Burton Mack, Hans-Dieter Betz, Frank Hughes, Duane Watson). Many who engage in epistolary analysis, of course, claim also the importance of rhetorical criticism. Stanley Stowers, for example, in his study of letter writing in the ancient world speaks of the need 'to compare Christian letters to the whole range of letters and to approach them with a knowledge of ancient epistolary and rhetorical theory'.[1] Similarly, John White states: 'The use of rhetorical techniques, especially in the theological body of St. Paul's letters, indicates that a knowledge of these traditions is quite relevant to the study of early Christian letters.'[2] Other than such token comments, however, there is little attempt by epistolographers to engage seriously in rhetorical criticism or to define its relationship to epistolary analysis.

The situation in the 'rhetorical camp' is not much different. A few of those involved in rhetorical criticism attempt to justify their approach by highlighting the weaknesses of epistolary analysis. Robert Jewett, for example, in his rhetorical study of 1 Thessalonians, claims that 'the difficulty with studies of epistolary form is that the component parts are difficult to relate to each other.'[3] Similarly, Frank Hughes, in his rhetorical analysis of 2 Thessalonians, states:

> The question that rhetorical analysis of letters can answer, that epistolographic analysis alone does not appear to answer very well, is this: Just how are the structure and the function of a letter related to its content and the intention of its writer?[4]

In the main, it seems that those working with the categories of ancient rhetoric usually do not dialogue with those engaged in epistolary analysis.

It is not my intention to define in detail the relationship between epistolary analysis and rhetorical criticism. A discussion of these two methodological approaches would take us well beyond the scope of my specific concern. Rather, the purpose here is much more modest, namely, to specify how the kind of epistolary analysis proposed in this study relates to the current state of affairs within biblical studies. For in

1. Stowers, *Letter Writing in Greco-Roman Antiquity*, p. 23.
2. White, *Light from Ancient Letters*, p. 3.
3. R. Jewett, *The Thessalonian Correspondence: Pauline Rhetoric and Millenarian Piety* (Philadelphia: Fortress, 1986).
4. Hughes, *Early Christian Rhetoric*, p. 30.

choosing an epistolary analysis approach for the examination of Paul's letter closings, I recognize that I am going somewhat against the recent tide of rhetorical analyses of the apostle's letters. Nonetheless, it seems preferable to deal with Paul's letters first from the background of other letters of his day than to start with the rhetorical rules that were developed for oral discourse. This is not to suggest that epistolary analysis and rhetorical criticism are in any way at odds with each other. The two approaches, rather, are complementary, with each providing its own insights in the quest to understand more fully Paul's writings.

Indeed, if epistolary analysis and rhetorical criticism are complementary methods, then it may prove helpful—even though my concern in this work is more epistolary than rhetorical—to give some attention here— even though briefly—to how the ancient rhetoricians viewed the end part of a discourse. For in ancient rhetorical theory the function of the closing of a speech parallels in large measure the function of the closing of Paul's letters, as I will attempt to demonstrate in what follows.

The ancient rhetoricians discussed the ending of a speech under the second of the five major parts of rhetoric: arrangement.[1] The different terms used to describe a closing section were, in Greek, ἐπίλογος or ἀνακεφαλαίωσις, and, in Latin, *conclusio* or *peroratio*. Aristotle claimed that the ἐπίλογος possessed four functions: 'to dispose the hearer favourably towards oneself and unfavourably towards the adversary; to amplify and depreciate; to excite the emotions of the hearer; to recapitulate (ἀνάμνησις)'.[2] Cicero maintained that the *peroratio* consisted of three parts: the 'summing-up' (*enumeratio*), the 'exciting of indignation' against one's adversary (*indignatio*), and the 'arousal of pity and sympathy' (*conquestio*).[3] Quintilian divided the *peroratio* into two types: one that involves a repetition and recapitulation of the facts

1. The five major parts of rhetoric as set out in the classical handbooks are: (1) Invention (εὕρησις, *inventio*): the planning of a discourse and the arguments to be employed; (2) Arrangement (τάξις or φράσις, *dispositio*): the ordering of this material; (3) Style (λέξις, *elocutio*): the selection of words, figures of speech, metaphors to fit the desired style; (4) Memory (μνήμη, *memoria*): the process of memorizing the material; and (5) Delivery (ὑπόκρισις, *pronunciatio*): the choice of vocal variation and gestures.
2. Aristotle, *The 'Art' of Rhetoric* (trans. J.H. Freese; Loeb Classical Library; Cambridge, MA: Harvard University Press, 1926), 3.19.1.
3. Cicero, *De Inventione, De Optimo Genere Oratorum, and Topic* (trans. H.M. Hubbell; Loeb Classical Library; Cambridge, MA: Harvard University Press, 1949), 1.98-100, 107-109.

(*enumeratio*); the other that makes an appeal to the emotions.[1] In discussing the relative importance of each type, Quintilian notes that the majority of Athenians and philosophers 'have held that the recapitulation is the sole form of peroration'.[2] The unknown author of *Rhetorica ad Herennium* identifies three parts of the *conclusio*: the summary (*enumeratio*) that 'gathers together and recalls the points which have been made', the amplification (*amplificatio*), and the appeal to pity (*commiseratio*).[3]

The Greco-Roman rhetorical handbooks exhibit some degree of variation regarding the content and purpose of the final part of a discourse. The one element common to all of them, however, is the function of recapitulating (ἀνάμνησις) and summarizing (*enumeratio*) the main points previously raised in the dialogue. Ancient rhetoricians, in fact, proposed that good speakers do exactly what this epistolary analysis suggests that Paul did in the closings of his letters: that Paul adapted the epistolary conventions of his day in writing his letter closings, with a view to having the final sections of his letters synthesize the major arguments previously developed in the respective bodies of his letters.

3. *Summary*

The purpose of this introductory chapter has been to demonstrate both the need for and the value of a comprehensive treatment of the Pauline letter closings. The need for such an inquiry is apparent from a survey of the development of epistolary analysis. For despite impressive results from recent epistolary examinations of the openings, thanksgivings and bodies of the Pauline letters, the closings of the apostle's letters have been virtually ignored. The value of a detailed analysis of these final sections lies in the proposition that the letter closings recapitulate the major concerns of their respective letters and therefore provide important clues for understanding the main issues addressed in the bodies of each of those letters. This suggested function of the Pauline letter closings receives support from the fact that the ancient rhetorical handbooks expected the closing of a good speech to perform a similar task.

---

1.   Quintilian, *Institutio Oratoria* (trans. H.E. Butler; Loeb Classical Library; Cambridge, MA: Harvard University Press, 1920–22), 6.1.1.

2.   Quintilian, *Institutio Oratoria*, 6.1.7.

3.   *Rhetorica ad Herennium* (trans. H. Caplan; Loeb Classical Library; Cambridge, MA: Harvard University Press, 1954), 2.47.

To establish the validity of this thesis regarding the Pauline letter closings, I begin by examining the epistolary practices of the world in which the apostle lived. This will involve a detailed analysis of closing conventions in ancient Hellenistic letters (Chapter 2) and ancient Semitic (Aramaic/Hebrew) letters (Chapter 3). After examining these epistolary backgrounds and influences, attention will then be directed to the apostle's own letters (Chapter 4). A basic assumption of this study, of course, is that Paul was influenced, to varying degrees, by the letter-writing conventions of his day. So I will seek to identify the epistolary conventions or stereotyped formulae found within his letter closings and to demonstrate the high degree of sophistication with which his closings have been constructed. Having established the form and function of various closing conventions, I will then proceed to examine how Paul adapts and uses these conventions to point back to key issues addressed in the bodies of his letters, arguing that, to the discerning reader, the closings contain significant clues for interpreting Paul's letters (Chapter 5).

Chapter 2

CLOSING CONVENTIONS IN ANCIENT HELLENISTIC LETTERS

An examination of the Hellenistic epistolary tradition reveals the presence of several stereotyped formulae belonging to the closing sections of ancient letters. While some of these closing conventions occur with a high degree of frequency and exhibit a relatively fixed form, others do not. This lack of uniformity suggests that there was no single or rigidly established pattern used to close a letter. Rather, the evidence points to the existence of a number of diverse stock phrases and expressions from which a letter writer could choose, depending on his own personal style or the requirements of the epistolary situation itself.

A detailed study of closing conventions in the Greek papyrus letters has already been undertaken by Francis Exler,[1] and so much of what follows is indebted to his ground-breaking work. Yet since Exler's monograph of 1923, a large number of additional papyrus letters have been published. As the basis for my study of closing conventions in ancient Hellenistic letters, I have, therefore, carefully examined about five hundred of these subsequently published letters in order to determine whether Exler's observations continue to be true in light of this new evidence.

The vast majority of the letters I have studied belong to the 'non-literary' or 'documentary' tradition (i.e., correspondence not intended for publication). This is in keeping with the now generally accepted axiom that the documentary letter is 'the primary literary *Gattung* to which the Pauline letters belong'.[2] Still, despite being the most important, the documentary or common letter is not the only tradition on which Paul depends. So I have investigated a number of letters belonging to the 'literary' tradition as well.[3]

---

1. Exler, *Ancient Greek Letter*, pp. 69-77, 113-27.
2. So White, *Body of the Greek Letter*, p. 3.
3. References to papyrus letters given below follow the abbreviations proposed

1. *The Farewell Wish*

The epistolary convention that occurs most frequently in letter closings is the 'farewell wish'.[1] This stereotyped formula served to signal the definitive end of a letter and functions somewhat akin to the expressions 'sincerely' or 'yours truly' used to close our modern correspondence. The farewell wish is expressed in two basic forms: ἔρρωσο[2] ('Be strong!') or εὐτύχει[3] ('Prosper!').[4] Exler maintained that it was the opening formula that determined which of these two closing formulae was used.[5] The opening formula A (= letter sender) to B (= letter recipient) normally uses ἔρρωσο to mark the end of the letter, while the opening formula B from A typically uses εὐτύχει. Since the former type of opening formula occurs far more frequently than the latter, the closing formula ἔρρωσο appears far more commonly than εὐτύχει. This pattern, with only a few exceptions, is validated by the more recently published papyri, as seen, for example, in the following cases:

P. Princ. 72	Letter Opening:	Λευκάδιος Εὐπόρωῳ χαίρειν
	Letter Closing:	ἔρρωσο
P. Princ. 163	Letter Opening:	Γαῖος Ὠρίωνι τῷ φιλτάτῳ χαίρειν
	Letter Closing:	ἔρρωσο
P. Oxy. 2786	Letter Opening:	Σαραπίων Ἰούστῳ τῷ υἱῷ χαίρειν
	Letter Closing:	ἔρρωσο

by J.F. Oates, R.S. Bagnall and W.H. Willis in the second edition of their *Checklist of Editions of Greek Papyri and Ostraca* (Bulletin of the American Society of Papyrologists, Suppl. 1; Missoula, MT: Scholars, 2nd edn, 1978).

1.   See the discussion of this form in Ziemann, *De Epistularum Graecarum*, pp. 334-56; Exler, *Ancient Greek Letter*, pp. 73-77, 103-107; Koskenniemi, *Des griechischen Briefes*, pp. 151-54; Gamble, *Textual History*, pp. 58-59; J.L. White, 'Epistolary Formulas and Clichés', pp. 289-29; *idem*, 'The Greek Documentary Letter Tradition: Third Century BCE to Third Century CE', *Semeia* 22 (1981), pp. 92-95; *idem*, 'New Testament Epistolary Literature in the Framework of Ancient Epistolography', *Aufstieg und Niedergang der römischen Welt*, II, 25.2 (Berlin: de Gruyter, 1984), pp. 1733-34; and *idem*, *Light from Ancient Letters*, pp. 198-202.

2.   The perfect passive imperative of ῥώννυμι ('to be strong, vigorous').

3.   The present active imperative of εὐτυχέω ('to be lucky, well off, succeed, prosper'). By the first century AD this form was expanded to διευτυχέω.

4.   Because of its function in bringing a letter to a close, most papyrologists translate both forms simply as 'farewell'.

5.   Exler, *Ancient Greek Letter*, pp. 69-74.

P. Oxy. 2980	Letter Opening:	Θέων ᾿Αμμωνίῳ τῷ ἀδελφῷ χαίρειν
	Letter Closing:	ἔρρωσο
P. Tebt. 41	Letter Opening:	Κρονίῳ ἀρχιφυλακίτῃ Κερκεοσίρεως
		παρὰ ῾Αρμιύσιος κωμάρχου
	Letter Closing:	εὐτύχει
P. Tebt. 53	Letter Opening:	Πετεσούχῳ κωμογραμματεῖ Κερκεοσίρεως
		παρ᾿ ῎Ωρου τοῦ κοννῶτος
	Letter Closing:	εὐτύχει
P. Oxy. 2342	Letter Opening:	Γαίῳ Μινικίῳ ᾿Ιτάλῳ τῷ κυρίῳ ἡγεμόνι
		παρὰ ᾿Απίωνος τοῦ ᾿Απίνος
	Letter Closing:	διευτύχει
P. Oxy. 2713	Letter Opening:	᾿Αριστίῳ ᾿Οπτάτῳ διασημοτάτῳ ἐπάρχῳ
		τῆς Αἰγύπτου παρὰ Αὐρηλίας Διδύμης
		θυγατρὸς Διδύμου
	Letter Closing:	διευτύχει

Another way of distinguishing between the two forms of the farewell wish is according to letter type. Family, business and official letters, which all typically begin with an A to B opening formula, virtually always close with ἔρρωσο. By contrast, petitionary letters, which typically begin with the B from A opening formula, normally close with εὐτύχει. Because letters of petition are addressed to those of a higher rank, this has led some to posit that ἔρρωσο was used in letters to peers or inferiors and εὐτύχει in letters to superiors.[1] The high number of exceptions to this pattern, however, suggests that such a distinction cannot be sustained.[2]

Although the majority of ancient Hellenistic letters end with a farewell wish, this form is not so firmly established as to suggest that it was considered an essential element in the closing of every letter. A good many letters, in fact, exist in which a farewell wish is absent. This occurs especially in business letters, that is, agreements of sale, loans, receipts, contracts and tenders written in letter form. It also occurs in other types of letters as well. Fred Francis, therefore, is correct when he asserts:

> Attention must be called to the fact that many Hellenistic letters, both private (P. Tebt. 34) and public (P. Tebt. 29), both secondary (Ant. VIII, 50-54; I Macc. 10.25ff.) and primary (P. Tebt. 34), both early (P. Tebt. 29, II BC) and late (P. Oxy. 1071, V AD)—many Hellenistic letters of all types have no closing formulas whatsoever; they just stop.[3]

1. So Roller, *Das Formular*, pp. 481-82.
2. See Ziemann, *De Epistularum Graecarum*, pp. 350-56.
3. F.O. Francis, 'The Form and Function of the Opening and Closing

When a final wish, however, does occur—and this is true for the majority of ancient letters—its form is simple and fixed. In the older papyrus letters, the farewell wish is expressed in the verb itself: ἔρρωσο or εὐτύχει. But toward the end of the first century AD, the more expansive ἐρρῶσθαί σε εὔχομαι[1] ('I pray that you may be well') began to replace the simple form, and in the second and third centuries AD it became the standard closing formula. But this expansive phrase is not really an elaboration; rather, it is the result of combining the farewell wish with a closing health wish.[2]

Although the farewell wish is characteristically brief and occurs in a rather fixed form, it frequently appears, in fact, with various additions or elaborations. These tend to be of three types. The first involves a reference to the recipient, usually in the vocative case. The recipient has already been identified in the letter opening and there is no need, therefore, to mention him or her by name once again in the farewell wish. Nevertheless, a term of relationship or endearment such as ἀδελφέ ('brother'), πάτερ ('father'), κύριε ('lord'), φίλτατε ('most loved'), τιμιώτατε ('most honoured') or ἥδιστε ('sweetest') is often added.[3] For example:

BGU 417	ἔρρωσο μοι γλυκύτατε
P. Ryl. 233	ἔρρωσο κύριε
P. Oxy. 2980	ἔρρωσο ἄδελφε ἥδιστε
P. Oxy. 3063	ἔρρωσο φίλτατε
P. Ryl. 238	ἐρρῶσθαί σε εὔχομαι τιμιώτατε
P. Oxy. 1296	ἐρρῶσθαί σαι εὔχομαι πάτερ
P. Oxy. 1664	ἐρρῶσθαί σε εὔχομαι κύριέ μου χρηστὲ καὶ εὐγενέστατε
P.Princ. 68	ἐρρῶσθαί σε εὔχομαι φίλτατε
P.Princ. 69	ἐρρῶσθαί σε εὔχομαι κύριε μου ἄδελφε

Family designations such as 'brother' and 'sister' usually do not refer to actual siblings, but rather reflect a writer's friendship with the recipient. Reverential designations such as 'lord' are commonly used as a respectful way to address one's parent. The presence of such non-essential superlatives as 'most loved', 'most honoured', or 'sweetest',

---

Paragraphs of James and I John', *ZNW* 61 (1970), p. 125.

1.   The substitution of εὔχομαι by βούλομαι sometimes appears, as do also a few other minor variations.

2.   See discussion of the 'health wish' below.

3.   See Exler, *Ancient Greek Letter*, pp. 74-77.

which appear not just in family letters but also business and official letters, provides evidence of what Koskenniemi referred to as the 'philophronetic' element of a Greek letter, i.e., the development of friendly relations between two parties by means of a letter.[1] The second type of elaboration commonly found in a farewell wish is a prepositional phrase such as μετὰ τῶν σῶν πάντων ('with all of yours'), σὺν τοῖς σοῖς πᾶσι ('with you all'), or ἐν πανοικησίᾳ ('in [your] whole household'). Such prepositional phrases serve to broaden the scope of the farewell wish to include others besides the recipient of the letter. This can be seen, for example, in the following cases:

P. Giss. 24	ἔρρωσο μοι σὺν τοῖς σοῖς πᾶσι
P. Hamb. 54	ἔρρωσο μου παλλοῖς χρονοῖς μετὰ καὶ τῶν σῶν
P. Amh. 135	ἐρρῶσθαί σε εὔχομαι μετὰ τῶν τέκνων
P. Princ. 68	ἐρρῶσθαί σε εὔχομαι φίλτατε πανοικεί
P. Oxy. 2274	ἐρρῶσθαί σαι εὔχομαι σὺν πάντοις

A third way of expanding a farewell wish is by means of an adverbial phrase such as διὰ ὅλου βίου ('throughout [your] whole life'), εἰς τὸν ἀεὶ χρόνον ('for all time'), εἰς μακροὺς αἰῶνας ('for many years'), or, most commonly, πολλοῖς χρόνοις ('many times'). These adverbial phrases function to enlarge the temporal scope of the wish and so intensify its expression of good will. The following provide some typical examples:

P. Oxy. 2275	ἔρρωσό μοι κύριε πολλοῖς χρόνοις εὖ πρατύτοντα διὰ βίου
P. Fay. 117	ἐρρῶσθαί σαι εὔχομαι εἰς τὸν ἀεὶ χρόνον
PSI 286	ἐρρῶσθαί σε εὔχομαι εὐκόπουντα διὰ ὅλου βίου
P. Oxy. 2982	ἐρρῶσθαί σε εὔχομαι εἰς μακροὺς αἰῶνας
P. Oxy. 3065	ἐρρῶσθαι ὑμᾶς εὔχομαι πολλοῖς χρόνοις

All three of these types of elaborations begin to appear about the second century BC. They increase greatly in frequency, however, in subsequent years, so that by Paul's day they have become a common feature of the farewell wish. The fact that these additions to the farewell wish are more characteristic of the Roman than the Ptolemaic period suggests the influence of Latin letter writing in this area on Greek epistolary style.[2]

---

1.   Koskenniemi, *Des griechischen Briefes*, pp. 35-37.
2.   See White, 'Epistolary Formulas and Clichés', p. 291; *Light from Ancient Letters*, p. 200.

In keeping with its function of bringing a letter to a definitive close, the farewell wish normally occupies the final position in a letter. Nothing usually follows it, except the date—if one is given. Ancient letter writers, however, did not slavishly follow the common pattern, for there are a number of examples of secondary greetings or postscriptive remarks given after the farewell wish.[1] In these instances the farewell wish is sometimes repeated,[2] though such repetition can occur even without any intervening material.[3] The farewell wish also appears with great frequency in a second hand, being written, presumably, by the sender of the letter as opposed to the secretary or amanuensis who wrote down the material on behalf of the author.[4]

A connection between the closing section of a letter and its body section may be evident in letters of rebuke. In P. Tebt. 758, for example, a minor official is severely reprimanded for overstepping the limits of his own authority as well as his drunkenness. The omission of a farewell wish in the closing of this letter may well be due to the sharp rebuke expressed in the body of the letter. Similarly, in P. Oxy. 3085, Hermias censures his friend Sarapion for grossly overcharging him for a pig and threatens him with further action if he fails to pay back the overcharged amount. The fact that Hermias closes the letter with the brief farewell wish ἔρρωσο instead of the more expansive phrase ἐρρῶσθαί σε εὔχομαι so common of his day (third century AD), and also omits any kind of positive elaborating phrase usually found with this formula, suggests that the closing has been deliberately written in such a way as to match the threatening tone of the body of the letter.

Another example of the concern among ancient writers to construct a letter closing appropriate to both the contents and tone of the letter

1. See, e.g., BGU 249, 601, 665, 824, 884, 1079; P. Bad. 35; P. Cair.Zen. 59618, 59626; P. Fay 110, 112, 115, 119, 123; P. Hib. 201, 202, 235, 265; P. Lond. 897; P. Lips. 106; P. Mich. 201, 212, 216, 218; P. Mert. 12, 63, 81, 82, 84; P. Oslo 47, 161; P. Oxy. 3199; P. Princ. 69; P. Ryl. 231, 558, 604, 692; P. Tebt. 58; P. Wash. 30; P. Wisc. 74.
2. See, e.g., BGU 249, 665, 815, 1875; P. Lond. 413, 897; P. Oxy. 298; P. Fay. 115, 119; Ignatius, *Smyrn.* 13.2; *Pol.* 8.3; Cicero, *ad Fam.* 14.3, 16.4,9,15.
3. See, e.g., P. Brem. 5, 9, 21, 22, 50, 54; P. Giess. 16; P. Oxy. 931; P. Princ. 67.
4. See, e.g., BGU 37, 665, 844; P. Cair.Zen 59618, 59626; P. Mich. 523, 524, 527, 530; P. Mert. 28; P. Oxy. 2985, 3086, 3123, 3124, 3129, 3182, 3253, 3313, 3314; P. Ryl. 577, 603, 604, 607, 675, 690. The phenomenon of closing a letter by means of writing in one's own hand will be dealt with more fully below under the heading of 'autograph'.

body can be seen in a letter of consolation. In P. Oxy. 115, a woman by the name of Eirene writes to her friends who have recently lost a son. Eirene expresses her sympathy to the grieving parents and shares with them words of consolation. The significant aspect of this letter, as far as this thesis is concerned, is that both the letter opening and the letter closing have been adapted to reflect better the contents and tone of the letter body. The customary opening formula χαίρειν ('Greetings') has been replaced by εὐψυχεῖν ('Be of good courage')—an expression commonly found among tomb inscriptions.[1] Similarly, the customary closing formula ἔρρωσθε ('Farewell') has been replaced by εὖ πράττετε ('May you fare well'). That these two changes are not fortuitous but deliberate in light of the nature of the letter is confirmed by the fact that Eirene, in another letter to the same couple in which financial matters are being discussed, uses the customary formulae (P. Oxy. 116).

2. *The Health Wish*

A second epistolary convention often found in the closings of ancient Hellenistic letters is a 'health wish'.[2] This formula primarily expresses concern about the welfare of the letter recipient with an assurance of the letter writer's own well-being often included as well. Exler treated the health wish, along with secondary greetings, as an epistolary convention belonging to the body of a Hellenistic letter.[3] Yet the fact that a health wish either directly follows an initial formula of address or occurs immediately prior to a farewell wish suggests that it more properly belongs to the opening and closing of a letter than its body. Such a possibility is confirmed by at least two facts. First, health wishes and greetings serve to maintain relations between a letter sender and a letter recipient—a function that belongs primarily to the opening and closing sections of letters rather than to their bodies. Second, the not infrequent presence of a health wish and greetings *after* a farewell wish[4] suggests

1.   See LSJ, s.v. εὐψυχέω, II; BAGD, s.v. εὐψυχέω.
2.   See the discussion of this form in Ziemann, *De Epistularum Graecarum*, pp. 302-325; Exler, *Ancient Greek Letter*, pp. 107-111; Koskenniemi, *Des griech-ichen Briefes*, pp. 130-139; Roller, *Das Formular*, pp. 62-65; Gamble, *Textual History*, pp. 60-61; White, 'Epistolary Formulas and Clichés', pp. 295-99; *idem*, 'Greek Documentary Letter Tradition', pp. 94-95; *idem*, 'New Testament Epistolary Literature', pp. 1734-35; *idem*, *Light from Ancient Letters*, pp. 200-202.
3.   Exler, *Ancient Greek Letter*, pp. 101-113.
4.   For examples, see the letters cited above p. 33 n. 1.

that these two epistolary conventions do, in fact, belong to the closings of letters and not to their bodies as Exler maintained.

When one first looks at papyrus letters, it appears difficult to discern a definitive pattern in a health wish. For not only does a health wish possess a bewildering array of variations in form, it also occurs in different locations: in the opening section, in the closing section, and frequently in both. Closer examination of the Greek letters, however, reveals a basic form for a health wish which seems to have undergone distinctive stages of development. Phrases characteristic of different historical periods can, in fact, be discerned in the Greek papyrus letters. In this regard, the health wish in ancient Greek letters differs from its counterpart in ancient Latin letters, the *formula valetudinis*, whose form remained relatively constant.[1]

Although a Greek epistolary health wish exhibits a great deal of variety, it still possesses a relatively fixed basic form, depending on whether it is located at the opening or the closing of a letter. The root form of the health wish in a letter opening is taken by Exler to be εἰ ἔρρωσαι, εὖ ἂν ἔχοι· ἐρρώμεθα (ὑγιαίνομεν) καὶ ἡμεῖς (αὐτοί) ('If you are well, it would be good. We too are well').[2] Koskenniemi suggests an original form that differs only slightly: εἰ ἔρρωσαι (ὑγίαινες), εὖ ἂν ἔχοι· καὶ αὐτὸς δ'ὑγίαινον ('If you are well, it would be good. I myself am well too').[3] This formula evidently served as a base form by which a writer could express concern for the letter recipient's health, and which could then be adapted and expanded according to the letter writer's own personal taste. Some of the most common variations include the substitution of καλῶς for εὖ, ἐρρώμεθα for ὑγιαίνομεν, αὐτοί for ἡμεῖς, as well as the addition of πρὸ μὲν πάντων or πρὸ τῶν ὅλων, τὰ λοιπά or τἆλλα, βούλομαι or θέλω, κατὰ λόγον, κατὰ νοῦν or κατὰ γνώμην. Because the health wish was an established epistolary convention, it frequently was given in a shortened or elliptical form. P. Paris 43, for example, has the abbreviated form: εἰ ἔρρωσθαι, ἔρρωμαι δὲ καὐτοί ('If you are well, I myself am well too').[4]

A survey of ancient papyrus letters reveals the following development of the Greek health wish as it occurs in letter *openings*. From the third century BC to the middle of the second century BC, the opening health

1. I.e., *Si vales, bene est; ego valeo* ('If you are well, it is good; I am well').
2. Exler, *Ancient Greek Letter*, p. 106.
3. Koskenniemi, *Des griechischen Briefes*, p. 131.
4. For further examples, see Exler, *Ancient Greek Letter*, pp. 105-106.

wish was expressed as a separate formula. It was given in the basic form indicated above and followed immediately after the opening greeting. Some examples of these independent, opening health wishes include the following:[1]

PSI 331   εἰ ἔρρωσαι εὖ ἂν ἔχοι· ἐρρώμεθα δὲ καὶ ἡμεῖς
('If you are well, it would be good. We also are well')

PSI 364   εἰ ἔρρωσαι καλῶς ἂν ἔχοι· ὑγιαίνομει δὲ καὶ αὐτοί
('If you are well, it would be good. We ourselves are also well')

UPZ 64   εἰ ἐρρωμένως σοι καὶ τἆλλα κατὰ λόγον ἐστίν, τὸ δέον ἂν εἴη· καὐτοὶ δὲ ὑγιαίνομεν
('If you are well and everything else is agreeable, it is as it should be. We also are well')

UPZ 68   εἰ ἔρρωσαι, ἔρρωμαι δὲ καὐτός
('If you are well, I myself am also well')

PCairZen   εἰ αὐτός τε ὑγιαίνεις καὶ τὰ λοιπά σοι κατὰ λόγον γέγονεν, ἐρρώμεθα δὲ καὶ αὐτός
('If you yourself are well and if all your other affairs have been as you want, I myself am also well').

By the mid-second century BC and up to the early second century AD, the health wish began to be combined with the opening greeting. This resulted in the rather fixed formula, χαίρειν καὶ ἐρρῶσθαι or χαίρειν καὶ ὑγιαίνειν ('Greeting and good health'), commonly given with the qualifying phrase διὰ παντός ('continual,' 'always') or the adverb πλεῖστα ('many'):[2]

P. Tebt. 12   χαίρειν καὶ ἐρρῶσθαι
P. Oxy. 2979   χαίρειν καὶ ὑγιαίνειν
BGU 1204   χαίρειν καὶ ὑγιαίνειν διὰ παντός
P. Mert. 62   πλεῖστα χαίρειν καὶ διὰ παντός

In the latter part of the second century AD and the third century AD, the health wish once again appeared as a separate formula. Its form, however, differed slightly from that followed in an earlier period. Now the health wish was almost universally expressed in the formula πρὸ μὲν πάντων εὔχομαί σε ὑγιαίνειν ('Above all, I pray that you are well'). An alternate or additional way of expressing concern for the addressee's health during this period was by making obeisance to the god(s) on the recipient's behalf: e.g., ὑπὲρ σου τὸ προσκύνημα ποιῶ παρὰ τοῖς

1.   For further examples, see Exler, *Ancient Greek Letter*, pp. 103-105.
2.   See also e.g., BGU 597, 1078, 1206, 1207, 1208, 1209; P. Fay. 117; P. Oxy. 293, 294, 746, 1061, 1480, 1672; P. Tebt. 409.

ἐνθάδε θεοῖς ('For you I make supplication before the gods of this place'). The following opening health wishes are typical of this period:[1]

P. Mich. 481   πρὸ μὲν πάντων εὔχομαί σε ὑγιαίνειν μετὰ τῶν σῶν πάντων
('Above all, I pray that you are well together with your family')

P. Lond. 479   πρὸ μὲν πάντων εὔχομαί σε ὑγιαίνειν πανοικησίᾳ
('Above all, I pray that you with your whole household are well')

P. Oxy. 3065   πρὸ μὲν πάντων εὔχομαι τῷ θεῷ περὶ τῆς σωτηρίας ὑμῶν καὶ τοῦ ἀδελφοῦ μου Στεφάνου
('Above all, I pray to the god for your health and for my brother Stephen')

P. Ryl. 244   πρὸ μὲν πάντων εὔχομαι θεοῖς πᾶσιν ὅπως ὑγιαίνοντας ὑμᾶς ἀπολάβω
('Above all, I pray to all the gods that I may receive you back in good health')

BGU 38   πρὸ παντὸς εὔχομαι ὑγιαίνειν· τὸ προσκύνημα σου ποιῶ παρὰ πᾶσι τοῖς θεοῖς
('Above all, I pray that you may be well. I make your supplication before all the gods')

P. Oxy. 1670   πρὸ μὲν πάντων εὔχομαί σαι ὁλοκληρεῖν καὶ τὸ προσκύνημά σου ποιῶ καθ' ἑκάστην ἡμαίραν παρὰ τῷ κυρίῳ θεῷ Σαράπιδι
('Above all, I pray that you may be well and I make your supplication each day to the lord god Sarapis')

The health wish in Greek letter *closings* also underwent certain discernable stages of development. In the third and second century BC, it occurred in letter closings less frequently than in letter openings. This may be due to the fact that the farewell wish during this period, ἔρρωσο or εὔτυχει, retained its literal meaning ('Be strong!'; 'Prosper!'), with some writers therefore considering it redundant to close a letter with an additional health wish. When a health wish does occur, however, it usually comes just before the farewell wish and has the basic form: ἐπιμέλου σεαυτοῦ ἵν' ὑγιαίνῃς ('Take care of yourself in order that you may be healthy').[2]

The Greek closing health wish, therefore, shares with its counterpart, the opening health wish, concern for the recipient's well-being. It differs, however, in that it makes no reference to the letter writer's own health. Another difference is that the basic form of the Greek closing health wish exhibits much less variety than its counterpart in the opening of the letter.

1. For further examples, see Exler, *Ancient Greek Letter*, pp. 107-109.
2. Exler, *Ancient Greek Letter*, pp. 113-114.

Nevertheless, it does allow some variation, either by way of substitution (ὅπως for ἵνα, σώματος for σεαυτοῦ, the participle ἐπιμελόμενος for the imperative ἐπιμέλου) or by way of addition (τὰ δ'ἄλλα, πρὸ πάντων, μάλιστα). Generally speaking, the use of σώματα belongs to letters of the earlier Ptolemaic period, with the second person reflexive pronoun σεαυτοῦ being more popular in the later Ptolemaic and early Roman periods. Similarly, the participle ἐπιμελόμενος (which is dependent on another verb that usually expresses 'favor'[1]) occurs in letters of the earlier Ptolemaic period, with the imperatival form ἐπιμέλου belonging to the later Ptolemaic and early Roman periods. A further item occasionally added to a Greek closing health wish from the beginning of the first century AD onward is the expression τὰ ἀβάσκοντα—a wish that the 'evil eye' may not come upon nor harm the letter recipient.[2]

The following examples serve to illustrate the variations that commonly occur in the Greek closing health wish:

P. Mert. 62	ἐπιμέλου σεαυτοῦ ἵν' ὑγιαίνῃς
P. Petr. 2	ἐπιμέλου δὲ καὶ σεαυτοῦ ὅπως ὑγιαίνῃς
P. Oslo 47	τὰ δ'ἄλλα ἐπιμέλου δὲ σεαυτοῦ ἵν' ὑγιαίνῃς
P. Oxy. 294	πρὸ μὲν πάντων σεαυτοῦ ἐπιμέλου ἵν' ὑγιαίνῃς
P. Lond. 42	χαίρει δὲ καὶ τοῦ σώματος ἐπιμελόμενος ἵν' ὑγιαίνῃς
P. Yale 42	εὐχαρίστησις οὖν μοι ἐπιμελόμενος τοῦ σώματος σοῦ ἵν' ὑγιαίνῃς

By the end of the first century AD and the beginning of the second, the basic form of a Greek closing health wish disappears. Its absence is apparently due to the assimilation of the health wish to the farewell wish, thereby producing the form ἐρρῶσθαί σε εὔχομαι ('I pray that you may be well'). Although the farewell wish, which had been expanded from its original ἔρρωσο to ἐρρῶσθαί σε εὔχομαι, functioned as the definitive close to a letter, its literal meaning was almost identical to that

---

1.   The main verbs used to express 'favor' as part of the closing health wish are εὐχαρίστησις, χαρίζοισθε, and χαίρει: e.g., P. Yale 41 (229 BC): εὐχαρίστησις οὖν μοι ἐπιμελόμενος τοῦ σώματος σου ἵν' ὑγιαίνῃς ('Therefore, you would favor me by taking care of your body in order that you may be healthy'). For other examples, see BGU 1208; P. Grenf. II 36; P. Lond. 42; P. Tebt. 12; P. Yale 40; UPZ 64.

2.   See, e.g., BGU 811; P. Giss 29; P. Oxy. 292, 528, 930, 1666, 2981, 3312, 3313; P. Princ. 70; Sel.Pap. 133. This stereotyped phrase is frequently located in the middle of a secondary greeting rather than as part of the health wish. See below, p. 45.

of the health wish, thereby rendering this latter epistolary convention superfluous. Thus from some time early in the second century AD on, the formula used to close the vast majority of Greek letters was ἐρρῶσθαί σε εὔχομαι—a formula that both expressed a wish for health and took on the function of bidding good-bye.

3. *The Greeting*

A third epistolary convention commonly found in the closings of ancient Hellenistic letters is the 'greeting'.[1] It would be more precise to speak of this closing greeting as a 'secondary' greeting, since it is to be distinguished from the primary greeting (χαίρειν) given in the letter openings. The main function of both the opening and closing greetings was to establish and maintain relationships. As such, they possess little intellectual content but are more emotionally orientated. The greeting was, in fact, one of the key means of expressing 'philophronesis'—i.e., the friendly relationship that existed between the sender of the letter and its recipient.

Unlike epistolary farewell wishes and health wishes, the Greek closing greeting did not undergo any real development in form. Closing greetings are rarely found prior to the first century BC[2] and so seem not to have existed long enough for any significant development to have occurred. When secondary greetings do appear about the time of Augustus' reign, they quickly become a regular feature in the closing sections of letters. Otto Roller attributed this dramatic rise in the use of greetings in letter closings to Paul and the use of this stereotyped formula in his letters.[3] The evidence, however, suggests that the greeting formula was becoming a regular feature of letters already before the apostle's time and in circles where his letters would not have been known. In keeping with its function, secondary greetings occur most frequently in private or familiar letters.

1. See the discussion of this form in Ziemann, *De Epistularum Graecarum*, pp. 325-26; Exler, *Ancient Greek Letter*, pp. 111-12; Koskenniemi, *Des griechischen Briefes*, pp. 148-51; Gamble, *Textual History*, pp. 59-60; White, 'Epistolary Formulas and Clichés', pp. 298-99; Mullins, 'Greeting', pp. 418-23.
2. Some of the earliest examples of secondary greetings are found in P. Oxy. 745 (ca. 25 BC); P. Oxy. 1061 (22 BC); P. Oxy. 1479 (late 1st century BC); and Cicero, *ad Fam*. 14.4, 5 (ca. 50 BC). There is also at least one earlier example where a greeting occurs—not independently, but combined with a health wish: P. Tebt. 768 (116 BC).
3. Roller, *Das Formular*, pp. 67-68.

Greetings in letter closings are virtually always expressed by the verb ἀσπάζεσθαι ('to greet, welcome, salute'). Two exceptions to this almost universal practice include the infrequent use of προσαγορεύειν ('to address, call by name')[1] and ἐπισκόπεισθαι ('to look after, watch over').[2] Although the literal meaning of ἐπισκόπεισθαι does not express greeting, most papyrologists and epistolographers treat this verb as a technical term of greeting with the meaning 'send regards to'.[3] John White concurs with this understanding when the indicative form of the verb is used, but disagrees when the imperative is found. In the latter situation, White argues that the literal meaning of 'take care of' ought to be retained and that the imperative form thus functions in a manner similar to the health wish.[4] Such a distinction, however, seems too nuanced to be convincing. If, as the evidence suggests, ἐπισκόπεισθαι functioned as a technical term of greeting, it would seem best to translate and understand the imperative form in the same way as the indicative.

Secondary greetings can be classified according to the different persons of the verb,[5] thereby resulting in three basic types.

First-Person Type of Greeting
In a first-person type of greeting, the writer of the letter greets someone directly: e.g., P. Wash. 30: ἀσπάζομαί σε ἄδελφε Νεικῆτα ('I greet you, brother Neicetes'). Because of its form (always first-person indicative), this is the most direct and personal of the three types of greeting formulae. It is also the most infrequent. Since the addressee has already been greeted in the opening salutation (χαίρειν), there is no need for the letter writer to repeat this. Thus when the first-person greeting is found, it often stresses the friendliness and closeness of the

1. See, e.g., BGU 948, 984; P. Ant. 44; P. Oslo 154; P. Oxy. 526, 928, 1070, 1162, 1492, 1664, 2731, 2785, 2862, 3314; P. Ryl. 604.
2. See, e.g., P. Geiss, 12; P. Mert. 63; P. Tebt. 58, 768; P. Oslo 153; P. Oxy, 293, 294, 743.
3. See, e.g., the translation used in P. Mert. 63 (note also the editor's comments on p. 45) and P. Oslo 153.
4. White, 'Epistolary Formulas and Clichés', pp. 298-99; also his *Light from Ancient Letters*, p. 202, n. 63.
5. So Mullins, 'Greeting', p. 418. Koskenniemi (*Des griechischen Briefes*, pp. 148-51) also suggested that the greeting formula has three forms but delineated the three types of greeting somewhat differently: (1) the writer greets the addressee; (2) the writer greets others through the addressee; and (3) the writer conveys greetings from another party to the recipient.

relationship between the sender and recipient of the letter.

First-person greetings directed to the addressee are frequently located at the beginning of the letter, immediately following the opening salutation. This occurs predominantly in later letters belonging to the second and third centuries AD.[1] It appears that the greeting has been moved from its original position in the letter closing to the letter opening in order to expand and intensify the χαίρειν wish that begins the correspondence.

Personal greetings of the writer to someone or some group other than the person named in the opening are rather infrequent, since this type of greeting was normally mediated through the addressee (see discussion of 'second-person type of greeting' below). But when first-person greetings directed to someone not identified in the letter opening do occur, they are always located in the letter closing.[2] These greetings indicate that the author has a larger audience in mind for the letter than the opening salutation indicates. Although only one person may be listed as the addressee, the direct greetings of the writer to other people indicates that the writer expects the letter to be read by them as well. Thus first-person greetings potentially aid in discerning the intended audience of a letter.[3]

Second-Person Type of Greeting
In a second-person type of greeting, which is the most common of the three types, the writer exhorts the addressee to greet someone else on his behalf. The recipient of the letter thus becomes an agent of the sender of the letter in establishing and maintaining communication with a third party: e.g., P. Tebt. 412: ἀσπάζου τὴν μετέρα σου καὶ τὸν πατέρα σου ('Greet your mother and your father'). The form of this type of greeting is either the present imperative, ἀσπάζου, or the aorist imperative, ἀσπάσαι, with both forms almost always given in the singular to match the letter recipient.

Whereas a first-person greeting is sometimes located in a letter opening and, less frequently, in a letter closing, second-person greetings consistently occur in the final section of a letter.[4] They are somewhat

---

1. In addition to examples cited in Exler, *Ancient Greek Letter*, pp. 111-12, see P. Amh. 133; P. Mert. 28; P. Mich. 201, 496; P. Oxy. 2984.
2. See, e.g., BGU 276; P. Fay. 116; P. Mert. 81, 82, 85; P. Oxy. 123, 1067, 1494; P. Princ. 70; P. Tebt. 415.
3. So Mullins, 'Greeting', p. 420.
4. See, e.g., BGU 632; P. Fay. 112, 123; P. Mert. 22, 81, 82; P. Oslo 47, 48, 49,

less personal than first-person types, since the greeting of the writer is not given directly but only mediated through the addressee. It would be dangerous to conclude from this, however, that a second-person greeting implies a closer relationship between the writer and the addressee than that between the writer and the person(s) greeted. Judgments about the closeness of the relationship between parties referred to in a letter cannot be established by the greeting formula alone but must be made in light of the epistolary situation.[1] Nevertheless, this type of greeting is important in providing information about relationships that exist between the writer and others not addressed directly in the letter opening.

Third-Person Type of Greeting
In a third-person type of greeting, the letter writer becomes an agent through whom a third party greets the addressee or even some fourth party: e.g., P. Mich. 464: ἀσπάζονταί σέ σου τὰ παιδία ('Your children greet you'). The form is always the third-person indicative, either singular or plural depending on the number of those sending greetings. Like a second-person greeting, it is consistently located in the letter closing.[2] Another similarity with the aforementioned type of greeting lies in its help in providing information about relationships that exist beyond that of the letter writer and the addressee.

An examination of the various types of secondary greetings reveals that they consist of three basic elements: (1) the greeting verb (some form of ἀσπάζεσθαι, προσαγορεύειν or ἐπισκόπεισθαι, the latter two verbs only rarely used); (2) the giver of the greeting (most commonly the author of the letter but sometimes another person[s]); and (3) the recipient of the greeting (either the addressee or some other person[s]). Secondary greetings also contain a number of additions or elaborating phrases that serve to modify and call attention to one of the three basic elements. Some of these elaborations are common in farewell wishes and health wishes as well, while others are unique to secondary greetings.

In order to heighten the effect of the first basic element of the greeting formula, that is, the greeting verb, a number of adverbs and prepositional phrases are frequently added: μεγάλως ([to greet] 'earnestly'), πλεῖστα ('most of all'), πρὸ πάντων ('above all'), πρὸ τῶν ὅλων ('by all

---

150, 161; P. Oxy. 114, 295, 300, 1061, 1489, 2981, 2982, 3199, 3312, 3313; P. Princ. 68, 70; P. Ryl. 230, 231; P. Tebt. 412.
    1.   See the comments of Mullins, 'Greeting', pp. 420-21.
    2.   See, e.g., P. Mert 22, 81, 82, 83; P. Oxy. 2981, 2982, 3312; P. Princ. 70.

means'), πρὸς ἀλήθειαν ([to greet] 'sincerely'), and, most commonly, πολλά ('many times', i.e., [to greet] 'warmly'):

P. Oxy. 1067	ἀσπάζομαι ὑμᾶς πολλά
	('I send you many greetings')
P. Iand. 9	πλεῖστα ἀσπάζεται ὑμᾶς πάντας κατ' ὄνομα Λοπεινᾶς
	('Lopeinas most of all greets you all by name')
P. Fay. 118	ἀσπάζου τοὺς φιλοῦντές σε πάντες πρὸς ἀλήθειαν
	('Greet sincerely all those loving you')
BGU 1079	ἀσπάζου Διόδωρον μεγάλως
	('Greet Diodoros earnestly')

At first, these elaborations on the greeting verb seem to have been intended to impart a warmer and more personal tone. With the passing of time, however, their wide use caused them to become virtually another conventional element of the greeting formula. This explains why, for example, πολλά is sometimes used twice in a greeting: e.g., P. Mich. 201: ἀσπάζεται ἡμᾶς Θερμουθᾶς πολλὰ πολλά ('Thermouthas greets you many, many times'). Because πολλά had lost its literal meaning and become only a standard element of the greeting formula, the writer had to repeat the word in order to indicate the intensity and sincerity of his greeting.

Elaboration also takes place in the second basic element of the greeting formula: the giver of the greeting. For example, instead of the simple ἀσπάζομαι ὑμᾶς ('I greet you'), P. Oxy. 1067 reads: κἀγὼ 'Αλέξανδρος ὁ πατὴρ ὑμῶν ἀσπάζομαι ὑμᾶς ('I, Alexandros, your father, greet you'). Here we witness the addition of the personal pronoun (ἐγώ), the name ('Αλέξανδρος), and an adjectival statement of relationship (ὁ πατὴρ ὑμῶν). These supplementary items are clearly not essential for the recipient of the greeting to identify the one greeting him, given the parent-child relationship that exists between them. The presence of these additional items, therefore, appears to stem from the author's desire to give his greeting a more intimate tone.

The most frequent elaborations take place in the third basic element of the greeting formula: the recipient of the greeting. These elaborations tend to add to the proper name either a statement of relationship (e.g., ἡ θυγάτηρ μου ['my daughter'], ὁ υἱός μου ['my son'], ὁ πατήρ σου ['your father']) or a term of endearment (e.g., γλυκύτατος ['most sweet'], ἀξιολογώτατος ['most estimable'], φίλτατος ['most loved']). Quite often, the greeting contains no proper name and the identification of the recipient is made by a statement of relationship or endearment only:

P. Oxy. 1676   ἀσπάζεταί σε ὁ υἱός μου καὶ ἡ μήτηρ αὐτοῦ
                ('My son and his mother greets you')
P. Tebt. 412   ἀσπάζου τήν μετέρα σου καὶ τὸν πατέρα σου
                ('Greet your mother and your father')
P. Oxy. 1218   ἄσπαζε πολλὰ τὸν φίλτατον Φούλλωνα
                ('Greet warmly most loved Phullon')
P. Lond. 404   ἀσπάζομαι τὴν Νονναν καὶ τὸν γλυκύτατον Κωνσταντιν
                ('I greet Nonna and the most sweet Constantius')
P. Mich. 499   ἀσπάζομαι ᾽Αβάσκαντον τὸν χρησιμώτατον
                ('I greet the most worthy Abascantus')
P. Oxy. 1664   προσαγορεύω τὸν ἀξιολογώτατον γυμνασίαρχον
                ᾽Ωρίωνα
                ('I greet the most estimable gymnasiarch Horion')

   Even more frequently, the recipient is identified by means of a generalized statement such as πάντας τοὺς ἐν οἴκῳ ('everyone in [your] house'), τοὺς φιλοῦντάς σε ('those loving you'), ὁλοὺς τοὺς ὑμῶν ('all those belonging to you'), or τὴν σύμβιον ('your companion'). In order to make these generalized greetings more specific or personal, the phrase κατ᾽ ὄνομα ('by name') is often added. Some examples of these more generalized statements in greetings include the following:

P. Lond. 243   ἀσπάζομαί σε καὶ πάντας τοὺς ἐν τῷ οἴκῳ σου
                ('I greet you and all those in your house')
P. Tebt. 413   αἱ φίλαι σου πᾶσαι ἀσπάζονται τούς σε φιλοῦντας
                ('All your friends greet those loving you')
P. Oxy. 1677   ἄσπασαι τοὺς σοὺς πάντας κατ᾽ ὄνομα
                ('Greet all of yours by name')
P. Oxy. 2275   ἄσπασε πολλὰ τοὺς ὑμῶν πάντας κατ᾽ ὄνομα
                ('Greet warmly all those belonging to you by name')
P. Giss. 12   ἐπισκοποῦμαι τὴν σὴν σύνβιον καὶ τοὺς φιλοῦντάς
                σε πάντας
                ('I greet your companion [i.e., wife] and all those loving you')

   The extreme lengths to which these generalized greetings could go is illustrated in P. Mich. 206: ἀσπάζου τοὺς σοὺς πάντας κατ᾽ ὄνομα· ἀσπάζονταί σε καὶ τοὺς σοὺς πάντας οἱ ἐμοὶ πάντας κατ᾽ ὄνομα ('Greet everyone with you by name. Everyone with me also greets everyone with you by name'). Greetings such as this clearly stem more from the epistolary form of the greeting than the actual epistolary situation. For while many of the elaborations originally served to convey a more personal and intimate tone, in time they became only standard elements of the greeting formula.

One other item frequently added to secondary greetings is τὰ ἀβάσκοντα—a wish that the 'evil eye' may not harm the person(s) being greeted. This 'good luck' wish is most frequently connected with the greeting of children:[1]

P. Oxy. 2981   ἄσπασαι τὰ ἀβάσκοντά σου παιδία
('Greet your children whom the evil eye will not harm')

P. Princ. 70   ἀσπάζομαι τὰ ἀβάσκοντα σου τέκνα καὶ τὴν σύμβιόν σου καὶ πάντας τοὺς ἐν οἴκῳ κατ᾽ ὄνομα
('I greet your children—whom the evil eye will not harm—and your wife and all in your house by name')

P. Oslo 161   ἀσπάζου μοι τὴν κυρίαν μου ἀδελφὴν καὶ Ἡρακλέαν καὶ Μίαν καὶ τὰ ἀβάσκαντα αὐτῶν τέκνα
('Greet for me my lord sister and Heraklea and Mia and their children whom the evil eye will not harm')

P. Wisc. 74   ἀσπάζωμεν τὴν ἀδελφὴν τὴν Ἐλευθέρα σου καὶ τὰ ἀβάσκαντα αὐτῆς παιδία καὶ τοὺς ὑμῶν πάντας κατ᾽ ὄνομα
('We greet our sister, your wife, Eleuthera and her children whom the evil eye will not harm and all those of yours by name'

In terms of its relationship to other epistolary conventions belonging to the letter closing, the greeting is normally located after the health wish (if one is present) and before the farewell wish. But while this is the normal pattern, it is by no means rigidly followed—as evidenced by the many examples where the greeting formula follows the farewell wish.[2]

4. *The Autograph*

Another epistolary convention in the closing sections of ancient Hellenistic letters is the autograph.[3] A secretary or amanuensis was frequently

---

1.   See also, e.g., BGU 714; P. Mich. 208; P. Oxy. 292, 300, 930, 1159, 1218, 1666, 3312, 3313; P. Ryl. 604; P. Wisc. 76. This wish for the 'evil eye' not to come upon nor harm the letter recipient is also occasionally interjected into a health wish: e.g., BGU 811; P. Giss. 23; P. Oxy. 3312, 3313.

2.   See papyrus letters cited above in n. 1, p. 33.

3.   See the discussion of this epistolary convention in Ziemann, *De Epistularum Graecarum*, pp. 362-65; Roller, *Das Formular*, pp. 70-78; Gamble, *Textual History*, pp. 62-63; Bahr, 'Subscriptions', pp. 27-33; R.N. Longenecker, 'Ancient Amanuenses and the Pauline Epistles', in *New Dimensions in New Testament Study* (ed. R.N. Longenecker and M.C. Tenney; Grand Rapids: Zondervan, 1974), pp. 282-88.

employed to assist in the writing of letters.[1] In such situations, the letter sender would often write some closing remarks in his or her own hand. Since this change of script would have been obvious to the reader of the letter, there was no reason to state explicitly that the author was now writing rather than a secretary. We do not find among the ancient Greek letters, therefore, an autograph formula or fixed phrase typically given to indicate that the author has begun writing.[2] Similarly, with respect to Latin letters, though they may contain passing remarks to the effect that the sender is now writing in his or her own hand,[3] there is no standard autograph formula. It would appear, therefore, that if a sender desired to write the ending of a letter in his or her own hand, one or more of the closing epistolary conventions would simply be used.

The extent of an autograph section varies greatly among the extant Greek papyri. Most commonly, it is very brief and consists just of a farewell wish. For example, the autograph material in the closing section of P. Oxy. 1491 is obvious not only from the change of script but also from the repetition of the farewell wish:[4]

1st hand:	ἐρρῶσθαί σε εὔχομαι ἀδελφέ
2nd hand:	ἐρρῶσθαί σε εὔχομαι ἀδελφέ

Much less frequently, however, an autograph section includes other items such as greetings, a date, or postscriptive remarks. For example, in P. Lond. 897, after a farewell wish given in the same hand as the rest of

---

1.   There are several reasons why a secretary was used in antiquity for the writing of letters. The most common was the illiteracy of the sender(s) (see discussion of 'The Illiteracy Formula' below). Other factors include such things as the physical difficulty of writing on papyrus and the lack of easy access to writing materials, so making the use of an amanuensis a common practice of the day. For an extended discussion of the use of a secretary in Greco-Roman antiquity, see E.R. Richards, *The Secretary in the Letters of Paul* (Tübingen: Mohr-Siebeck, 1991), pp. 1-127.

2.   Note, however, the following two examples where the author makes explicit reference to the fact that he has written the whole letter in his own hand: P. Gren. II 89 ὁλόγραφον χειρὶ ἐμῇ ('I have written all in my own hand'); also a letter cited by Ziemann, *De Epistularum Graecarum*, p. 365: ταῦτά σοι γέγραφα τῇ ἐμῇ χειρί ('I have written these things to you in my own hand').

3.   See, e.g., Cicero, *ad Att.* 8.1, 12.32, 13.28.

4.   See also, e.g., BGU 37; P. Amh. 131; P. Mert. 28; P. Oslo 49; P. Oxy. 118, 1664, 1665, 1676, 2152, 2192, 2862, 2983, 3066, 3067, 3124, 3129, 3182, 3253, 3313, 3314.

the letter, there occurs a greeting, another farewell wish, and a date in a slightly smaller and lighter script that is also more cursive and careless:[1]

1st hand:	ἔρρωσο	
2nd hand:	ἀσπάζου 'Αφροδουν τὴν μικρὰν καὶ	
	τοὺς ἐν οἴκῳ	ἔρρωσο
	Λ γ αὐτοκράτορος καίσαρος Δομιτιανοῦ Σεβαστοῦ	
	Γερμανικοῦ	Φάρμουθι γ

If an autograph section contains any final remarks, these are usually brief, consisting of no more than a couple of lines. For example, P. Oxy. 3063 closes with the following note written in a second hand, presumably that of the sender:

ἐκομισάμην δὲ [...
τὸ κεράμιον τῆς ἐλαίας τὰ δὲ ἄλλα [...
γέγραφα· φύλασσε ἕως ἄν παρὰ σοὶ γένωμαι
ἔρρωσο φίλτατε 'Απολλογένη
('I received
the jar of oil. The other things
I have written about, keep them until I join you.
Farewell, most loved Apollogenes')

A few examples can be found, however, where as much as a paragraph or two of postscriptive comments are given.[2]

It is significant to note that, contrary to our modern convention, the name signature in a writer's own hand does not occur in the closings of ancient letters.[3] The absence of a personal signature possibly stems from the fact that the author has already formally identified him- or herself in the letter opening and so has no need to repeat this. Koskenniemi argues that it was the equating of the letter-writing situation with a personal meeting that accounts for the absence of a name signature in letter closings.[4] For if a letter was understood as a substitute for personal presence, then there was no need to give one's signature since a conversational partner obviously does not say his or her name after each contribution to the dialogue. Schnider and Stenger, however, assert that

1. See also, e.g., BGU 665; P. Ant. 44; P. Cair.Zen. 59618; P. Hib. 201, 202, 235, 265; P. Mich. 490; P. Oslo 150, 151; P. Oxy. 1063, 1674, 2191, 2709, 2985.
2. See, e.g., BGU 183, 526, 910; P. Geiss. 97; P. Princ. 71; Cicero, *ad Att.* 11.24, 12.32, 13.28.
3. This is not true, however, of business records, contracts and leases where the name signature is consistently given.
4. Koskenniemi, *Des griechischen Briefes*, p. 168.

the autograph closing of a letter substitutes for the writer's signature.[1]

This raises the question concerning an autograph's function or purpose—an issue that has generated some debate. One popular view is that the writing of part of a closing in the author's own hand served to testify to the letter's authenticity.[2] This motive, which is only implied in the papyrus letters, is explicitly stated in some of the literary letters. Plancus, for example, in a letter to Cicero (*ad Fam.* 10.21), says: *Credidi chirographis eius* ('I put my trust in his autographic letters').[3]

Others have argued that an autograph has the function of making a letter a legally binding document. Gordon Bahr comments: 'The subscription served to make legally binding the agreement which the scribe has cast in an appropriate written form'.[4] This legal function is evident in letters of petition where the body of the appeal is frequently written in one hand (the secretary's) and closed in another (the sender's). The petition P. Oxy. 2712, for example, closes with the following autograph statement that is often found in letters of this type: Αὐρηλία Διοσκουρίαινα ἐπιδέδωκα ('I, Aurelia Dioscuriaena, submitted [the petition]'). It appears that the purpose of adding such a brief comment in the sender's own hand is to make the petition an official or legally binding document. The same purpose seems to be at work in business letters which also typically close with an autograph statement or signature.

These motives of (1) establishing authenticity and (2) making a letter legally binding are certainly present in some of the extant letters of antiquity, most notably in official or business letters. They do not, however, explain the presence of a closing autograph in informal, private correspondence written to family and friends, where such functions would presumably be neither necessary nor appropriate. In these familiar or friendly letters, an autograph seems to have a philophronetic function of giving the correspondence a more personal touch.[5] As the classical

---

1. Schnider and Stenger, *Neutestamentlichen Briefformular*, p. 135.
2. So Ziemann, *De Epistularum Graecarum*, pp. 362-65; Roller, *Das Formular*, p. 74; Deissmann, *Light from Ancient East*, pp. 166-67.
3. For further examples and comments, see Gamble, *Textual History*, p. 63, n. 43.
4. Bahr, 'Subscriptions', p. 31. See also Schnider and Stenger, *Neutestamentlichen Briefformular*, pp. 136-37.
5. Koskenniemi, *Des griechischen Briefes*, pp. 168-69; Gamble, *Textual History*, p. 63. Although Bahr stresses the legal function of the autograph, he also recognizes its personalizing aspect: 'After the secretary has completed the letter which the author wished to send, the author himself writes to the addressee in personal intimate terms' ('Subscriptions', p. 33).

rhetorician Julius Victor noted in his fourth-century work on letter writing: 'As a rule, to those closest to them, the ancients wrote in their own hands, or at least frequently appended a postscript'.[1] This explains why in dictated letters the farewell wish is so often written by the letter sender in his or her own hand.[2] Yet it still remains somewhat surprising that we do not find more examples of an autograph health wish or secondary greeting, since such epistolary conventions were the principal means of expressing friendship.[3]

Another motivation for writing in one's own hand was to ensure confidentiality: matters of private and personal concern could be safely dealt with. Evidence for this function comes predominantly from the literary tradition. In *ad Att.* 11.24, for example, Cicero states: *sed ad meam manum redeo; erunt enim haec occultius agenda* ('Here I take the pen myself, for I have to deal with confidential matters'). Or again in *ad Att.* 4.17: *quae tantum habent mysteriorum ut eas ne librariis quidem fere committamus ne quid quo excidat* ('They [my letters] contain so many secrets that I don't usually trust them even to my clerks for fear something might leak out').

The fact that a closing autograph occurs in letters of quite diverse types (e.g., business, personal, official, petition) and in both the non-literary and literary traditions suggests that it possessed a rather fixed stylistic function. The rule seems to have been that letters dictated to or drafted by a secretary were generally expected to close in the hand of the author. This does not preclude, however, the possibility that an autograph, as a relatively fixed element in the closing of a letter, could also be used to accomplish a specific task, such as to authenticate a letter, to make a letter legally binding, to give a letter a more personal touch, or to ensure confidentiality. Thus the specific function of any given

---

1. Julius Victor, 'Ars Rhetorica (De Epistolis),' in *Rhetores Latini Minores* (ed. C. Halm; Leipzig: Teubner, 1863). Gamble (*Textual History*, p. 63, n. 44) draws attention to a couple of literary letters that suggest correspondence written in the author's own hand were more favorably received than those written by a secretary. See Cicero, *ad Att.* 7.12: 'Your letters are each more delightful than the last—I mean those in your own handwriting'; and 7.3: 'I was pleased at first glance to see that your letter was in your own hand.' Also Fronto, *ad Marc.* 3.3: 'Indeed, I dote on the very characters of your writing; so whenever you write, do so in your own hand.'

2. See the letters cited in n. 1, p. 47.

3. There are, of course, many letters where a secretary was not employed and the author penned the entire letter, including the health wish and the greeting.

autograph must be determined by a close examination of the epistolary situation of the particular letter itself.

5. *The Illiteracy Formula*

Many people in the Greco-Roman world did not possess the ability to write. Although they could send a letter through the assistance of a secretary, they were unable to close the letter in their own hand. In such situations, a secretary would often attach to the end of the letter an 'illiteracy formula'—a brief note explaining that a secretary had written the document because of the illiteracy of the person who commissioned the letter.[1] The illiteracy formula does not occur in purely private letters. It appears, however, to have been a requirement of legal and official letters, for a large number of examples can be found in ancient letters of this type. For example:[2]

BGU 92   ἔγραψα ὑπὲρ αὐτοῦ Νεικίας Ἰσιδώρου μὴ εἰδότος
               γράμματα
               ('I wrote for Neikia Isidoros because he did not know how to write')

P. Ryl. 73   ἔγραψεν ὑπὲρ αὐτῶν Δίδυμος κοινὸς γραμματεὺς
               ἀξιωθεὶς διὰ τὸ ἡμεῖν μὴ ἐπίστασθαι γράμματα
               ('Didymos, a public scribe, wrote for them because they did
               not know how to write')

P. Oxy. 267   Θέων Πααήτος γέγραφα ὑπὲρ αὐτοῦ μὴ εἰδότος γράμματα
               ('Theon Paaetos wrote for him because he did not know how
               to write')

P. Oxy. 2713   Αὐρήλιος Θῶνεις ἔγραψα ὑπὲρ αὐτῆς μὴ ἰδυείης γράμματα
               ('I, Aurelia Thoneis, wrote for her because she does not know
               how to write')

The illiteracy formula possessed a relatively fixed form, though allowed for some variation. In the first half of the formula the verb γράφειν ('to write'), in either the aorist or perfect tense, is consistently used, with the name of the scribe as well as the sender of the letter being normally given. In a few letters, the third-person form of the verb occurs: e.g., P. Ryl. 183: ἔγραψεν ὑπὲρ αὐτοῦ Μάρων γραμματεὺς αὐτοῦ διὰ

---

1.   See the discussion of this closing convention in Exler, *Ancient Greek Letter*, pp. 124-27; Bahr, 'Subscriptions', pp. 28-29; White, 'Greek Documentary Letter Tradition', 2.141; *idem*, 'New Testament Epistolary Literature', pp. 1735–36. Schnider and Stenger (*Neutestamentlichen Brie,fformular*, pp. 142-44) refer to the illiteracy formula as the 'secretary's note' ('Sekretärvermerk').

2.   For additional examples, see Exler, *Ancient Greek Letter*, pp. 124-26.

τὸ βραδύτερον αὐτὸν γράφειν ('Maron, his scribe, wrote for him because he writes too slowly'). It is much more common, however, to find the first-person: e.g., P. Ryl. 94: Ἀφροδίσιος ὁ προγεγράμμενος ἔγραψα ὑπὲρ αὐτοῦ Ἡρακλῆου διὰ τὸ μὴ εἰδέναι αὐτὸν γράμματα ('I, Aphrodisios, the one who has written the above, wrote for Herakleos because he did not know how to write').

The second half of an illiteracy formula gives the reason why the scribe has written on behalf of the letter sender. As noted in the examples above, the reason normally lies in the inability of a sender to write competently or to write at all. With the passing of time, this latter explanatory part of the illiteracy formula seems to have undergone a slight development. For in letters stemming from the Ptolemaic and early Roman periods, a prepositional infinitive construction is used: διὰ τὸ μὴ εἰδέναι (ἐπίστασθαι) αὐτὸν γράμματα ('because he does not know how to write letters'). By the beginning of the first century AD, however, this form became slowly supplanted by the participial construction μὴ εἰδότος γράμματα ('not knowing [how to write] letters'). Also common among letters from the second and third centuries AD is the somewhat abbreviated formula ἔγραψα ὑπὲρ αὐτοῦ ἀγραμμάτου ('I wrote for him who was unlettered', i.e., one who does not know how to write).

The illiteracy formula is always the final element of the letter closing. It comes after the farewell wish and the date, being sometimes separated from the rest of the letter by a few blank lines.

6. *The Dating Formula*

Another epistolary convention belonging to a letter closing is the date.[1] This differs from the practice found in business receipts or in official notices not drawn up in an epistolary style, where the date is given at the beginning of a document rather than at its end.

In terms of form, a dating formula is regularly introduced by the word ἔτους ('year') or its equivalent representative symbol 'L'. Ancient papyrus letters exhibit a clear development in the dating formula, from simple to more complex. In the Ptolemaic and early Roman periods, the

1.   See the discussion of this closing convention in Exler, *Ancient Greek Letter*, pp. 78-100; B. Olsson, *Papyrusbriefe aus der Frühesten Römerzeit* (Uppsala: Almqvist & Wiksells, 1925), pp. 18-20; Gamble, *Textual History*, pp. 61-62; White, *Light from Ancient Letters*, pp. 5, 8.

date was expressed by a brief formula consisting of the year and the month, sometimes also the day: e.g., P. Mich. 48 (251 BC): L λε Μεσορὴ ζ ('Year 35, Mesore 7'). In the later Roman period, this formula was expanded to include the names and titles of the reigning emperor or emperors, thus resulting in a quite lengthy expression of time: e.g., P. Mich. 464 (AD 99): L β Αὐτοκράτορος Καίσαρος Νέρουσα Τραιανοῦ Σεβαστοῦ Γερμανικοῦ Φαμενὼθ κ ('Year 2, of the Emperor Caesar Nerva Trajanus Augustus Germanicus, Phamenoth 20'). Other items frequently added to the dating formula include the word μηνός ('month') before the name of the month and θεός ('god', 'divine') to the name of emperors, particularly those who had already passed away.

Not all letters, however, were dated. The dating formula occurs in most official or business letters, though not always. But letters of a more personal nature frequently omitted giving the date. Exler notes: 'It is approximately correct to say that in private letters the date is missing almost as frequently as it is given.'[1]

No firm rules or generally accepted practice for the dating of letters can be determined.[2] A degree of freedom was apparently allowed as to whether to include a date or not. When it does occur, however, the dating formula normally occupies the final position in the closing section of the letter, after the farewell wish.

7. *The Postscript*

Although Greco-Roman letters normally end with a farewell wish and date (if one was given), there occasionally appears also a 'postscript'[3] following these closing conventions. A postscript consists of final remarks that, for one reason for another, have been omitted from the formal letter closing, and so are appended to the end. A postscript is by definition not a normative letter-closing convention, but a feature that arises out of the necessity to include some final information that was not earlier included.

These parting comments were usually written at the bottom of the page. If space was limited, however, the postscript would be written

1. Exler, *Ancient Greek Letter*, p. 98.
2. See Olsson, *Papyrusbriefe*, pp. 18-20, who refutes earlier attempts to determine epistolary rules concerning the presence and form of the dating formula.
3. See the discussion in Gamble, *Textual History*, p. 64.

vertically in the left-hand margin[1] (rarely on the right).[2] Contrary to what one might assume, postscriptive remarks are found not only in non-literary letters but also in the correspondence of more sophisticated and learned writers as well.[3]

In terms of content, postscriptive remarks are typically brief and often consist of one of the formal conventions belonging to the letter closing, such as a greeting or a health wish. In P. Tebt. 58, for example, the postscript involves a health wish given after the farewell wish and the date:[4] ἔρρωσο· ἔτους ϛ Παχὼν κϛ· ἐπειμένου τοῖς ἐν οἴκῳ ('Farewell. The 6th year, Pachon 26. Take care of your household').

But there are also many examples where a postscript contains non-conventional material. Sometimes the writer may give some new information that has come to light immediately following the writing of the letter. For example, the postscript in P. Mich. 490 reads as follows: γείνωσκε ὅτι ἰς Μεισηνοὺς διετάγην, ὕστερον γὰρ ἐπέγνων ('Know that I have been assigned to Misenum, for I learned this later on' [i.e. after the letter was written]).[5] Sometimes the postscript contains a final comment or command that has apparently come to the mind of the writer after the letter was finished.[6] In P. Oxy. 1063, for example, a father closes a letter to his son with a farewell wish and a final command written in his own hand: ἐρρῶσθαί σε εὔχομαι· τὸ πιττάκιον ἀναγνοὺς μὴ ἀναδῷς τῷ Ἡρώδῃ ('I pray that you may be well. After you have read the letter do not give it to Herodes').

A postscript can also reinforce a command previously given in a

1. See, e.g., BGU 423, 1097; P. Lond. 243, 409, 418; P. Mich. 212, 466, 476, 692; P. Oxy. 298, 530, 933, 1069, 1154, 1666, 2151, 2783, 3061; P. Paris 43; P. Princ. 71, 72; P. Ryl. 692; UPZ 66.
2. See, e.g., P. Mich. 466. The use of the right-hand margin here, however, is only due to the fact that the left-hand margin was already filled. For a postscript written at the top of a letter, above the prescript, see P. Lond. 893.
3. Many examples of postscripts can be found in the letters of Cicero, Fronto and others. See, e.g., Cicero, *ad Fam.* 10.21; 11.1; 12.12; 14.1; 15.5; 16.15, 19; *ad Att.* 3.22; 8.12, 11.4; 12.11; 15.6, 29; 16.15; Fronto, *ad Marc.* 3.8; 4.2; *ad Anton.* 1.1.
4. For additional examples, see the papyrus letters cited in n. 1, p. 33.
5. See also P. Tebt. 41; P. Oxy. 937. The arrival of new information after the completion of a letter is the reason for many of Cicero's postscripts. See, e.g., *ad Fam.* 12.12; 16.15; *ad Att.* 8.12; 15.6, 29; 16.15.
6. See, e.g., BGU 423, 1204, 1207; P. Amh. 37; P. Mich. 201; P. Oslo 161; P. Oxy. 113, 530, 933, 1067, 1069, 1220, 2155, 2783, 2985, 3061; P. Princ. 19; P. Ryl. 236; P. Tebt. 314; UPZ 66.

letter. P. Oxy. 1481 is a letter from a soldier to his mother reassuring her about his health and acknowledging the receipt of various gifts that she sent. In the body of the letter, the son exhorts his mother: μὴ ὀχλοῦ δὲ πέμπειν τι ἡμῖν ('Do not trouble yourself to send me anything'). A postscript written in the left-hand margin repeats this command almost verbatim: μὴ ἐπιβαροῦ πέμπειν τι ἡμῖν ('Do not burden yourself to send me anything'). Here the postscript clearly echoes and reinforces the earlier command.

Another example of a postscript that echoes material found in the body of the letter can be seen in P. Wisc. 74. Two sisters write to their brother with an urgent request for him to return home:

> Put all things aside and come immediately (ἐκσαυτῆς ἀπαντήσων) to us because our mother has died and we badly need your presence. Do not (μὴ θελήσῃς) stay at your place but come (ἀπαντῆσαι) to us... We have also sent our brother Martyrius so that you may come immediately (ἐκσαυτῆς ἀπαντήσῃς) to us with him.

Following the closing of the letter, which contains a secondary greeting and a farewell wish, a two-line postscript is added: 'Do not (μὴ θέλῃς) neglect it and feel repentance afterwards. Come immediately (ἐκσαυτῆς ἀπαντήσων) to us so that you may arrange everything.' Once again we see a closing postscript serving to echo and reinforce an appeal given earlier in the letter body.

One other type of postscript is of particular significance for my thesis regarding the recapitulating function of the Pauline letter closings. For in some letters, especially those of a business or financial nature, the postscript serves as a summary of the main details contained in the body of the letter. The summarizing function of a postscript in business letters was first observed by Gordon Bahr,[1] who cited as an example P. Oxy. 264, a business letter concerning the sale of a loom:[2]

> Ammonius, son of Ammonius, to Tryphon, son of Dionysius: Greetings. I agree that I have sold to you the weaver's loom belonging to me, measuring three weavers' cubits less two palms, and containing two rollers and two beams, and I acknowledge the receipt from you through the bank of Sarapion, son of Lochus, near the Serapeum at Oxyrhynchus, of the price of it agreed upon between us, namely 20 silver drachmae of the Imperial and Ptolemaic coinage; and that I will guarantee to you the sale

---

1. See Bahr, 'Subscriptions', esp. pp. 28-29.
2. The same letter is cited by Schnider and Stenger, *Neutestamentlichen Briefformular*, p. 143, and Richards, *Secretary*, pp. 81-82.

with every guarantee, under penalty of payment to you of the price which I have received from you increased by half its amount, and of the damages. This note of hand is valid. The 14th year of Tiberius Claudius Caesar Augustus Germanicus Imperator, the 15th of the month Caesareus.

[2nd hand] I, Ammonius, son of Ammonius, have sold the loom, and have received the price of 20 drachmae of silver and will guarantee the sale as aforesaid. I, Heraclides, son of Dionysius, wrote for him as he was illiterate.

In this business letter, as in others like it,[1] the postscript repeats the key points of the letter so that it can be said to summarize or recapitulate the letter as a whole. Although not as common as in Greek letters, a number of Latin letters also contain such summarizing postscripts.[2]

8. *Summary*

Our survey of Hellenistic letters has shown that a number of epistolary conventions belong to the closings of ancient letters: a farewell wish, a health wish, secondary greetings, an autograph, an illiteracy formula, the date, and a postscript. The instances in which all—or even most—of these closing conventions occur simultaneously, however, are rare. This indicates that, other than the farewell wish, none of these epistolary conventions was considered essential to the closings of ancient letters. Rather, a letter writer had a number of closing conventions that could be employed, depending on his or her personal style or the requirements of the specific epistolary situation.

When several closing elements occur in the same letter, they exhibit a relatively consistent order: secondary greetings, health wish, farewell wish, date, illiteracy formula, postscript. This seems to have been the usual order, though it was by no means rigidly followed—a fact attested in many letters where a secondary greeting and a health wish come after the farewell wish and date.

In letters of the Greco-Roman world, a number of links between the closing sections and the body sections exist. For example, if the content of the body deals with personal matters (family or familiar letters), the closing section typically contains greetings and a health wish, since these closing conventions served to heighten the philophronetic function of the

1. See the letters cited by Bahr, pp. 28-29, nn. 6-7.
2. L. Mitteis, *Römisches Privatrecht bis auf die Zeit Diokletians* (2 vols.; Leipzig: Duncker & Humblot, 1908), I, pp. 292-314. See esp. his comments on pp. 304-305.

letter. On the other hand, if the content of the body deals with a request
to a superior or government official to rectify some injustice (petitionary
letters) or to deal with some administrative matters (official letters), the
letter normally closes with a farewell wish that differs from the one used
in other types of letters. And if the content of the body contains a sharp
warning or rebuke, closing conventions such as the farewell wish, health
wish and secondary greeting, along with the positive elaborating phrases,
are deliberately omitted. And if the content of the body deals with
financial matters or issues related to law and order (business and official
letters), the closing section virtually always contains a dating formula.

Yet though such links between the closing sections and the body
sections of ancient letters exist, the connections are rather general in
nature. We do not find, for example, the kind of clever adaptation of
closing conventions that I will later propose exists in Paul's letters, which
serve to echo specific material in the body. The closest parallel to this in
Greco-Roman letters are the postscripts in business or financial letters
that summarize the bodies of such letters. The absence of more direct
links between the closing sections and the body sections of Hellenistic
letters is not too surprising, however, given the rather short and
simplistic nature of these letters in comparison to the letters of Paul.
What is clear, however, from even the more general links between the
letter closings and their respective letter bodies, is that writers did not
end their correspondence in a careless manner but rather attempted to
construct closings that were appropriate to each letter's contents.

Our study of Greco-Roman letters has also been important for establishing a standard to be used in determining to what degree Paul was
dependent on the epistolary conventions of his day having to do with
letter closings, and how he adapts or deviates from these conventions.
Indeed, the distinctive features of the Pauline letter closings can only be
discovered *vis-à-vis* such a comparative analysis.

Chapter 3

CLOSING CONVENTIONS IN ANCIENT SEMITIC LETTERS

The influence of Hellenistic epistolary practice on the writings of Paul is clear from even a cursory examination of his letters. The obvious parallels between ancient Greco-Roman letters and the Pauline letters demonstrate quite convincingly the apostle's indebtedness to the epistolary practices of his day. But as crucial as the Hellenistic letters are for understanding the content and form of Paul's letters, they may not be the only source influencing his letter-writing style. The fact that Paul consistently identifies himself as a Jew[1] and makes several references to the zealousness of his pre-conversion activities as a Pharisee[2] raises the possibility of his also being influenced by Semitic epistolary practice.[3] Thus a comprehensive examination of the epistolary conventions in the Pauline letter closings also requires a study of the closing conventions found in ancient Semitic letters.

Such an inquiry, however, faces a number of serious difficulties. First and foremost is the paucity of extant Aramaic and Hebrew letters. Compared to the thousands of examples of Hellenistic letters available, the number of Semitic letters that have been discovered is exceedingly small. This problem is exacerbated by the fact that only a small percent-

1. Rom. 11.1; 2 Cor. 11.22; Phil. 3.5. See also the statements attributed to Paul in Acts 21.39, 22.3, as well as the evidence that he spoke and understood Aramaic (Acts 21.40, 22.2, 26.14).
2. Phil. 3.5-6; Gal. 1.13-14; 1 Cor. 15.9. See also Acts 22.3, 23.6, 26.5, 9, 11.
3. This raises, of course, the complicated question of relations between Hellenistic and Semitic epistolary practices. In general, Hellenism had a strong impact on Judaism, even in those institutions and areas of Jewish life that were passionately nationalistic (see M. Hengel, *Judaism and Hellenism* [trans. J. Bowden; 2 vols.; Philadelphia: Fortress, 1974). Semitic letters were no doubt also influenced by Greco-Roman letter writing. Nevertheless, there is evidence that Semitic epistolary practice contained unique literary features under the influence of an older letter-writing tradition that dates to 5th and 6th century BC (see, e.g., the Aramaic letters from Elephantini and the Hebrew letters from Arad and Lachish).

age of such extant letters can be dated within the lifetime of the apostle. Furthermore, many of these letters exist in fragmentary form with the closing section of the letter missing. Finally, parallels between ancient Semitic letters and the Pauline letters are not always obvious. As William Doty notes: 'It is difficult, if not impossible, to establish any direct lines of borrowing by Paul from Jewish epistolary materials in terms of their form and structure.'[1]

Despite these difficulties, however, an examination of the epistolary form of Semitic letters is not without some benefit. For although not as numerous or obvious as they are in Hellenistic letters, a few parallels between Semitic letters and Paul's letters can be discovered. Joseph Fitzmyer, for example, concludes his study of Aramaic letters by noting that 'certain items in NT epistolography find illustration in some elements of the Aramaic letters'.[2] And Irene Taatz's recent examination of early Jewish letters concludes that there are parallels in form and content between these writings and the Pauline letters.[3]

Semitic epistolography, it is true, has not received the same degree of attention that Hellenistic letters have enjoyed. With a few exceptions,[4] Aramaic and Hebrew letters have only recently come under the critical eye of biblical scholars. Furthermore, recent epistolographic studies of Semitic letters have tended to separate the relevant documents into two groups based on the language of the text. There exists, therefore, a number of formal analyses of Aramaic letters[5] and Hebrew letters.[6] Yet

1. W.G. Doty, *Letters in Primitive Christianity* (Philadelphia: Fortress, 1973), p. 22.

2. J.A. Fitzmyer, 'Some Notes on Aramaic Epistolography', *JBL* 93 (1974), p. 220.

3. I. Taatz, *Frühjüdische Brief: Die paulinischen Briefe im Rahmen der offiziellen religiösem Briefe des Frühjudentums* (Göttingen: Vandenhoeck & Ruprecht, 1991).

4. A cursory treatment of Semitic epistolography can be found in G. Beer, 'Zur israelitisch-jüdischen Briefliteratur', in *Alttestamentliche Studien Rudolf Kittel zum 60. Geburtstag dargebracht* (ed. A. Alt *et al.*; Leipzig: Hinrichs, 1913), pp. 20-41. Also see J. Marty, 'Contribution à l'étude de fragments épistolaires antiques, conservés principalement dans la Bible hébraïque: Les formules de salutation', in *Mélanges syriens offerts à Monsieur René Dussaud* (2 vols.; Paris: Geuthner, 1939), II, pp. 845-55; I.H. Cazelles, 'Formules de politesse en hébreu ancien', *Groupe linguistique d'études chamito-sémitiques, Comptes rendus* 7 (1954–57), pp. 25-26.

5. Fitzmyer, 'Aramaic Epistolography'. This article is reprinted with only slight revision in *A Wandering Aramean: Collected Aramaic Essays* (Missoula, MT: Scholars, 1979), pp. 183-204, and reprinted again with a brief postscript and

as important as these studies are, the majority of these Semitic letters come from the period of 630–586 BC, and are therefore much too early to be of use for a comparison with the Pauline letters.

In what follows, therefore, the first task will be to isolate those Semitic letters that belong to the period of approximately 200 BC to AD 200. Once this corpus of letters has been established, it will be possible to examine the epistolary conventions that belong to the closings.

1. *Corpus of Semitic Letters*

Semitic letters that fall within the historical period delineated above can be divided into two groups. The first group is composed of all the 'primary' letters, i.e., those letters that were discovered in their original manuscript form. The remaining Semitic letters are best identified as 'secondary' letters, for these letters have been incorporated into existing documents and are not available in their original form.

a. *Primary Letters*

Twenty-eight Semitic letters in their original form have been discovered thus far, though some are very fragmentary. With three exceptions, these letters all belong to the period of the Bar Kokhba revolt (AD 132–135) and originate from four relatively close sites in the Judaean desert: Murabba'at, Nahal Hever, Nahal Se'elim, and Masada.[1]

bibliography in *Semeia* 22 (1981), pp. 25-57. See also P.E. Dion, 'La lettre Araméenne passe-partout et ses sous-espèces', *RB* 80–81 (1973–74), pp. 183-95; *idem*, 'A Tentative Classification of Aramaic Letter Types', in *SBL Seminar Papers* 11 (Missoula, MT: Scholars, 1977), pp. 415-41; *idem*, 'Les types épistolaires hébréo-araméens jusqu'au temps de Bar-Kokhbah', *RB* 86 (1979), pp. 544-79; P.S. Alexander, 'Remarks on Aramaic Epistolography in the Persian Period', *JSS* 23 (1978), pp. 155-70.

6.   D. Pardee, 'An Overview of Ancient Hebrew Epistolography', *JBL* 97 (1978), pp. 321-46; *idem*, *Handbook of Ancient Hebrew Letters* (Missoula, MT: Scholars, 1982).

1.   E. Qimron and J. Strugnell claim that the document 4QMMT discovered in Cave 4 at Qumran is also a letter ('An Unpublished Halakhic Letter from Qumran', in *Biblical Archaeology Today: Proceedings of the International Congress on Biblical Archaeology, April 1984, Jerusalem* [Jerusalem: Israel Exploration Society, 1985], pp. 400-407). There are, however, serious difficulties with their assertion. First and foremost, the document does not contain any epistolary conventions, either in the opening—which is wholly lost—or in the closing. Furthermore, the fact that six

Murabba'at. Wadi Murabba'at, located about twenty-five kilometers southeast of Jerusalem and eighteen kilometers south of Qumran Cave 1, has yielded a total of 173 texts in Aramaic, Hebrew, Greek, Latin and Arabic.[1] Among these documents are eleven letters (Mur 42–52), all written in Hebrew on papyrus at the time of the Second Jewish revolt.[2] The final four letters (Mur 49–52) are too fragmentary to be of any use, thereby leaving eight letters from Murabba'at that are of value for analysis and comparison. Joseph Fitzmyer identifies an ostracon (Mur 72) as an additional letter,[3] but this seems highly unlikely.

Nahal Hever. Approximately twenty kilometers farther south along the western shore of the Dead Sea, about six kilometers slightly southwest of En-gedi, lie the caves of Nahal Hever. Here fifteen letters in three different languages have been discovered:[4] eight in Aramaic (5/6 Hev 1, 2, 4, 8, 10, 11, 14, 15); five in Hebrew (5/6 Hev 5, 7, 9, 12, 13); and two in Greek (5/6 Hev 3, 6). Although the texts of the Aramaic and Greek letters have been published,[5] so far only one of the Hebrew letters (5/6 Hev 12) has been released and this only in an incomplete form.[6]

copies of this document were found in the same cave suggests that 4QMMT was not originally composed as a real letter. Finally, the contents of this document (a cultic calender, a list of about twenty halakhic topics, and a discussion of the reasons for the sect's withdrawal from the rest of the Jewish people) suggest that 4QMMT is more of theological treatise than a genuine letter. Strugnell has recently withdrawn his original claim about the genre of 4QMMT, stating that this document is instead a legal treatise or collection of laws somewhat analogous to the Biblical book of Deuteronomy (E. Cook, 'The Latest on MMT: Strugnell vs. Qimron', *BARev* 20 (1993), pp. 68-69.

1.   For details concerning the discovery, purchase and publication of the Murabba'at texts, see *Discoveries in the Judaean Desert.* II. *Les Grottes de Murabba'at* (ed. P. Benoit, J.T. Milik and R. de Vaux; Oxford: Clarendon, 1961). A detailed bibliography of the Murabba'at texts is provided by Pardee, *Handbook*, pp. 114-19.

2.   The Murabba'at letters were edited by Benoit *et al.*, *Discoveries in Judean Desert*, II, pp. 155-69.

3.   Fitzmyer, 'Aramaic Epistolography', p. 224.

4.   For further information about the discoveries at Nahal Hever, see the bibliography provided by Pardee, *Handbook*, pp. 139-41.

5.   For the text of the Aramaic letters, see Y. Yadin, 'Expedition D', *IEJ* 11 (1961) pp. 40-50. The two Greek letters were published by B. Lifshitz, 'Papyrus grecs du desért de Juda', *Aeg* 42 (1962), pp. 240-58.

6.   Yadin, 'Expedition D', pl. 22c; *idem, Bar Kokhba* (New York: Random House, 1971) p. 133.

Nahal Se'elim. In a cave at Nahal Se'elim still farther south along the shore of the Dead Sea, J.T. Milik reported finding a short letter in Hebrew written to Bar Kokhba from Matatyah with the sender's signature appended at the bottom of the document.[1] This letter, however, has still not been published, not even in preliminary form. And Milik has provided only a general description of its contents.

Masada. Two fragmentary letters have been discovered by Yigael Yadin at Masada.[2] The first letter (papMas Ep gr 1039–307/1) is written in Greek on papyrus and deals with the supply of liquids and vegetables. The second letter (MasOstr 16–89) is an ostracon written in Aramaic and is concerned with the payment of money. Unfortunately, these two letters have not been published; only their contents and opening lines have been given. Whereas the rest of the primary letters belong to the period of the Bar Kokhba revolt, these two letters have a slightly earlier date, being pre-73 AD.

b. *Secondary Letters*
A number of Jewish literary writings from the Second Temple period contain letters that have been incorporated into them.[3] Although the use of such 'secondary' letters is not free from difficulty (see discussion below), these letters potentially aid in an understanding of Semitic letters, and so need to be included in our corpus of texts.

Not surprisingly, the largest number of secondary letters is found in the writings of Josephus. Incorporated within his writings are some thirty-seven letters, thirteen of which have been taken from the biblical text or other known literary works of the period.[4] The largest source of

---

1.   J.T. Milik, 'Le travail d'édition des manuscrits du Désert de Juda', in *Volume du Congès Internationale pour l'Etude de l'Ancien Testament* (ed. J.A. Emerton *et al.*; VTSup, 4; Leiden: Brill, 1957), p. 21. See also J.A. Fitzmyer, 'The Bar Cochba Period', in *Essays on the Semitic Background of the New Testament* (London: Chapman, 1971), pp. 308, 344.

2.   See Y. Yadin, 'The Excavation of Masada—1963/64, Preliminary Report', *IEJ* 15 (1965), pp. 110-111.

3.   See P.S. Alexander, 'Epistolary Literature', in *Jewish Writings of the Second Temple Period* (ed. M.E. Stone; Assen: Van Gorcum, 1984), pp. 579-82.

4.   *War* 1.643; *Life* 217-18; 226-27; 229; 235; 365; 366; *Ant.* 8.50-52; 8.53-54; 11.12-17; 11.22-25 (= 1 Esdr. 2.16-24; Ezra 4.7-16); 11.104 (see 1 Esdr. 6.34; Ezra 6.12); 11.118-19 (see 1 Esdr. 6.27-31; 6.6-10); 11.123-30 (= 1 Esdr. 8.9-24; Ezra

secondary letters within a single document is 1 Maccabees. This late second century BC work contains eleven letters. A couple of these were written by Jews (5.10-13; 12.6-18), but most were drafted by various Seleucid kings and other foreign rulers to the Jewish people (10.18-20; 10.25-45; 11.30-37; 11.57; 12.20-23; 13.36-40; 14.20-22; 15.2-9; 15.16-21). 2 Maccabees incorporates seven letters within its text: two letters from the Jewish leaders in Jerusalem concerning the proper celebration of Hanukkah (1.1-10; 1.10–2.18); three from Antiochus Epiphanes (9.19-27; 11.23-26; 11.27-33); one from Antiochus' officer Lysias (11.17-21); and one from the Roman ambassadors Quintus Memmius and Titus Manius (11.34-38). 3 Maccabees contains two letters, both from Ptolemy IV Philopator to his generals (3.12-29; 7.1-9).

Secondary Semitic letters can be found in other diverse literary works as well. The so-called 'Letter of Aristeas,' despite its title, is not written in the form of a letter, nor was it recognized as such by other authors of that day.[1] Nevertheless, within the document three letters are recorded: a note from the librarian Demetrius to Ptolemy II Philadephus (29–33); a letter from Ptolemy to the Jewish High Priest Eleazar (35–40); and the epistolary response of Eleazar (41–46). Eusebius records a fragment of the Jewish historian Eupolemus that contains four letters from Solomon, Hiram and Pharaoh (*Praeparatio Evangelica* 9.31-34). Among the additions found in the Greek text of Esther are two official decrees of Ahasuerus (Xerxes) written in epistolary form (3.13a-g; 8.12a-x). The final chapters of the Syriac *Apocalypse of Baruch* contain a letter sent by Baruch to the Jews of the Dispersion in order to encourage them to remain faithful (*2 Apoc. Bar.* 78.1–86.1). The *Paraleipomena of Jeremiah*, also known as *4 Baruch*, records two letters: one sent by Baruch via an eagle to Jeremiah in Babylon (6.17-23); the other is the prophet's reply (7.23-29). Finally, thirteen letters can be found in the

---

7.11-24); 11.273-83 (= Esther [Gk. text] 8.12a-x); 12.36-39 (see *Ep. Arist.* 28-32); 12.45-50 (*Ep. Arist.* 35-40); 12.51-56 (*Ep. Arist.* 41-46): 12.138-44; 12.148-53; 12.226-27 (= 1 Macc. 12.20-23); 12.258-61; 12.262-63; 13.45 (= 1 Macc. 10.18-20); 13.48-57 (= 1 Macc. 10.25-45); 13.65-68; 13.70-71; 13.126-28 (= 1 Macc. 11.30-37); 13.166-70 (= 1 Macc. 12.6-18); 14.225-27; 14.241-43; 14.244-46; 17.134-35; 17.137; 17.139; 18.304; 20.10-14.

1.   Josephus refers to the document as a βιβλίον (*Ant.* 12.100); Epiphanius calls it a σύνταγμα (*De Mensuris et Ponderibus* 9); Eusebius gives it the title Περὶ τῆς Ἑρμηνείας τοῦ τῶν Ἰουδαίων Νόμου (*Praeparatio Evangelica* 9.38).

rabbinic literature.[1] Unfortunately, these rabbinic letters are very fragmentary and not one of their closing sections appears to have survived.

Of the two types of the letters, primary and secondary, the former is
obviously of greatest importance for an inquiry into the closing conventions of Semitic letters. This fact arises from the difficulties encountered
in using secondary or incorporated letters.[2] First, some of these letters
no longer exist in their original language. The letters recorded in
1 Maccabees, for example, were translated first from Greek into Hebrew
in its original version and then from Hebrew back into Greek when the
original text was subsequently translated. With such flip-flopping in
translation, the danger of epistolary formulae being replaced or distorted
is great.[3] Second, it is difficult to determine how faithfully the author has
quoted the letter in his document. He may have recorded only the part
of the letter germane to his interests, or he may have simply paraphrased the letter's contents. Third, the opening and closing formulae of
many incorporated letters are missing due to their being assimilated into
the narrative framework. In terms of importance, therefore, those letters
that have been discovered in their original manuscript form—namely,
the Bar Kokhba and Masada letters—clearly take precedence over
letters known only as part of an existing literary work. And this importance of the primary letters will be reflected in the greater attention given
to them in my study of Semitic letter closings.

2. *Formal Analysis of Semitic Letters*

a. *Primary Letters*
An examination of the extant primary Semitic letters reveals that they
possess the same tri-partite pattern as found in Hellenistic letters: opening,
body, and closing. This pattern can be observed in the following three

1.   The most important of the rabbinic letters are: two Hebrew letters under the
joint authorship of Rabbi Shimon b. Gamaliel and Yohanan b. Zakkai (Midrash
Tannaim to Deut. 26.23); three Aramaic letters sent by Rabbi Gamaliel (*t. Sanh.* 2.6;
p. Sanh. 18d; *y. Ma'as.* 56c; *b. Sanh.* 11.a); a Hebrew letter from the Jews of
Jerusalem to their countrymen in Alexandria concerning Judah b. Tabbai (*y. Hag.*
77d; see *y. Sanh.* 23c; *b. Sanh.* 107b; *b. Sota* 47a); and a letter from Judah ha-Nasi to
the Emperor Antoninus (Gen. Rab. 75,5). For a detailed discussion of these texts, see
Pardee, *Handbook*, pp. 183-211.
2.   See Alexander, 'Epistolary Literature', pp. 582-83.
3.   Similarly, the Hanukkah letters recorded in 2 Macc. 1.1-10 were originally
written in Aramaic or Hebrew, but only a Greek version survives.

papyrus letters, all belonging to the period of the Bar Kokhba revolt and
written in Hebrew, Aramaic, and Greek, respectively:

> From Shimon to Yeshua son of Galgula:
> Greetings. You are to send five
> kor measures of wheat by men of my house
> who are known to you. Prepare for them
> an empty place. They will be with you
> this sabbath, if they desire to come.
> Keep up your courage and strengthen that place.
> Farewell. I have designated the person
> who is to give you his wheat. They may
> take it after the sabbath. (Mur 44)

> Simeon to Judah, son of Manasseh, of Qiryat 'Arabayah:
> I have sent to you two asses with which you are to send
> two men to Jonathan, son of Ba'yan, and to Masabbalah,
> that they should gather
> and send to the camp, to you, palm branches and
> citrons. And you, send others from your own place
> and let them bring to you myrtle branches and willow boughs.
> Prepare them and send them to the camp [...
> ...] Farewell. (5/6 Hev 15)

> Soumaios to Jonathes,
> [son] of Baianos, and to Ma-
> sabala: Greetings.
> Since I have sent to
> you Agrippa, make
> haste to send to me
> shafts and citrons,
> and furnish them
> for the Citron celebration
> of the Jews; and do not do
> otherwise. Now it [this letter] has
> been written in Greek because
> the motivation has not been
> found to write
> in Hebrew. Send
> him quickly
> because of the feast;
> and do not do
> otherwise.
> Soumaios.
> Farewell. (5/6 Hev 3)

The closing section in each of these letters is short and rather simple in form. Yet a study of these and other Semitic letters reveals at least two epistolary conventions characteristic of the letter closings of such letters.

Farewell Wish. The most common formula found in Semitic letter closings is the 'farewell wish'. The form of this wish differs slightly depending on the language in which the letter was composed. In Hebrew letters the farewell wish is הוא שלום (Mur 42, 44, 46, 48), in Aramaic letters הוא שלם (5/6 Hev 4, 11, 15), while in Greek letters ἔρρωσο (5/6 Hev 3, 6). The farewell wish occurs in all the complete letters except two,[1] and so appears to be a standard, although not essential, convention of Semitic letter closings. This formula marks the end of the letter, and nothing normally follows it except for a signature by the letter sender and any postscriptive remarks if they are required.

As noted above, elaborations on the form of a farewell wish are common in Hellenistic letters. It is not surprising, therefore, to find the same phenomenon taking place in Semitic letters as well. For example, in Mur 42 the farewell wish reads: אהוה שלום וכל בית ישראל ('Farewell to you and to all the house of Israel'). Here the recipient of the wish is expanded from the simple 'to you' to 'and to all the house of Israel'. This type of elaboration commonly occurs in Hellenistic letters as a means of broadening the scope of a farewell wish so that it includes others beyond the recipient identified in the letter opening.

Another Semitic example of the expansion of a farewell wish is found in 5/6 Hev 6: ἔρρωσο ἀδελφέ ('Farewell, brother'). The addition of 'brother' does not, it would seem, originate from any sibling relationship between sender and recipient. Family terms were commonly used to express the philophronetic aspect of the letter, i.e., the friendly relationship that exists between the sender of the letter and its recipient.

There are no precise parallels to these closing farewell wishes in the earlier Semitic letters. The only possible link with previous Aramaic and Hebrew letters is the formula found in several of the Hermopolis papyri: לשלמכי שלחת ספרא זכה ('For your peace [i.e., well-being] I have sent this letter').[2] A closer parallel is the almost ubiquitous ἔρρωσο or ἔρρωσθε

---

1. 5/6 Hev 8; Mur 43. For further comments about the potential significance of the omission of the farewell wish in these letters, see discussion below.

2. See nos. 1.12-13; 2.17; 3.13; 5.9; 6.10; 7.4 in E. Bresciani and M. Kamil, *Le lettere aramaiche di Hermopoli* (Rome: Atti dell' Accademia Nazionale dei Lincei, 1966).

wish of Greek letters (also found in 5/6 Hev 3, 6). So it appears that the farewell wish of Semitic letters originates from the farewell wish of Greek letters. This line of dependency reflects the influence of Hellenistic epistolary practices on Semitic letter writing—even in such a zealously nationalistic circle as that of Bar Kokhba.

The function of a farewell wish seems clear enough: to say 'Good-bye' and so bring the letter to a definitive close. This closing function is strengthened by the *inclusio* that is formed between the opening greeting שלום and the closing farewell wish שלום. In this manner, the boundaries of the letter are clearly marked out.

The literal meaning of שלום ('peace', 'health', 'well-being') suggests, however, that a farewell wish functioned not merely to say 'Good-bye' but also to express concern for the health and welfare of the letter's recipient. Thus the closing שלום wish of Semitic letters appears to have served a double function, just like that of a farewell wish in Hellenistic letters of the second and third centuries AD (εὔχομαί σε ἐρρῶσθαι): to express both a word of good-bye ('Farewell') and a wish for health ('Fare well').

The fact that a farewell wish served not only to say good-bye but also to express concern for the recipient's well-being probably explains the absence of this epistolary formula in two Semitic letters. As noted above, the farewell wish is found in all the complete Semitic letters except two: 5/6 Hev 8 and Mur 43. The non-friendly, even threatening, tone of both these letters suggests that the absence of the farewell wish may be deliberate. Mur 43 reads as follows:

> From Shimon, son of Kosiba, to Yeshua,
> son of Galgula, and to the men of your company:
> Greetings. I swear by the heavens:
> Should harm come to any one of the Galileans
> who are with you, I'll put your feet
> in chains as I did
> to the son of Aflul.
> Shimon, son of [Kosiba, writer].

If the absence of a farewell wish in this letter is, in fact, deliberate, then we have here an example of a letter closing that has been adapted in such a way as to reflect more directly the contents and tone of the letter body.

Signature. A second epistolary convention of the closings of Semitic letters is a signature (5/6 Hev 1[?], 3, 6, 8; Mur 42, 43, 46, 48, unpublished letter from Nahal Se'elim). Semitic letters differ in this regard from Hellenistic letters, which rarely include a signature but rather have the closing conventions frequently written in the author's own hand (the 'autograph'). Thus, when Paul includes his signature in the formula used to indicate to his readers that he is now taking over from his amanuensis and writing for himself ('I, Paul, write this in my own hand': Phlm. 19; 1 Cor. 16.21; Gal. 6.11; 2 Thess. 3.17; Col. 4.18), it may be that he is being influenced in this specific area by Semitic, rather than Hellenistic, epistolary practice.

In Semitic letters written in Greek, the closing signature is clearly that of the letter sender and occurs prior to the farewell wish. For example, 5/6 Hev 6 closes as follows: "Αννανος· ἔρρωσο ἀδελφέ ('Annanos. Farewell, brother'). In letters written in Hebrew and Aramaic, however, the situation is complicated slightly by the fact that the signature is always accompanied by the word כתבה. One would expect כתבה to be a designation of the secretary and to be translated as '[So-and-so] wrote it [i.e., the letter]' or '[So-and-so] was the scribe'. The signature would then be that of the amanuensis rather than that of the sender.[1] This interpretation does, in fact, work for 5/6 Hev 8:

> Simeon, son of Kosiba,
> to Jonathan, son of Ba'yan,
> and Masabbalah, son of Simeon.
> You are to send to me Eleazer,
> son of Hitah, immediately, before
> the Sabbath.
> Simeon, son of Judah, wrote it (כתבה).

Since the name of the closing signature differs from the name identified in the letter opening, it would be natural to assume that the closing signature of Simeon, son of Judah, refers to the secretary who wrote the letter on behalf of Simeon, son of Kosiba.

Such an interpretation of כתבה, however, that it refers to the amanuensis, is contradicted by Mur 42 and Mur 46:

---

1. So Fitzmyer, 'Aramaic Epistolography', p. 217; implicitly, Yadin, 'Expedition D', p. 45.

From the village managers of Beth-Mashko, from Yeshua and Elazar,
to Yeshua, son of Galgula, camp commander: Greetings. We (hereby) apprise
you that the cow which Yehosef, son of Ariston, took from Yaaqov,
son of Yehuda, whose residence in Beth-Mashko, is his [i.e., Yehosef's].
If the 'Gentiles' were not so close to us, I would have gone up
and declared you free of obligation on this account.
For I don't want you to say that it is through neglect that
I have not come up to see you. Best wishes to you and to all Beth-Israel.
Yeshua, son of Elazar, writer (כתבה).
Elazar, son of Yehosef, writer (כתבה).
Yaaqov, son of Yehuda, principal party (על נפשה).
Shaul, son of Elazar, witness (עד).
Yehosef, son of Yehosef, witness (עד).
Yaaqov, son of Yehosef, notary (מעיד). (Mur 42)

From Yonatan, son of [MHNYM] to Yose, [son of...]
Greetings. [I] don't need your [...]
son of Eliezer that you'll give him [...]
that he is here with me in Ein-Gedi [...]
the poor and buries the dead [...]
he needs nothing but what is his [...]
at all. In what comes to him [...]
everything which [...]
'MR upon him that he dismiss by it/him [...]
Yehonatan, son of MH[NYM] writ[er] (כתבה)
Farewell. (Mur 46)

Two things need be noted here. First, that the names of the closing
signatures are the same as the names of the senders found in the letter
opening. Second, that the closing signatures are written in a different
hand than that found in the main body of the letter. Consequently, the
word כתבה cannot be referring to an amanuensis and be translated as
'[So-and-so] wrote it'. Rather, כתבה must be referring to the sender of
the letter and ought to be translated as '[So-and-so] sent it' or '[So-and-
so] issued it'.[1] Thus it must be assumed (1) that secretaries wrote the
bodies of both Mur 42 and Mur 46, and (2) that the senders themselves
closed their respective letters with their own signatures followed by the

1.   Note Milik's translation of כתבה in Benoit *et al.*, *Discoveries in Judean Desert*, II, p. 158: 'l'a (fait) écrire', 'l'a dicté (à un scribe professionel)'. See also the discussion in Pardee, 'Hebrew Epistolography', pp. 341-42; *idem, Ancient Hebrew Letters*, pp. 125-26; Alexander, 'Epistolary Literature', p. 591, n. 48.

word כתבה—a notation affirming that the person just named had issued or sent the letter.

Aramaic letter 5/6 Hev 8 (for text of this letter, see above), however, does not fit this pattern, for it opens with the sender being identified as 'Simeon, son of Kosiba' but closes with the signature 'Simeon, son of Judah'. There are two explanations that could possibly solve this apparent discrepancy: (1) that בר כוסבה should not be understood as a patronymic ('son of Kosiba') but as a title; or (2) that the person identified in the closing signature ('Simon, son of Judah') dictated the letter to an amanuensis, but did so in the name of (i.e., with the authority of) Simon, son of Kosiba.[1] But whatever happened in this particular letter, the common practice in Semitic letters as a whole was, quite clearly, for a letter to be signed by the sender, not his secretary.

But what was the purpose of closing a letter with one's own signature? That it was not intended simply to identify the letter sender is obvious from the fact that not all letters close with a signature. Furthermore, that function had been fulfilled already in the letter opening which explicitly names the sender.

In a couple of letters, the closing signature clearly possesses a legal function. Most illustrative in this regard is Mur 42 (for the text of this letter, see above). This letter was written by two officials of the village Beth-Mashko to an official of another village. Its contents either demand the return of a stolen cow[2] or, as is more likely the case, confirm the purchase of the animal.[3] At the close of the letter, following an expanded farewell wish, there are six signatures, each coupled with a descriptive word identifying the named person. The first two signatures, 'Yeshua, son of Elazar' and 'Elazar, son of Yehosef,' are followed by the word כתבה. As we have seen above, the word כתבה identifies these two men as the senders of the document—a fact that is confirmed by the letter opening. The third signature is that of 'Yaaqov, son of Yehuda,' who is the previous owner of the cow. His signature is followed by the phrase על נפשה, a formula common in the Murabba'at documents for

1. E. Volterra, 'Intorno a AP. 131 in. 17–18', in *Mélanges Eugène Tisserant*. I. *Ecriture sainte—Ancien Orient* (Studie Testi 231; Città del Vaticano: Biblioteca apostolica vaticana, 1964), pp. 443-48. See also E. Koffmahn, *Die Doppelurkunden aus der Wüste Juda* (Leiden: Brill, 1968), *passim*.

2. Pardee, 'Hebrew Epistolography', p. 342; *idem, Ancient Hebrew Letters*, p. 125.

3. So Yadin, *Bar Kokhba*, p. 136.

designating the adherence of one or more of the principal parties of the document to the stipulations contained therein.[1] This brief phrase functioned like an oath formula and can be paraphrased as: '[So-and-so] hereby takes it upon himself to accede to the provisions of this document'.[2] The fourth and fifth signatures, 'Shaul, son of Elazar' and 'Yehosef, son of Yehosef', are each followed by the word עד, which means 'witness'. The sixth and final signature is that of 'Yaaqov, son of Yehosef', who is identified by the title מעיד. This word, unattested elsewhere as a designation of a social office or function, probably describes a person who serves as a verifier of witnesses' signatures, i.e., a notary.[3]

The legal function of these six closing signatures is confirmed by a number of facts. First, the letter was written by officials of one village to an official of another village. Second, two of the men who signed their names are explicitly identified as witnesses. Third, the term על נפשה frequently appears next to signatures in legal documents. Finally, the content of the letter describes a legal transaction involving the purchase of an animal. The activities of the Roman army had made it impossible for the parties involved in the selling and purchasing of a cow to meet in person. So a meeting was replaced by a letter, which was signed by village officials, the seller, witnesses, and a notary. The closing signatures, therefore, serve to make the letter a legally binding document.

A slightly different function of a closing signature appears to be at work in Mur 43:

> From Shimon, son of Kosiba, to Yeshua,
> son of Galgula, and to the men of your company:
> Greetings. I swear by the heavens:
> Should harm come to any one of the Galileans
> who are with you, I'll put your feet
> in chains as I did
> to the son of Aflul.
> Shimon, son of [Kosiba, writer].

1. So Benoit *et al.*, *Discoveries in Judean Desert*, II, pp. 155-59.

2. Pardee, 'Hebrew Epistolography', p. 342; *idem*, *Ancient Hebrew Letters*, pp. 125-26.

3. Milik (in Benoit *et al.*, *Discoveries in the Judean Desert*, II, p. 158) claims that the מעיד signature belongs to that of the scribe who penned the letter ('C'est sans doute la signature du scribe'). He explains the difference in handwriting between the letter and the final signature as the result of one person using two styles: a formal style for his role as a scribe; a cursive style for his own signature. If Milik is correct, then the scribe would be functioning as both the writer of the letter and its notary.

The letter opening identifies the sender as the commander-in-chief of the Jewish rebellion, Shimon, son of Kosiba (Simon bar Kokhba), and the recipient as Yeshua, son of Galgula, along with the men who are part of his company. After the initial greeting, the letter body opens with an oath: 'I swear by the heavens' (see Deut. 4.26; 30.19; 31.28; 1 Macc. 2.37). This biblical oath sets the threatening tone of the letter. Shimon demands that his readers not harm the 'Galileans' who are with them. Failure to comply with this command will result in the penalty of imprisonment. To demonstrate that this is no idle warning, Shimon reminds Yeshua and his men of the fate of the son of Aflul.

This threatening letter then closes with a signature written in a different hand from that of the rest of the document. Unfortunately, the final letters of this signature are difficult to discern, thereby resulting in some confusion about (1) the family name, and (2) the accompanying title originally found in the text. For the title, Milik restores the text to read על נפשה ('principal witness') on the basis of the oath quality and imprecatory tone of the letter.[1] The proper use of על נפשה, however, appears to be restricted to business documents, and so there is no valid reason for reading this word in Mur 43 instead of the expected כתבה ('[So-and-so wrote it').

For the family name, Yadin suggests that the letter originally closed with the signature of a person that differs from the sender identified in the letter opening.[2] Yadin does this on the basis of 5/6 Hev 8, which is another letter from Shimon, son of Kosiba. Since 5/6 Hev 8 closes with the signature 'Simeon, son of Judah', Yadin argues that the signature of the same person should be understood in Mur 43. If correct, a scribe of Shimon son of Kosiba would have drafted the letter and another party (Shimon, son of Judah) signed it. In this interpretation, the signature has something of a legal function: the command is certified by the signature.[3]

If the handwriting of the signatures of 5/6 Hev 8 and Mur 43 were similar, this would support Yadin's restoration of the text. Yadin makes no comment about the handwriting of the respective signatures; and, since 5/6 Hev 8 has not been published, it is impossible to make the comparison ourselves.

A simpler and more plausible view, however, would be to restore the

1. Benoit *et al.*, *Discoveries in the Judean Desert*, II, p. 161.
2. Yadin, 'Expedition D', p. 45.
3. So Schnider and Stenger (*Neutestamentlichen Briefformular*, pp. 140-41), who argue that all the signatures of the Semitic letters have a legal function.

closing of Mur 43 to read: 'Shimon, son of Kosiba, writer'. This reading would also agree with the pattern found in other letters containing a closing signature. For in all other letters with a signature (with the notable exception of 5/6 Hev 8), the name of the signature in the closing is identical with that of the sender identified in the letter opening.[1] It seems most probable, therefore, that a scribe wrote the body of Mur 43 and that Shimon, son of Kosiba signed it in his own hand. The signature in this case would appear to have an authenticating and/or authoritative function. Shimon leaves out the farewell wish (in keeping with the threatening tone of the letter) but includes his own signature, thereby proving that the letter has come from him and ensuring that it will be obeyed.

Another possible function of a closing signature, besides legalizing or authenticating a letter, was to give the correspondence a more personal touch. This purpose may have been at work in the Greek letter of 5/6 Hev 6:

> Annanos to brother Jonathes: Greetings.
> Since Simon, son of Chosibas, has written back again
> (i.e. has ordered) to send...
> [for] the needs of our brothers...
> ....
> and to send these things immediately in safety.
> Annanos.
> Farewell, brother.

This letter's poor state of preservation make definitive statements about its contents impossible. The general sense, however, appears to be as follows: Annanos has just received a letter from Simon, son of Chosibas, which orders him to send supplies immediately to meet the needs of his fellow countrymen; after receiving this letter, Annanos writes to Jonathes, presumably to enlist his help in answering this written request for aid. If the use of ἀδελφός in the letter opening and closing is to be understood literally, with Jonathes being a genuine sibling of Annanos, the closing signature would serve to make the letter more personal.

---

1. It might also be noted that the parallel between 5/6 Hev 8 and Mur 43 is not exact, for these two letters were written in different locations and in different languages. Furthermore, other letters possibly written by Bar Kokhba (e.g., Mur 44) do not have the signature 'Shimon, son of Judah' in the closing.

Family designations such as ἀδελφός, however, were commonly used in letters as a friendly way of describing others, even though of no family relationship. If Annanos and Jonathes were not brothers, then the closing signature probably has the function of authenticating or making officially binding the commands given in the body of the letter.

The paucity of extant Semitic letters makes it difficult to establish with certainty the purpose or function of a closing signature. From the few letters available, however, it appears that a closing signature probably had a number of diverse functions. In letters pertaining to financial matters or concerns, the signature seems to have had a legal function, turning the letter into a binding contract. In letters dealing with various commands and instructions from village officials or military superiors to others, the signature appears to have had an authenticating and/or authoritative function, proving that the letter did indeed come from the person identified in the opening, thereby ensuring that its contents would be obeyed. In letters concerning private or family matters, the signature may possibly have had a personalizing function, giving the letter a more friendly and intimate tone.

Postscript. At least one of the primary Semitic letters contains some postscriptive remarks:

> From Shimon to Yeshua son of Galgula:
> Greetings. You are to send five
> kor measures of wheat by men of my house
> who are known to you. Prepare for them
> an empty place. They will be with you
> this sabbath, if they desire to come.
> Keep up your courage and strengthen that place.
> Farewell. I have designated the person
> who is to give you his wheat. They may
> take it after the sabbath. (Mur 44)

Shimon (bar Kokhba?) sends a letter to Yeshua with instructions concerning a shipment of wheat. Yeshua should expect the arrival of Shimon's men, who will require lodging and five kors (about twenty-five bushels) of wheat to be transported elsewhere. After a final word of encouragement, the letter closes with a farewell wish. Since a farewell wish in other ancient letters, both Hellenistic and Semitic, is always the final epistolary convention in the closing, the material that follows must be considered a postscript. Here a postscript is necessary because

Shimon has forgotten to mention in the body of the letter that he had made arrangements to have the required grain deposited with Yeshua. Also, to ensure that his men would not violate the sabbath, Shimon appends a final command about when they should transport the wheat.

A postscript is obviously not a normative closing convention of Semitic letters. It occurs here, however, out of a desire to include some additional information that has not been given in the body of the letter.

b. *Secondary Letters*

To complete my analysis of epistolary conventions belonging to the closing sections of Semitic letters, I turn next to secondary letters that have been incorporated into the texts of various literary works. Although the closing sections in many of these letters are missing due to their assimilation into the narrative framework of their host compositions, a number of closing conventions still remain and can be readily identified.

Farewell Wish. As in primary letters, the most common epistolary convention of the closing section of secondary letters is the farewell wish. The form of the wish is identical to the Greek Bar Kokhba letters (5/6 Hev 3, 6) and to Hellenistic letters in general: ἔρρωσο or ἔρρωσθε (Josephus, *Life* 227; *Ant.* 11.104; 11.130; 12.56; 2 Macc. 11.21; 11.33; *3 Macc.* 7.9; *Ep. Arist.* 40, 46; see *2 Apoc. Bar.* 86.1). In one letter, however, the farewell wish is expressed by ὑγιάνετε (2 Macc. 11.38). The use of this word for the farewell wish is rather striking. For although the verb ὑγιάνειν can be found in closing health wishes of the third and second century BC (ἐπιμέλου σεαυτοῦ ἵν' ὑγιαίνῃς: 'Take care of yourself in order that you may be well'), it is never used as a substitute for the closing farewell wish ἔρρωσθε.

Elaboration of the farewell wish also occurs in secondary Semitic letters. Two letters expand the temporal aspect of the wish: 'Farewell always (ἀεί)' (*Ep. Arist.* 33); 'And at all times (Syriac: *b^ekhulz^ebhan* [Codex Ambrosianus]) fare well' (*2 Apoc. Bar.* 86.1). One letter includes within the farewell wish a term of endearment: 'Farewell most loved (φίλτατε) friend' (Josephus, *Life* 365).

Date. A number of the closing sections of secondary letters list the date following the farewell wish. For example, the letter of Antiochus to the Jews recorded in 2 Macc. 11.33 closes as follows: ἔρρωσθε· ἔτους ἑκατοστοῦ τεσσαρακοστοῦ ὀγδόου, Ξανθικοῦ πέμπῃ καὶ δεκάτῃ

('Farewell. Year one hundred and forty eight, the fifteenth [day] of Xanthicus').[1] This agrees with the shorter dating formula found in Greek letters of the Ptolemaic and early Roman periods: the word ἔτους or its equivalent representative symbol 'L' followed by the calendar year, month and day. The presence of the dating formula in certain letters is likely due to the official nature of their contents. For all the letters that include the date are official letters written by various kings or government rulers.

Health Wish. There are quite a few examples among the secondary letters of an *opening* health wish. Some are combined with the opening salutation and are rather brief: e.g., *Ep. Arist.* 35, χαίρειν καὶ ἐρρῶσθαι ('Greetings and good health'); 2 Macc. 1.10, χαίρειν καὶ ὑγιαίνειν ('Greetings and good health'). Other opening health wishes are given independently and are more elaborate: e.g., 2 Macc. 11.28, εἰ ἔρρωσθε, εἴη ἂν ὡς βουλόμεθα· καὶ αὐτοὶ δὲ ὑγιαίνομεν ('If you are well, it would be as we wish; we ourselves also are well').[2] The influence of Greek epistolary practice here is obvious, for these opening health wishes are identical to those found in the Greek papyrus letters.

While the opening health wish is common in secondary Semitic letters, there exists only one possible occurrence of a *closing* health wish: that found in Josephus, *Ant.* 17.135, σὺ δ'εὐτυχοίης περὶ τὸ πρᾶγμα ('May you have success in the matter'). The absence of more closing health wishes can be explained by two factors. First, as noted above, the farewell wish not only expressed a word of parting but also a word of concern for the well-being of the letter recipient. This additional function of the farewell wish is confirmed by the elaboration 'always' (*Ep. Arist.* 33; *2 Bar.* 86.1), for the letter writer is obviously not giving an eternal goodbye but rather a wish for perpetual well-being. Thus there was no need for a separate closing health wish since this concern for the recipients' health was already expressed in the farewell wish. Second, it is quite probable that some letters did originally have a closing health wish but that this wish, like other epistolary conventions of the closing, has been omitted when the letter was incorporated into its host text.

---

1. For secondary Semitic letters that include a closing date, see also 2 Macc. 1.10a; 11.21 and 11.38; Josephus, *Ant.* 20.14.

2. For other opening health wishes, see 2 Macc 9.19; *3 Macc.* 3.13; 7.2; Josephus, *Ant.* 12.51; 12.148; 13.166; *Life* 226; *Ep. Arist.* 41.

3. *Summary*

Our study of ancient Semitic letters has highlighted the presence of a few epistolary conventions commonly found in the closings of these letters. In the primary letters, the closing consists of a farewell wish and often a signature of the letter sender. In the secondary or incorporated letters, the closing also has a farewell wish and occasionally includes the date. The closings of Semitic letters are shorter and less elaborate than the closings in Hellenistic letters, even though the latter are themselves rather brief and simple.

There is some evidence in the Semitic letters of a connection between the body and the closing sections. For example, a letter of warning or rebuke may omit the farewell wish so that the closing echoes the threatening tone of the body. Or letters from kings or government officials may include the date following the farewell wish so that the closing reflects the official nature of the material in the body. Or again, a letter may end with the personal signature of the sender so that the closing either legalizes, authenticates or personalizes the correspondence.

These links between the closing and body sections of ancient Semitic letters, however, are only general. As we found with respect to ancient Hellenistic letters, there does not appear among the Semitic letters to be any deliberate and careful adaptation of closings so that they summarize and echo key issues previously taken up in their respective bodies. The closings of Semitic letters are too short to allow for this degree of clever manipulation. Nevertheless, the few links that do exist between Semitic letter closings and their respective letter bodies indicate that their letter writers did not haphazardly end their letters but rather were sensitive in choosing closing epistolary conventions appropriate to the document's contents.

Chapter 4

CLOSING CONVENTIONS IN THE PAULINE LETTERS:
FORMS AND VARIATIONS

This study so far has been focused on the closing conventions of
Hellenistic and Semitic letters in order to understand more exactly the
epistolary practice of the ancient world in which Paul lived and wrote. I
now turn my attention to the apostle's own correspondence so as to
discover the various epistolary conventions that he used to close his
letters. Although the influence of Hellenistic and, to a lesser degree,
Semitic letters on Paul will become obvious, so also will become clear
Paul's adaptation of existing epistolary conventions and his creation of
forms unparalleled in ancient letters.

The primary concern of this chapter is to establish the form of the
various epistolary conventions found in Paul's letter closings and to note
variations within these forms. For though some of these variations may
appear at first glance insignificant, further analysis will reveal how Paul
in many cases has deliberately and carefully adapted such closing conventions so that they echo and point back to key issues previously
addressed in their respective letters. Only a brief explanation will be
given here about the significance of an altered form in a Pauline letter
closing and about its connection with material found in the body of that
letter. A more exhaustive treatment of how Paul's closing conventions
echo—sometimes, in fact, even summarize—earlier material will be
taken up in Chapter Five that follows.

My analysis will be concerned primarily with the undisputed letters of
Paul: Romans, 1 and 2 Corinthians, Galatians, Philippians, 1 and 2
Thessalonians,[1] and Philemon. References to the disputed Pauline letters

---

1. The Pauline authorship of 2 Thessalonians has been an issue of great dispute,
being questioned as early as 1801 by J.E.C. Schmidt ('Vermuthungen über die
beiden Briefe an die Thessalonicher', in *Bibliothek für Kritik und Exegese des Neuen
Testaments und ältesten Christengeschichte* 2.3 [Hadamar: Gelehrtenbuchhandlung,

(Ephesians, Colossians, 1 and 2 Timothy, Titus) and to the non-Pauline letters of the NT (Hebrews, 1 and 2 Peter, 2 and 3 John, Jude, Revelation) will also be made for the sake of completeness and comparative study, although comments on these writings will be minimal. The order in which the various closing conventions will be treated loosely follows their frequency, beginning with those formulae that are most common.

1. *The Grace Benediction*

The most common epistolary convention of a Pauline letter closing is the 'grace benediction'. It closes every one of Paul's letters, including those whose authenticity is questioned. But not only is the grace benediction the most frequent of the closing conventions, it is formally the most

1801], pp. 380-86). The first major attack against its authenticity, however, was launched by W. Wrede (*Die Echtheit des zweiten Thessalonicherbriefes* [Leipzig: Hinrichs, 1903]), who based his argument primarily on literary parallels between the two Thessalonian letters. Although Wrede's conclusions were followed by others, the majority of biblical scholars up until the late sixties of this century affirmed that 2 Thessalonians was the work of Paul. The appearance of W. Trilling's *Untersuchungen zum 2 Thessalonicherbrief* (Leipzig: St. Benno) in 1972, however, marked a shift in the tide of critical opinion in favor of the letter's inauthenticity (see also Trilling's *Der zweite Brief an die Thessalonicher* [Neukirchen: Neukirchener, 1980], and more recently, G.S. Holland, *The Tradition that You Received from Us: 2 Thessalonians in the Pauline Tradition* [Tübingen: Mohr-Siebeck, 1988]). I.H. Marshall, in his 1983 commentary (*1 and 2 Thessalonians* [Grand Rapids: Eerdmans, 1983], pp. 29-45), re-examined Trilling's argument in detail and came out decidedly in support of the letter's authenticity. This position was later upheld by Jewett (*Thessalonian Correspondence*, pp. 1–46) in his study of the issue. Although there are many who deny the authenticity of 2 Thessalonians, the tide appears to have come full circle so that the majority once again affirms its Pauline authorship: e.g., W.G. Kümmel, *Introduction to the New Testament* (Nashville: Abingdon, 1973), pp. 264-69; E. Best, *A Commentary on the First and Second Epistles to the Thessalonians* (London: A. & C. Black, 1977), pp. 50-58; F.F. Bruce, *1 and 2 Thessalonians* (Waco, TX: Word Books, 1982), pp. xxxii-xxxiv; J.C. Hurd, 'Concerning the Authenticity of 2 Thessalonians' (unpublished paper, SBL Pauline Seminar, 1983); C.A. Wanamaker, *The Epistles to the Thessalonians* (Grand Rapids: Eerdmans, 1990), pp. 17-28. For a detailed discussion on the complex issues involved in determining the authenticity of Paul's letters, see K.J. Neumann, *The Authenticity of the Pauline Epistles in the Light of Stylostatistical Analysis* (Atlanta: Scholars, 1990). Significantly, Neumann's own analysis supports the Pauline authorship of 2 Thessalonians.

consistent. The grace benediction exhibits a striking uniformity (see Table 1), consisting of three basic elements: the wish, the divine source, and the recipient.[1]

a. *Elements of the Grace Benediction*
The Wish. The wish or content of a Pauline closing benediction is expressed in the nominative case, with χάρις ('grace') appearing in every instance. Because of the fixed form of the grace benediction throughout the Pauline letters, the two supplemental wishes found in 2 Cor. 13.13 are rather striking. For in addition to the expected χάρις, this benediction also contains a reference to ἀγάπη ('love') and κοινωνία ('fellowship'). This expansion of the standard shorter form evidently stems from the specific situation of the Corinthian church, where unrest and quarreling characterized relations between believers.[2] The additional elements of 'love' and 'fellowship', therefore, should probably be seen as not merely a fortuitous expansion but a deliberate alteration of the standard form by Paul, thereby causing this grace benediction to relate more directly to the specific epistolary situation. The closing wish for grace, in fact, fits the thrust of the entire closing section of 13.11-13, which likewise emphasizes the need for peace and harmony within the Corinthian church.

The Divine Source. Paul identifies the divine source of the wish by means of a genitive phrase that possesses a remarkably constant form: τοῦ κυρίου (ἡμῶν) Ἰησοῦ (Χριστοῦ) ('of [our] Lord Jesus [Christ]'). The identification of the divine giver of the blessing is present in all the undisputed letters of Paul. It is, however, noticeably absent in all the disputed letters.

1.   The order of these three elements is constant in all the Pauline closing grace benedictions. A different order, however, is followed in those benedictions found in the opening and body sections of Paul's letters. Mullins ('Benediction,', pp. 59-61) uses the order of the elements to classify the benedictions into various 'types': an opening type (wish, recipient, wish, divine source); an intermediate type (divine source, wish, recipient), and a closing type (wish, divine source, recipient).
2.   A. Plummer (*Second Epistle of St. Paul to the Corinthians* [New York: Charles Scribner's Sons, 1915], p. 383) notes that 'a community in which there had been so much party-spirit and contention required an outpouring of the love of God and of the fellowship of the Holy Spirit'.

	Wish	Divine Source	Recipient
Rom. 16.20b	ἡ χάρις	τοῦ κυρίου ἡμῶν Ἰησοῦ	μεθ' ὑμῶν
1 Cor. 16.23	ἡ χάρις	τοῦ κυρίου Ἰησοῦ	μεθ' ὑμῶν
2 Cor. 13.13	ἡ χάρις ἡ ἀγάπη ἡ κοινωνία	τοῦ κυρίου Ἰησοῦ Χριστοῦ καὶ τοῦ θεοῦ καὶ τοῦ ἁγίου πνεύματος	μετὰ πάντων ὑμῶν
Gal. 6.18	ἡ χάρις	τοῦ κυρίου ἡμῶν Ἰησοῦ Χριστοῦ	μετὰ τοῦ πνεύματος ὑμῶν ἀδελφοί
Phil. 4.23	ἡ χάρις	τοῦ κυρίου Ἰησοῦ Χριστοῦ	μετὰ τοῦ πνεύματος ὑμῶν
1 Thess. 5.28	ἡ χάρις	τοῦ κυρίου ἡμῶν Ἰησοῦ Χριστοῦ	μεθ' ὑμῶν
2 Thess. 3.18	ἡ χάρις	τοῦ κυρίου ἡμῶν Ἰησοῦ Χριστοῦ	μεθ' ὑμῶν
Phlm. 25	ἡ χάρις	τοῦ κυρίου Ἰησοῦ Χριστοῦ	μετὰ τοῦ πνεύματος ὑμῶν
Eph. 6.24	ἡ χάρις		μετὰ πάντων τῶν ἀγαπώντων τὸν κύριον ἡμῶν Ἰησοῦν Χριστὸν ἐν ἀφθαρσίᾳ
Col. 4.18b	ἡ χάρις		μεθ' ὑμῶν
1 Tim. 6.21b	ἡ χάρις		μεθ' ὑμῶν
2 Tim. 4.22b	ἡ χάρις		μεθ' ὑμῶν
Tit. 3.15b	ἡ χάρις		μετὰ πάντων ὑμῶν
Heb. 13.25	ἡ χάρις		μετὰ πάντων ὑμῶν
Rev. 22.21	ἡ χάρις	τοῦ κυρίου Ἰησοῦ	μετὰ πάντων

Table 1. Grace Benedictions

The genitive phrase is clearly used in a subjective sense denoting source, i.e., the grace that Jesus Christ has and gives.[1] Although Paul ordinarily refers to God as the source of grace, he occasionally speaks of Christ in this fashion (2 Cor. 8.9; 12.9; Gal. 1.6; [5.4]; 2 Thess. 1.12). On the whole, however, the depiction of Christ as the source of grace is a characteristic feature of the letter closings.[2]

The one grace benediction that differs from the rest in terms of its divine source is 2 Cor. 13.13, where the two additional wishes of ἀγάπη and κοινωνία are coupled with τοῦ θεοῦ and τοῦ πνεύματος respectively. The motivation for this elaboration probably did not lie in the intention of Paul to teach anything about the threefold nature of God or about the relation of Father, Son, and Holy Spirit to one another. If such were the case, Paul would have referred to God as 'Father' and mentioned Jesus second rather than first, following the pattern he uses in his letter openings. Nor did Paul likely borrow from any existing formula circulating among the churches of his day, for this tripartite reference does not appear in any of the apostle's other letters.[3] Instead, this benediction seems to be a spontaneous creation of Paul, originating out of a desire to identify the divine source from whom the Corinthians receive 'love' and 'fellowship' in sharp contrast to the enmity and division currently found in their church.

The Recipient. The recipient of the wish or benediction is always introduced in Paul's letters by the preposition μετά ('with') and followed by the plural of the second-person personal pronoun ὑμῶν ('you').[4] Two additional elements sometimes found in the prepositional phrase include: (a) the identification of the recipient by τοῦ πνεύματος ὑμῶν ('your spirit': Gal. 6.18; Phil. 4.23; Phlm. 25), and (b) the adjective πάντων

1. See BDF §162; N. Turner, *A Grammar of the New Testament*, vol. 3 (Edinburgh: T. & T. Clark, 1963), p. 210.
2. The letter openings also identify Christ as the source of grace, but there Christ possesses a secondary role to 'God our Father': Rom. 1.7; 1 Cor. 1.3; 2 Cor. 1.2; Gal. 1.3; Phil. 1.2; 2 Thess. 1.2; Phlm. 1.3.
3. See Plummer, *Corinthians*, p. 383. J. Jeremias (*Jerusalem zur Zeit Jesu* [Göttingen: Vandenhoeck & Ruprecht, 1958], II, p. 109) thinks that the trinitarian reference is derived from a baptismal formula.
4. The only exception is Eph. 6.24 where the personal pronoun has been replaced with a more expansive description: μετὰ πάντων τῶν ἀγαπώντων τὸν κύριον ἡμῶν Ἰησοῦν Χριστὸν ἐν ἀφθαρσίᾳ ('with all those who love our Lord Jesus Christ in eternity').

('all': Rom. 16.24; 2 Cor. 13.13; 2 Thess. 3.18). The former element is
used in an anthropological sense, and so 'your spirit' means exactly the
same as 'you'.[1] It would be reading too much into the singular
πνεύματος used with the plural ὑμῶν to argue that the singular noun
stresses 'the unity of the body of believers in which one spirit is to be
found'.[2] All one can say with justification is that the addition of the genitive is a more emphatic way of identifying the recipients of the grace
benediction: Paul's closing wish is that the grace of Jesus Christ will rest
on the spirit of *each one* of his readers.[3]

The addition of πάντων in the grace benedictions of 2 Cor. 13.13 and
2 Thess. 3.18[4] also has an emphatic function. In ancient letters, the
adjective πᾶς in a prepositional phrase was commonly added to expand
the scope of a farewell wish or greeting.[5] In similar fashion, Paul uses
πᾶς to stress the fact that his final grace benediction is intended for *all*
his readers, even those whom he rebuked earlier in the letter. As
Leon Morris notes in his discussion of 2 Thess. 3.18, 'the addition of
"all" is significant, and is in view of the specific disturbances noted
earlier.'[6] That this addition is to be viewed as intentional seems
confirmed by the fact that πᾶς occurs four more times in this letter's
brief closing of 3.16-18, thereby highlighting the fact that Paul was
concerned not to leave anyone out of his benediction.

Another grace benediction that identifies the recipient of the wish in a
somewhat distinctive fashion is Gal. 6.18, for it adds the vocative

---

1.   So E. Schweizer, 'πνεῦμα', *TDNT*, VI, p. 435; R. Bultmann, *Theology of the
New Testament* (London: SCM, 1952), I, p. 206.

2.   So R.P. Martin, *Philippians* (Grand Rapids: Eerdmans, 1980), p. 171.

3.   See G.F. Hawthorne, *Philippians* (Waco, TX: Word Books, 1983), pp. 215-
16; F.F. Bruce, *Philippians* (Peabody: Hendrickson, 1989), p. 160.

4.   The addition of πάντων is also found in Rom. 16.24, which is textually
suspect, and in 1 Cor. 16.24, which is not a grace benediction but a postscript in
which Paul expresses his personal love for his Corinthian readers.

5.   For examples of ancient Greco-Roman letters that use πᾶς to expand the
scope of the farewell wish, see discussion of the 'farewell wish' in Chapter 2.

6.   L. Morris, *The First and Second Epistles to the Thessalonians* (Grand
Rapids: Eerdmans, 1959), p. 262 n. 27. See also W. Hendriksen, *I–II Thessalonians*
(Grand Rapids: Baker, 1955), p. 209; D.E.H. Whiteley, *Thessalonians in the Revised
Standard Version, With Introduction and Commentary* (Oxford: Oxford University
Press, 1969), p. 112. For a similar evaluation of the addition of πάντων in the grace
benediction of 2 Cor. 13.13, see Plummer, *Corinthians*, p. 384; F. Fisher,
Commentary on 1 & 2 Corinthians (Waco, TX: Word Books, 1975), p. 446;
R.P. Martin, *2 Corinthians* (Waco, TX: Word Books, 1986), pp. 496, 506.

ἀδελφοί ('brothers') and a final ἀμήν ('Amen').[1] In light of Paul's harsh tone in this letter, the addition of 'brothers' in the vocative may have been intended to reassure the apostle's readers of his continued love and concern for them. This possibility is strengthened by the fact that the vocative ἀδελφοί appears at strategic places throughout the letter (1.11; 3.15; 4.12, 28, 31; 5.11,13; 6.1).

b. *The Verb in the Grace Benediction*

A feature of the grace benediction in Paul's letter closings that warrants attention is the omission of the main verb. For although the copula εἰμί is clearly implied, it is less obvious which mood of the verb was intended. There are three possibilities: (1) If the indicative (ἐστίν) is understood, then the benediction would have the sense of a declarative statement: 'The grace of the Lord Jesus *is* with you'. (2) Another option is the optative (εἴη) in which the benediction would express a holy or pious wish: '*May* the grace of the Lord Jesus be with you'. (3) A third possibility is that the ellipsis of the verb has in view the imperative mood (ἔστω): 'The grace of the Lord Jesus *be* with you'.[2] Support can be found for all three views. The *indicative* has appealed to some because it captures the confidence with which Paul presumably would have spoken. Willem van Unnik, for example, argues that understanding the grace benediction as a wish 'falls short of the certitude of Paul's faith'.[3] Support for the *optative*, however, can be derived from other benedictions or wishes in Paul's letters, most of which use the optative (Rom. 15.5-6; 15.13; 1 Thess. 3.11; 3.12-13; 5.23; 2 Thess. 2.16-17; 3.5; 3.16).[4]

---

1.   Although some reject ἀμήν as a later addition by a copyist in accordance with liturgical practice, it has extremely strong textual support (it is omitted only by a few less important witnesses: G itg Marius Victorinus Ambrosiaster). Similarly, there is good manuscript support for the ἀμήν found in the grace benediction of 1 Corinthians and Philippians. But even if original, the ἀμήν probably serves as a confirmatory response to the whole letter and not simply to the grace benediction.

2.   Most translations understand the imperative to be implied in the grace benediction: e.g., KJV, RSV, NIV (but see 2 Cor. 13.13), JB, NAS.

3.   W.C. van Unnik, '"Dominus Vobiscum": The Background of a Liturgical Formula', in *New Testament Essays in Memory of T.W. Manson* (ed. A.J. Higgins; Manchester: Manchester University Press, 1959), p. 291. See also C.F.D.Moule, *Worship in the New Testament* (London: Lutterworth, 1961), pp. 78-79; G. Delling, *Worship in the New Testament* (London: Darton, Longman & Todd, 1962), p. 75.

4.   Note, however, the use of the indicative (future tense) in the peace benediction of Rom. 16.20, 2 Cor. 13.11, and Phil. 4.9.

By analogy, this practice suggests that the same mood is implied in the grace benedictions as well. Furthermore, although the opening benedictions of Paul's letters also omit the verb, the opening benedictions of other NT letters have the optative (1 Pet. 1.2; 2 Pet. 1.2; Jude 2). Yet it need be noted that an *imperative* understanding is supported by parallels with ancient Greco-Roman letters. For Paul's grace benedictions serve to bring his letters to a definitive close, and so correspond to the common Hellenistic farewell wish ἔρρωσο that is always expressed in the imperative mood.

It is impossible to know with certainty which of the three moods was intended by Paul. Yet total agnosticism on the question is not appropriate either. For the parallels cited above from both Paul's own letters and the Greco-Roman letters of his day suggest that either the optative or the imperative mood is more appropriate than the indicative.[1] And of these two options a choice may not be necessary since the optative in the NT often takes on a force similar to that of the imperative. Bastiaan Van Elderen, for example, speaks of an 'imperatival optative'—an optative that expresses a stronger sense than mere volition: 'The speaker intends more than a wish ("may it be so-and-so"); he expresses this with a strong confidence of fulfilment ("let it be so-and-so").'[2] Although Van Elderen does not go on to state the converse, it would seem that that was also sometimes true in ancient letter writing: that the imperative expressed the nuance of the optative. This is evident, for example, in the closing formula ἔρρωσο of ancient Greek letters which, although given in the imperative mood, expressed a wish for the letter recipient's health. Thus, whether Paul intended the optative or the imperative in his grace benedictions, the sense remains the same: it is a wish that the apostle confidently expects will be received and realized in the lives of his readers.

c. *The Origin and Purpose of the Grace Benediction*
An inquiry into the origin of Paul's grace benedictions opens up the complex issue of the relation between the apostle's letters and early

---

1. A. Robertson and A. Plummer (*First Epistle of St. Paul to the Corinthians* [New York: Charles Scribner's Sons, 1911], p. 402) argue against the indicative in 1 Cor. 15.24, and therefore also in 15.23 for the following reason: 'He [Paul] would not have said πάντων if ἐστί(ν) were understood, for some offenders were too flagrant to be at present included; but as a wish, an aspiration and a prayer, his message may embrace all'.
2. B. Van Elderen, 'The Verb in the Epistolary Invocation', *CTJ* 2 (1967), p. 48.

Christian worship. Since this matter falls outside of the primary focus of our interest, I shall limit myself here to a few summary observations.

The rather fixed nature of the various epistolary conventions found in Paul's letter closings, coupled with the fact that these closing formulae often contain words and phrases that do not appear in the body of their respective letters, has caused some to conclude that the grace benedictions and other closing conventions of Paul's letters were not creations of Paul himself, but rather traditional materials that he appropriated from the liturgy of the primitive church. Leonard Champion, for example, in an extensive study of the benedictions and doxologies of Paul's letters, concludes:

> This examination has shown quite clearly that they [benedictions and doxologies] are not essential to the thought of the epistles and that they can be separated quite easily from their context. They are used chiefly to provide a fitting conclusion to the various sections of the letters. This use points to the [sic!] Christian worship as the place of their immediate origin.[1]

The closing of 1 Cor. 16.20-23 has been used to take the argument one step further. For the closing conventions found here—the kiss greeting, the 'anathema' warning, the 'maranatha' prayer, and the grace benediction—are claimed to be evidence of an early Christian liturgical sequence.[2] Furthermore, on the basis of such parallels as found in Justin Martyr's *Apology*[3] and the *Didache*,[4] it has been argued that Paul deliberately shaped the closing of 1 Corinthians to serve as a transition from the public reading of the letter to the celebration of the eucharist.[5]

---

1. Champion, *Benedictions and Doxologies*, p. 34. Wiles (*Paul's Intercessory Prayers*, p. 301) entitles his chart of the various closing elements in Paul's letters 'Liturgically Oriented Closing Pattern'. See also Delling, *Worship*, pp. 74-75; W. Kramer, *Christ, Lord, Son of God* (Naperville, IL: Allenson, 1966), pp. 90-91; P.-É. Langevin, *Jésus Seigneur et l'eschatologie: exégèse de textes prepauliniens* (Paris: Desclee, 1967), pp. 191-92.

2. See J.A.T. Robinson, 'Traces of a Liturgical Sequence in 1 Cor. 16.20-24', *JTS* 4 (1953), pp. 38-41.

3. *Apology* 1.65: 'When we have ceased from prayer, we salute one another with a kiss. There is then brought to the president bread and a cup of wine.'

4. *Didache* 10.6: 'Let grace come and let this world pass away. Hosanna to the God of David. If any man is holy, let him come. If any be not, let him repent. Maranatha. Amen.'

5. This theory was first proposed by R. Seeberg, *Aus Religion und Geschichte* (Leipzig: Deichert, 1906), pp. 118-20. Since then it has been accepted by numerous other scholars: e.g., H. Lietzmann, *The Mass and the Lord's Supper* (trans.

But though such a postulated connection between the closing of
1 Corinthians and the celebration of the eucharist is intriguing, the
evidence cited in support remains tenuous.[1] Willem van Unnik has
warned against the danger of a '"pan-liturgism" which sees everywhere
in the Pauline epistles the background of the liturgy whenever a simple
parallel is found'.[2] And even if grace benedictions and other closing conventions in Paul's letters were derived from the liturgy of the early
church, it does not follow from this that these closing formulae could not
have been used in a purely epistolary function. The distinction between
source and function must not be blurred. As Harry Gamble notes:

> A liturgical *form* may indeed be derivative, but in the letters may perform a
> strictly epistolary *function*. To the extent that such formulae can be seen to
> serve purely epistolary needs and/or to possess contextual relationships,
> and thus to be integral to the letters as *letters*, there is no reason to seek out
> a non-epistolary rationale for their use.[3]

A proper understanding of Paul's grace benedictions, therefore, ought
primarily to be derived from their epistolary function. For just as their
counterpart in Greco-Roman letters, the farewell wish, functioned to
close a letter, so grace benedictions served to bring Paul's letters to a
definitive close. Thus a grace benediction normally occupies the final
position in Paul's letter closings. There are only two instances in the

D.H.G. Reeve; Leiden: Brill, 1979 [1926]), p. 229; G. Bornkamm, 'Das Anathema in
der urchristlichen Abendmahlsliturgie', *TLZ* (1950), pp. 227-30; Robinson, 'Traces
of a Liturgical Sequence', pp. 38-41; O. Cullmann, *Early Christian Worship* (London:
SCM, 1953), pp. 13-14; Wiles, *Intercessory Prayers*, pp. 150-55; P. Vielhauer,
Geschichte der urchristlichen Literatur (Berlin: de Gruyter, 1975), p. 67.
   1.   In response to the view that 1 Cor. 16.19-24 served as a liturgical sequence
for the celebration of the eucharist, C.F.D. Moule pointedly asks: 'But how much of
this is really cogent? If I Corinthians was really intended to be (as it were) the homily,
leading on into the eucharist, why is there so little trace of this in other New Testament
epistles? Why does the "maranatha" in I Cor. xvi. 22 come at this particular point,
before the grace (and the apostle's love)? Why does it occur where it does in the
Didache? In spite of all that is said, is there sufficient evidence to suggest that it was
meant to lead straight into the eucharist proper?' ('A Reconsideration of the Context
of "Maranatha"', *NTS* 8 [1959/60], p. 307). See also the criticisms by Gamble,
Textual History, pp. 143-44; G. Fee, *The First Epistle to the Corinthians* (Grand
Rapids: Eerdmans, 1987), pp. 836-37; Schnider and Stenger, *Neutestamentlichen
Briefformular*, pp. 132-33.
   2.   Van Unnik, '"Dominus Vobiscum"', p. 272.
   3.   Gamble, *Textual History*, p. 144 (italics his).

Pauline corpus where this is not the case: 1 Cor. 16.24, where a final
personal expression of love by Paul to the Corinthians follows the benediction; and Rom. 16.21-27, which contains final greetings and, if
authentic, a closing doxology. Such postscriptive comments or greetings,
however, are a common occurrence in the Greco-Roman letters of that
day.

One might ask why Paul changed the rather simple farewell wish of
ancient letters to the more elaborate wish for the grace of Jesus Christ to
be with his readers. The answer may lie in the fact that farewell wishes
at the end of the first century AD were beginning to be assimilated to
health wishes.[1] As a result, the farewell wish came to express more than
a simple or civil good-bye; it also expressed concern for the *physical*
welfare of the letter recipient. In light of Paul's pastoral interests, however, this may explain why he transformed the standard expression of
farewell into the more elaborate grace benediction so that this closing
convention functions not only to signal the end of the letter but also to
express concern for the *spiritual* welfare of his readers.

It could further be asked why this concern for the spiritual welfare of
his readers was expressed by Paul in terms of 'the grace of our Lord
Jesus Christ' rather than a wish for something else. Paul's desire for
Christ's grace to be received by his readers would make sense in light of
his general christological focus. A more specific epistolary reason, however, seems evident. For by making the content and divine source of the
wish 'the grace of our Lord Jesus Christ', Paul was able to construct an
inclusio with the opening salutation ('Grace to you and peace from God
our Father and the Lord Jesus Christ'). Paul's closing grace benedictions, therefore, give evidence of how he skillfully transformed the
standard closing formula of his day to serve better his own theological,
literary and pastoral interests.

2. *The Peace Benediction*

In addition to the grace benediction, the Pauline letter closings contain
another type of wish or benediction, which, on the basis of its content,
may best be identified as a 'peace benediction'. With the exception of
1 Corinthians and Philemon, a peace benediction occurs in all the
undisputed letters and therefore can be regarded as a regular part of the
Pauline letter closings.

1.   See discussion of the farewell wish above, pp. 29-34.

a. *Elements of the Peace Benediction*

A comparison of the various peace benedictions (see Table 2) reveals that this closing convention is not nearly as frequent nor as tightly structured as the grace benediction. Nevertheless, it does exhibit a clear and rather consistent pattern involving four basic elements: an introductory element, the wish, the divine source, and the recipient. The latter three elements are identical to those found in the grace benediction; but the order of the three in the peace benediction is altered slightly, with the wish being subordinate to the divine source. So instead of saying 'The peace of God be with you', as the form of the grace benediction would suggest, the peace benediction has 'The God of peace be with you'. From a strictly grammatical perspective, of course, the two statements are different. From a functional or sense perspective, however, they are the same since peace may be said to be the wish in each.[1] The reversing of order, therefore, does not indicate a fundamental change in meaning but only a difference in emphasis: the former stresses the wish; the latter, the divine source.

In order to determine more clearly the form of the peace benediction, as well as any significant Pauline deviations from its usual form, it is necessary to study in a more detailed manner the four basic elements of this closing formula.

The Introductory Element. Peace benedictions are normally introduced by the particle δέ in the post-positive position. This particle sometimes has a connective force, and so could serve to link the peace benediction with the material that precedes it.[2] More commonly, however, δέ possesses an adversative sense (although more moderate than ἀλλά), which would serve to set peace benedictions somewhat apart from what has just been written.[3] This latter sense is supported by the fact that a peace benediction normally occupies the first position in a Pauline letter

1. See Mullins, 'Benediction', p. 61. Hawthorne (*Philippians*, p. 190) comments: 'The expression "God of peace" means that God is the source and origin of peace'.

2. The connective force of δέ is stressed by Jewett ('Homiletic Benediction', pp. 22-23), who argues that the peace benedictions of the Thessalonian letters are closely linked with their respective preceding homilies.

3. For the use of δέ in general, see J.D. Denniston, *The Greek Particles* (Oxford: Clarendon, 1934), pp. 162-89; M.E. Thrall, *Greek Particles in the New Testament* (Leiden: Brill, 1962); BDF, §447. For the use of δέ in the Pauline peace benedictions, see Frame, *Thessalonians*, p. 210; Gamble, *Textual History*, p. 69.

	Introductory Element	Divine Source	Wish	Recipient
Rom. 15.33	ὁ δὲ	θεὸς τῆς	εἰρήνης	μετὰ πάντων ὑμῶν
Rom. 16.20a	ὁ δὲ	θεὸς τῆς	εἰρήνης	συντρίψει τὸν Σατανᾶν ὑπὸ τοὺς πόδας ὑμῶν ἐν τάχει
2 Cor. 13.11	καί	ὁ θεὸς τῆς ἀγάπης καὶ	εἰρήνης	ἔσται	μεθ' ὑμῶν
Phil. 4.9b	καί	ὁ θεὸς τῆς	εἰρήνης	ἔσται	μεθ' ὑμῶν
1 Thess. 5.23	αὐτὸς δὲ	ὁ θεὸς τῆς	εἰρήνης	ἁγιάσαι ὑμᾶς ὁλοκελεῖς καὶ ὁλόκληρον ὑμῶν τὸ πνεῦμα καὶ ἡ ψυχὴ καὶ τὸ σῶμα ἀμέμπτως ἐν τῇ παρουσίᾳ τοῦ κυρίου ἡμῶν Ἰησοῦ Χριστοῦ τηρηθείη
2 Thess. 3.16	αὐτὸς δὲ	ὁ κύριος τῆς	εἰρήνης	δῴη τὴν εἰρήνην διὰ παντὸς ἐν παντὶ τρόπῳ	ὑμῖν
Gal. 6.16	καὶ ὅσοι τῷ κανόνι τούτῳ στοιχήσουσιν εἰρήνη ἐπ' αὐτοὺς καὶ ἔλεος καὶ ἐπὶ τὸν Ἰσραὴλ τοῦ θεοῦ

Table 2. *Peace Benedictions*

closing and so serves as a literary heading, marking the transition from the letter body to the letter closing.

The adversative sense of the particle δέ in peace benedictions explains why in 2 Cor. 13.11b, Gal. 6.16 and Phil. 4.9b the wish for peace is introduced instead by the simple conjunction καί. For the peace wish in these three instances, rather than being set apart, is linked with the immediately preceding material.[1] Thus the shift from δέ to καί should be seen as a subtle, yet significant, clue signifying that the closing section of the letter begins not with the peace benediction but with the material preceding the wish.

The Divine Source. After the introductory element, the divine source of the wish in the Pauline peace benedictions is given in the nominative case.[2] Whereas the divine source of the grace benedictions is always identified as '(our) Lord Jesus (Christ)', in the peace benedictions it is typically 'God' (ὁ θεός).[3] This pattern of aligning a grace benediction with Christ and a peace benediction with God follows naturally from the opening salutation, where the same two wishes are linked in chiastic fashion with the same two divine figures: 'Grace and peace be to you from God our Father and the Lord Jesus Christ'.

Because the pattern of grace/Christ and peace/God is followed so consistently by Paul in his closing benedictions, the reference in 2 Thess.

1. The significance of the shift from δέ to καί in these three peace benedictions is recognized by R. Bultmann, *The Second Letter to the Corinthians* (trans. R.A. Harrisville; Minneapolis: Augsburg, 1976, 1985 [Eng.]), p. 250; V.P. Furnish, *II Corinthians* (Garden City, NY: Doubleday, 1984), p. 586; Martin, *2 Corinthians*, pp. 493, 500.

2. In a couple of instances, the third-person intensive pronoun αὐτός is added to the noun. G. Harder (*Paulus und das Gebet* [Gütersloh: Bertelsmann, 1936], p. 26, n. 4) argues for a connection between the third-person address 'God himself' with the second-person address 'You God' or 'You yourself' found in the Psalms (LXX) and the Talmud. M. Black (*An Aramaic Approach to the Gospels and Acts* [Oxford: Clarendon, 1946], p. 70) proposes that the expression αὐτὸς δὲ ὁ is an Aramaism in which the intensive pronoun is used proleptically to emphasize the following noun. G. Wiles (*Paul's Intercessory Prayers*, pp. 30-31) claims that αὐτός 'had an accepted liturgical significance, adding a note of majesty to the address'. Although the origin of the intensive pronoun in the peace benediction remains a disputed point, the occasional addition of αὐτός to the divine source of the wish seems to have an emphasizing function.

3. The two exceptions are Gal. 6.16, where the divine source is omitted, and 2 Thess. 3.16, where the giver or source of the wish is ὁ κύριος ('the Lord').

3.16 to 'the Lord (κύριος) of peace' is rather striking.[1] But while the phrase here differs from the form found in all the other peace benedictions, it agrees with a certain tendency in 2 Thessalonians to ascribe to Christ qualities and activities elsewhere ascribed to the Father.[2] Furthermore, the substitution of κύριος for θεός is in keeping with the emphasis throughout this brief letter on Christ, particularly on his expected return.[3] Thus, even with this small change, it can be seen how Paul in 2 Thessalonians adapts a standard closing convention so that it better relates to the christological concerns expressed throughout that letter.

Added consistently to the identification of the divine source is the qualifying genitive phrase τῆς εἰρήνης ('of peace'). The term εἰρήνη occurs some twenty-nine times in Paul's undisputed letters,[4] with virtually all these occurrences found in the opening salutations and closing peace benedictions. The fuller expression ὁ θεὸς τῆς εἰρήνης is rare in the literature of Paul's day, with only two occurrences (*T. Dan.* 5.2; Heb. 13.20) outside of his final wish for peace.

The expression 'the God of peace' describes God as the source and giver of peace. Consequently, when this phrase is used with the verb εἰμί whether stated or implied, it expresses the wish of the benediction. Paul's statement 'May the God of peace be with you' is tantamount to saying 'May the God of peace give you peace'.[5] In fact, the peace benediction of 2 Thess. 3.16 states this wish explicitly: 'May the Lord of peace himself give you peace.' Since the genitive phrase frequently indicates the content of the wish, I will leave a more detailed discussion of

1. This fact explains why a few manuscripts have θεός instead of κύριος (G L 1912 1319 642 1610 bo Ambrst).
2. See Marshall, *Thessalonians*, p. 230.
3. Within this short three-chapter letter, there are twenty-two references to κύριος: 1.1, 2, 7, 8, 9, 12 (2×); 2.1, 2, 8, 13, 14, 16; 3.1, 3, 4, 5, 6, 12, 16 (2×), 18.
4. The word εἰρήνη also occurs eight times in Ephesians, twice in Colossians, and four times in the Pastorals.
5. Most commentators take the genitive phrase to denote not so much a characteristic of God as a gift that he gives to his people. For example, in his discussion of the peace benediction, Martin (*2 Corinthians*, p. 494) states that he 'takes "peace" and "love" to be gifts of God, given by him to the Corinthians'. Similarly, E. Best (*Second Corinthians* [Atlanta: John Knox, 1987], p. 136) comments on 2 Cor. 13.11b: 'He is the God of love and peace and in situations of conflict what is needed above all is the peace and love that he alone can give.'

this expression to the section below dealing with the third element of the grace benediction.

The Wish. Identifying the content or wish of the peace benediction is complicated somewhat by the fact that some of these closing benedictions use the copula εἰμί (given or implied) while others have a transitive verb. As noted above, the content of the wish is taken from the qualifying genitive phrase. The benediction 'May the God of peace be with you,' therefore, can be understood as meaning 'May the God of peace give you peace' (Rom. 15.33; 2 Cor. 13.11b; Phil. 4.9b; see Gal. 6.16). But the same wish is found as well in one of the benedictions using a transitive verb: 'May the Lord of peace himself give you peace at all times in all ways' (2 Thess. 3.16). And in the two other benedictions, while still identifying the source of the wish as 'the God of peace', the content of the wish is for something additional or other than peace (Rom. 16.20a; 1 Thess. 5.23).

More significantly, however, it need be noted that a number of the Pauline peace benedictions deviate from the typical form because of material that is altered or added to bring these benedictions into line with material found earlier in the bodies of their respective letters. For example, the peace benediction of 2 Cor. 13.11 contains an extra qualifying genitive, τῆς ἀγάπης, with the result that this closing formula reads: 'The God of love and peace will be with you.' Although the addition of 'love' may not appear important at first glance, it becomes noteworthy because of the fact that the expression 'the God of peace' alone appears in all the other Pauline peace benedictions. The addition of 'love' becomes even more noteworthy when it is observed that the same word has also been added in the closing of this letter to the grace benediction—a formula that elsewhere in Paul's letters exhibits an otherwise consistent pattern. Furthermore, it should be noted that the expression 'God of love' does not occur anywhere else in Paul's writings, nor does it appear anywhere else in the NT or the LXX.

Ralph Martin suggests that the insertion of 'love' into the peace benediction of 2 Cor. 13.11 anticipates the upcoming grace benediction of 13.13, which also includes the phrase 'the love of God'.[1] A more likely explanation, however, is that the addition of 'love' here (as well as in v. 13) is due to Paul's emphasis on love that appears throughout his

---

1.   Martin, *2 Corinthians*, p. 500; also Fisher, *1 & 2 Corinthians*, p. 445.

correspondence to the Corinthians.[1] Particularly in light of his immediately preceding exhortations to 'rejoice, aim for restoration, encourage one another, be of the same mind, live in peace' (13.11)—as well as his earlier exhortations to avoid 'quarreling, jealousy, anger, selfishness, slander, gossip, conceit and disorder' (12.20)—it can be hardly doubted that 'love' has been added by Paul to strengthen the exhortations concerning reconciliation and peace given elsewhere in his Corinthian correspondence, especially those of 2 Corinthians 10–13.

Another distinctive wish element in the Pauline peace benedictions is that found in 2 Thess. 3.16: 'May the Lord of peace himself give you peace at all times and in all ways.' Ernest Best rightly notes that this description of Christ as the 'Lord of peace' seems appropriate to the situation at Thessalonica where there was disorderliness and division. Yet Best goes on to downplay the connection of this peace benediction with its preceding material on the grounds that Paul regularly closes his letters with this formula.[2] Such an evaluation, however, fails to recognize that the prayer for peace in 2 Thess. 3.16 is clearly emphasized by virtue of the double reference to 'peace'—a feature not found in any of the other closing benedictions of this type. Furthermore, this wish that the 'Lord of peace himself give you peace' relates directly not only to the tensions and potential division between the idlers and the rest of the community (3.6-13), but also to the anxiety and fears within the Thessalonian church that stemmed from the claim that the Day of the Lord had come (2.1-17). 2 Thess. 3.16 is, therefore, another example of how Paul has clearly adapted a closing convention so that it addresses issues raised earlier in that particular letter.

The most significant of the Pauline peace benedictions in terms of both its form and its function of echoing key themes in the letter body is 1 Thess. 5.23-24. In form, it is by far the most expanded of Paul's peace benedictions. For instead of the simple and relatively fixed formula 'May the God of peace be with you,' we find the following expanded wish: 'May the God of peace himself sanctify you wholly; and may your spirit, soul and body be kept whole and blameless at the coming of our Lord Jesus Christ' (v. 23). Another unique formal feature of the wish is the word of encouragement that immediately follows the benediction: 'Faithful is the one who is calling you; and he will do it' (v. 24).

---

1. See 1 Cor. 4.21; 8.1; 13.1-4, 8, 13; 14.1; 16.14, 24; 2 Cor. 2.4, 8; 5.14; 6.6; 8.7-8, 24.

2. Best, *Thessalonians*, p. 345.

The connections between this peace benediction and the content of 1 Thessalonians are both numerous and rich, though they can only be summarily treated here. One important link lies in the theme of sanctification. In the peace benediction, this concern is expressed by means of two optative verbs: ἁγιάσαι ('may he sanctify') and ἀμέμπτως τηρηθείη ('may it [your spirit, soul and body] be kept blameless'). In the letter body, a stress on living a holy life is found in the first half of the letter (2.10, 12; 3.13; see 1.3, 7-9), but is especially emphasized in the second half in the paraenetic section (4.1, 3, 4, 7, 8, 9-12; also the light/darkness and day/night imagery of 5.4, 5, 8). Likewise, the closing commands of 5.12-22 highlight the practical consequences of what this theme of sanctification means for believers, making extended use of the adjective πᾶς (vv. 14, 15 [2×], 16, 18, 21, 22), and so stressing the comprehensive nature of living a holy life—a point also emphasized in the peace wish.[1]

A second important link between this closing peace benediction and the rest of 1 Thessalonians is found in the theme of Christ's parousia. 1 Thess. 5.23 is the only peace benediction that includes an explicit reference to the return of Christ: ἐν τῇ παρουσίᾳ τοῦ κυρίου ἡμῶν Ἰησοῦ Χριστοῦ ('at the coming of our Lord Jesus Christ').[2] To the careful reader, the mention of the parousia in the closing wish recalls numerous allusions, references, and even extended discussions in the letter concerning Christ's return (1.3,10; 2.19; 3.13; 4.13-18; 5.1-11).

A third bridge between the peace benediction of 1 Thessalonians and earlier material in this letter involves the references to πνεῦμα, ψυχή and σῶμα (5.23). Paul is not here espousing a new, tripartite anthropological position, but rather has in view the Thessalonians' concern about the fate of those believers who have died before Jesus' return (4.13-18). Their fear was of not fully participating in the triumphal return of Christ. By means of the tripartite reference, however, Paul reassures his readers that their whole (ὁλόκληρον) person—spirit, soul and body—will participate in Christ's parousia.

1.   The two words that form an alliteration, ὁλοτελεῖς and ὁλόκληρον, as well as the tripartite reference to πνεῦμα, ψυχή and σῶμα, stress that sanctification involves the whole person and his or her whole life.
2.   Although no other peace benediction contains an explicit reference to Christ's return, there is an implied eschatological aspect to the peace benediction of Rom. 16.20a which describes what God will do to Satan by means of the believers at Rome ('The God of peace will crush Satan under your feet speedily').

Other important links between the peace benediction of 1 Thess. 5.23-24 and the body of that particular letter could be cited. Enough has been said for now, however, to demonstrate that 1 Thess. 5.23-24 is another example of how Paul adapts a closing convention so that it echoes topics and concerns previously addressed in its respective letter.[1]

The Recipient. The fourth element in a Pauline peace benediction is the recipient of the wish. The recipient is frequently introduced by the preposition μετά ('with') and followed by the second-person plural personal pronoun ὑμῶν ('you'). This form of identifying the recipient, identical to that used in the grace benediction, occurs in the peace benedictions of Rom. 15.33, 2 Cor. 13.11b, and Phil. 4.9b. Although the remaining four wishes of Rom. 16.20a, 1 Thess. 5.23, 2 Thess. 3.16 and Gal. 6.16 exhibit some degree of diversity and expansion, the identity of the recipient is still indicated by the second-person plural personal pronoun.

A closer examination of those peace benedictions that deviate somewhat from the simple and standard form of identifying the recipient of the wish reveals potential links with the preceding material in their respective letter bodies. For example, 2 Thess. 3.16 expands the peace wish by means of a double prepositional phrase: διὰ παντὸς ἐν παντὶ τρόπῳ ('at all times in all ways'). And this additional phrase, as Robert Jewett notes, 'refers more naturally to the discussion of the times and seasons that dominated earlier sections of the letter (1.5-10; 2.1-12; 2.13–3.5)'.[2]

Another noteworthy peace benediction with respect to the identification of the recipient is Rom. 15.33 where the adjective πάντων ('all') is added. As noted above in discussing grace benedictions, Paul occasionally expanded the scope of a wish by means of this adjective—a practice also commonly followed in the papyrus letters of his day. The addition of πάντων here in Rom. 15.33, therefore, probably stems from Paul's treatment in the previous chapters of the unrest and divisions that were

1. Note again the following evaluations of the peace benediction in 1 Thess. 5.23-24: 'The unit [benediction] in 1 Th. 5.23…serves in fact to summarize and climax the entire epistle' (Jewett, 'Homiletic Benediction', p. 24); 'Cette bénédiction fait écho à plusieurs thèmes ou préoccupations majeures de la lettre. Elle en fournit même une certain synthèse' (Langevin, 'L'intervention de Dieu', p. 90); 'The *peroratio* and epistolary closing (5.23-27) emphatically recapitulates the principal theme of the letter' (Wanamaker, *Thessalonians*, p. 50)

2. Jewett, *Thessalonian Correspondence*, p. 81. See also *idem*, 'Homiletic Benediction', p. 25.

developing between 'the strong' and 'the weak' in the Roman church. The addition of πάντων would thus be a subtle attempt by Paul to tailor the peace benediction so that it reinforces his previous calls for peace and unity among *all* members of the church. The peace benediction of Rom. 16.20a is also striking for a number of reasons. First, it is the only example of a second peace benediction within the same letter closing. Second, it is the only instance where Paul places the peace benediction immediately prior to the grace benediction without any intervening material.[1] Third, it is the only closing benediction that calls for God to do something to someone other than Paul's readers ('The God of peace will crush Satan under your feet speedily'). The immediate context is a hortatory section (16.17-19) in the letter closing where Paul likely takes up the pen himself and addresses in very strong language the problem of 'those who create dissensions and difficulties' (16.17). If, then, the peace benediction of 16.20a were seen to close this section rather than the whole letter, this would go a long way to account for its unique occurrence, placement and form.

The peace benediction that deviates most from the standard form is Gal. 6.16.[2] It differs not only in the wish (note the addition of ἔλεος ['mercy'], which along with εἰρήνη is expressed by means of the nominative case rather than by a qualifying genitive phrase) and divine source (which is omitted), but especially in the identification of the recipient. Instead of the expected μεθ' ὑμῶν the recipient is introduced by a relative clause (ὅσοι τῷ κανόνι τούτῳ στοιχήσουσιν ['all those who walk by this rule']), followed by a double prepositional phrase (ἐπ' αὐτοὺς... καὶ ἐπὶ τὸν Ἰσραὴλ τοῦ θεοῦ ['on them...and on the Israel of God']).

1.   Although some manuscripts locate the grace benediction either in 16.24, after some further greetings, or in 16.27, after the doxology, the majority of witnesses support 16.20b as its original location.

2.   This peace benediction has some affinity with the 19th Benediction of the *Shemoneh 'Esreh* (the Babylonian Talmud lists nineteen blessings while the Palestinian has eighteen): 'Bring peace, goodness and blessing, grace and favour and mercy over us and over all Israel, thy people' (see E. Schürer, *The History of the Jewish People in the Age of Christ* [ed. G. Vermes *et al.*; Edinburgh: T. & T. Clark, 1979], II, p. 458). A simpler parallel can be found in Psalm 125.5 (LXX 124): 'Peace be upon Israel'. If Paul is borrowing here from one of these benedictions, this would explain why Gal. 6.16 differs in form so greatly from the other peace benedictions. The differences between Gal. 6.16 and the two parallels, however, should not be overlooked. At best, one can only speak of a possible dependence of Paul on one of these benedictions.

Unlike the other Pauline peace benedictions, the wish in Gal. 6.16 contains a conditional aspect: only those who follow the rule laid down by Paul will enjoy the blessing of peace and mercy.[1] This conditional formulation of the peace benediction reflects the strained relations between Paul and his readers that are so evident throughout the Galatian letter.

Another unique feature of this particular peace benediction is Paul's reference to the recipients of the wish as 'the Israel of God'. On the basis of Paul's use of 'Israel' in other letters as well as other claimed parallels, several commentators conclude that the phrase 'the Israel of God' refers to Jews, either a non-judaizing group of Jewish Christians in Galatia,[2] a believing Jewish remnant within the broader Christian church,[3] or an eschatological Israel that will be saved at Christ's return.[4]

It is difficult to believe, however, that in a letter where Paul has been breaking down the distinctions that separate Jewish and Gentile Christians and stressing the equality of both groups, that he in the closing would give a peace benediction addressed to believing Jews as a separate group within the church. If one takes the context of the letter seriously, it seems much better to conclude that the phrase 'the Israel of God' refers to those Gentile Christians in Galatia who walk according to Paul's rule.[5] Furthermore, by using this particular designation, Paul

1. The conditional character of the peace benediction probably accounts for the subjunctive form στοιχήσωσιν found in P[46], thereby making the clause agree with the classical construction of a conditional relative (although the particle ἄν also should be added). The conditional character of the benediction has been noted by a number of commentators; e.g., P. Richardson, *Israel in the Apostolic Church* (Cambridge: Cambridge University Press, 1969), p. 76; Gamble, *Textual History*, p. 73; Betz, *Galatians*, pp. 320-21; Schnider and Stenger, *Neutestamentlichen Briefformular*, p. 150. Note also the conditional character of the peace benediction of 2 Cor. 13.11 indicated by the use of the future tense.

2. So, e.g., G. Schrenk, 'Was bedeutet "Israel Gottes"?' *Judaica* 5 (1949), pp. 81-94; *idem*, 'Der Segenwunsch nach der Kampfepistel', *Judaica* 6 (1950), pp. 170-90; D.W.B. Robinson, 'Distinction between Jewish and Gentile Believers in Galatians', *AusBR* 13 (1965), pp. 29-44.

3. See Burton, *Galatians*, pp. 357-58; Richardson, *Israel in the Apostolic Church*, pp. 74-84; W.D. Davies, 'Paul and the People of Israel', *NTS* 24 (1977), pp. 4-39, esp. pp. 9-11.

4. So, e.g., F. Mussner, *Der Galaterbrief* (Freiberg: Herder, 1974), p. 417; F.F. Bruce, *The Epistle to the Galatians* (Grand Rapids: Eerdmans, 1982), p. 275.

5. So, e.g., N.A. Dahl, 'Der Name Israel, I: Zur Auslegung von Gal. 6,16', *Judaica* 6 (1950), pp. 161-70; Betz, *Galatians*, pp. 322-23; C.B. Cousar, *Galatians* (Atlanta: John Knox, 1982), p. 150; Longenecker, *Galatians*, pp. 297-99.

addresses once more the important question dealt with earlier in the letter of who rightfully are the children of Abraham (see esp. 3.6-9, 14, 16, 26-29; 4.21-23).

It appears, therefore, that Paul in the letter closing of Galatians has deliberately adapted the conventional peace benediction so that it better addresses the concerns of the letter as a whole in two ways. First, the conditional nature of the wish reflects somewhat generally the strained relations between Paul and his readers. Second, the phrase 'the Israel of God' recalls more specifically the issue of who rightfully are the heirs of Abraham.

Before concluding this discussion of the elements of the peace benediction, I note again the omission of this wish in both 1 Corinthians and Philemon. There is no obvious reason for its absence in these letters. In fact, one would expect that such a closing benediction would be very appropriate in both letters. For in Philemon, the subject of peace and reconciliation between the master and his slave, Onesimus, constitutes the heart of the letter's subject matter. Similarly, a peace benediction would be fitting in 1 Corinthians where a growing tension existed between Paul and some in that church. The absence of a wish for peace in these letters, therefore, should caution against speaking of any fixed number of closing conventions that had to be used by Paul in any given letter. It is more accurate to view the apostle as having a number of closing conventions at his disposal that could be selected and adapted so as best to accomplish his specific goals.

b. *The Origin of the Peace Benediction*
Having examined the various components of a Pauline peace benediction, I turn next to the question of its origin. Is Paul here borrowing from an established form and practice, or is this closing formula his *de novo* creation?

One possibility is that the peace benediction of Paul's letter closings stems from some liturgical practice. A number of examples can be found in Judaism where a petition for peace closes the worship service. The Aaronic blessing of Num. 6.24-26, which, in its final section, invokes God to give peace to his people, regularly functioned in Jewish circles to close both the temple and synagogue service.[1] The final benediction of

1.   See *m. Ber.* 5.4; *m. Meg.* 4.3, 5, 6, 7; *m. Sota* 7.6. The blessing consists of three sections: (1) 'The Lord bless you and keep you'; (2) 'The Lord make his face shine upon you and be gracious to you'; (3) 'The Lord turn his face toward you and

the *Shemoneh 'Esreh*, which expresses a wish for peace, also was occasionally used at the end of a worship service.[1] Some of the old rabbinic prayers close with a petition for peace,[2] and synagogue inscriptions also point to the use of a peace wish in a liturgical setting.[3] Thus there are a number of precedents within Judaism for a wish for peace at the close of a worship service.

Although parallels with Jewish liturgical practice are suggestive, a closer analogy to the peace benediction in the epistolary closings of Paul can be found in the Semitic letters of his day. The study of Semitic letters undertaken in Chapter 3 revealed that the most common closing formula was the farewell wish, expressed in Aramaic and Hebrew letters by a wish for 'peace'.[4] Since this formula occurs in all the extant, complete letters except two, it seems to have been a standard, although not essential, closing convention of Semitic letters. The influence of Semitic epistolary practice with regard to closing formulae is evident in the NT letters of 1 Peter and 3 John which likewise close with a final wish for peace.[5] It may be assumed, therefore, that Paul's use of a peace benediction to close his letters has precedent in the Semitic letters of his day. So while Paul feels free to adapt, sometimes greatly, the form of the peace wish so that it better serves his own particular interests, it may be postulated that the origin of the wish itself stems from an epistolary convention of Aramaic and Hebrew letters of his day rather than any specific liturgical practice.

---

give you peace.' In the temple service, the blessing was pronounced all together as one part with the people responding with 'Amen', while in the synagogue service it was pronounced in three parts with the people responding with 'Amen' after each section (*m. Sota* 7.6).

1. The 18th benediction (Palestinian Talmud) expresses the following prayer to God: 'Bring thy peace over Israel, thy people, and over thy city and over thine inheritance; and bless all of us together. Blessed art thou, Lord who makest peace' (Schürer, *History of Jewish People*, II, p. 461).

2. See D. de Sola Pool, *The Kaddish* (New York: Bloch, 1929), pp. 70-71.

3. See C.H. Kraeling, *The Synagogue* (New Haven: Yale University Press, 1956), p. 263; H. Lietzmann, 'Zwei Notizen zu Paulus', *Kleine Schriften. II. Studien zum Neuen Testament* (ed. K. Aland; Berlin, 1958), pp. 284-91, esp. p. 286.

4. Mur 42, 44, 46, 48; 5/6 Hev 4, 11, 15. For a discussion of this closing formula in the Semitic letters, see above pp. 65-66.

5. 1 Pet. 5.14: εἰρήνη ὑμῖν πᾶσιν τοῖς ἐν Χριστῷ ('Peace to all of you who are in Christ'); 3 John 15: εἰρήνη σοι ('Peace to you').

c. *The Function of the Peace Benediction*
The origin of the peace benediction in Semitic epistolary practice helps clarify the function that this closing convention has in Paul's letters. In Aramaic and Hebrew letters, the wish for peace served to mark the end of the correspondence, bringing the letter to a definitive close. The literal meaning of שׁלום, however, suggests that the final peace wish also had the function of expressing concern for the health and well-being of the letter recipient—a function fulfilled in Greco-Roman letters by the health wish (the *formula valetudinis*). It seems probable, therefore, that the peace benediction in Paul's letters also possesses this double function of (1) closing the correspondence, and (2) expressing concern for the spiritual welfare of the readers.

The peace benediction in Paul's letters, however, does not bring a letter to a definitive close. This function is fulfilled by the grace benediction. Rather, the peace benediction serves to mark the beginning of the letter closing and so separate the subsequent material from that which precedes the wish. The peace benediction in Paul's letters, therefore, naturally occupies the first position in a letter closing.[1]

Some scholars view the peace benediction in Paul's letters as marking the formal closure of the letter body rather than of the whole letter.[2] This view, however, founders on the fact that both the peace wish of Semitic letters and the health wish of Greco-Roman letters (to which the peace benediction is analogous) clearly belong to the closing of the whole letter and not the body. Even stronger evidence lies in the deliberate *inclusio* that is formed with the opening salutation: 'grace to you and peace', which appears at the opening of the letter, is echoed in chiastic fashion at its closing—first by the peace benediction and then by the grace benediction. This bracketing of Paul's letters by a chiastic repetition of the grace and the peace wish in the opening and closing sections demonstrates decisively that the peace benediction belongs properly to the epistolary closing.

1.   Hence the use of the adversative δέ to open the wish. In those few instances where material precedes the peace benediction but yet belongs to the letter closing, the introductory δέ is substituted for the simple conjunction καί (2 Cor. 13.11b; Phil. 4.9b; Gal. 6.16). See discussion of 'Introductory Element' above (pp. 88-90).
2.   So Roller, *Das Formular*, pp. 66-67, 196-97; White, 'Ancient Greek Letters', p. 97; *idem*, 'Apostolic Letter Tradition', p. 442. A number of commentaries on Paul's letters also treat the peace benediction as part of the letter body rather than as part of the letter closing.

d. *'Other' Benedictions*

Before ending this examination of the Pauline peace benedictions, it is important to recognize that a number of other benedictions or wishes can be found in Paul's letters that do not belong to either of the two types studied so far. As evident in Table 3, these so-called 'other' benedictions are not nearly as tightly structured as either the grace benedictions or the peace benedictions. Despite their diversity, however, they possess a common structure consisting of four basic elements: the divine source, the wish, the recipient, and the purpose.[1]

These 'other' benedictions occur only in the bodies of Paul's letters, not the closings, and so are of little significance for this thesis. Consequently, only a brief comment about each of the four constituent elements of these wishes will be given:

1.   Unlike the grace and peace benedictions where the divine source is always 'the Lord Jesus (Christ)' and 'God', respectively, in these other benedictions the giver of the wish can be either one of the divine persons or both. The divine source, given in the nominative case, is usually elaborated on by means of a genitive phrase or a participial clause.

2.   The wish, normally expressed by the verb in the optative mood, does not fall into any recognizable pattern in terms of its content, but expresses a variety of diverse hopes.

3.   In contrast to the grace and peace benedictions, where the recipient is typically expressed by the preposition μετά and the second-person personal pronoun ὑμῶν, no two of these other benedictions are identical in their identification of the receiver of the wish.

4.   Finally, a unique characteristic of these benedictions belonging to the letter body is a statement giving the intended purpose of the wish, expressed by a ἵνα or εἰς clause.

---

1.   Wiles (*Paul's Intercessory Prayers*, p. 29) refers to these benedictions as 'wish-prayers' and likewise delineates 'four parts: (1) The prayer begins with the subject God (described with various attributes), (2) continues with a predicate having one or more verbs usually in the optative, (3) together with a noun or pronoun for the one to be benefited. (4) An "additional benefit" is then expressed either by a purpose clause (using ἵνα, εἰς τό), or by an additional clause joined by καί, or by an adjectival or prepositional phrase.'

	Divine Source	Wish	Recipient	Purpose
Rom. 15.5-6	ὁ δὲ θεὸς τῆς ὑπομονῆς καὶ τῆς παρακλήσεως	δῴη τὸ αὐτὸ φρονεῖν	ὑμῖν ἐν ἀλλήλοις κατὰ Χριστὸν Ἰησοῦν	ἵνα ὁμοθυμαδὸν ἐν ἑνὶ στόματι δοξάζητε τὸν θεὸν καὶ πατέρα τοῦ κυρίου ἡμῶν Ἰησοῦ Χριστοῦ
Rom. 15.13	ὁ δὲ θεὸς τῆς ἐλπίδος	πληρώσαι πάσης χαρᾶς καὶ εἰρήνης	ὑμᾶς ἐν τῷ πιστεύειν	εἰς τὸ περισσεύειν ὑμᾶς ἐν τῇ ἐλπίδι ἐν δυνάμει πνεύματος ἁγίου
1 Thess. 3.11	αὐτὸς δὲ ὁ θεὸς καὶ πατὴρ ἡμῶν καὶ ὁ κύριος ἡμῶν Ἰησοῦς	κατευθύναι τὴν ὁδὸν ἡμῶν	πρὸς ὑμᾶς	

1 Thess. 3.12-13	ὁ δὲ κύριος	πλεονάσαι περισσεύσαι τῇ ἀγάπῃ	ὑμᾶς καὶ εἰς ἀλλήλους καὶ εἰς πάντας καθάπερ καὶ ἡμεῖς εἰς ὑμᾶς	εἰς τὸ στηρίξαι ὑμῶν τὰς καρδίας ἐν ἀμέμπτους ἐν ἁγιωσύνῃ ἔμπροσθεν τοῦ θεοῦ καὶ πατρὸς ἡμῶν ἐν τῇ παρουσίᾳ τοῦ κυρίου ἡμῶν Ἰησοῦ μετὰ πάντων τῶν ἁγίων αὐτοῦ [ἀμήν]
2 Thess. 2.16-17	αὐτὸς δὲ ὁ κύριος ἡμῶν Ἰησοῦς Χριστὸς καὶ ὁ θεὸς ὁ πατὴρ ἡμῶν ὁ ἀγαπήσας ἡμᾶς καὶ δοὺς παράκλησιν αἰωνίαν καὶ ἐλπίδα ἀγαθὴν ἐν χάριτι	παρακαλέσαι τὰς καρδίας καὶ στηρίξαι	ὑμῶν ἐν παντὶ ἔργῳ καὶ λόγῳ ἀγαθῷ	
2 Thess. 3.5	ὁ δὲ κύριος	κατευθύναι τὰς καρδίας	ὑμῶν	εἰς τὴν ἀγάπην τοῦ θεοῦ καὶ εἰς τὴν ὑπομονὴν τοῦ Χριστοῦ

Table 3. *Other Benedictions*

The few similarities that exist in Paul's letters between these 'other' benedictions and the peace benedictions have caused some to view these two types as belonging to the same category.[1] There are several reasons, however, for treating the peace benediction as a distinct type. First, whereas the content of the wish in the peace benediction is relatively constant (a wish for peace), in the other benedictions no two wishes are alike. Second, every one of the peace benedictions identifies the divine source ('God') with the qualifying genitive phrase 'of peace'. This is in marked contrast to the other benedictions where the divine source is variously described as the God 'of patience and encouragement' (Rom. 15.5), 'of hope' (Rom. 15.13), or 'who loved us' (2 Thess. 2.16). Third, not only do the peace benedictions lack the fourth element (a purpose clause) regularly found in the other benedictions, they also exhibit a high degree of stylistic uniformity in the other three elements (divine source, wish, recipient) compared to the much looser form of the other benedictions. Finally, whereas the other benedictions occur at various points in the letter body, the peace benedictions are consistently located in the letter closing. Therefore, there is compelling evidence for treating the closing peace benedictions as a wish distinct from the other benedictions found in the bodies of Paul's letters.

3. *The Greeting*

With the boundaries of the Pauline letter closings clearly marked out by the peace and grace benedictions, a number of other closing conventions can also be discovered in these final sections. The item that occurs most frequently between the two closing benedictions is the 'greeting'. This closing convention appears in all the undisputed letters of Paul with the notable exception of Galatians.[2]

---

1. For example, Jewett ('Homiletic Benediction', pp. 18-34) classifies the two types together as 'homiletic benedictions'. Wiles (*Paul's Intercessory Prayers*, pp. 45-107) views both types as belonging to the same category and refers to them as 'wish-prayers'. Mullins ('Benediction', p. 61), following Champion (*Benedictions and Doxologies*, pp. 29-30), classifies the benedictions according to their location in the letter and so treats the two types together under the heading of 'intermediate' benedictions in contrast to 'opening' and 'closing' benedictions.
2. For the significance of this omission, see discussion below. Among the disputed letters of Paul, the greeting is missing only in Ephesians and 1 Timothy. In other NT letters, the greeting occurs in Heb. 13.24 (2×), 1 Pet. 5.13-14, 2 Jn 13 and 3 Jn 15 (2×).

a. *Types of Greetings*

Of all the different conventions found in a Pauline letter closing, the greeting exhibits the closest parallels with the same formula in Hellenistic letters. As in our study of greetings in Greco-Roman letters, here too it is possible to classify the greetings in Paul's letters into three types according to the different persons expressed in the verb: first-, second-, or third-person types (see Table 4).

First-Person Type of Greeting. Paul himself never uses the first-person type of greeting ἀσπάζομαι ('I greet'). The only occurrence of this type of greeting is found in Rom. 16.22 where the apostle's secretary, Tertius, personally greets the readers of the letter: ἀσπάζομαι ὑμᾶς ἐγὼ Τέρτιος ὁ γράψας τὴν ἐπιστολὴν ἐν κυρίῳ ('I, Tertius, the one who wrote this letter, greet you in the Lord'). The absence of the first-·person greeting in Paul's letters agrees with the restricted use of this type of greeting in Hellenistic letters. For since Paul conveys his personal greeting in the opening salutation (χάρις ὑμῖν καὶ εἰρήνη), it would be redundant to repeat his personal greeting in the letter closing.

Gamble claims that 'the imperative form of the greeting verb functions as a surrogate for the first-person indicative form, and so represents a direct personal greeting of the writer himself to the addressees'.[1] It is true, of course, that the second-person greeting (ἀσπάσασθε) can serve to express the greeting of the writer—a greeting normally given in the first-person form. It would be wrong, however, to equate completely these two distinct types of greeting, since the first-person type communicates the greeting in a more direct and personal manner than the second-person type.

Although Paul's letters contain no explicit examples of a first-person greeting given by Paul himself, there is a distinctive formula that belongs to this greeting type: ὁ ἀσπασμὸς τῇ ἐμῇ χειρὶ Παύλου ('The greeting [is written] with my own hand': 1 Cor. 16.21; 2 Thess. 3.17; Col. 4.18). Paul's use of this phrase to express a greeting seems to be unparalleled in other letters of his day. Some want to view ὁ ἀσπασμός as referring to a closing convention outside of the clause such as the grace benediction. According to this interpretation, the grace benediction should be understood as expressing Paul's personal greeting.[2] This view,

1. Gamble, *Textual History*, p. 93.
2. So Ziemann, *De Epistularum Graecarum*, pp. 364-65; Roller, *Das Formular*, pp. 70, 165-66.

Table 4. *Greetings*

(1) First-Person Type of Greetings

Rom. 16.22	ἀσπάζομαι ὑμᾶς ἐγὼ Τέρτιος ὁ γράψας τὴν ἐπιστολὴν ἐν κυρίῳ	
1 Cor. 16.21	ὁ ἀσπασμὸς τῇ ἐμῇ χειρὶ Παύλου	
2 Thess. 3.17	ὁ ἀσπασμὸς τῇ ἐμῇ χειρὶ Παύλου, ὅ ἐστιν σημεῖον ἐν πάσῃ ἐπιστολῇ	
Col. 4.18	ὁ ἀσπασμὸς τῇ ἐμῇ χειρὶ Παύλου	

(2) Second-Person Type of Greetings

Rom. 16.3-5a	ἀσπάσασθε	Πρίσκαν καὶ Ἀκύλαν τοὺς συνεργούς μου ἐν Χριστῷ Ἰησοῦ, οἵτινες ὑπὲρ τῆς ψυχῆς μου τὸν ἑαυτῶν τράχηλον ὑπέθηκαν, οἷς οὐκ ἐγὼ μόνος εὐχαριστῶ ἀλλὰ καὶ πᾶσαι αἱ ἐκκλησίαι τῶν ἐθνῶν, καὶ τὴν κατ' οἶκον αὐτῶν ἐκκλησίαν
Rom. 16.5b	ἀσπάσασθε	Ἐπαίνετον τὸν ἀγαπητόν μου, ὅς ἐστιν ἀπαρχὴ τῆς Ἀσίας εἰς Χριστόν
Rom. 16.6	ἀσπάσασθε	Μαρίαν, ἥτις πολλὰ ἐκοπίασεν εἰς ὑμᾶς
Rom. 16.7	ἀσπάσασθε	Ἀνδρόνικον καὶ Ἰουνιᾶν τοὺς συγγενεῖς μου καὶ συναιχμαλώτους μου, οἵτινές εἰσιν ἐπίσημοι ἐν τοῖς ἀποστόλοις, οἳ καὶ πρὸ ἐμοῦ γέγοναν ἐν Χριστῷ
Rom. 16.8	ἀσπάσασθε	Ἀμπλιᾶτον τὸν ἀγαπητόν μου ἐν κυρίῳ
Rom. 16.9	ἀσπάσασθε	Οὐρβανὸν τὸν συνεργὸν ἡμῶν ἐν Χριστῷ καὶ Στάχυν τὸν ἀγαπητόν μου
Rom. 16.10a	ἀσπάσασθε	Ἀπελλῆν τὸν δόκιμον ἐν Χριστῷ
Rom. 16.10b	ἀσπάσασθε	τοὺς ἐκ τῶν Ἀριστοβούλου
Rom. 16.11a	ἀσπάσασθε	Ἡρῳδίωνα τὸν συγγενῆ μου
Rom. 16.11b	ἀσπάσασθε	τοὺς ἐκ τῶν Ναρκίσσου τοὺς ὄντας ἐν κυρίῳ
Rom. 16.12a	ἀσπάσασθε	Τρύφαιναν καὶ Τρυφῶσαν τὰς κοπιώσας ἐν κυρίῳ
Rom. 16.12b	ἀσπάσασθε	Περσίδα τὴν ἀγαπητήν, ἥτις πολλὰ ἐκοπίασεν ἐν κυρίῳ
Rom. 16.13	ἀσπάσασθε	Ῥοῦφον τὸν ἐκλεκτὸν ἐν κυρίῳ καὶ τὴν μητέρα αὐτοῦ καὶ ἐμοῦ
Rom. 16.14	ἀσπάσασθε	Ἀσύγκριτον, Φλέγοντα, Ἑρμῆν, Πατροβᾶν, Ἑρμᾶν καὶ τοὺς σὺν αὐτοῖς ἀδελφούς
Rom. 16.15	ἀσπάσασθε	Φιλόλογον καὶ Ἰουλίαν, Νηρέα καὶ τὴν ἀδελφὴν αὐτοῦ, καὶ Ὀλυμπᾶν καὶ τοὺς σὺν αὐτοῖς πάντας ἁγίους
Rom. 16.16a	ἀσπάσασθε	ἀλλήλους ἐν φιλήματι ἁγίῳ
1 Cor. 16.20b	ἀσπάσασθε	ἀλλήλους ἐν φιλήματι ἁγίῳ
2 Cor. 13.12a	ἀσπάσασθε	ἀλλήλους ἐν ἁγίῳ φιλήματι
Phil. 4.21a	ἀσπάσασθε	πάντα ἅγιον ἐν Χριστῷ Ἰησοῦ
1 Thess. 5.26	ἀσπάσασθε	τοὺς ἀδελφοὺς πάντας ἐν φιλήματι ἁγίῳ
Col. 4.15	ἀσπάσασθε	τοὺς ἐν Λαοδικείᾳ ἀδελφοὺς καὶ Νύμφαν καὶ τὴν κατ' οἶκον αὐτῆς ἐκκλησίαν
2 Tim. 4.19	ἄσπασαι	Πρίσκαν καὶ Ἀκύλαν καὶ τὸν Ὀνησιφόρου οἶκον
Tit. 3.15b	ἄσπασαι	τοὺς φιλοῦντας ἡμᾶς ἐν πίστει
Heb. 13.24a	ἀσπάσασθε	πάντας τοὺς ἡγουμένους ὑμῶν καὶ πάντας τοὺς ἁγίους
1 Pet. 5.14	ἀσπάσασθε	ἀλλήλους ἐν φιλήματι ἀγάπης
3 Jn 15b	ἀσπάζου	τοὺς φίλους κατ' ὄνομα

Table 4. *Greetings* (cont.)

(3) Third-Person Type of Greeting

Rom. 16.16b	ἀσπάζονται	ὑμᾶς	αἱ ἐκκλησίαι πᾶσαι τοῦ Χριστοῦ
Rom. 16.21	ἀσπάζεται	ὑμᾶς	Τιμόθεος ὁ συνεργός μου καὶ Λούκιος καὶ Ἰάσων καὶ Σωσίπατρος οἱ συγγενεῖς μου
Rom. 16.23a	ἀσπάζεται	ὑμᾶς	Γάϊος ὁ ξένος μου καὶ ὅλης τῆς ἐκκλησίας
Rom. 16.23b	ἀσπάζεται	ὑμᾶς	Ἔραστος ὁ οἰκονόμος τῆς πόλεως καὶ Κούαρτος ὁ ἀδελφός
1 Cor. 16.19a	ἀσπάζονται	ὑμᾶς	αἱ ἐκκλησίαι τῆς Ἀσίας
1 Cor. 16.19b	ἀσπάζεται	ὑμᾶς	ἐν κυρίῳ πολλὰ Ἀκύλας καὶ Πρίσκα σὺν τῇ κατ' οἶκον αὐτῶν ἐκκλησίᾳ
1 Cor. 16.20a	ἀσπάζονται	ὑμᾶς	οἱ ἀδελφοὶ πάντες
2 Cor. 13.12b	ἀσπάζονται	ὑμᾶς	οἱ ἅγιοι πάντες
Phil. 4.21b	ἀσπάζονται	ὑμᾶς	οἱ σὺν ἐμοὶ ἀδελφοί
Phil. 4.22	ἀσπάζονται	ὑμᾶς	πάντες οἱ ἅγιοι, μάλιστα δὲ οἱ ἐκ τῆς Καίσαρος οἰκίας
Phlm. 23	ἀσπάζεταί	σε	Ἐπαφρᾶς ὁ συναιχμάλωτός μου ἐν Χριστῷ Ἰησοῦ, Μᾶρκος, Ἀρίσταρχος, Δημᾶς, Λουκᾶς, οἱ συνεργοί μου
Col. 4.10-11	ἀσπάζεται	ὑμᾶς	Ἀρίσταρχος ὁ συναιχμάλωτός μου καὶ Μᾶρκος ὁ ἀνεψιὸς Βαρναβᾶ (περὶ οὗ ἐλάβετε ἐντολάς, ἐὰν ἔλθῃ πρὸς ὑμᾶς, δέξασθε αὐτόν) καὶ Ἰησοῦς ὁ λεγόμενος Ἰοῦστος, οἱ ὄντες ἐκ περιτομῆς, οὗτοι μόνοι συνεργοὶ εἰς τὴν βασιλείαν τοῦ θεοῦ, οἵτινες ἐγενήθησάν μοι παρηγορία
Col. 4.12-13	ἀσπάζεται	ὑμᾶς	Ἐπαφρᾶς ὁ ἐξ ὑμῶν, δοῦλος Χριστοῦ [Ἰησοῦ], πάντοτε ἀγωνιζόμενος ὑπὲρ ὑμῶν ἐν ταῖς προσευχαῖς, ἵνα σταθῆτε τέλειοι καὶ πεπληροφορημένοι ἐν παντὶ θελήματι τοῦ θεοῦ. μαρτυρῶ γὰρ αὐτῷ ὅτι ἔχει πολὺν πόνον ὑπὲρ ὑμῶν καὶ τῶν ἐν Λαοδικείᾳ καὶ τῶν ἐν Ἱεραπόλει
Col. 4.14	ἀσπάζεται	ὑμᾶς	Λουκᾶς ὁ ἰατρὸς ὁ ἀγαπητὸς καὶ Δημᾶς
2 Tim. 4.21	ἀσπάζεταί	σε	Εὔβουλος καὶ Πούδης καὶ Λίνος καὶ Κλαυδία καὶ οἱ ἀδελφοὶ πάντες
Tit. 3.15a	ἀσπάζονταί	σε	οἱ μετ' ἐμοῦ πάντες
Heb. 13.24b	ἀσπάζονται	ὑμᾶς	οἱ ἀπὸ τῆς Ἰταλίας
1 Pet. 5.13	ἀσπάζεται	ὑμᾶς	ἡ ἐν Βαβυλῶνι συνεκλεκτὴ καὶ Μᾶρκος ὁ υἱός μου
2 Jn 13	ἀσπάζεταί	σε	τὰ τέκνα τῆς ἀδελφῆς σου τῆς ἐκλεκτῆς
3 Jn 15a	ἀσπάζονταί	σε	οἱ φίλοι

however, does not agree with the content of a typical grace benediction (which is a wish for grace, not a word of greeting) nor with its function in bringing the letter to a definitive close. It is simpler, and therefore better, to understand ὁ ἀσπασμὸς τῇ ἐμῇ χειρὶ Παύλου as an 'autograph greeting': a genuine greeting of Paul that he pens in his own hand,[1] and so a Pauline type of first-person greeting.

Second-Person Type of Greeting. In the second-person type of greeting found in papyrus letters, the addressee becomes the agent of the sender of the letter, establishing and maintaining communication with a third party. The use of this type of greeting in Paul's letters seems to suggest that the people being specifically greeted were not part of the congregation to whom the letter was addressed.[2] If that were the case, the use of the second-person greeting in, for example, Romans would imply that only one of several house churches at Rome was the actual recipient of the letter, and that Paul authorizes them to pass on his personal greetings to specific persons who belonged to other house churches in the capital city.[3]

It is clear, however, that Paul expected his letter to be read in all the churches of Rome,[4] and that, as a result, he could greet members in those churches directly himself. So, as noted above, a second-person greeting functions almost as a surrogate for a first-person greeting. For Paul to exhort the Roman congregation to greet specific persons is, therefore, virtually equivalent to Paul greeting them himself. If it is asked, 'Why then did Paul not use the more personal first-person greeting?', the answer seems to be that the involvement of the congregation in passing on his greetings to others expressed a stronger sense of public commendation for those individuals being specifically greeted by the apostle.

The form of second-person greetings throughout Paul's letters remains

---

1. H. Windisch ('ἀσπάζομαι', *TDNT*, I, p. 502) states that 'the greeting in the apostle's own hand…is materially identical with ἀσπάζομαι'. See also Gamble, *Textual History*, p. 74.
2. Mullins ('Greeting', pp. 425-26) states that the use of the second-person greeting in Romans implies that Paul 'had close enough rapport with that congregation to act for him' and that this type of greeting 'means that the persons greeted might not be among those who read the letter'.
3. See Kim, *Greek Letter of Recommendation*, pp. 139-40.
4. The recipients of the Roman letter are identified in 1.7 as '*all* those in Rome'. See also 1 Thess. 5.27 and Col. 4.16.

constant: the plural aorist imperative ἀσπάσασθε.[1] This is the most frequent of the greeting types, the form occurring twenty times in the undisputed letters compared to ten occurrences of the third-person greeting. These figures, however, are somewhat misleading, as a comparison of the individual letters to each other indicates. For if the greetings in Romans are omitted, only four examples of a second-person type are left. And of these four remaining examples, 1 Cor. 16.20, 2 Cor. 13.12, and 1 Thess. 5.26 belong to the rather fixed formula exhorting the exchange of a holy kiss—which leaves only Phil. 4.21 of a second-person greeting type outside of Romans.

Third-Person Type of Greeting. In the third-person type of greeting, Paul passes on greetings of others who are with him to the recipients of the letter. The form of this type of greeting is always the present indicative, given either in the singular (ἀσπάζεται) or the plural (ἀσπάζονται) depending on the number of those sending greetings. Paul therefore serves as an agent expressing greetings on behalf of specific individuals (Rom. 16.21, 23; 1 Cor. 16.19b; Phlm. 23), of well-defined groups (1 Cor. 16.19a; Phil. 4.22), or of very general groups (1 Cor. 16.20; 2 Cor. 13.12b; Phil. 4.21). The fact that Paul can speak for 'the church in Asia' (1 Cor. 16.19a) or for 'all the saints' (2 Cor. 13.12b)—or even more broadly yet for 'all the churches of Christ' (Rom. 16.16b)—reflects his own perception of his apostolic and authoritative status.

b. *Elements of the Greeting Formula*
The form of closing greetings found in Paul's letters contains the same three basic elements common to the greetings in Greco-Roman letters: (1) the greeting verb (some form of ἀσπάζεσθαι); (2) the giver of the greeting (either Paul [first-person and second-person greetings] or some other person or group [third-person greeting]); and (3) the recipient of the greeting (either the addressee or some other specifically named person or group). Paul actually follows a more rigid pattern in his greeting formula than other writers of the ancient world, for he

---

1. The only exceptions are found in the disputed Pauline letters where the singular form is used: 2 Tim. 4.21; Tit. 3.15. This change is understandable in light of the singular addressees of these letters.

consistently uses the verb ἀσπάζεσθαι[1] and his order of the three elements always remains the same.

Paul has included in his greetings a number of additions or elaborating phrases that serve to modify and stress one or more of the three elements making up this closing formula. The first element of the greeting formula, the verb, for example, is emphasized in 1 Cor. 16.19b by the addition of the adverb πολλά. This particular adverb was also regularly added to greetings in Hellenistic letters in order to give them a warmer and more personal tone. Another addition to the first element of Paul's greeting formula are the prepositional phrases ἐν κυρίῳ ('in the Lord') and ἐν Χριστῷ ('in Christ'). It remains unclear, however, whether these prepositional phrases should be read with the greeting verb ('Greet *in the Lord/Christ*') or with the recipient of the greeting ('Greet so and so *who is* in the Lord/Christ'). Yet since the prepositional phrase in several examples clearly serves to modify the person rather than the verb (see Rom. 16.5b, 11b, 12a, 12b), it would seem wise to understand at least most of the more ambiguous examples in the same manner. Nevertheless, in 1 Cor. 16.19b and Phil. 4.21 the prepositional phrase certainly does seem to modify the verb.

Elaboration of the second element of the greeting formula, the giver of the greeting, also takes place, especially in third-person greetings. This expansion frequently consists of a short descriptive phrase that makes the identification of the sender of the greeting more exact—for example, 'Gaius, who is host to me and to the whole church, greets you' (Rom. 16.23a); 'Erastus, the city treasurer...greets you' (Rom. 16.23b); 'All the saints, especially those of Caesar's household, greet you' (Phil. 4.22); 'I, Tertius, who wrote the letter, greet you' (Rom. 16.22). Many of these supplemental descriptive phrases exhibit the pattern of a nominative in apposition to the person's name followed by the first-person personal pronoun in the genitive—for example, ὁ συνεργός μου ('my fellow worker'); οἱ συγγενεῖς μου ('my kinsmen'); ὁ ξένος μου ('my host'); ὁ συναιχμάλωτός μου ('my fellow prisoner'). These additional phrases are helpful in indicating the nature of the relationship that exists between the sender of the greeting and Paul.

Such descriptive phrases also occur in the third element of the greeting formula: the recipient. As with the sender of the greeting, the identity of

---

1. The verbs προσαγορεύειν and ἐπισκόπεισθαι, although not nearly as frequent as ἀσπάζεσθαι, were also used in letters of the day to express closing greetings.

the person being greeted is further clarified by means of an appositive noun or adjective followed by the first-person personal pronoun in the genitive. Here, however, there are a number of unique features. First, the descriptive phrase of the recipient expresses a stronger statement of endearment or commendation—e.g., τὸν ἀγαπητόν μου ('my beloved': Rom. 16.5b; 16.8; 16.9; 16.12b); τὸν δόκιμον ἐν Χριστῷ ('esteemed in Christ': Rom. 16.10a); τὸν ἐκλεκτὸν ἐν κυρίῳ ('chosen in the Lord': Rom. 16.13). Second, there is the frequent addition of ἐν κυρίῳ or ἐν Χριστῷ ('Ιησοῦ).[1] As noted above, although this prepositional phrase could in some cases modify the verb ('Greet *in the Lord/Christ*'), there is greater evidence that it refers to the recipient ('Greet so and so *who is* in the Lord/Christ'). This addition adds a strong element of commendation to the description of the recipient, for Paul explicitly recognizes the person's relationship to the Lord.

Third, the descriptive phrase is expanded, sometimes greatly, by means of a relative clause—e.g., οἵτινες ὑπὲρ τῆς ψυχῆς μου τὸν ἑαυτῶν τράχηλον ὑπέθηκαν ('who risked their necks for my life': Rom. 16.4a); οἷς οὐκ ἐγὼ μόνος εὐχαριστῶ ἀλλὰ καὶ πᾶσαι αἱ ἐκκλησίαι τῶν ἐθνῶν ('to whom not only I but also all the churches of the Gentiles give thanks': Rom. 16.4b); ὅς ἐστιν ἀπαρχὴ τῆς Ἀσίας εἰς Χριστόν ('who is the first convert of Asia for Christ': Rom. 16.5b).[2] These prepositional phrases were obviously not intended to help the addressees identify the person(s) being greeted, for such a person(s) would have been well known to the Christian community. Rather, as their laudatory content makes clear, these lengthy elaborative phrases possess a commendatory function.[3]

c. *The Greeting with the 'Holy Kiss'*
In Rom. 16.16a, 1 Cor. 16.20b, 2 Cor. 13.12a and 1 Thess. 5.26, Paul explicitly states the manner in which the greeting is to be given: 'with a

1. In the twenty greeting formulae that identify the recipient of the greeting, this prepositional phrase occurs eleven times: Rom. 16.3, 5b, 7, 8, 9, 10a, 11b, 12a, 12b, 13; Phil. 4.21a.
2. Other examples include the following: ἥτις πολλὰ ἐκοπίασεν εἰς ὑμᾶς ('who has worked hard among you': Rom. 16.6); οἵτινές εἰσιν ἐπίσημοι ἐν Χριστῷ ('who are outstanding among the apostles': Rom. 16.7b); οἳ καὶ πρὸ ἐμοῦ γέγοναν ἐν Χριστῷ ('who also were in Christ before me': Rom. 16.7c); ἥτις πολλὰ ἐκοπίασεν('who has worked hard in the Lord': Rom. 16.12b).
3. See Kim, *Greek Letter of Recommendation*, pp. 133-39; Gamble, *Textual History*, pp. 91-92.

112   *Neglected Endings*

holy kiss' (see also 1 Pet. 5.14). The wording of this command is relatively constant: ἀσπάσασθε ἀλλήλους ἐν φιλήματι ἁγίῳ ('Greet one another with a holy kiss'). The only variations involve the reversed order of ἁγίῳ φιλήματι in 2 Cor. 13.12a and the replacement of ἀλλήλους with τοὺς ἀδελφοὺς πάντας in 1 Thess. 5.26. Gamble suggests that Phil. 4.21a (ἀσπάσασθε πάντα ἅγιον ἐν Χριστῷ Ἰησοῦ ['Greet every saint in Christ Jesus']) should also be understood as a command to greet one another with a holy kiss, since this is the only place, other than the explicit requests for the exchange of a holy kiss cited above, where the second-person greeting occurs with a general object.[1] But instead of the expected ἀλλήλους, Phil. 4.21a has πάντα ἅγιον as well as the additional phrase ἐν Χριστῷ Ἰησοῦ—so it deviates substantially from the rather constant pattern of the 'kiss greeting' found elsewhere. Furthermore, the exhortation can stand on its own as a simple request for the readers to greet one another. Thus there does not appear to be sufficient evidence to warrant adopting Gamble's proposal.

The practice of giving a kiss as part of a greeting was widespread in the Orient.[2] Jewish examples of greeting others with a kiss, either when arriving or departing, can be found in the oldest books of the OT right up to those dated to the intertestamental period.[3] Furthermore, greeting another person with a kiss continued to be a common practice in Jesus' day (Mk 14.45; Lk. 7.45; 15.20; 22.47) and in Paul's (Acts 20.37). Thus

1.   Gamble, *Textual History*, p. 75, n. 88.
2.   G. Stählin, 'φιλέω', *TDNT*, IX, pp. 119-24, 125-27, 138-46. For further study of the 'holy kiss', as well as the kiss in general, see A. Wünsche, *Der Kuss in Bibel, Talmud und Midrasch* (Breslau: Marcus, 1911); I. Löw, 'Der Kuss', *MGWJ* 65 (1921), pp. 253-76, 323-49; K.M. Hofmann, *Philema Hagion* (Beiträge zur Förderung christlicher Theologie 38; Gütersloh: Bertelsmann, 1938); G. Dix, *The Shape of the Liturgy* (Glasgow: Glasgow University Press, 1945), pp. 105-110; K. Thraede, 'Ursprünge und Formen des "Heiligen Kusses" im frühen Christentum', *JAC* 11/12 (1968/1969), pp. 124-80; N.J. Perella, *The Kiss: Sacred and Profane* (Berkeley: University of California Press, 1969); S. Benko, 'The Kiss', in his *Pagan Rome and the Early Christians* (Bloomington: Indiana University Press, 1984), pp. 79-102; E. Kreider, 'Let the Faithful Greet Each Other: The Kiss of Peace', *Conrad Grebel Review* (Waterloo, Ontario) 5 (1987), pp. 28-49; W. Klassen, 'The Sacred Kiss in the New Testament', *NTS* 39 (1993), pp. 122-35.
3.   E.g., Gen. 29.11, 13; 31.28; 32.1; 33.4; Exod. 4.27; 18.7; 2 Kgs 19.4 (LXX); 20.9 (LXX); 3 Kgs 19.20 (LXX); Tob. 5.17; 10.12; *3 Macc.* 5.49; Add. Est. 15.8-12; *Par. Jer.* 6.2; *T. Ben.* 3.7; *T. Reub.* 1.5; *T. Simon* 1.2; *T. Dan* 7.1; *T. Naph.* 1.7; *Joseph and Asenath*, 4.1, 7; 18.3; 22.9.

the command in Paul's letters to greet one another with a kiss reflects a widespread custom of that time, which explains why the command can be given in a rather simple and constant formulaic expression without any accompanying word of explanation.

What is new, however, is that Paul explicitly refers to this greeting kiss as being a 'holy' kiss. Paul could be referring to the importance of maintaining proper and holy motives while practicing a kiss greeting. The early church evidently experienced problems with the kiss greeting, the exchange of the kiss becoming for some an erotic experience.[1] In such a situation, the exhortation to greet one another with a 'holy' kiss would serve as a warning against its improper practice.

But though this concern is surely part of Paul's thought in the exhortation, the reference to a 'holy' (ἅγιος) kiss suggests that the apostle wants to distinguish the greeting kiss of believers (ἅγιοι) from that practiced by those outside the faith. For others, the greeting kiss 'could be simply an expression of friendship and good will, but among Christians it assumed a deeper meaning; it symbolized the unity, the belonging together of Christians, in the church of Jesus Christ'.[2] The kiss expressed not merely friendship and love, but more specifically reconciliation and peace (see Gen. 33.4; 45.15; 2 Kgs 14.33 [LXX]; Lk. 15.20). In fact, the kiss exchanged between believers soon was referred to by early Christians as the *osculum pacis* ('the kiss of peace').[3] As a con-

---

1. It is this concern that likely lies behind Tertullian's comment that a pagan husband would not allow his wife 'to meet any one of the brethren to exchange the kiss'. *Ad uxorem* 2.4. (ET in *The Anti-Nicene Fathers*, 4.34). Similarly, the apologist Athenagoras, a contemporary of Tertullian, states: 'We feel it a matter of great importance that those, whom we thus think of as brother and sister and so on, should keep their bodies undefiled and uncorrupted. For the Scripture says again, "If one kisses a second time, because he found it enjoyable..." [rest of line is missing]. Thus the kiss, or rather the religious salutation should be very carefully guarded. If it is defiled by the slightest evil thought, it excludes us from eternal life.' *Legatio pro Christianis* 32 (ET in C.C. Richardson, *Early Christian Fathers*, I [Philadelphia: Westminster, 1953], p. 337). Clement of Alexandria also warned against the improper practice of the kiss greeting 'which occasions foul suspicions and evil reports' (*Paed.* 3.11).
2. Benko, 'The Kiss', p. 98.
3. Tertullian, *De oratione* 18 (14). The kiss greeting became a test to ensure that peace and harmony existed among believers. In the East during the third century AD, it was explicitly asked while the kiss was being exchanged whether anyone harbored anger towards another so that even at the last moment the bishop might make peace between them. See Dix, *Shape of the Liturgy*, pp. 106-107.

crete expression of the oneness that exists between followers of Jesus, the exchange of the holy kiss naturally became an introductory step leading up to the celebration of the eucharist—a further outward act that also powerfully symbolized the unity of believers as the body of Christ.[1]

Paul's command to 'greet one another with a holy kiss', therefore, expresses more than an exhortation simply to greet one another. It serves, rather, as a challenge to his readers to remove any hostility that may exist among them and to exhibit the oneness that they share as fellow members of the body of Christ. Furthermore, it is significant to note that Paul's four closing exhortations to greet others with a holy kiss all occur in contexts where some degree of conflict exists within the congregation.[2]

d. *The Origin and Function of the Greeting Formula*

By closing his letters with parting greetings, Paul clearly reflects the epistolary practice of his day. In contrast to his grace and peace benedictions, where he has adapted and 'Christianized' the standard health and farewell wishes of Hellenistic and Semitic letters, Paul follows quite closely in his greetings the patterns found in the secular letters of his day.[3] This dependency can be witnessed both in the types of greetings used and in the constituent elements of the greeting formula.

The extensive elaborations and additions found in his greetings, however, indicate that Paul did not follow in any wooden fashion the standard secular form, but rather tailored his greetings so that they better related to particular situations. For example, the commendatory tone of the long elaborating phrases added to the second-person greetings addressed to particular individuals at Rome is one of several means by which Paul

1. For further discussion of the celebration of the eucharist and its relationship to epistolary conventions in the closings of Paul, see above pp. 84-87.
2. Gamble (*Textual History*, p. 76) notes that the kiss greeting serves to highlight the unity that exists not only within a congregation itself, but also the fellowship of a congregation with Paul as well as with other congregations: 'The close connection between the kiss-greeting and the greetings from other communities is to be noted (Rom 16.16; 1 Cor 16.20; 2 Cor 13.12-13; cf. Phil 4.1-22)'.
3. Roller argued for a reverse version of dependency in which it was Paul's practice of closing his letters with greetings that led to the popular use of this formula to close secular letters (*Das Formular*, pp. 67-68). The presence of greetings in letters dated to the first century BC, however, indicates that the greeting formula was becoming a common feature of secular letters well before Paul's time and in circles where his letters would not have been known.

seeks to win the acceptance of his apostleship and gospel by the Roman Christians.

The primary function of Paul's closing greetings was that of expressing 'philophronesis', that is, the friendly relations that existed between Paul and his letter recipients. Since the apostle could not always personally visit the various churches, greetings were an important means of maintaining—even establishing—relations between himself and his readers. This philophronetic function was, of course, fulfilled to an extent by the letter as a whole. Closing greetings, however, were an even more direct and personal way of expressing and developing an intimate bond between Paul and his readers, as well as promoting unity and fellowship among the various churches.

In view of its important philophronetic function, the absence of any greetings in the letter closing of Galatians is significant. It is possible, of course, that this omission stems from the fact that Galatians was meant to be a circular letter.[1] The more obvious and likely reason for the omission of any closing greetings, however, lies in the strained relations that existed between Paul and his Galatian converts. This tension is evident not only in the content of the letter but in many of its epistolary forms: the extended defense of Paul's apostolic calling in the letter opening (1.1); the absence of any positive description of the letter recipients (1.2); the expanded salutation that stresses the complete nature of the salvific work of Christ (1.3-5); the substitution of a thanksgiving section with a rebuke section (1.6-10); the long autobiographical defense of Paul's apostleship (1.11–2.14); the lengthy autograph section in which Paul takes up the pen himself and addresses in a summary fashion the major issues raised in the letter body (6.11-18); and the conditional nature of the closing grace benediction (6.16). Thus the absence of final greetings—the only omission of this closing convention in all the undisputed letters of Paul—ought to be interpreted in line with the many other rebuking features to be found in the Galatian letter.[2]

The closing greetings in Paul's letter to the Romans are distinctive for a number reasons. First, Romans contains more greetings (21) than all the other undisputed letters combined (14). Second, Romans is the only letter with two lists of greetings: one in 16.3-16, another in 16.21-23.

1.   Note the absence of greetings in Ephesians, also widely considered to be a circular letter.

2.   The deliberate omission of closing greetings in letters expressing displeasure or rebuke occurs in Greco-Roman and Semitic letters as well.

The greetings in the first list are highlighted by virtue of the list's position (it comes in the first and therefore the emphatic position) and its size (seventeen greetings in the first list compared to four greetings in the second). Furthermore, the greetings in the first list all follow the form of second-person greetings—a type not normally used by Paul.[1] Third, the greetings in Romans are unique because of the commendatory element found throughout the first list. No other Pauline greetings, in fact, have such elaborate phrases that praise the person(s) being greeted. Thus the closing greetings in Romans, particularly those of 16.3-16, are unique compared to those found in Paul's other letters.

A principal reason for the unique character of the greetings in Romans can be found in the specific epistolary situation. For since Paul is writing to a church that he neither founded nor visited (1.10, 13; 15.22), he needs to win the trust of the Roman Christians so that his gospel, as it has been shared with them in the body of the letter, will be accepted. One effective way for Paul to gain their trust was for him to align himself with as many believers at Rome as possible, especially those in leadership positions. Paul does this by not only greeting a number of people at Rome by name, but also by commending each one through laudatory phrases attached to the greeting. A careful examination of these laudatory phrases reveals that they emphasize the relations between the person being praised and the apostle. In this fashion, Paul marshals support for himself at Rome by praising specific individuals located there, but also by associating himself so closely with these individuals that he himself indirectly shares the commendations that they receive. As Gamble perceptively observes:

> It is especially striking how, in the descriptive phrases, a heavy emphasis is placed on the relationship between the individuals mentioned and Paul himself. He ties them to himself, and himself to them. From these features it can be seen that Paul's commendatory greetings to specific individuals serve to place those individuals in a position of respect vis-à-vis the community, but also, by linking the Apostle so closely to them, place Paul in the same position.[2]

This attempt at self-commendation found in the first list of the closing greetings of Romans reinforces Paul's concern in the rest of the epistolary framework (opening, thanksgiving and apostolic parousia) to

---

1. Other than in the formulaic kiss greeting, the second-person type of greeting occurs only in Phil. 4.21a.
2. Gamble, *Textual History*, p. 92.

underscore the authority of his apostleship and gospel over the Roman Christians, thereby ensuring that his gospel—conveyed to them in the body of the letter—will be accepted. The greetings in the letter closing of Romans, therefore, have been carefully constructed and used by Paul in such a way that they further support his overriding purpose in the letter as a whole, i.e., to share his gospel with the believers in Rome.

Other significant closing greetings include Paul's commands to 'greet one another with a holy kiss'. As noted above, these 'kiss greetings' were not simply an expression of farewell but a challenge by the apostle to his readers to let peace and harmony characterize their relations with each other. If one keeps this function in mind, then the deeper significance of kiss greetings—given normally, it need be emphasized, in letters where congregational conflict exists—will be recognized.

In 2 Corinthians, for example, the tensions between Paul and certain leaders at Corinth resulted in divided loyalties and discord within the church. Paul therefore closes his letter with five final commands that focus on the need for mutual peace and harmony (13.11a). He then reinforces these closing exhortations with a peace benediction that has been elaborated slightly with the addition of ἀγάπη to emphasize further the need for love and peace within the church (13.11b). Paul next commands his readers to 'greet one another with a holy kiss' (13.12). In this context, such a command echoes the concern of the previous verses and challenges the readers to greet each other in a manner that publicly testifies to the forgiveness and reconciliation that ought to characterize their relations with each other.[1]

Similarly, the Roman congregation experienced internal tensions and conflict that resulted from differing opinions over the propriety of believers eating certain foods and observing special days. Paul treats this problem of division between 'the weak' and 'the strong' within the Roman church at length in 14.1–15.13, and again with quite strong language in 16.17-20. Between these two passages, and at the end of a long series of greetings, Paul commands his readers to 'greet one another with a holy kiss' (16.16a). Given the context of this exhortation, it is hardly going too far to suggest that Paul uses the kiss greeting to echo his previous call for unity and peace within the church.

---

1. *Contra* Best (*2 Corinthians*, p. 136), who states that 'this [the kiss greeting] is not a deliberate attempt to counter disputations.'

4. *The Autograph*

The Greek papyri indicate that ancient letters frequently ended with an autograph statement. Whereas the letter body was dictated to a secretary, the letter closing—or, at least, part of the closing—was written by the sender in his own hand. It is not surprising, therefore, that the same phenomenon occurs in Paul's letters.

a. *The Autograph Formula*
The existence of an autograph is expressly stated in the following verses, all located in the closing sections of Paul's letters:

1 Cor. 16.21	ὁ ἀσπασμὸς τῇ ἐμῇ χειρὶ Παύλου
Gal. 6.11	ἴδετε πηλίκοις ὑμῖν γράμμασιν ἔγραψα τῇ ἐμῇ χειρί
2 Thess. 3.17	ὁ ἀσπασμὸς τῇ ἐμῇ χειρὶ Παύλου, ὅ ἐστιν σημεῖον ἐν πάσῃ ἐπιστολῇ
Phlm. 19	ἐγὼ Παῦλος ἔγραψα τῇ ἐμῇ χειρί
Col. 4.18a	ὁ ἀσπασμὸς τῇ ἐμῇ χειρί

The phrase τῇ ἐμῇ χειρὶ (Παύλου) ('in/with my own hand [of Paul]') occurs four times in the undisputed letters of Paul (1 Cor. 16.21; Gal. 6.11; 2 Thess. 3.17; Phlm. 19) and once in the disputed Pauline letter to the Colossians (4.18a). This phrase implies that Paul had to this point been using a secretary to write the letter, but now takes up the pen himself to write personally to his readers. In three instances, the autograph statement is found as part of a greeting formula already examined above: ὁ ἀσπασμὸς τῇ ἐμῇ χειρὶ Παύλου (1 Cor. 16.21; 2 Thess. 3.17; Col. 4.18a). Whereas these examples lack a main verb,[1] the two remaining occurrences of an autograph statement have ἔγραψα (Gal. 6.11; Phlm. 19).[2]

Paul exhibits a degree of flexibility in the manner in which he

---

1.   The implied verb is likely γέγραπται or some similar form which is then followed by the dative of means: 'The greeting is written with my own hand.'

2.   ἔγραψα is usually understood as an epistolary aorist. For the use of the past tense to describe an action that is present from the letter writer's view, but past by the time the letter is read by its recipient(s), see A.T. Robertson, *A Grammar of the Greek New Testament in the Light of Historical Research* (New York: Hodder & Stoughton, 3rd edn, 1919), p. 846; W.D. Chamberlain, *An Exegetical Grammar of the Greek New Testament* (New York: Macmillan, 1941), p. 78; N. Turner, *Syntax*, Vol. III in *A Grammar of New Testament Greek* (ed. J.H. Moulton; Edinburgh: T. & T. Clark, 1963), pp. 72-73.

indicates to his readers that he has begun writing himself rather than his secretary. It may therefore be misleading to speak too quickly of an 'autograph formula' in the sense of a fixed, stereotyped phrase. Nevertheless, the five-fold occurrence of the phrase τῇ ἐμῇ χειρί gives us some justification to speak of this expression as just that: an 'autograph formula'.[1]

Although very infrequent, a few parallels in Greco-Roman letters to this formula can be found. Ferdinandus Ziemann cited a Greek letter that closes: ταῦτά σοι γέγραφα τῇ ἐμῇ χειρί ('I have written these things to you in my own hand').[2] The sender of P. Gren. II 89 states: ὁλόγραφον χειρὶ ἐμῇ ('I wrote all in my own hand'). The letters of Cicero contain a number of references to *mea manu* ('in my own hand'), apparently a preferred formula signaling the shift from the secretary to his own hand.[3] Despite these examples, Greco-Roman letters rarely speak of a change of hand, for such a shift would have been obvious to the reader. Paul, however, knew that his letters would be read aloud in public gatherings, and so he needed to make an explicit reference to the closing material that he had written in his own hand.[4]

b. *The Frequency of the Autograph*
The evidence strongly suggests that Paul used a secretary in the writing of all his letters. The assistance of an amanuensis is obvious in Rom. 16.22 where the secretary himself greets the readers, as well as in those letters which contain an explicit reference to Paul writing 'in my own hand' in contrast to the previous material written in a secretary's hand (1 Cor. 16.21; Gal. 6.11; 2 Thess. 3.17; Phlm. 19; Col. 4.18a). This testi-

1. Richards (*Secretary*, p. 173) refers to τῇ ἐμῇ χειρί as a 'typical formula'.
2. Ziemann, *De Epistularum Graecarum*, p. 365.
3. E.g., *Ad Att.* 8.1; 13.28. See comment of Richards, *Secretary*, p. 173.
4. The issue does not center on the fact that Paul's letters were read out loud, for all literature in that day, with rare exception, was read out loud (see, e.g., J. Balogh, 'Voces paginarum: Beiträge zur Geschichte des lauten Lesens und Schreibens', *Philologus* 82 [1927], pp. 84-109, 202-240; B.M.W. Knox, 'Silent Reading in Antiquity', *GRBS* 9 (1968), pp. 421-35; P.J. Achtemeier, '*Omne verbum sonat*: The New Testament and the Oral Environment of Late Western Antiquity', *JBL* 109 [1990], pp. 3-27; M. Slusser, 'Reading Silently in Antiquity', *JBL* 111 [1992], p. 499; F.D. Gilliard, 'More Silent Reading in Antiquity: *Non Omne Verbum Sonabat*', *JBL* 112 [1993], pp. 689-94). The point, rather, is that Paul's letters were read in gatherings where the size of the group prevented everyone from observing the change of handwriting.

mony, coupled with the wide-spread use in that day of secretaries in the drafting of letters, make it virtually certain that Paul had the assistance of various amanuenses in the writing of all his letters.[1] Given this fact, it may then be asked whether Paul regularly ended his letters with an autograph statement. Is the autograph a regular feature of the Pauline letter closing?

The answer to this question depends in large part on how one understands 2 Thess. 3.17. In this verse the autograph greeting formula ὁ ἀσπασμὸς τῇ ἐμῇ χειρὶ Παύλου is followed by the relative clause ὅ ἐστιν σημεῖον ἐν πάσῃ ἐπιστολῇ ('which is the sign in every letter'). Since the relative pronoun ὅ is neuter, its antecedent cannot be the masculine ὁ ἀσπασμός but rather must be the whole preceding clause. This leaves two possibilities: (1) that Paul is emphasizing the greeting itself, or (2) that he is stressing the fact that the greeting is in his own handwriting.

The first option is unlikely given the fact that the greeting formula, whether in its verbal or noun form, is not found in every letter of Paul. Furthermore, if σημεῖον is understood in a technical sense as an official 'sign' indicating authenticity,[2] the referent of the relative clause would be to the handwritten script of Paul and not the greeting. The terse two-word phrase that concludes this verse supports such an interpretation, for οὕτως γράφω ('thus I write') refers to the manner in which Paul closes his letters (i.e., with an autograph) and not to the content of his closing (i.e., with a greeting). The phrase ἐν πάσῃ ἐπιστολῇ suggests, therefore, that Paul always ended his letters with an autograph statement, and, further, that this fact should be assumed to be true even in

---

1.   So the majority of commentators (see especially the extended discussion in Richards, *Secretary*, pp. 169-98). The few who object typically do so on the grounds that (1) the autograph formula should be understood to mean that Paul wrote the whole letter in his own hand rather than that he was just beginning to write, or (2) the ἔγραψα in Gal. 6.11 and Phlm. 19 should not be read as an epistolary aorist but as a regular aorist that refers to the entire letter. See, e.g., Roller, *Das Formular*, pp. 187-91; G.S. Duncan, *The Epistle of Paul to the Galatians* (London: Hodder & Stoughton, 1934), p. 189; D. Guthrie, *Galatians* (Grand Rapids: Eerdmans, 1969), p. 148. Note also A.Q. Morton and J. McLeman (*Paul: The Man and the Myth* [New York: Harper & Row, 1966]), who, on the question of whether Paul used a secretary, wrongly claim that 'this is something which we do not know' (pp. 94-95).

2.   K.H. Rengstorf ('σημεῖον', *TDNT*, VII, p. 259) proposes that Paul uses σημεῖον in this verse in the same sense as σύμβολον—an addition to a letter in the author's own hand to indicate the authenticity of the correspondence.

those letters that make no such explicit reference to the apostle's own handwriting.

This conclusion receives further support from the papyrus letters, the vast majority of which indicate that the sender closed the correspondence in his own hand without expressly saying so.[1] Recognizing the weight of these parallels, Adolf Deissmann concluded that it would be begging the question to assume that Paul 'only finished off with his own hand those letters in which he expressly says that he did'.[2] Therefore, on the basis of explicit indications in Paul's writings as well as the common epistolary practice of his day, the autograph does, in fact, appear to be a regular feature of Paul's letter closings.

c. *The Extent of the Autograph*

Once it is recognized that Paul regularly ended his letters in his own hand, the question immediately arises as to the extent of these closing autographs. The answer to this issue must remain somewhat uncertain, since no letter of Paul has yet been discovered in its original form—thereby, of course, making it impossible to determine visually the change from one person's handwriting to that of another. Nevertheless, the extent of autograph material can be made with a high degree of certainty in the five letters that contain the phrase τῇ ἐμῇ χειρί.

The natural sense of this autograph formula implies a break with the preceding material. For it would seem highly improbable that Paul had been writing himself for several verses and then finally admitted to the readers that he was now doing so.[3] A much more plausible view is that Paul made reference to his own handwriting at precisely the point in the letter where he took over from his amanuensis. Randolph Richards notes that 'the evidence in antiquity strongly indicates that such authorial references *always begin* the autographed section.'[4] This understanding is

1. See the examples and discussion of closing autographs found above, pp. 45-50. None of these autographs explicitly state that the letter sender has taken over from the secretary.

2. Deissmann, *Light from Ancient East*, pp. 158-59.

3. *Contra* Bahr ('Subscriptions', pp. 33-41), who extends the size of the autograph to include material that occurs well before the reference to writing 'in my own hand': Rom. 12–16; 2 Cor. 10–13; Gal. 5.2–6.18; Phil. 3.1–4.23; 1 Thess. 4.1–5.28; 2 Thess. 3.1-18. For a criticism of Bahr's position, see Gamble, *Textual History*, p. 78 n. 105; A.J. Bandstra, 'Paul, the Letter Writer', *CTJ* 3 (1968), pp. 176-80; Richards, *Secretary*, pp. 176-79.

4. Richards, *Secretary*, p. 173 (italics his).

further strengthened by the fact that the explicit references to writing 'in my own hand' all occur at a natural break with the preceding material. Overwhelming evidence exists, therefore, for viewing the formula τῇ ἐμῇ χειρί as a sign that marks the beginning of the closing autograph.[1]

Although the formula τῇ ἐμῇ χειρί provides an important guide for determining the beginning of an autograph, there is no corresponding formula or other evidence for determining with certainty where this section ends. In the vast majority of Greco-Roman letters that betray the presence of an autograph, the author writes all the subsequent material in the closing (i.e., greetings, farewell wish, postscript), giving the pen back to the secretary only to write the address on the outside of the letter. Unless there is clear evidence to the contrary, it seems logical to assume that the same practice was operative in Paul's letters as well.

With the boundaries of the autograph marked out in these five Pauline letters, it becomes clear that the material written in the apostle's own hand occurs in varying length. Some of the autographs are rather short, consisting of such matters as Paul's personal greetings, a short warning or exhortation, the grace benediction, and a postscript (1 Cor. 16.21-24; 2 Thess. 3.17-18; Col. 4.18). Paul's practice here agrees with the majority of closing autographs found in Hellenistic letters, which tend to be rather brief. Other closing autographs in Paul's letters, however, are longer. Galatians, for example, contains a lengthy section in Paul's hand (6.11-18) in which the apostle personally addresses the key issues previously raised in the body of the letter. Similarly, Philemon possesses a rather extended autograph (19–25), containing a promissory note, confidence formula, apostolic parousia, greetings and grace benediction.[2]

---

1. White ('NT Epistolary Literature', p. 1740) comments that the autograph formula 'functions like the illiteracy formula, indicating that Paul has been employing a secretary up to this point at which he takes the pen in his hand'.
2. Although most scholars agree that all of vv. 19–25 should be understood as an autograph, a few maintain that only v. 19a is written in Paul's own hand: e.g., M. Dibelius, *An die Kolossar, Epheser; an Philemon* (rev. H. Greeven; Tübingen: Mohr, 1953), pp. 106-107. Still others, however, claim that the letter is so brief that a secretary was not required and that Paul wrote the whole letter himself: e.g., J.B. Lightfoot, *St. Paul's Epistles to the Colossians and Philemon* (London: Macmillan, 1875), p. 342 [note, however, Lightfoot's admission that it would be 'quite exceptional' for Paul to have written the whole letter himself]; Roller, *Das Formular*, p. 592; J.J. Müller, *The Epistles of Paul to the Philippians and to Philemon* (Grand Rapids: Eerdmans, 1955), p. 188; N.T. Wright, *Colossians and Philemon* (Grand Rapids: Eerdmans, 1986), p. 188.

Although these longer sections written in the hand of Paul differ from the typical length of most autographs, parallels can be found in other letters of the day.[1]

In those Pauline letter closings that do not contain an autograph formula, there is no certain means of determining the extent of the material that the apostle has written himself. In the five letters where the existence and extent of the autograph can be clearly determined, the one closing convention common to them all is the grace benediction. There is good justification, therefore, for concluding that Paul wrote all the grace benedictions in his own hand.

Although the identification of other autograph units can only be conjectured, a careful study of the remaining Pauline letter closings is suggestive of further material personally written by the apostle. For example, there are hints in the final chapter of Romans that it contains autograph material. The disjunction between 15.33 and 16.1-27, the personal commendation of Phoebe (16.1-2), the anomaly of two greeting units (16.3-16, 21-24), the highly personal tone of the first greeting unit (16.3-16) coupled with the assumption that all of Paul's letters originally revealed his own hand, caused Harry Gamble to believe that 16.1-20 was written in Paul's hand.[2] This position, however, is probably too ambitious in terms of the extent of the autograph. More convincing is the view that just 16.17-20 was written in the hand of Paul.[3] Not only would this explain the somewhat sudden shift in these verses to a harsher tone, but it also parallels Paul's practice elsewhere of giving a closing warning in his own hand (Gal. 6.11-18; 1 Cor. 16.22).

Another possible autograph section can be found in the closing of Paul's letter to the Philippians. Most commentators view the letter closing as beginning with the greetings of 4.21. However, the presence in 4.9b of a peace benediction—elsewhere in Paul's letters always an epistolary convention belonging to the closing—suggests that the letter closing begins here or, more likely, in the final exhortations of 4.8-9a. A

1.   E.g., BGU 183, 526, 910; P. Geiss. 97; P. Princ. 71; Cicero, *ad Att.* 11.24, 12.32, 13.28.

2.   Gamble, *Textual History*, pp. 93-94. So also Jervis, *Purpose of Romans*, p. 139.

3.   So H. Lietzmann, *An die Römer* (Tübingen: Mohr, 4th edn, 1933 [1906]), pp. 121-22; K.H. Schelkle, *The Epistle to the Romans* (Freiburg: Herder & Herder, 1964), p. 262; Wiles, *Paul's Intercessory Prayers*, p. 93; L. Morris, *The Epistle to the Romans* (Grand Rapids: Eerdmans, 1988), p. 538; J.D.G. Dunn, *Romans* (2 vols.; Dallas: Word Books, 1988), pp. 902, 906.

detailed discussion of the boundaries of the closing section in Philippians, as well as the literary integrity of this letter, cannot be treated here. What is of significance for this discussion at this point is the strong possibility that 4.10-23 was originally written in the hand of Paul even though not explicitly stated.[1]

A number of factors support this view of the autograph in Philippians. First, it provides a sound explanation as to why Paul's 'thank-you note' for the Philippian gift appears so late in the letter: Paul waits till the end of the letter so that he can personally convey his gratitude for their financial support. Second, Paul uses in 4.10-20 a number of technical terms commonly found in the papyri of business receipts (v. 15: δόσις, λῆμψις; v. 18: ἀπέχω).[2] This suggests that a parallel exists between this section and the legal acknowledgment of payment in business letters that required an autograph certification. Third, the highly personal tone of the language used in this section, as well as the personal nature of its subject matter, make 4.10-23 a strong candidate for autograph material.

There are good reasons for also seeing an autograph section at the closing of 1 Thessalonians. For following an expanded grace benediction (5.23-24), an exhortation for prayer (5.25) and a challenge to greet fellow believers with a holy kiss (5.26), Paul gives his readers a solemn adjuration: 'I charge (ἐνορκίζω) you by the Lord that this letter be read to all the brothers' (5.27). Since stereotyped formulae throughout this letter occur in the plural,[3] the petition given here in the singular seems to have a particular significance.[4] And in light of Paul's practice in his other

---

1.   This view was apparently first suggested by Bahr ('Subscriptions', p. 38): 'The thank-you note for the gift which Epaphroditus brought him was a highly personal matter for Paul, and so he wrote about that in his own hand.' Bahr, however, takes the autograph section to include not only 4.10-20 but also all the material beginning with 3.1. Gamble (*Textual History*, pp. 94, 145-46) also recognizes the presence of an autograph in the closing of Philippians, but he properly limits the material in Paul's own hand to 4.10-20 or 4.10-23. So also Hawthorne, *Philippians*, p. 210 (tentatively) and P.T. O'Brien, *The Epistle to the Philippians* (Grand Rapids: Eerdmans, 1991), p. 17.

2.   See BAGD, s.v. 'ἀπέχω'; Deissmann, *Light from Ancient East*, pp. 110-12; F. Preisigke, *Wörterbuch der griechischen Papyrusurkunden* (ed. E. Kiessling; Berlin: Grete Preisigke, 1925), I, pp. 162-63; Lightfoot, *Philippians*, p. 165; Martin, *Philippians*, p. 181.

3.   E.g., thanksgiving (1.2; 2.13); disclosure (2.1; 4.9; 4.13; 5.1); and petition (4.1; 5.14).

4.   Although a couple of personal interjections of Paul are given in the letter

letter closings, it would seem natural to view this shift from the plural to
the singular as evidence for an autograph. As F.F. Bruce notes, 'the
most probable explanation is that Paul took over the pen at this point
and added the adjuration and the concluding benediction with his own
hand.'[1] Paul's remark in 2 Thess. 3.17 about his custom of closing all his
letters in his own hand implies that *at least* his previous letter to the
Thessalonians also contained a closing autograph, as probably to be
found in 1 Thess. 5.27-28.

   2 Corinthians is another letter that contains no explicit reference to an
autograph. On the analogy of Paul's other letters, a reasonable conjec-
ture is that at least the final grace benediction was written in his own
hand. A much bolder proposal, however, would be to view the whole of
chs. 10–13 as an autograph.[2] It is not my intention to enter here into the
complex issue of the literary integrity of 2 Corinthians and the many
reconstructions that have been proposed. Nevertheless, the proposal that
chs. 10–13 were written in Paul's own hand in contrast to the
secretary's work in chs. 1–9 is one that should not be immediately dismissed as impossible. Such a view would explain many of the tensions
that scholars feel between the two major sections of the letter. The
emphatic wording of 10.1, αὐτὸς δὲ ἐγὼ Παῦλος παρακαλῶ ('I,
Paul, myself appeal'), is more in keeping with the opening of an autograph than a new letter (as many view 10.1 to be). The predominant use
of the first-person plural in chs. 1–9 and the first-person singular in

(2.18; 3.5), they are not found in any of the stereotyped formulae.
   1.   F.F. Bruce, *1 & 2 Thessalonians* (Waco, TX: Word Books), p. 135. So also
Best, *Thessalonians*, p. 246; Marshall, *Thessalonians*, p. 165; Richards, *Secretary*,
pp. 179-80; Wanamaker, *Thessalonians*, p. 208. Best allows for the possibility that
the autograph begins with the greeting of 5.25. Similarly, White ('NT Epistolary
Literature', p. 1741, n. 27) comments: 'Though Paul does not actually state that he is
writing the greeting in 1 Th. 5.26f., the manner in which the greeting is joined to a
strong pronouncement suggests that he himself may be closing the letter.'
   2.   This view has been proposed and adopted by a number of scholars: e.g.,
H.A.W. Meyer, *Kritisch-exegetischer Handbuch über den zweiten Brief an die
Korinther* (Göttingen: Vandenhoeck & Ruprecht, 1840), p. 183; Deissmann, *Light
from Ancient East*, pp. 153, 167, n. 7; O. Holtzmann, *Das Neue Testament nach der
Stuttgarter griechischer Text übersetzt und erklärt* (Giessen: Töpelmann, 1926), II,
p. 717; M. Dibelius, *A Fresh Approach to the New Testament and Early Christian
Literature* (trans. D.S. Noel and G. Abbott; New York: Charles Scribner's Sons,
1936), p. 157; W.H. Bates, 'The Integrity of II Corinthians', *NTS* 12 (1965), p. 67;
Bahr, 'Subscriptions', pp. 37-38; Richards, *Secretary*, pp. 180-81.

chs. 10–13 would be easily explained if the final section of the letter were written personally by the apostle. The sharp tone of chs. 10–13 agrees with the harsh language found in Paul's other closing autographs (1 Cor. 16.22-24; Gal. 6.11-18; Rom. 16.17-20; 1 Thess. 5.27). The length of this material (33 per cent of the letter), although certainly longer than Paul's normal autographs, is not impossible. Cicero, for example, commonly has handwritten postscripts that are relatively longer.[1] But even though the suggestion that chs. 10–13 constitute an autograph section of Paul is a legitimate possibility, there is not the kind of explicit support in the text needed to make such a proposal convincing.

d. *The Function of an Autograph*
My study of autographs in ancient Greco-Roman letters pointed out that the practice of closing a letter in the sender's own hand was a fixed epistolary custom: letters written with the help of a secretary were expected to close with an autograph. At the same time, however, a closing autograph served to accomplish various specific tasks—for example, to authenticate a letter, to make a letter legally binding, to give a letter a more personal touch, to ensure confidentiality.[2] Similarly, by writing part of the letter closing in his own hand, Paul not only follows the epistolary custom of his day but also uses this closing convention to serve various specific purposes.

In 2 Thessalonians, for example, the intention of the closing autograph (3.17) seems to be to prove the letter's authenticity. The possible existence of forged correspondence claiming to be from Paul and his fellow workers (2.2) caused the apostle to write part of the closing in his own hand, thereby establishing the letter's genuineness.[3] A closer examination of the letter, however, suggests a slightly different, or at least additional purpose. The Thessalonian church was experiencing internal conflict stemming from problems with the 'idlers' (3.6-15).

---

1. See Richards, *Secretary*, p. 180. Bahr ('Subscriptions', p. 28, n. 6) lists several papyri with lengthy summary subscriptions in proportion to the size of the document.
2. See discussion of autograph above, pp. 48-50.
3. So virtually all commentators. See, e.g., Milligan, *Thessalonians*, p. 188; J.E. Frame, *A Critical and Exegetical Commentary on the Epistles of St Paul to the Thessalonians* (Edinburgh: T. & T. Clark, 1912), p. 311; W. Neil, *The Epistle of Paul to the Thessalonians* (London: Hodder & Stoughton, 1950), p. 199; Rigaux, *Thessaloniciens*, p. 718; Best, *Thessalonians*, p. 347.

Because Paul recognizes the strong possibility that these idlers will not obey the exhortations contained in his letter (3.14), he closes the letter in his own hand, thereby emphasizing the authority of the letter and the need for the idlers to obey its injunctions.[1] The function of the autograph in 2 Thessalonians, then, is to emphasize the authority of Paul's letter, not so much its authenticity.

In the letter to Philemon the autograph serves quite a different purpose. In the context of discussing the financial restitution that Onesimus must make to Philemon, the statement ἐγὼ Παῦλος ἔγραψα τῇ ἐμῇ χειρί· ἐγὼ ἀποτίσω ('I, Paul, write this in my own hand. I will repay it') becomes an official promissory note or IOU.[2] Here the autograph possesses a legal function in which Paul commits himself to make full compensation for whatever the slave Onesimus may owe his master Philemon.

A unique autograph statement occurs in Galatians. For immediately preceding the reference to his own handwriting, Paul states: ἴδετε πηλίκοις ὑμῖν γράμμασιν ἔγραψα ('See with what large letters I write to you'). Several diverse explanations have been forwarded to explain why Paul gives this autograph with 'large letters'[3] and what purpose he intends by drawing his readers' attention to this feature of his handwriting:

1.   Some postulate that the large letters were due to Paul's poor eyesight—a physical defect implied in 4.15 ('For I bear witness that, if possible, you would have plucked out your eyes and given them to me'). This proposal suffers from the fact that 4.15 likely is a popular idiom expressing one's willingness to

1.   The function of the autograph in 2 Thessalonians in stressing the authority of Paul's letter rather than its authenticity is recognized by Marshall, *Thessalonians*, p. 232.

2.   The verb ἀποτίνω, used only here in the NT but frequently in the papryi (e.g., P. Oxy. 275.27; BGU 759.23), is a legal term meaning 'to make compensation', 'to pay the damages'. See BAGD §101; Deissmann, *Light from Ancient East*, p. 332; E. Lohse, *Colossians and Philemon* (trans. W.R. Poehlmann and R.J. Karris; Philadelphia: Fortress, 1971), p. 204.

3.   The KJV takes the plural γράμματα in the singular sense of 'a letter' (i.e., a document) rather than letters of the alphabet: 'See how large a letter I have written.' This view, however, is surely wrong since: (1) Paul always uses the word ἐπιστολή to refer to his correspondence; (2) Galatians is not a long letter compared to many of Paul's letters; and (3) the plural γράμματα, although occasionally used to refer to a written correspondence, more naturally refers to letters of the alphabet.

provide for another person's needs rather than an allusion to
the visual impairment of Paul.[1]

2.   Adolf Deissmann argued that 'the apostle's "large letters" are
best explained as the clumsy, awkward writing of a workman's
hand deformed by toil.'[2] Deissmann translated πηλίκοις
γράμμασιν as 'clumsy letters' and takes Paul's words 'as a
piece of amiable irony': his clumsy letters contrast those who
make a fine outward show in their insistence on circumcision.[3]
The adjective πηλίκος, however, refers to size only, not to
poor quality of shape or style.[4]

3.   Appealing to 2.19 ('I have been crucified with Christ') and
6.14, 17 ('I [have been crucified] to the world'; 'I bear on my
body the marks of Jesus'), Nigel Turner claims that Paul 'had
actually been crucified at Perga in Pamphylia' and sustained
permanent damage to his hand.[5] This view founders, however,
on a too literal and fanciful interpretation of those verses in
Galatians that Turner cites in support.

4.   John Nijenhuis attempts to explain the 'large letters' in light of
Paul's psychological condition. In order to overcome his
internal timidity and shyness, Paul 'overcompensated' with the
external act of writing large letters.[6] But this explanation seems

1.   Longenecker, *Galatians*, pp. 193, 290. There probably is a connection here to
the τὰ ἀβάσκοντα wish (i.e., a wish that the 'evil eye' would not cause someone
harm) commonly found in the health wishes and greetings of Hellenistic letters. See
discussion above, pp. 38, 45.

2.   Deissmann, *St. Paul*, p. 51; see also *Light from Ancient East*, p. 166 n. 7.

3.   Deissmann, *Bible Studies*, p. 348. Deissmann also talks about Paul 'playfully
trusting that surely the large letters will touch their hearts' and that 'the feeling of
coolness that might have remained behind [from the sharp tone of the letter] was now
happily wiped away by Paul's thrice-welcomed good-natured irony' (p. 349). So too
R.A. Cole, *Epistle of Paul to the Galatians* (Grand Rapids: Eerdmans, 1965) pp. 179-
80.

4.   See C.J. Ellicott, *Epistle to the Galatians* (Andover, MA: Draper, 1880)
pp. 148-49; W.K.L. Clarke, 'St. Paul's "Large Letters"', *ExpTim* 24 (1912–13),
p. 285; J.S. Clemens, 'St. Paul's Handwriting', *ExpTim* 24 (1912–13), p. 380;
R.Y.K. Fung, *The Epistle to the Galatians* (Grand Rapids: Eerdmans, 1988), p. 301.

5.   N. Turner, *Grammatical Insights into the New Testament* (Edinburgh:
T. & T. Clark, 1965), p. 94.

6.   J. Nijenhuis, 'This Greeting in My Own Hand—Paul', *Bible Today* 19
(1981), pp. 255-58. Nijenhuis appeals to 2 Cor 10.1, 10-11 for support.

    more influenced by modern psychological analysis than any solid evidence from Paul's letters.

5.   The most plausible view understands the 'large letters' as a means of emphasizing and underscoring the importance of Paul's closing words.[1] As E. Dewitt Burton notes, 'The size of the letters would have somewhat the effect of bold-face type in a modern book, or double underlining in a manuscript, and since the apostle himself called attention to it, it would impress not only the one person who might be reading the letter to a congregation, but the listening congregation also.'[2] Lukyn Williams cites evidence from Pisidian Antioch and Pompeii supporting the notion that writing in large letters was used to accentuate in much the same way as italics function today.[3] A possible parallel with the autograph of 2 Thessalonians thus emerges. For the closing autograph in Galatians serves to provide emphasis and so stress the authority of Paul's words in contrast to the claims of his opponents.

It was argued above that there is good justification for identifying an autograph in the closings of Romans, Philippians and 1 Thessalonians. Assuming the validity of this position, what function does the autograph have in these letters? Both Rom. 16.17-20 and 1 Thess. 5.27-28 contain a final, passionate appeal or challenge of Paul, and so are similar to 2 Thessalonians and Galatians where the autograph serves to stress the authority of Paul's letter. A different purpose, however, is intended in the autograph of Phil. 4.10-23, which contains Paul's personal thanks for the financial gifts he has received. This autograph has a personalizing function: by closing in his own hand, Paul better expresses the depth and sincerity of his gratitude.

By closing his letters in his own hand, Paul not only follows the

1.   Apparently first proposed by Theodore of Mopsuestia (see Lightfoot, *Galatians*, p. 221). This interpretation enjoys the support of most modern commentators: e.g., H. Schlier, *Der Brief an die Galater* (Göttingen: Vandenhoeck & Ruprecht, 1951) p. 280; Mussner, *Der Galaterbrief*, p. 410; Betz, *Galatians*, p. 314; Bruce, *Galatians*, p. 268; Cousar, *Galatians*, p. 148; Fung, *Galatians*, p. 301; Longenecker, *Galatians*, p. 290.

2.   E.D. Burton, *A Critical and Exegetical Commentary on the Epistle to the Galatians* (Edinburgh: T. & T. Clark, 1921), p. 348.

3.   A.L. Williams, *The Epistle of Paul the Apostle to the Galatians* (Cambridge: Cambridge University Press, 1910), p. 136.

epistolary practice of his day but also uses this closing convention to serve various specific purposes—that is, to stress the authority of his words, to validate in a legal fashion a promise of payment, and to express a warmer, more personal tone. My argument for the multi-purposed function of the autograph, however, contradicts the work of Franz Schnider and Werner Stenger, who argue that *all* the autographs should be understood as serving a legal or juridical function.[1] Although Schnider and Stenger recognize that closing a letter in the sender's hand was a common practice of the day, they stress that a handwritten name signature was rare, occurring primarily in legal or business documents. Thus on the basis of parallels with handwritten name signatures in Hellenistic and Jewish letters, they conclude that the closing autographs in Paul's letters serve to validate the contents in a quasi-juridical manner and make it legally binding on its hearers.

The difficulties with this view are threefold. First, only three of the closing autographs of Paul's letters have his signature (1 Cor. 16.21; 2 Thess. 3.17; Phlm. 19). It would be wrong, therefore, to conclude, as Schnider and Stenger do, that *all* the autographs have a legal function. Second, two of the three instances where Paul includes his name in the autograph occur in a greeting formula (1 Cor. 16.21; 2 Thess. 3.17), with the presence of Paul's name in these instances more naturally stating who is sending the greeting than making the letter legally binding on the readers. Third, apart from Philemon, the content of those letters of Paul that contain a closing autograph cannot be considered in any remote or indirect way as legalistic.[2] Consequently, the parallels drawn by Schnider and Stenger with Hellenistic and Jewish business or official letters lose their force, and the conclusion reached above concerning the

---

1.   Schnider and Stenger (*Neutestamentlichen Briefformular*, p. 137): 'Von hier gesehen darf man fragen, ob auch da, wo Eigenhändigkeitsvermerk und namentliche Unterschrift im Eschatokoll begegnen, eine wie auch immer im einzelnen zu präzisierende, *juristische Funktion* anzunehmen ist' ('From this perspective, one might also ask whether the handwritten endorsements and signatures that appear here and there may also have a legal function that needs to be specified for each case' [Italics theirs, translation mine]). See their extended discussion, pp. 135-67.

2.   In an attempt to get around the weight of this objection, Schnider and Stenger (*Neutestmentlichen Briefformular*, p. 150) claim that Paul, because of the seriousness with which he viewed his admonitions and exhortations, considered his letter some-what akin to 'holy law'. For example, in Galatians, they argue that Paul's vehement opposition to those who insisted on the priority and permanence of the law caused him, paradoxically, to turn the gospel into law.[!]

multi-purposed function of the Pauline autograph is not invalidated.

Before ending this discussion of the autograph, a few observations ought to be made concerning the central concern of my thesis, namely that there are important links that exist between the Pauline closings and the rest of the material that appears in their respective letters. Much of what Paul has written in his own hand includes conventional formulae such as grace benedictions and greetings. Since both of these closing conventions have already been discussed in some detail, there is no need to repeat this material here. Closing autographs also contain, however, other miscellaneous items that are likewise related to key issues addressed in their respective letter bodies.

The most striking autograph by far is Gal. 6.11-18. The extended length of this closing section (the longest of all the unquestioned autographs)[1] as well as its emphatic introduction ('See with what large letters I write to you') serve in tandem to underscore the importance of this closing passage written personally by Paul. The feature of greatest significance for our present interest, however, is the way Paul uses this autograph to recapitulate the main concerns previously taken up in the body of the Galatian letter. Although a detailed examination of Gal. 6.11-18 must be left till the subsequent chapter, the following observations are sufficient to demonstrate the summarizing function of this closing autograph.

Following the autograph formula (v. 11), Paul draws his readers' attention to the false motives of his opponents who selfishly seek to boast in the circumcision of the Galatians, thereby avoiding persecution for the cross of Christ (vv. 12-13). Paul, therefore, immediately takes up in the closing autograph the problem of his opponents in Galatia, whom he has been attacking throughout the letter—as in 1.7, 8, 9; (2.12); 3.1; 4.17, 21; 5.7, 10, 12. All the key words in this closing rebuttal are terms that have played a central part in his argument in the letter body: (1) The word σάρξ ('flesh'), found twice in the autograph at vv. 12 and 13, occurs repeatedly in the letter (physical sense: 1.16; 2.16, 20; 3.3; 4.13, 14, 23, 29; ethical sense: 5.13, 16, 17 [2×], 19, 24; 6.8 [2×]). (2) The double reference to τῷ σταυρῷ τοῦ Χριστοῦ ('the cross of Christ') of vv. 12 and 14 serves as a direct link to Paul's previous statement about the centrality of the cross to the Christian gospel in 2.19; 3.1, 13; 5.11, 24 (1.4; 2.20c, 21). (3) The five references to circumcision in the auto-

---

1. The only exception would be 2 Cor. 10–13 if this material were in fact written in Paul's own hand.

graph at vv. 12, 13 [2×], 15 [2×] echo Paul's previous discussion concerning this OT rite in 2.3, 7, 8, 9, 12; 5.2, 3, 6, 11, (12)—in particular, note the striking parallel between 6.15, οὔτε γὰρ περιτομή τί ἐστιν οὔτε ἀκροβυστία ('For neither circumcision nor uncircumcision is anything'), and the earlier words of 5.6, οὔτε περιτομή τι ἰσχύει οὔτε ἀκροβυστία ('Neither circumcision nor uncircumcision means anything'). (4) The idea of persecution, important in the closing autograph at vv. 12 and 17, also is a subject addressed earlier in the letter in 4.29 and 5.11 (see also 1.13, 23). And (5) the enigmatic phrase καινὴ κτίσις ('a new creation') in v. 15, probably a well-known maxim of the early church expressing the new order brought about by Christ, serves as an appropriate climax to Paul's argument throughout the letter against those who insist on hanging on to the old order with its nomistic lifestyle in conformity to the Mosaic commandments.

Even in such a brief analysis of Gal. 6.11-18 one cannot help but be struck by the masterful way in which Paul uses his closing autograph to summarize the primary concerns addressed earlier in the letter. This recapitulating or synthesizing function of the Galatian autograph has been recognized by several commentators. Already a century ago Joseph Lightfoot observed that 6.11-18 functions by way of 'summing up the main lessons of the epistle'.[1] Donald Guthrie refers to this passage as a 'concluding summarizing appeal'.[2] And Richard Longenecker comments that '6.11-18 must be seen as something of a prism that reflects the major thrusts of what has been said earlier in the letter.'[3]

---

1. Lightfoot, *St. Paul's Epistle to the Galatians* (New York: Macmillan, 1890), p. 220.

2. Guthrie, *Galatians*, p. 149.

3. Longenecker, *Galatians*, p. 288. A number of other commentators also recognize the summary character of the autograph in Galatians: e.g., H.A.W. Meyer, *Kritisch-exegetischer Handbuch über den Brief an die Galater* (Göttingen: Vandenhoeck & Ruprecht, 1841): 'Eigenhändiger Endabschnitt des Briefes. Die polemischen Hauptpunkte werden recapituliert...' (p. 208); H.W. Beyer, 'Der Brief an die Galater', in *Die kleineren Briefe des Apostels Paulus* (Göttingen: Vandenhoeck & Ruprecht, 1949), p. 54; Williams, *Galatians*, p. 136; R. Bring, *Commentary on Galatians* (trans. E. Wahlstrom; Philadelphia: Muhlenberg, 1961): 'The Letter to the Galatians ends with a few final words in which Paul summarizes the matter of most importance in the letter' (p. 282; see also pp. 285-87); Holtzmann, *Das Neue Testament*, p. 67; Burton, *Galatians*, pp. 347, 349; Bahr, 'Subscriptions': 'These few concluding verses are a kind of summary of the entire epistle' (p. 32); Mussner, *Galaterbrief*, p. 410: '[6.11-16] fast wie ein abschliessendes Summarium der vorausgehenden

Another autograph that contains more than just a grace benediction and a greeting in Paul's own hand is Philemon 19–25. Although not as obvious as in Gal. 6.11-18, here too one can discern a summarizing function.[1] The autograph formula in v. 19a repeats in an official or legally binding fashion Paul's promise of the previous verse (18) to cover any debts that Onesimus may owe Philemon. The word play on Onesimus' name in v. 20a recalls not only the general subject matter of the letter body (i.e., Paul's appeal for Onesimus) but also the words of v. 11 ('Formerly he was useless to you, but now he is indeed useful to you and to me'). Paul's command of v. 20b that Philemon 'refresh my heart in Christ' (ἀνάπαυσόν μου τὰ σπλάγχνα) is reminiscent of his description of Philemon in v. 7b as one through whom 'the hearts of the saints have been refreshed' (τὰ σπλάγχνα τῶν ἁγίων ἀναπέπαυται διὰ σοῦ) and of his description of Onesimus in v. 12b as 'this one is my heart' (τοῦτ' ἔστιν τὰ ἐμὰ σπλάγχνα). So also Paul's address of Philemon in v. 20 as ἀδελφέ recalls the apostle's earlier appeal in v. 16 for Philemon to welcome Onesimus back as a ἀδελφὸν ἀγαπητόν. The 'confidence formula'[2] of v. 21 and the 'apostolic parousia'[3] of v. 22 are

Partien des Briefes wirkt' ('it functions almost as a concluding summary of the preceding passages of the letter'); Bruce, *Galatians*: 'Some of these comments [in 6.11-18] recapitulate the main emphases of the letter' (p. 268); B.H. Brinsmead, *Galatians—Dialogical Response to Opponents* (Chico, CA: Scholars, 1982): '[Gal. 6.11-18] is striking in the way it recapitulates the main themes of the epistle' (p. 48; see also pp. 63-67); Cousar, *Galatians*: 'Paul chooses to return to the primary reason for writing and to several terms already mentioned in the body of the letter... The section, in fact, epitomizes the heart of the letter' (p. 148); G.W. Hansen, *Abraham in Galatians* (Sheffield: JSOT Press, 1989): '6.11-18 contains the summary of the cardinal points of the letter' (p. 53; see also pp. 65-66, 69-70).

1. So Bahr, 'Subscriptions', pp. 35-36; *idem*, 'Paul and Letter Writing', pp. 467-68. Although critical of Bahr's view of the closing in Philemon, Richards (*Secretary*, p. 178) nevertheless admits that 'what follows [i.e., Phlm. 19–25] could be loosely termed a summary subscription.'

2. The term 'confidence formula' was apparently first coined by White (*Body of the Greek Letter*, pp. 104-106) who, on the basis of Phlm. 21, Gal. 5.10, and Rom. 15.14, identified four standard elements in this formula: '(1) the emphatic use of the pronoun (ἐγώ); (2) the perfect form of the verb (πείθω), by which Paul alleges his "confidence"; (3) the specification of the basis of confidence defined as residing either in the Lord (Gal. 5.10) or in Paul's addressees (Philem. 21 and Rom. 15.14); and (4) explicit mention of the object concerning which Paul is confident (introduced by ὅτι)' (see also White, 'Structural Analysis of Philemon', pp. 40-41). The confidence formula was later examined in greater detail by S.N. Olson who, despite

also intimately related to the letter's central concern—the first reinforcing the granting of Paul's request in a positive manner by praising
Philemon in advance for his expected obedience;[1] the second reinforcing
the letter's request in a more negative fashion, since the announcement
of Paul's impending arrival serves as an indirect threat suggesting that
his coming will be to see whether his wishes have been carried out.
Therefore, as in Galatians, so also here in Philemon we see how Paul
uses his closing autograph to highlight and summarize the key concern
previously raised in the body of that letter.

It was suggested above that Rom. 16.17-20 was written in Paul's own
hand, even though he does not explicitly draw attention to that fact. If
so, this passage provides yet another example of a summarizing
autograph. For though 16.17-20 does not restate the argument of the
whole letter, it does echo the concerns of 14.1–15.13. Paul's autograph
warning against 'those who create dissensions and divisions' (16.17)
recalls, albeit in a stronger tone, his earlier appeals against a disunity
within the Roman congregation that stemmed from sharp disagreements
between the 'weak' and the 'strong'. Karl Donfried observes that

arguing against speaking of any stereotyped formula as such because of the variation
of such expressions, nevertheless identifies five elements that are typically present:
(1) an indication of a first-person subject in the verb or pronoun, or in the antecedent
to the participle; (2) the confidence term or terms; (3) a reference to the addressees as
the object of confidence, using a second-person pronoun; (4) a conjunction linking
the expression (causally) with what precedes; and (5) an indication of the content of
the confidence, usually with ὅτι, but also a direct prepositional phrase. See S.N. Olson,
'Pauline Expressions of Confidence in His Addressees', *CBQ* 47 (1985), pp. 282-95,
esp. p. 295; *idem*, 'Epistolary Uses of Expressions of Self-Confidence', *JBL* 103
(1984), pp. 585-97; 'Confidence Expressions in Paul: Epistolary Conventions and the
Purpose of 2 Corinthians' (PhD dissertation; New Haven: Yale University Press,
1976).

3.   For discussions of the 'apostolic parousia' in Paul's letters, see R.W. Funk,
'The Apostolic *Parousia*: Form and Significance', in *Christian History and
Interpretation: Studies Presented to John Knox* (ed. W.R. Farmer, C.F.D. Moule and
R.R. Niebuhr; Cambridge: Cambridge University Press, 1967), pp. 249-69; Doty,
Letters, pp. 12, 36-38; White, 'Structural Analysis of Philemon', pp. 41-45; Jervis,
Purpose of Romans, pp. 52-53, 110-131. For a slightly critical view of the apostolic
parousia as a fixed formula, see T.Y. Mullins, 'Visit Talk in New Testament Letters',
CBQ 35 (1973), pp. 350-58.

1.   Olson ('Pauline Expressions of Confidence', p. 288) comments: 'In Phlm 21
the confidence of compliance functions to reinforce the appeal of the *whole* letter'
(italics mine).

'Rom. 16.17-20 is a concluding summary' of issues raised in the previous chapters, and that 'it is these themes which Paul is summarizing in the form of a final warning in Rom. 16.17-20 and thus, there is nothing "new" about the subject matter.'[1] Paul Achtemeier likewise comments that 16.17-20 'summarizes the theme that had preoccupied Paul not only in his section on admonitions (chs. 12–16), but which also underlies the whole of his theology, namely the unity in Christ of Jews and Gentiles'.[2]

The remaining Pauline autographs will not be discussed here, but will be taken up in the next chapter. Enough has been said, however, to show that the closing material that Paul wrote in his own hand in his various letters is intimately related to the bodies of those letters. In fact, the closing autographs frequently serve as summaries of the key issues developed earlier in their respective letters.

5. *The Doxology*

Another epistolary convention that is frequently claimed to be a regular feature of Paul's letter closings is the doxology.[3] Although the doxology has some affinity with the benediction, there is good warrant for distinguishing between these two conventional formulae.[4] For they differ not only in form (see discussion of basic elements of the doxology below) but also in focus or direction. Whereas the benediction is an invocation to God to bestow a blessing on some person(s), the doxology is an

1. K.P. Donfried, 'A Short Note on Romans 16', *JBL* 89 (1970), p. 449 (article reprinted in *idem* [ed.], *The Romans Debate*, pp. 44-52).

2. P.J. Achtemeier, *Romans* (Atlanta: John Knox, 1985), p. 238. Achtemeier also goes on to say: 'In short, verses 17–20...sum up the core of what Paul has wanted to communicate to the Romans' (p. 239).

3. So Funk, *Language, Hermeneutic, and Word of God*, pp. 257, 270; F.V. Filson, *'Yesterday': A Study of Hebrews in the Light of Chapter 13* (Naperville, IL: Allenson, 1967) pp. 22-24; Doty, *Letters*, p. 27; H. Boers, 'A Form-Critical Study of Paul's Letters: 1 Thessalonians as a Case Study', *NTS* 22 (1976), p. 140; R.P. Martin, *New Testament Foundations* (2 vols.; Grand Rapids: Eerdmans, 1978), II, pp. 246-47; *idem, 2 Corinthians*, p. 492; Russell, 'Pauline Letter Structure', pp. 303, 305; Wanamaker, *Thessalonians*, p. 205.

4. *Contra* Champion (*Benediction and Doxologies*) who, in his extensive study of these two conventional formulae, tends to blur the distinction between them: e.g., 'both benedictions and doxologies have common characteristics and are built up in a similar manner, and thus they may be considered together' (p. 19).

expression of praise to God. Thus the benediction possesses more of an anthropocentric focus (although God clearly is the source of the blessing) while the doxology has a purely theocentric view.

a. *The Elements of the Doxology*

A doxology occurs four times in the authentic letters of Paul, four times in the disputed Pauline letters, and eight times in the remaining NT letters. If all NT occurrences of a doxology are included for the sake of comparative analysis (see Table 5), it becomes clear that the doxology exhibits a relatively fixed pattern, consisting of four basic elements: the object of praise, the element of praise, the indication of time, and the confirmatory response.

The Object of Praise. The first element of any NT doxology identifies the object or recipient of praise. This is always given in the dative case, usually the third-person personal pronoun αὐτῷ or, more commonly, the relative pronoun ᾧ. The precise identity of the one being praised must be determined from the antecedent of the pronoun. In doxologies belonging to the undisputed letters of Paul, the object of praise is always God.[1] The remaining doxologies normally follow this pattern, although a number of exceptions can be found in which praise is instead directed to Christ (2 Tim. 4.18;[2] 2 Pet. 3.18; Rev. 1.5b-6; 5.13b).

Of the four basic elements of a NT doxology, the object of praise is the constituent part that undergoes the most elaboration. Additional phrases describing the recipient of praise can occur either within the doxology itself or, more commonly, outside the formula in the preceding verses that provide the antecedent of αὐτῷ or ᾧ. Elaboration sometimes involves a rather brief listing of divine attributes, for example, 1 Tim. 1.17: τῷ δὲ βασιλεῖ τῶν αἰώνων, ἀφθάρτῳ, ἀοράτῳ, μόνῳ θεῷ ('To the king of ages, immortal, invisible, the only God'). In other instances, elaboration can be much more extensive, for example, Jude 24-25:

---

1.   The statement of C.K. Barrett (*The Epistle to the Romans* [New York: Harper & Row, 1957], p. 287) that Paul in the doxology of Rom. 16.25-27 'ascribes glory to Christ' is surely wrong, since the true antecedent of ᾧ is not Ἰησοῦ Χριστοῦ but θεῷ (16.27). See also the parallel pattern in Heb. 13.21 and 1 Pet. 4.11.

2.   J.N.D. Kelly (*A Commentary on the Pastoral Epistles* [Grand Rapids: Baker, 1963], p. 220) maintains that the object of praise (κύριος: see 4.14, 17, 18) is God rather than Christ, and that this doxology is therefore consistent with the pattern found elsewhere in Paul's letters. This is highly unlikely, however, given that the apostle virtually always uses the title κύριος to refer to Christ.

	Object of Praise	Element of Praise	Indication of Time	Confirmatory Response
Rom. 11.36b	αὐτῷ	ἡ δόξα	εἰς τοὺς αἰῶνας	ἀμήν
Rom. 16.25-27	τῷ δὲ δυναμένῳ ... ᾧ	ἡ δόξα	εἰς τοὺς αἰῶνας	ἀμήν
Gal. 1.5	ᾧ	ἡ δόξα	εἰς τοὺς αἰῶνας τῶν αἰώνων	ἀμήν
Phil. 4.20	τῷ δὲ θεῷ καὶ πατρὶ ἡμῶν	ἡ δόξα	εἰς τοὺς αἰῶνας τῶν αἰώνων	ἀμήν
Eph. 3.20-21	τῷ δὲ δυναμένῳ ... αὐτῷ	ἡ δόξα ἐν τῇ ἐκκλησίᾳ καὶ ἐν Χριστῷ Ἰησοῦ	εἰς πάσας τὰς γενεὰς τοῦ αἰῶνος τῶν αἰώνων	ἀμήν
1 Tim. 1.17	τῷ δὲ βασιλεῖ ...	τιμὴ καὶ δόξα	εἰς τοὺς αἰῶνας τῶν αἰώνων	ἀμήν
1 Tim. 6.16	ᾧ	τιμὴ καὶ κράτος	αἰώνιον	ἀμήν
2 Tim. 4.18	ᾧ	ἡ δόξα	εἰς τοὺς αἰῶνας τῶν αἰώνων	ἀμήν
Heb. 13.21b	ᾧ	ἡ δόξα	εἰς τοὺς αἰῶνας τῶν αἰώνων	ἀμήν
1 Pet. 4.11	ᾧ ἐστιν	ἡ δόξα καὶ τὸ κράτος	εἰς τοὺς αἰῶνας τῶν αἰώνων	ἀμήν
1 Pet. 5.11	αὐτῷ	τὸ κράτος	εἰς τοὺς αἰῶνας	ἀμήν
Jude 24-25	τῷ δὲ δυναμένῳ ...	δόξα μεγαλωσύνη κράτος καὶ ἐξουσία	πρὸ παντὸς τοῦ αἰῶνος καὶ νῦν καὶ εἰς πάντας τοὺς αἰῶνας	ἀμήν
Rev. 1.5b-6	τῷ ἀγαπῶντι ἡμᾶς ... αὐτῷ	ἡ δόξα καὶ τὸ κράτος	εἰς τοὺς αἰῶνας τῶν αἰώνων	ἀμήν
Rev. 5.13b	τῷ καθημένῳ ...	ἡ εὐλογία καὶ ἡ τιμὴ καὶ ἡ δόξα καὶ τὸ κράτος	εἰς τοὺς αἰῶνας τῶν αἰώνων	
Rev. 7.12	τῷ θεῷ ἡμῶν	ἡ εὐλογία καὶ ἡ δόξα καὶ ἡ σοφία καὶ ἡ εὐχαριστία καὶ ἡ τιμὴ καὶ ἡ δύναμις καὶ ἡ ἰσχύς	εἰς τοὺς αἰῶνας τῶν αἰώνων	ἀμήν

Table 5. *Doxologies*

τῷ δὲ δυναμένῳ φυλάξαι ὑμᾶς ἀπταίστους καὶ στῆσαι κατενώπιον τῆς δόξης αὐτοῦ ἀμώμους ἐν ἀγαλλιάσει, μόνῳ θεῷ σωτῆρι ἡμῶν διὰ Ἰησοῦ Χριστοῦ τοῦ κυρίου ἡμῶν ('Now to him who is able to keep you from falling and to present you without blemish before the presence of his glory with rejoicing, to the only God, our Savior through Jesus Christ our Lord'). Both types of elaborations, brief and extensive, can be found in the doxologies used in Paul's letters.

The Element of Praise. The nominative case identifies the element of praise to be ascribed to God (or Christ). In every occurrence of the doxology in the NT letters, the element of praise is δόξα ('glory')— hence the title of this stereotyped formula. Many doxologies belonging to the disputed and non-Pauline letters, however, contain additional elements of praise. By far, the most common of these is κράτος ('power'), but τιμή ('honor'), ἐξουσία ('authority'), εὐλογία ('blessing') and so on, also appear. The ascribing of glory or some other element of praise to God does not imply the adding of something not currently present, but rather acknowledges an existing divine attribute. The doxology, therefore, is a declarative statement rather than a pious wish.[1]

There are no elaborations on the element of praise, unless one considers the additional elements of praise contained in some doxologies to be elaborations. The one exception is the doxology of Eph. 3.20-21 that contains the double prepositional phrase ἐν τῇ ἐκκλησίᾳ καὶ ἐν Χριστῷ Ἰησοῦ ('in the church and in Christ Jesus'), thereby identifying the sphere in which glory is to be ascribed to God.

The Indication of Time. Every NT doxology contains an indication of how long the element of praise is to be given. This is expressed by the prepositional phrase εἰς τοὺς αἰῶνας τὸν αἰώνων, an idiom meaning 'for ever and ever'. Only slight variations and elaborations of this phrase take place. In a few doxologies, αἰών occurs only once (Rom. 11.36; 16.27; 1 Pet. 5.11; 1 Tim. 6.16) rather than twice. In a few other

---

1.   The doxologies presuppose, therefore, the indicative ἐστί(ν) rather than the optative εἴη, a fact confirmed by the presence of the indicative in the doxology of 1 Pet. 4.11. See also BDF §128.5; G. Kittel, 'δόξα' *TDNT*, II, p. 248; A. Stuiber, 'Doxology', *RAC* 4 (1959), p. 215; D.H. Milling, 'The Origin and Character of the NT Doxology' (PhD dissertation, Cambridge University, 1972), pp. 268-71. For a contrary view, see R. Deichgräber, *Gotteshymnus und Christushymnus in der frühen Christenheit* (Göttingen: Vandenhoeck & Ruprecht, 1967), pp. 30-32.

doxologies, the expression of time has been intensified by the addition of πάσας τὰς γενεάς ('for all generations': Eph. 3.21) or καὶ νῦν καί ('both now and': 2 Pet. 3.18; also Jude 25). The greatest elaboration, however, occurs in Jude 25: πρὸ παντὸς τοῦ αἰῶνος καὶ νῦν καὶ εἰς πάντας τοὺς αἰῶνας ('before all time and now and for ever').

In the LXX, the singular εἰς τὸν αἰῶνα served to indicate an indefinite past or future. In order to bring out more fully the concept of eternity, the plural εἰς τοὺς αἰῶνας (e.g., Ps. 41.4; 77.8; 2 Chron. 4.2) was used or the doubling of the singular: εἰς τὸν αἰῶν τοῦ αἰώνου (e.g., Ps. 89.29; 111.3). The NT, however, stresses even further the notion of eternity by combining both these intensive practices of the LXX, thereby resulting in εἰς τοὺς αἰῶνας τῶν αἰώνων commonly found in the doxologies.[1] Therefore, the deviations and expansions of the NT doxological formula should not be analyzed too precisely, for they are all part of the sonorous language used to express the permanence with which glory is to be ascribed to God.

The Confirmatory Response. NT doxologies consistently close with ἀμήν ('amen').[2] This is a Semitic word whose root has the sense of firmness, consistency, truthfulness. In the OT, 'amen' functions as a formula of confirmation, either in the acceptance of an oath or curse (Num. 5.22; Deut. 27.15-26; Jer. 11.5; Neh. 5.13) or in the affirmation of praise to God as in the doxologies that close the first four books of the Psalms (Ps. 41.13; 72.19; 89.52; 106.48; see also 1 Chron. 16.36).

The confirmatory sense of 'amen' is also evident in the LXX, which translates this word as γένοιτο ('May it be!') or, less frequently, ἀληθῶς ('truly').[3] In the Jewish synagogue the worshippers responded with an 'amen' to each of the three sections of the Aaronic blessing, as well as to any prayer or praise uttered by another, thereby voicing their public affirmation of what was just spoken. In the worship service of Christians, the 'amen' naturally expressed 'the congregation's appropriation and confirmation of what has been uttered on their behalf by

1. H. Sasse ('αἰών', *TDNT*, I, p. 200) concludes: 'Hence, it may be seen that the usage of the NT is distinguished from that of the LXX only by an intensification of the tendency already displayed in the LXX to replace the simple formulae by the more complicated.'

2. See H. Schlier, 'ἀμήν', *TDNT*, I, pp. 335-38; Moule, *Worship in the New Testament*, pp. 73-76.

3. Luke also translates 'amen' as ἀληθῶς (Lk. 9.27; 12.44; 21.3; see also 4.25), unlike most NT writers who simply transliterate the word.

the leader of the worship'.[1] Thus in light of its uniform use in both Judaism and early Christianity, the presence of 'amen' at the end of a doxology in Paul's letters served to anticipate the natural response of his readers in ascribing glory to God.

b. *The Origin of the Doxology*

A doxology was not an epistolary convention of either Greco-Roman or Semitic letters. It may, therefore, be asked: From where did this stereotyped formula derive and what function does it have in the letters of the NT, particularly those written by Paul?

The answer to both these questions is not difficult, for the origin of the NT doxology clearly lies in Judaism and Jewish worship. Each of the four basic elements of the NT doxologies reflects Semitic influence.

1. The one to whom glory belongs (the object of praise) is always identified by the dative case. But the use of the dative with the implied verb ἐστί(ν) to express possession is rare in secular Greek. Rather, this construction reflects Hebrew usage where the preposition לְ can appear without a verb to express possession, particularly the fact that people, things or qualities belong to God.[2]

2. The word δόξα (the element of praise) is used in the LXX in the sense of a glorious quality belonging to God (from the Hebrew כָּבוֹד) rather than in the classical Greek sense of 'opinion' or 'view.'[3]

3. The phrase εἰς τοὺς αἰῶνας τῶν αἰώνων (the indication of time), as discussed above, clearly reflects LXX practice and is derived from Semitic phrases such as לְעוֹלָם וָעֶד.[4]

4. The Semitic loan word 'amen' (the confirmatory response) used to close the doxology likewise betrays the Jewish origin of this stereotyped formula.

So there can be little doubt that the form of doxologies found in the NT stems from Jewish worship, and that Paul and the other NT writers appropriated that Jewish form for use in their letters.

---

1. Moule, *Worship in the New Testament*, p. 75.
2. See Deichgräber, *Gotteshymnus*, p. 25.
3. Kittel, 'δόξα', pp. 233-53; S. Aalen, 'Glory, Honour', *NIDNTT*, pp. 44-48.
4. See Sasse, 'αἰών', pp. 198-202; Moule, *Worship in the New Testament*, pp. 76-77.

c. *The Function of the Doxology*

An examination of the various NT contexts in which doxologies occur reveals that a doxology serves to conclude previous material. The concluding function of a doxology is most evident in those letters where this formula occurs as part of the closing or as the last convention within this final section (Rom. 16.25-27; Phil. 4.20; 2 Tim. 4.18; Heb. 13.21b; 1 Pet. 5.11; 2 Pet. 3.18; Jude 24-25). Even in those instances where a doxology occurs within the body of a letter, it always concludes previous material and so marks the end of one section or unit and the beginning of another (Rom. 11.36; Gal. 1.5; Eph. 3.20-21; 1 Tim. 1.17; 6.16; 1 Pet. 4.11; Rev. 1.5b-6; 5.13b; 7.12). The concluding function of a doxology in NT letters probably stems from its similar function in the liturgy of worship, both Jewish and Christian.[1]

In the undisputed letters of Paul, a doxology occurs four times: twice within a letter body or letter opening (Rom. 11.36; Gal. 1.5) and twice in a letter closing (Rom. 16.25-27; Phil. 4.20). Since a doxology occurs rather infrequently in Paul's letters—and in those few occurrences is not limited to the final section of his letters—the assertion of several scholars[2] that a doxology constitutes a closing convention of Paul's letters is suspect. Other writers of the NT frequently closed their letters with a doxology, but Paul did not *typically* use it in this fashion.

Yet though a doxology is not a regular feature of his letter closings, Paul does include doxologies in the final section of two of his letters. The doxology of Phil. 4.20 contains no striking or distinctive features in terms of its form, but matches the pattern of a 'standard' doxology. Paul uses this formula here at 4.20 as a fitting conclusion to the preceding (autograph?) section of personal thanks for financial support (4.10-19)[3] and to the Philippian letter as a whole.[4]

---

1. Note the doxologies found at the end of four of the books of Psalms (Pss. 41.13; 72.19; 89.52; 106.48). In Rev. 5.13b-14 and 7.11-12 doxologies appear at the end of the heavenly liturgy, which possibly parallels the earthly liturgy used by early Christians. See Champion, *Benedictions and Doxologies*, pp. 103-106; Schnider and Stenger, *Neutestamentlichen Briefformular*, pp. 180-81.

2. E.g., Funk, Filson, Doty, Boers, Martin, Russell, and Wanamaker, as cited above in n. 3, p. 135.

3. The preceding section (4.10-19) already contains a fitting conclusion in the prayer-wish of v. 19: 'And my God will supply every need of yours according to his riches in glory in Christ Jesus.'

4. Martin (*Philippians*, p. 184) states that 'the doxology flows from the joy of the whole epistle', and so 'is Paul's fitting response to all the things

The only other doxology found in the closings of Paul's letters is Rom. 16.25-27, a passage whose authenticity has been questioned on both textual and literary grounds. The MSS indicate that this doxology has been variously placed after 14.23, 15.33 and 16.23.[1] And many claim its language and style to be un-Pauline. The issues concerning the authenticity of 16.25-27 are complex and have generated extended discussion. A detailed examination of the issue need not be undertaken here. For now I would simply note that, despite the consensus raised against the doxology being from Paul, some scholars continue to support its authenticity.[2]

The doxology of Rom. 16.25-27 is of interest and potential significance for this thesis because of the way in which it echoes earlier material in Paul's letter to the Romans. The identification of God as 'the one who is able to strengthen you' (16.25a) reflects previous references to the power of God and the strength that he gives to believers (1.11; 1.16; 9.17; 15.13, 19). The expression 'according to my gospel' (16.25a, κατὰ τὸ εὐαγγέλιόν μου), not found in Paul's other letters,[3] is paralleled exactly in 2.16. These references in the opening of the doxology to the empowering work of God, Paul's gospel and the 'preaching of Jesus Christ,' echo, in particular, the key statement of 1.16 that refers to the gospel as the power of God that Paul was commissioned to preach.

The notion of the gospel as a 'mystery hidden for ages but now revealed' (16.25b-26a) parallels the thought of 3.21, which also is a key statement in the overall theme of the letter. This mystery was 'made known through the prophetic writings according to the command of the eternal God' (16.26) as Paul has clearly demonstrated throughout the letter by means of repeated OT quotations and allusions.[4] More specifically, the phrase 'through the prophetic writings' (16.26, διὰ γραφῶν

which cause him joy in his prison experience'.

1. In some MSS the doxology occurs twice after both 14.23 and 16.23, while in a few other MSS it is omitted altogether.

2. See especially L.W. Hurtado, 'The Doxology at the End of Romans', in *New Testament Textual Criticism: Its Significance for Exegesis. Essays in Honor of Bruce M. Metzger* (ed. E.J. Epp and G.D. Fee; Oxford: Clarendon, 1981), pp. 185-99.

3. In other occurrences of this prepositional phrase, Paul always uses the plural form (ἡμῶν) of the first-person personal pronoun: 2 Cor. 4.3; 1 Thess. 1.5; 2 Thess. 2.14. See, however, 2 Tim. 2.8.

4. Paul quotes the OT at least 53 times in his letter to the Romans, more than in all his other letters combined (36 times).

προφητικῶν) is a deliberate allusion to the opening words of the letter, 'through his prophets in the holy scriptures' (1.2, διὰ τῶν προφητῶν αὐτοῦ ἐν γραφαῖς ἁγίαις). The goal or purpose of making the mystery of the gospel known is 'to bring about the obedience of faith for all the nations' (16.26, εἰς ὑπακοὴν πίστεως εἰς πάντα τὰ ἔθνη). This phrase from the doxology provides another direct verbal link with the prescript: 'to bring about the obedience of faith for all the nations' (1.5, εἰς ὑπακοὴν πίστεως ἐν πᾶσιν τοῖς ἔθνεσιν). It also reflects Paul's concern throughout the letter to show that the gospel extends equally to the Gentiles[1] as well as to the Jews, so that both are now one in Christ.

These links between the doxology and the rest of the letter have been noticed by a number of scholars. William Sanday and Arthur Headlam observed almost a century ago that 'the doxology sums up all the great ideas of the epistle.'[2] Similarly, Reginald Parry states that the doxology 'sums up, tersely but completely, the main conception of the Epistle, and reproduces its most significant language'.[3] Although denying its Pauline authorship, Harry Gamble also recognizes that in the writing of the doxology 'special attention was paid to the Roman letter'.[4] Peter Richardson states that 'the conclusion [vv. 25-27] may also be a Pauline summary of the content of the letter.'[5] So also James Dunn observes in his recent commentary that 'the doxology succeeds quite well in summing up the central themes of the letter.'[6]

1. The word ἔθνη, used in the prescript and the doxology, is an important word in Romans, occurring 30 times.
2. W. Sandy and A.C. Headlam, *A Critical and Exegetical Commentary on the Epistle of the Romans* (New York: Charles Scribner's Sons, 1897), p. 436 (see also p. 432).
3. R. St. John Parry, *The Epistle of Paul the Apostle to the Romans* (Cambridge: Cambridge University Press, 1912).
4. Gamble, *Textual History*, p. 123.
5. Richardson, *Israel in the Apostolic Church*, p. 76.
6. Dunn, *Romans*, p. 913. Dunn also comments that 'the doxology has summarized well some of the basic concerns of the letter' (p. 917). Others who highlight the connections between the doxology and the rest of the letter include F.J.A. Hort, 'On the End of the Epistle to the Romans', in *Biblical Essays* (ed. J.B. Lightfoot; London: Macmillan, 1893), pp. 324-28 (reprinted from *Journal of Philology* 3 [1871], pp. 51-80); E. Kamlah, 'Traditionsgeschichtliche Untersuchungen zur Schlussdoxologie des Römerbriefes' (PhD dissertation, Tübingen University, 1955), pp. 29-65; L.G. Lönnermark, 'Till frågan om Romarbrevets integritet,' *SEÅ* 33 (1969),

In distinction from those who recognize links between the doxology and the rest of the letter as a whole, Larry Hurtado has argued that 16.25-27 echoes more specifically ch. 15 of Romans.[1] The reference to the mystery now revealed and made known through the prophetic writings (16.25) seems related to the thought of 15.4, that 'whatever was written in former days was written for our instruction'—i.e., that the writings of the OT have a special meaning to believers who currently live in the eschatological age of the gospel. Furthermore, as Hurtado points out, the phrase 'to bring about the obedience of faith for all the nations' (16.26, εἰς ὑπακοὴν πίστεως εἰς πάντα τὰ ἔθνη) echoes 15.18 where Paul claims that Christ is working through him 'to bring about the obedience of the nations' (εἰς ὑπακοὴν ἐθνῶν).

Hurtado, however, finds most striking of all the parallels that exist between the glory (δόξα) ascribed to God in 16.27 and the emphases on the glory due God for the salvation of the Gentiles that appear in 15.5-13. For in 15.5-6 the goal of Paul's prayer-wish is that Jewish and Gentile Christians 'may with one voice glorify (δοξάζητε) the God and Father of our Lord Jesus Christ'; in 15.7 he exhorts divisive believers at Rome to welcome one another 'for the glory of God' (εἰς δόξαν τοῦ θεοῦ); and in 15.8-9 he says that the purpose of Christ's ministry was 'that the Gentiles might glorify (δοξάσαι) God for his mercy'. And though the word 'glory' is not specifically used in 15.9-13, here there appears a catena of OT quotations that refer to praise and rejoicing over Gentile salvation.

The evidence of links between Rom. 16.25-27 and Romans 15, coupled with the evidence of other clear connections between this closing passage and the rest of the Romans letter, suggests that the doxology has been deliberately constructed so that it echoes central concerns previously raised in the letter. This, of course, is in keeping with Paul's practice in the closings of his other letters—namely, to adapt and shape his inherited closing conventions so that they better reflect the key issues discussed earlier in his letters.

pp. 141-48, esp. 143-44; D.B. Garlington, *The Obedience of Faith* (Tübingen: Mohr–Siebeck, 1991), p. 1 n. 1.

1.	Hurtado, 'The Doxology at the End of Romans', pp. 197-99. Hurtado's purpose in highlighting parallels between 16.25-27 and ch. 15 is to link the doxology with a 16-chapter form of Romans in opposition to Gamble's claim that the doxology originally began as a secondary conclusion to a 14-chapter form of Romans.

6. *The Hortatory Section*

Hortatory material can be found in the closings of all the undisputed Pauline letters, with the exception of 2 Thessalonians (see Table 6). It is clear that these final commands and exhortations are far less tightly structured than the other epistolary conventions that belong to Paul's letter closings. They appear to be *ad hoc* creations of the apostle, and so it would be wrong to speak of their 'form' in the same sense as that of the stereotyped formulae also found in his letter closings.

Nevertheless, there are a few features that are common to many of these hortatory sections. The most obvious is the use of the imperative mood, which is naturally to be expected in hortatory material. In those few instances where this mood does not occur, a verb of entreaty or adjuration expresses the imperative tone of Paul's words: παρακαλέω[1] (Rom. 16.17; 1 Cor. 16.15); ἐνορκίζω (1 Thess. 5.27). The exhortations are sometimes introduced by τὸ λοιπόν (2 Cor. 13.11; Gal. 6.17; Phil. 4.8), though more frequently by the vocative ἀδελφοί (Rom. 16.17; 2 Cor. 13.11; Phil. 4.8; 1 Thess. 5.25; Phlm. 20; see 1 Cor. 16.15).

b. *The Function of the Hortatory Section*
In some of Paul's letter closings, the hortatory section contains only general paraenetic remarks that have no specific relation to the concrete epistolary situation. For example, Paul's final appeal in his first letter to the Thessalonians, 'Brothers, pray for us' (1 Thess. 5.25), does not appear to be related in any significant way to the material found in the

---

1. The verb παρακαλέω is part of a stereotyped formula that plays an important role in Paul's letters. In his discussion of this formula, C.J. Bjerkelund notes two distinctive features about its occurrence in the closing sections of Paul's letters (Rom. 16.17; 1 Cor. 16.15; see also Phil. 4.2; 1 Thess. 5.14). First, παρακαλέω in the closing does not contain the prepositional phrase (διά plus the genitive) typically found with this formula. Second, the παρακαλέω formula in Paul's letter closings always addresses the relation between the congregation and specific individuals or groups within the congregation. There is some warrant, therefore, in speaking of a 'closing' παρακαλέω formula. See Bjerkelund, *Parakalô: Form, Funktion und Sinn der parakalô-Sätze in den paulinischen Briefen* (Oslo: Universitetsforlaget, 1967), pp. 128-29.

	Introductory Element	Hortatory Material
Rom. 16.17-18,19b	ἀδελφοί	παρακαλῶ δὲ ὑμᾶς σκοπεῖν τοὺς τὰς διχοστασίας καὶ τὰ σκάνδαλα παρὰ τὴν διδαχὴν ἣν ὑμεῖς ἐμάθετε ποιοῦντας, καὶ ἐκκλίνετε ἀπ' αὐτῶν· οἱ γὰρ τοιοῦτοι τῷ κυρίῳ ἡμῶν Χριστῷ οὐ δουλεύουσιν ἀλλὰ τῇ ἑαυτῶν κοιλίᾳ, καὶ διὰ τῆς χρηστολογίας καὶ εὐλογίας ἐξαπατῶσιν τὰς καρδίας τῶν ἀκάκων ... θέλω δὲ ὑμᾶς σοφοὺς εἶναι εἰς τὸ ἀγαθόν, ἀκεραίους δὲ εἰς τὸ κακόν
1 Cor. 16.13-16,22	ἀδελφοί	γρηγορεῖτε, στήκετε ἐν τῇ πίστει, ἀνδρίζεσθε, κραταιοῦσθε. πάντα ὑμῶν ἐν ἀγάπῃ γινέσθω. παρακαλῶ δὲ ὑμᾶς· οἴδατε τὴν οἰκίαν Στεφανᾶ, ὅτι ἐστὶν ἀπαρχὴ τῆς Ἀχαΐας καὶ εἰς διακονίαν τοῖς ἁγίοις ἔταξαν ἑαυτούς· ἵνα καὶ ὑμεῖς ὑποτάσσησθε τοῖς τοιούτοις καὶ παντὶ τῷ συνεργοῦντι καὶ κοπιῶντι ... εἴ τις οὐ φιλεῖ τὸν κύριον, ἤτω ἀνάθεμα. μαράνα θά
2 Cor. 13.11a	λοιπόν, ἀδελφοί	χαίρετε, καταρτίζεσθε, παρακαλεῖσθε, τὸ αὐτὸ φρονεῖτε, εἰρηνεύετε
Gal. 6.17	τοῦ λοιποῦ	κόπους μοι μηδεὶς παρεχέτω· ἐγὼ γὰρ τὰ στίγματα τοῦ Ἰησοῦ ἐν τῷ σώματί μου βαστάζω
Phil. 4.8-9a	τὸ λοιπόν, ἀδελφοί	ὅσα ἐστὶν ἀληθῆ, ὅσα σεμνά, ὅσα δίκαια, ὅσα ἁγνά, ὅσα προσφιλῆ, ὅσα εὔφημα, εἴ τις ἀρετὴ καὶ εἴ τις ἔπαινος, ταῦτα λογίζεσθε· ἃ καὶ ἐμάθετε καὶ παρελάβετε καὶ ἠκούσατε καὶ εἴδετε ἐν ἐμοί, ταῦτα πράσσετε
1 Thess. 5.25,27	ἀδελφοί	προσεύχεσθε [καὶ] περὶ ἡμῶν ... ἐνορκίζω ὑμᾶς τὸν κύριον ἀναγνωσθῆναι τὴν ἐπιστολὴν πᾶσιν τοῖς ἀδελφοῖς
Phlm. 20-22	ναὶ ἀδελφέ	ἐγώ σου ὀναίμην ἐν κυρίῳ· ἀνάπαυσόν μου τὰ σπλάγχνα ἐν Χριστῷ. πεποιθὼς τῇ ὑπακοῇ σου ἔγραψά σοι, εἰδὼς ὅτι καὶ ὑπὲρ ἃ λέγω ποιήσεις. ἅμα δὲ καὶ ἑτοίμαζέ μοι ξενίαν· ἐλπίζω γὰρ ὅτι διὰ τῶν προσευχῶν ὑμῶν χαρισθήσομαι ὑμῖν

Table 6. Hortatory Section

letter body, except perhaps to the general exhortation of 5.17.[1] In other
letters, however, the closing commands are directly related to concerns
addressed previously in the body.

The clearest example of this can be seen in 2 Cor. 13.11 where Paul
closes his last letter to the Corinthians with a series of five imperatives:
λοιπόν, ἀδελφοί, χαίρετε, καταρτίζεσθε, παρακαλεῖσθε τὸ αὐτὸ
φρονεῖτε, εἰρηνεύετε. There are a number of significant links between
these closing exhortations and the preceding material. The first exhortation of 13.11, χαίρετε ('rejoice!'), recalls not only Paul's words in 13.9
where he rejoices at the prospect of the Corinthians' being strong in
their faith in answer to his prayers, but also Paul's joy for them
expressed elsewhere in the letter (1.24; 2.3; 6.10; 7.4, 7, 9, 13, 16; see
also 8.2). The second exhortation of 13.11, καταρτίζεσθε ('aim for
restoration'), clearly echoes Paul's words in 13.9 where he prays for the
restoration (κατάρτισιν) of the Corinthians. The third exhortation of
13.11, παρακαλεῖσθε ('encourage one another'), has a verbal link
with the opening exhortation of 10.1, a key transitional verse in the
letter. Finally, the fourth and fifth exhortations ('be of the same mind',
and 'live in peace') serve with the three preceding exhortations to reflect
also the problem of disunity and disharmony in the Corinthian church
that Paul has been addressing, especially in chs. 10–13. Paul's closing
appeals to 'rejoice, aim for restoration, encourage one another, be of the
same mind, live in peace' relate directly to his concern that there exists
among the Corinthians 'quarreling, jealousy, anger, selfishness, slander,
gossip, conceit and disorder' (12.20).

A number of scholars have drawn attention to this phenomenon: that
Paul uses these final commands to echo and re-affirm his previous
appeals in the letter for unity and peace to exist within the Corinthian
church. Allan Menzies, for example, notes concerning 13.11: 'He [Paul]
gathers up the main points of what he has urged on them.'[2] Similarly,
Donald Carson comments: '2 Corinthians 13.11 casts a backward glance

---

1. So Frame, *Thessalonians*, p. 215. Best, however, assumes the καί to be
original ($\mathfrak{P}^{30}$ B D 33 81) and takes the exhortation for prayer in 5.25 to refer to the
immediately preceding prayer-wish (i.e., the peace benediction) of 5.23-24: 'Paul has
just prayed for the Thessalonians; let them also pray for him and his helpers'
(*Thessalonians*, p. 245).

2. A. Menzies, *The Second Epistle of the Apostle Paul to the Corinthians*
(London: Macmillan, 1912), p. 104.

148

Neglected Endings

at the rest of the epistle.'[1] And Victor Furnish, to cite but another among many, also recognizes that 'there are several significant links between v. 11 and the letter of chaps. 10–13'.[2]

Another closing hortatory section that points back to concerns raised earlier in a particular letter is Rom. 16.17-20. This passage was discussed above in connection with the probability that these verses should be seen as Paul's own autograph.[3] Rather than repeat this previous analysis, I want here simply to draw attention once again to the summary character of this passage: that Paul's autograph warning in 16.17-20 against those who create dissension and division recalls his earlier appeals against disunity in the Roman congregation stemming from tensions between the 'weak' and the 'strong'.

Other Pauline closing hortatory sections may also be related to a specific epistolary situation and highlight one or more key concerns of their respective letters, though a case made for each of them brings about only diminishing returns. The analyses of 2 Cor. 13.11 and Rom. 16.17-20, however, result in good evidence that at least certain hortatory sections found in Paul's letter closings have been carefully constructed with a view to the issues discussed in their respective letter bodies.

7. Miscellaneous Conventions

Grace benedictions, peace benedictions, greetings, autographs, doxologies and hortatory sections account for virtually all of the material found in

1. D.A. Carson, *From Triumphalism to Maturity: An Exposition of 2 Corinthians 10–13* (Grand Rapids: Baker, 1984), p. 183.
2. Furnish, *II Corinthians*, p. 585. See also Plummer (*Second Epistle to the Corinthians*, p. 379): 'There are fairly conspicuous links between these concluding verses and those which immediately precede them'; Fisher (*1 & 2 Corinthians*, p. 445): 'The conclusion of this letter fits the letter itself. There is a final appeal (v. 11) which reflects the troubles in Corinth'; F.T. Fallon (*2 Corinthians* [Wilmington, DE: Michael Glazier, 1980], p. 115): 'Paul enters into his final exhortations, which sum up his concerns in the preceding chapters and the needs of the community.' For a contrary view, however, see R.E. Picirilli (*1, 2 Corinthians* [Nashville: Randall House, 1987], pp. 431-32) who states: 'Some interpreters link these five injunctions with the immediately preceding. There is really no need for that...the injunctions are the kind of brief exhortations Paul often uses near the end of a letter, a more or less "standardized" kind of Christian "paraenesis".'
3. See above, pp. 123, 134-35.

Paul's letter closings. There remains, however, a small amount of closing material that does not belong to any of these epistolary conventions. This remaining closing material can be classified as belonging to one of the following three categories, all of which were common to letters of that day: the joy expression, the letter of commendation, and the postscript.

a. *The Joy Expression*

Three of Paul's letter closings contain an expression of joy, with each exhibiting the same basic form: the verb χαίρω followed by a causal construction introduced by ὅτι and/or ἐπί and the dative. 1 Cor. 16.17 reads: χαίρω δὲ ἐπὶ τῇ παρουσίᾳ Στεφανᾶ καὶ Φορτουνάτου καὶ Ἀχαϊκοῦ ('I rejoice because of the arrival of Stephanas and Fortunatus and Achaicus'). Phil. 4.10-20, which contains a long expression of joy for the gift of financial support, opens in essentially the same fashion: ἐχάρην δὲ ἐν κυρίῳ μεγάλως ὅτι ἤδη ποτὲ ἀνεθάλετε τὸ ὑπὲρ ἐμοῦ φρονεῖν, ἐφ' ᾧ καὶ ἐφρονεῖτε, ἠκαιρεῖσθε δέ ('I rejoice in the Lord greatly because you once again renewed your concern for me, because you were indeed concerned for me but had no opportunity'). And Rom. 16.19a has the same basic formula for expressing joy, although the order of the elements is reversed (first the causal phrase [ἐφ' ὑμῖν], then the principal verb [χαίρω]).

The Greek papyri contain numerous examples of stereotyped expressions of joy that typically consist of three elements: (1) the main verb, either χαίρω or ἔχω χαράν, given in the first-person indicative; (2) an adverb of magnitude (e.g., μεγάλως, λίαν, πολλά); and (3) a causal clause giving the reason for joy, introduced usually by ὅτι but sometimes by ἐπί and the dative.[1] The joy expressions in Paul's letter closings, therefore, rightly have been considered a distinct epistolary convention of the day,[2] with variations of this basic form appearing elsewhere as well in the NT.[3]

1. See, e.g., BGU 332.6-7; 632.9-10; P. Elephant. 13.2-3; P. Giss. 21.3-4; P. Lond. 42.7-9; 43.3-4; P. Mert. 12.3-6; P. Mich. 483.3-5; P. Yale 28.10-11.
2. For a discussion of the 'joy expression' as an epistolary convention in Greco-Roman letters, see Koskenniemi, *Des grieschischen Briefes*, pp. 75-77; J.L. White, 'Introductory Formulae in the Body of the Pauline Letters', *JBL* 90 (1971) pp. 95-96; *idem, Body of the Greek Letter*, pp. 39-40; *idem, Light from Ancient Letters*, p. 201; Stowers, *Letter Writing*, p. 186; Hansen, *Abraham in Galatians*, p. 28; Richards, *Secretary*, p. 204; Jervis, *Purpose of Romans*, p. 134.
3. A joy expression also is found in Phlm. 7, 2 John 4 and 3 John 3, all of which

The presence of a formula expressing joy at the *close* of Paul's letters, however, has been thought to conflict with contemporary Hellenistic letters where such stereotyped expressions of joy belong more properly to the opening of the letter body. John White, for example, has stated with regard to Paul's letter to the Philippians: 'Since expressions of joy usually introduce the body of the letter, the presence of such a formula in Phil. 4.10 supports Robert Funk's proposal that "this may...be an independent letter, now truncated".'[1] White, however, has subsequently recanted, saying: 'More recently, Nils Dahl convinced me that such phrases [i.e., joy expressions] tend to maintain contact between correspondents, which is more characteristic of the opening and closing of the letter.'[2] The position of joy expressions at the close of Paul's letters, therefore, is epistolarily proper, and need not give rise to theories of textual corruption.

b. *The Letter of Commendation*
Another epistolary convention found among the remaining material of Paul's letter closings is the letter of commendation. Rom. 16.1-2 has striking structural and verbal similarities to the many examples of the ἐπιστολὴ συστατική or *littera commendaticia* found in Greco-Roman letters. These ancient letters of commendation were earlier studied by Clinton Keyes,[3] and more recently by Chan-Hie Kim.[4] Their analyses reveal that Hellenistic letters of commendation have a relatively fixed form, consisting of the following structural elements:

1. verb of commendation
2. name of person being commended
3. identifying predicate
4. request clause
5. circumstantial clause
6. purpose or causal clause

Rom. 16.1-2 follows this pattern exactly, omitting only a circumstantial clause: (1) συνίστημι δὲ ὑμῖν ('I commend to you'), (2) Φοίβην ('Phoebe'), (3) τὴν ἀδελφὴν ἡμῶν, οὖσαν [καὶ] διάκονον τῆς ἐκκλησίας τῆς ἐν Κεγχρεαῖς ('our sister who also is a deaconess of

exhibit the same form as well. See also 2 Cor. 7.9, 16.
1. White, 'Introductory Formulae', p. 95. See also Funk, *Language*, p. 272.
2. White, *Light from Ancient Letters*, p. 201.
3. Keyes, 'Letter of Introduction', pp. 28-44.
4. Kim, *Letter of Recommendation*.

4. *Closing Conventions in Paul: Forms and Variations* 151

the church of Cenchreae'), (4) ἵνα αὐτὴν προσδέξησθε ἐν κυρίῳ ἀξίως τῶν ἁγίων καὶ παραστῆτε αὐτῇ ἐν ᾧ ἂν ὑμῶν χρῄζῃ πράγματι ('in order that you may receive her in the Lord in a manner worthy of the saints and that you may help her in whatever she may have need of you'), (5)..., and (6) καὶ γὰρ αὐτὴ προστάτις πολλῶν ἐγενήθη καὶ ἐμοῦ αὐτοῦ ('for she herself has also been a help of many and of me myself'). There can be no doubt, therefore, that Paul in 16.1-2 is constructing his introduction of Phoebe in a manner typical of contemporary letters of commendation, especially since he is personally familiar with this letter type (see 2 Cor. 3.1; also 1 Cor. 16.3).

The majority of ancient commendatory letters, however, are brief, independent letters, and not commonly found in the closing sections of existing letters.[1] This fact, along with a number of other difficulties claimed to be found in ch. 16, has led to the proposal that Romans 16 originally was an independent letter of recommendation.[2] Gamble, however, cites several examples from both Greek and Latin letters where a commendation occurs in the closing section of a letter.[3] The commendation of a third party in epistolary closings, therefore, is not without precedent. Consequently, the commendation of Phoebe in Rom. 16.1-2 is readily understandable as a closing convention, particularly if she was the bearer of the letter.[4]

1. In addition to the 83 Greek letters of commendation examined by Kim, see also the numerous Latin examples of *litterae commendaticiae* in Cicero's writings.
2. So Deissmann, *Light from Ancient East*, pp. 171, 235; J. Moffatt, *Introduction to the Literature of the New Testament* (New York: Charles Scribner's Sons, 1918), p. 135; E.F. Scott, *Paul's Epistle to the Romans* (London: SCM, 1947), p. 24; E.J. Goodspeed, 'Phoebe's Letter of Introduction', *HTR* 44 (1951), pp. 55-57; J. Fitzmyer, 'The Letter to the Romans', in *The Jerome Biblical Commentary* (ed. R.E. Brown, J.A. Fitzmyer and R.E. Murphy; Englewood Cliffs, NJ: Prentice–Hall, 1968), II, p. 292; J.I.H. McDonald, 'Was Romans XVI a Separate Letter?' *NTS* 16 (1969–70), pp. 369-72.
3. Gamble, *Textual History*, pp. 84-87.
4. A recommendation of the letter carrier, although not in the form of a standard letter of commendation, is found in Eph. 6.21-22 and Col 4.7-8. Some have argued that 1 Cor. 16.15-18 also ought to be viewed as a formal letter of recommendation on behalf of the letter carriers: see Gamble, *Textual History*, p. 97; L.L. Belleville, 'Continuity or Discontinuity: A Fresh Look at 1 Corinthians in the Light of First-Century Epistolary Forms and Conventions', *EvQ* 59 (1987), p. 34; Fee, *Corinthians*, p. 832.

c. *The Postscript*

The only part of Paul's letter closings not yet identified and formally classified are the final words of 1 Corinthians. Following the grace benediction, we find these closing words in 16.24: ἡ ἀγάπη μου μετὰ πάντων ὑμῶν ἐν Χριστῷ 'Ιησοῦ ('My love is with you all in Christ Jesus').

Since a grace benediction is the final convention in all of Paul's letter closings, signaling the definitive end of his letters, it seems best to consider 1 Cor. 16.24 as a postscript. This closing expression of personal affection by Paul ought to be seen against his severe rebukes and corrective appeals due to the divisions, immoralities and disorders that existed in the Corinthian congregation. Despite the growing tension between himself and some in Corinth—a tension that sometimes led to harsh words (see 16.22)—Paul wanted to assure the church of his love for them all (μετὰ πάντων ὑμῶν). This final expression of Paul's love for them all, in fact, mirrors his preceding exhortation in the letter closing to 'let everything you do be done in love' (16.14). So though the postscript of 1 Cor. 16.24 is unique to Paul's letter closings, it is typical of ancient Hellenistic and Jewish letters that frequently contain a brief remark following the farewell wish.[1] Furthermore, it echoes the exhortation to love found just a few verses earlier in the letter closing of 1 Corinthians.

8. *Summary*

At first glance, Paul's letter closings may appear to have a rather simple form and structure, consisting of some final remarks thrown together in a somewhat loose and disorderly fashion. Such a view of the final sections of the apostle's letters, however, is quickly dispelled on closer analysis. For the detailed study undertaken in this chapter has shown that Paul's letter closings consist of several epistolary conventions, all of which exhibit a high degree of formal and structural consistency, thereby testifying to the care with which these final sections have been constructed.

The most common and uniform closing convention is the grace benediction. It is found in all of Paul's letter closings and, with one exception, always occupies the final position in keeping with its principal function of bringing a letter to a definitive close. A second convention

---

1. See the discussions above on the 'postscript' in Chapters 2 and 3 (pp. 52-55; 73-74).

typically present in a Pauline letter closing is the peace benediction. This epistolary convention is distinguishable—not only from the grace benediction, but also from other benedictions or wishes found in the bodies of Paul's letters—in terms of its content, stylistic uniformity, and location. For the peace benediction holds an earlier position in a letter closing and forms an *inclusio* with the opening salutation: the 'grace to you and peace' uttered in the letter opening is echoed in chiastic fashion in the letter closing, first by the peace benediction and then by the grace benediction. Thus these two benedictions not only convey Paul's concern for the spiritual welfare of his readers, they also serve to mark the boundaries of Paul's letter closings.

Between these two closing benedictions, a number of other epistolary conventions can be found in Paul's letter closings. The most common of these is that of final greetings, with such greetings serving the important function of maintaining and developing ties between Paul and the various churches as well as promoting unity and fellowship among and within congregations. The exhortation to 'Greet one another with a holy kiss' is best understood as a sub-category of the greeting formula, which identifies the manner in which the greeting is to be given. The kiss greeting occurs in letters that reflect some degree of conflict existing within a congregation. This fact supports the notion that the command of Paul for his readers to greet one another with a holy kiss served as a challenge to remove all feelings of hostility and to exhibit the unity that believers share as fellow members of the body of Christ.

Paul's letter closings also contain an autograph section where the apostle takes over from his secretary and writes some final remarks in his own hand. Although there are only five explicit references to such autograph material, it may be postulated with confidence that Paul regularly penned part of his own letter closings himself—in keeping with then-current epistolary practice. Paul uses his closing autographs to serve a variety of functions, such as stressing the authority of his words, validating in a legal fashion a promise of payment, or expressing a warmer, more personal tone. Since the autograph does not regularly begin at any given point, it cannot be assigned to any constant place within the Pauline letter closings.

Another epistolary convention often claimed to be a regular feature of Paul's letter closings is the doxology. A study of the closings of the apostle's letters, however, does not substantiate this claim. Other NT writers, it is true, frequently closed their letters with a doxology. But

Paul did not typically use a doxology in this fashion. Nevertheless, the fact that he does close two of his letters with this stereotyped formula warrants including the doxology in a discussion of the Pauline letter closings.

Although final exhortations and warnings do not exhibit a fixed form as is characteristic of other closing conventions, hortatory remarks are also a regular feature of Paul's letter closings. The exhortations occur at various places in the closing sections, but typically are to be found between the greetings and the peace benediction. In those instances where hortatory remarks come before a peace benediction, there is a shift from δέ to καί as the introductory element to the wish for peace. The closings of Paul's letters also contain other epistolary conventions, such as a joy expression, a letter of commendation and a postscript. But these items do not constitute a regular feature of his letter closings.

In light of these observations, the following sequence or pattern of a typical Pauline letter closing comes into view:

1. Peace Benediction
2. Hortatory Section (can also come before a peace benediction)
3. Greetings
    3a. Greetings (first-, second-, or third-person types)
    3b. Kiss Greeting
    3c. Autograph Greeting
4. Grace Benediction

Even if additional items are found in a particular closing (e.g., joy expression, letter of commendation) or one of these epistolary conventions is missing, the sequence remains constant. This supports my contention that Paul's letter closings are not loose collections of final remarks, haphazardly thrown together, but rather are carefully constructed units.

A comparison of the closing conventions in Paul's letters with those found in Hellenistic and Semitic letters reveals that the apostle was heavily indebted to the epistolary practices of his day. The influence of Greco-Roman letters is particularly evident in Paul's closing greetings and in his autographs. Yet the apostle, evidently, did not feel completely bound to existing writing styles. For clearly he has 'Christianized' the standard farewell wish, and so develops a new closing convention: the grace benediction. In similar fashion he takes the greeting formula and creates a uniquely Christian greeting: 'Greet one another with a holy kiss.' And the peace benediction, a likely derivation from the final wish for peace in Semitic letters, is greatly expanded from the simple form found in the closings of Aramaic and Hebrew letters. In fact, Paul's extensive adaptations and creative additions to the rather hackneyed conventions so common in the ancient letters result in epistolary closings that are truly unparalleled among the extant letters of his day.

Chapter 5

CLOSING CONVENTIONS IN THE PAULINE LETTERS:
HERMENEUTICAL SIGNIFICANCES

Paul's letter closings are unique not only in form and structure, but also in the ways in which they echo concerns and issues dealt with in their respective letter bodies. Other ancient writers were concerned to construct closings appropriate to what they wrote in their letters. Paul, however, goes beyond their general concerns by deliberately adapting and shaping his closing conventions so that they function by way of highlighting the key themes of their respective letter bodies. In some instances, this adaptation of a closing convention is fairly obvious. The autograph of Gal. 6.11-18, for example, striking because of both its length and its emphatic introduction, serves to recapitulate Paul's attack against his opponents in Galatia and their errant gospel, which is the primary concern of the apostle throughout the Galatian letter. Likewise, the unique formal features of the peace benediction of 1 Thess. 5.23-24 recall the themes of sanctification and the return of Christ developed at some length throughout that letter.

The fact that the recapitulating function in these two above-cited closing conventions is so obvious suggests that other more subtle adaptations of Paul's closing conventions may also, on further investigation, prove to be quite telling. Indeed, this study of Paul's letter closings has revealed a number of instances where seemingly innocent changes in the form of the closing conventions actually point back to key issues raised in their respective letter bodies. The cumulative effect of this analysis has been to validate the claim that Paul's letter closings are carefully constructed units, being frequently adapted and shaped so that they relate directly to—sometimes, in fact, even summarize—the primary issues of their respective letters.

The previous chapter examined the forms of the various closing conventions in Paul's letters, taking note of the individual variations and tracing out the significance of those variations. The present chapter deals with much the same material, but rather than analyzing the various parts of Paul's letter closings seeks to study each letter closing as a whole. The purpose of this inquiry is not only to substantiate further the thesis that Paul's letter closings point back to key issues addressed in their respective letter bodies, but, more importantly, also to highlight the hermeneutical significance of this recapitulating function in the study of Paul's letters. In what follows, Paul's letters will be considered not in any necessary historical order, but in terms of the greater to lesser hermeneutical significance of their respective letter closings.

1. Galatians

a. *Extent of the Letter Closing*
The transition from the body of Galatians to its closing is clearly indicated by Paul's autograph statement of 6.11, 'See with what large letters I am writing to you in my own hand.' On the basis of the aorist ἔγραψα and in keeping with his thesis of expanded subscriptions, Gordon Bahr has argued that Paul closes Galatians in his own hand earlier at 5.2 ('See, I, Paul, am speaking to you').[1] Most exegetes, however, take ἔγραψα to be an epistolary aorist, as found elsewhere in Paul's letters (see Rom. 15.15 [probably]; 1 Cor. 5.11; 9.15; Phlm. 19, 21). Furthermore, the material from 5.2 to 6.10 does not contain any of Paul's usual closing conventions. There are, therefore, no good reasons for expanding the letter closing of Galatians to include anything prior to the autograph formula of 6.11.

b. *Structural Analysis of the Letter Closing*
The letter closing of Galatians seems to possess something of a concentric structure. Verse 12, which opens with the relative pronoun ὅσοι, is balanced by v. 16, which also begins with ὅσοι. Verse 12 describes the false motives of those who oppose Paul, in contrast to v. 16 with its description of the divine blessings of peace and mercy enjoyed by those who obey Paul. So v. 12 and v. 16 are parallel in that they set out Paul's negative and positive judgments. Verse 13 begins with a negated

---

1. Bahr, 'Subscriptions', p. 35. Although a few others also claim that Paul's autograph material begins at 5.2, unlike Bahr they do not assert that the letter closing begins at this point. See Deissmann, *Light from Ancient East*, pp. 166-67; Bring, *Galatians*, pp. 235, 282; H. Leitzmann, *An die Galater* (Tübingen: Mohr–Siebeck, 1971 [1910]), p. 40.

consecutive clause (οὐδὲ γὰρ) followed by an adversative clause (ἀλλά), with that same pattern found in v. 15 (οὔτε γάρ...ἀλλά). A further link between these two verses is the contrast highlighted in each: circumcision versus non-circumcision. At the center of this concentric structure stands v. 14, which contains Paul's forceful (note the use of the emphatic personal pronoun ἐμοί and the optative μὴ γένοιτο) claim that he boasts in nothing save 'the cross of our Lord Jesus Christ'. The structure of these verses, therefore, can be set out in terms of the following diagram:[1]

C	v. 12	ὅσοι—negative judgment on opponents of Paul
B	v. 13	οὐδὲ γάρ...ἀλλά (circumcision vs. non-circumcision)
A	v. 14	ἐμοὶ δὲ μὴ γένοιτο καυχᾶσθαι εἰ μὴ ἐν τῷ σταυρῷ τοῦ κυρίου ἡμῶν Ἰησοῦ Χριστοῦ
B′	v. 15	οὔτε γάρ...ἀλλά (circumcision vs. non-circumcision)
C′	v. 16	ὅσοι—positive judgment on supporters of Paul

The postulation of such a concentric structure is attractive not only because of the clear grammatical and thematic parallels in each of its corresponding parts, but also because it highlights v. 14 with its focus on the cross of Christ—a major concern of Paul throughout the letter (2.19; 3.1, 13; 5.11, 24; 6.12, 14, 17; see also 1.4; 2.19-20; 4.5). There are, however, two minor problems that this concentric structure faces: (1) it blurs somewhat the formal distinction between vv. 12-15, which consists of autograph statements, and v. 16, which contains the peace benediction; and (2) it minimizes somewhat the sharp contrast between vv. 12-13 with its description of Paul's opponents and vv. 14-15 with its description of Paul's position. Without denying an intentional concentric structure, it is possible also to outline the letter closing of Galatians as follows:

v. 11	Autograph Formula: Introduction
vv. 12-15	Autograph Statements
	v. 12 Paul's opponents
	v. 13 explanation (οὐδὲ γάρ...ἀλλά)
	v. 14 Paul's position
	v. 15 explanation (οὔτε γάρ...ἀλλά)
v. 16	Peace Benediction
v. 17	Hortatory Section
v. 18	Grace Benediction: Conclusion

---

1. See Schnider and Stenger, *Neutestamentlichen Briefformular*, pp. 145-46, for a somewhat similar concentric structure. J. Bligh (*Galatians: A Discussion of Paul's Epistle* [London: St. Paul's Publications, 1969], pp. 490, 493) presents a concentric structure for 6.12-14 and 6.14-18, but his outline is too forced to be convincing.

This latter, more topical, outline reveals both a basic similarity and a number of differences between the letter closing of Galatians and Paul's other letter closings. The similarity, of course, lies in the order in which the various closing conventions occur. The basic sequence or pattern of a typical Pauline letter closing is followed in the Galatian letter as well: a peace benediction, a hortatory section, greetings (which are here significantly omitted), and a grace benediction. But while there is a similarity between Galatians and Paul's other letters in the sequence of their respective closing conventions, there are also a great many dissimilarities between them in the form of their closing conventions.

A comparison of the various epistolary conventions in the letter closing of Galatians with those found in Paul's other letter closings reveals the strikingly unique character of Gal. 6.11-18. First, the closing of Galatians is introduced with an expanded autograph formula (v. 11) in which Paul writes with large letters to underscore the importance of his final words.[1] Second, it contains a disproportionately large section of closing statements (vv. 12-15) in which Paul rather angrily contrasts the false gospel and selfish motives of his opponents with the true gospel and selfless motives of himself—a major concern of Paul throughout the letter. Third, the peace benediction (v. 16) is conditional: only those who follow Paul's injunctions will receive the divine blessings of peace and mercy. Fourth, the peace benediction identifies those in Galatia who are faithful to Paul and his gospel by the striking and unparalleled phrase 'the Israel of God'. Fifth, the closing exhortation (v. 17) has a caustic tone and so serves as both a defense of Paul and a challenge to his opponents. Sixth, before the closing grace benediction (v. 18) there is the absence of any personal greetings, either from Paul or from any of 'the brothers' who were with him (1.2). Finally, the closing lacks any positive note of praise or thanksgiving as would be expressed in a closing doxology or joy expression. Beyond doubt, the combination of these features results in a closing that is truly distinctive among Paul's letters.

c. *Thematic Analysis of the Letter Closing*
The unique character of 6.11-18 clearly stems from the letter's specific epistolary situation. A judaizing theology—'another gospel, which is not at all the same gospel' (1.6-7)—was seriously challenging the spiritual

---

1. For a defense of this interpretation of 'large letters', as well as an examination of several other views that have been proposed, see above pp. 127-29.

welfare of the Galatians. Because this heretical seed had taken root among believers and was, in fact, continuing to grow, a serious conflict arose between Paul and his Galatian converts. This conflict manifests itself throughout the letter's opening and body sections, and so, not surprisingly, also in the closing. In fact, every one of the closing conventions of 6.11-18 appears to have been adapted and reshaped to echo better the major tensions and essential concerns expressed throughout the letter.

It is with justification, therefore, that a number of scholars have recognized the summarizing character of the Galatian letter closing. Franz Mussner, for example, says that 6.11-18 functions 'almost as a concluding summary of the preceding passages of the letter'.[1] Similarly, Bernard Brinsmead notes that 6.11-18 'is striking in the way it recapitulates the main themes of the epistle'.[2] Consequently, the letter closing of Galatians can in no way be considered a mere epistolary convention in contrast to the 'weightier' material in the rest of the letter. Rather 6.11-18 must be seen as a carefully constructed unit[3] in which Paul adapts and expands the usual closing conventions of the day so that they point back to the key issues of Galatians as a whole.

But while many scholars recognize the recapitulating function of the Galatian letter closing, almost all fail to move beyond this awareness and to a recognition of the hermeneutical significance that such a summarizing closing has. Hans Dieter Betz is one of the few exceptions. For despite approaching this closing section solely from the perspective of rhetorical criticism, without also investigating it in terms of epistolary analysis, Betz rightly notes that 6.11-18 is 'most important for the interpretation of Galatians. It contains the interpretive clues to the understanding of Paul's major concerns in the letter as a whole and should be employed as the hermeneutical key to the intentions of the Apostle.'[4] Following Betz's lead, my purpose in what follows is to examine the

1. Mussner, *Galaterbrief*, p. 410 (trans. mine).
2. Brinsmead, *Galatians*, p. 48. For others who recognize the summarizing character of 6.11-18, see previous chapter, p. 132 n. 3.
3. This would be especially be true if, as I believe, the concentric structure of 6.12-16 is intentional. In any case, Cousar's assessment (*Galatians*, p. 149) of the Galatian letter closing is entirely justified: 'Verses 11-18 are no hasty or ill-conceived postscript'.
4. Betz, *Galatians*, p. 313. Note also Longenecker's statement (*Galatians*, pp. 288-89) that 6.11-18 is like a 'paradigm set at the end of the letter that gives guidance in understanding what has been said before'.

main themes in the Galatian closing, showing how they not only echo major issues addressed earlier in the letter but also aid our understanding of Paul's purpose, arguments and exhortations—as well as our comprehension of the readers and their historical situation.

The letter closing of Galatians contains a series of antitheses or sharp contrasts between Paul and his opponents. The first focuses on the motives of each party: the opponents boast in their success of compelling the Galatians to be circumcised (v. 12, 'those who want to make a good showing in the flesh'; v. 13, 'in order that they may boast in your flesh'), whereas Paul boasts only in the cross of Christ (v. 14, 'But may I never boast except in the cross of our Lord Jesus Christ'). The second contrast has also to do with motives: the opponents seek to avoid persecution for the cross (v. 12, 'only in order that they might not be persecuted for the cross of Christ'), whereas Paul willingly accepts persecution for the cross (v. 17, 'for I bear on my body the marks of Jesus'). A third contrast sets out how the conflict between Paul and his opponents comes externally to expression: the opponents are compelling the Galatians to be circumcised (v. 12, 'these ones are compelling you to be circumcised'; v. 13, 'they want you to be circumcised'), whereas Paul argues against this Jewish rite, claiming that neither circumcision nor uncircumcision really matters (v. 15, 'For neither circumcision nor uncircumcision means anything)'. The final contrast highlights the broader theological perspective that separates the two parties: the opponents are still living under the influence of the old age, which is characterized by the term 'world' (v. 14, κόσμος), whereas Paul lives under the influence of the new age, which is characterized by the term 'new creation' (v. 15, καινὴ κτίσις). The key issue at stake in all four of these contrasts—an issue which serves, in fact, as the watershed between Paul and his opponents—is the cross of Christ (see v. 14 at the center of the concentric outline).

This series of contrasts is set out in the table below. When set out in this fashion, it becomes clear that in the letter closing of Galatians Paul is laying emphasis on contrasts between his opponents and himself. Paul draws attention to himself in v. 11 by means of an expanded autograph formula that stresses that the letter closing is written 'in my own hand'. Verse 14, itself emphasized by virtue of its location at the center of the concentric structure, opens with the emphatic first-person pronoun ἐμοί and repeats this pronoun two more times in the same sentence. Similarly, the first-person pronoun occurs three times in v. 17. Such a repetitive emphasis by Paul on himself within this series of contrasts results in a very powerful rebuttal in which the apostle, rather daringly, confronts his opponents and their claims head on.

Contrast:	OPPONENTS	versus	PAUL
Motive 1:	boast in the circum-cision of Galatians (vv. 12, 13)	C	boasts only in the cross of Christ (v. 14)
Motive 2:	avoid persecution for the cross (v. 12)	R	accepts persecution ('marks of Jesus') for the cross (v. 17)
		O	
External:	compel Galatians to be circumcised (vv. 12, 13)	S	claims circumcision and uncircumcision do not matter (v. 15)
Theological:	live in the 'world' (v. 14) under its powers	S	lives in the 'new creation' (v. 15) under the lordship of Christ

Such a confrontational approach has caused some scholars to feel uncomfortable, fearing in Paul a prideful aggression that tends to negate the very grace that his letter itself affirms. But rather than see here 'a less attractive side of St. Paul's personality',[1] we should recognize the seriousness of the threat that the opponents were, not only to his Galatian converts, but also to him personally. For the Galatian letter itself tells us that the opponents' judaizing theology was making inroads into the Galatian churches (see 1.6; 3.1; 4.11, 16; 5.7) and that they were also successful in undermining Paul's authority in the eyes of the Galatians, thereby requiring him to defend at great length his apostolic and authoritative status (1.10–2.14; see also the deliberate expansion of the letter opening in 1.1). The confrontational tone of the Galatian letter closing, therefore, reflects well the purpose and mood expressed in the rest of the letter.

Motivational Contrast 1: Boasting. The first of the contrasts, which focuses on a primary motive of Paul versus that of his opponents, deals with boasting. Paul begins by accusing his opponents of being motivated

---

1. Bligh, *Galatians*, p. 492. Bligh earlier comments: 'St. Paul could certainly have been kinder to his adversaries here' (p. 491).

by selfish intentions: although they outwardly claim to be interested in ensuring that Gentile believers are fully accepted by God as 'the Israel of God', their real goal is 'to make a good showing in the flesh' (v. 12).[1] This self-serving motive of his opponents is stressed by Paul as he repeats the same charge in v. 13: 'they want you to be circumcised in order that they might boast in your flesh.'

In interpreting this charge of Paul against his opponents (as well, of course, as his other accusations against them), commentators generally move in one of two directions, both of which unfortunately tend to miss the larger theological issue at stake.[2] One approach takes Paul's statements at face value and so understands the opponents to be preoccupied with increasing their own social standing among their fellow nationalistic Jews by boasting about how many Gentiles they have circumcised.[3] The other approach takes Paul's statements 'with a grain of salt' and stresses that the apostle's depiction of his opponents' motives may not correspond with reality. Betz, for example, states: 'This [6.12-13] looks very much like a caricature, and we must be cautious in assuming that this is what the opponents really have in mind.'[4]

Both approaches, however, fail to recognize in Paul's contrast of motives the larger theological issue at stake: the cross of Christ. This concern becomes clear when one turns to the other half of the contrast. For whereas his opponents boast in themselves and in their own success in compelling Gentiles to undergo circumcision, Paul in most emphatic

1. The phrase 'in the flesh' (ἐν σαρκί) can refer either to the opponents or the Galatians. In the former case, 'flesh' describes the outward or public appearance of the opponents (NIV: 'those who want to make a good impression outwardly'); in the latter, 'flesh' refers to the circumcision of the Galatians.

2. This point has been stressed by C.B. Cousar, 'Galatians 6.11-18: Interpretive Clues to the Letter', an unpublished paper given at the Pauline Epistles Section of the 1989 SBL annual meeting.

3. So, e.g., Bligh (*Galatians*, pp. 490-91) comments: 'Their [i.e., Paul's opponents] motive in preaching circumcision is a desire for social prestige—they wish to win the approval of the unconverted Jews in Jerusalem... [Paul] as much as says: "They collect foreskins like red Indians collecting scalps, so that they can return in triumph to Jerusalem—like David with his two hundred foreskins of the Philistines!"' See also Lightfoot, *Galatians*, pp. 221-22; Bring, *Galatians*, p. 283; Bruce, *Galatians*, p. 270; Fung, *Galatians*, pp. 304-305.

4. Betz, *Galatians*, p. 314. Note also the somewhat more reserved judgment of Longenecker (*Galatians*, pp. 290-91): 'In vv. 12-13 Paul states what he believes motivates his judaizing opponents.' Longenecker goes on to state that Paul's evaluation is a 'judgment call' that is 'highly subjective in nature'.

terms claims: 'But may I never boast except in the cross of our Lord Jesus Christ' (v. 14). The watershed between Paul and his opponents— not only in this first contrast, but in all the others as well—is the cross of Christ.

Motivational Contrast 2: Persecution. A second and closely related motivational contrast between Paul and his opponents that is set out in the Galatian letter closing involves the theme of persecution. For in addition to accusing his opponents of boasting in their own success concerning Gentile circumcision, Paul also charges that they are motivated out of a desire to avoid persecution: 'these ones are compelling you to be circumcised only[1] in order that they may not be persecuted for[2] the cross of Christ' (v 12).

Unfortunately, Paul says nothing about the historical circumstances that gave rise to this accusation. A plausible reconstruction, however, has been proposed by Robert Jewett.[3] On the basis of evidence drawn from Galatians itself, Jewett concludes that the opponents were an outside group that came to the Galatian churches from Jerusalem or, more generally, Judea. On the basis of external evidence drawn from Josephus and other ancient sources, Jewett further notes that Palestine was experiencing at this time a rising Zealot movement that became particularly intensive from the late forties up to the outbreak of the Jewish War in AD 66—Zealot activities that were especially fervent during the governorship of Tiberius Julius Alexander (AD 46–48) and his successor Ventidius Cumanus (AD 48–52). The Jewish Zealots were engaged in a militant program of purging Israel from all Gentile influence in the belief that such action would hasten, if not actually inaugurate, the Messianic age. And it was this Zealot activity, Jewett argues, that caused Jewish Christians of Judea to engage in a nomistic campaign among their fellow believers in the mistaken hope that the circumcision of Gentile Christians would somehow spare the church from Zealot reprisals.

1. Because another motive of the opponents has already been explicitly identified in the verse ('they want to make a good showing in the flesh'), the 'only' (μόνον) should not be taken literally but rather serves as a rhetorical device providing emphasis (see its use in 1.23; 2.10; 3.2; 4.18; 5.13). Betz (*Galatians*, p. 315) comments: 'the restrictive μόνον ("only") is argumentative and not simply informative.'

2. Virtually all commentators are agreed that the dative τῷ σταυρῷ expresses cause. See BDF §196.

3. R. Jewett, 'The Agitators and the Galatian Congregation', *NTS* 17 (1971), pp. 198-212.

Accepting Jewett's historical reconstruction, it can readily be understood why Paul attacks the motives of his Galatian opponents. For their actions do not stem from any sincere religious conviction, but rather arise from a self-serving desire to avoid persecution for the cross of Christ. As Jewett notes: 'If they could succeed in circumcising the Gentile Christians, this might effectively thwart any Zealot purification campaign against the Judean church!'[1] Such a historical reconstruction of the Galatian situation, in fact, explains how Paul's two motivational contrasts are interrelated: the Galatian opponents (1) intend to boast about Gentile Christians being circumcised, thereby (2) hoping to avoid persecution from their zealously minded fellow Jews.

Paul, however, willingly accepts such adversity as a feature of the Christian life, saying quite dramatically in v. 17: 'Finally, let no one continue to cause me trouble, for I bear in my body the marks of Jesus.' The cryptic nature of his comment here has resulted in some debate as to the precise meaning of these 'marks (στίγματα) of Jesus', with no shortage of proposed answers. Since στίγμα was a common term in the ancient world for the marks of religious tattooing,[2] Erich Dinkler has argued that Paul's body was marked at baptism with the Greek letter 'X' for Χριστός.[3] The difficulty with this view, however, is that religious tattoos were prohibited by both the Mosaic law (Lev. 19.28) and Pharisaic teaching.[4] Emanuel Hirsch claimed that Paul refers here to his eye-trouble resulting from his blinding encounter with Christ on the way to Damascus;[5] while John O'Neill asserted that 'Paul is about to be

---

1. Jewett, 'Agitators and the Galatian Congregation', p. 206. Jewett's reconstruction is accepted by Bruce, *Galatians*, pp. 31-32, 205; Longenecker, *Galatians*, pp. xciii-xcvi, 291.

2. See O. Betz, 'στίγμα', *TDNT*, VII, pp. 657-64.

3. E. Dinkler, 'Jesu Wort vom Kreuztrage', in *Neutestamentliche Studien für R. Bultmann* (BZNW 21 [1954], pp. 110-29, esp. p. 125). This article is reprinted in Dinkler's *Signum Crucis: Aufsätze zum Neuen Testament und zur christlichen Archäologie* (Tübingen: Mohr–Siebeck, 1967). See also F.J. Dölger, *Sphragis: ein altchristliche Taufbezeichnung in ihren Beziehungen zur profanen und religiosen Kultur des Altertums*, V, 3–4 (Paderborn: Ferdinand Schoningh, 1911), pp. 49-50, 105 n. 3; U. Wilckens, 'Zu den syrischen Göttern', in *Festgabe für Adolf Deissmann zum 60. Geburtstag* (Tübingen: Mohr, 1927), pp. 1-19, esp. pp. 7-9.

4. Betz, 'στίγμα', p. 663.

5. E. Hirsch, 'Zwei Fragen zu Gal 6', *ZNW* 29 (1930), pp. 196-97. See the critical response by O. Holtzmann, 'Zu Emanuel Hirsch, Zwei Fragen zu Gal 6', *ZNW* 30 (1931), pp. 82-83.

martyred; he is about to bear the marks of Jesus on his body.'[1] More likely, however, is the view held by most commentators that Paul here has in mind the physical wounds and scars left on his body as a result of the various sufferings he experienced as an apostle (see 2 Cor. 6.4-6 and 11.23-30; also 1 Cor. 4.9-13; perhaps Gal. 4.13-14).[2]

It is commonly claimed that these 'marks of Jesus' function in contrast to the mark of circumcision advocated by Paul's opponents. Ronald Fung, for example, states: 'The "brand-marks of Jesus" in Paul's body stand in antithesis to the mark of circumcision in the flesh of the Judaizers' converts.'[3] But while this connection cannot be excluded, the 'marks of Jesus' here primarily serve to contrast the persecution willingly experienced by Paul with the persecution deliberately avoided by his 'markless' opponents.[4] Thus 6.17 should not be seen as a further exhortation that is simply tacked on to the end of the Galatian letter with no relation to the immediately preceding verses.[5] Instead, v. 17 is an integral part of a series of sharp contrasts that Paul sets out between

1. J.C. O'Neill, *The Recovery of Paul's Letter to the Galatians* (London: SPCK, 1972), p. 82.

2. So, e.g., Burton, Lightfoot, Bring, Mussner, Betz, Bruce, Guthrie, Fung, Longenecker. A slightly different nuance is given to the verse by Deissmann (*Bible Studies*, pp. 349-60), who cites a striking parallel to Gal. 6.17 in the magical papyri in which a man says that he carries (βαστάζω) the mummy of Osiris (as an amulet) and thus warns his opponents against bringing any complaints (κόπους παρέχειν) against him. On the basis of this parallel, Deissmann argues that Paul intended his τὰ στίγματα τοῦ Ἰησοῦ, which literally refers to his physical sufferings as an apostle, to be metaphorically understood as 'protective-marks'. Deissmann's interpretation is supported by Betz, 'στίγμα', p. 663 and Bligh, *Galatians*, p. 497. For a more detailed survey and critique of the various proposed meanings of 'the marks of Jesus', see E. Güttgemanns, *Der leidende Apostel und sein Herr: Studien zur paulinischen Christologie* (Göttingen: Vandenhoeck & Ruprecht, 1966), pp. 126-35; U. Borse, 'Die Wundermale und der Todesbescheid', *BZ* 14 (1970), pp. 88-111; A.T. Hanson, *The Paradox of the Cross in the Thought of St. Paul* (Sheffield: JSOT Press, 1987), pp. 83-86.

3. Fung, *Galatians*, p. 314. Similar statements can be found in Deissmann, *Bible Studies*, p. 352 n. 3; Betz, 'στίγμα', p. 663; Bligh, *Galatians*, p. 496.

4. This important point has been recognized by Cousar (*Galatians*, p. 149), who notes that 'the underlying reason for Paul's appeal ["for I bear on my body the marks of Jesus"] relates to the earlier theme of persecution for the cross of Christ'.

5. *Contra* J.S. Pobee (*Persecution and Martyrdom in the Theology of Paul* [Sheffield: JSOT Press, 1985], p. 94), who argues that 6.17-18 ought to be viewed as a separate paragraph that is unrelated to the previous verses of the letter closing. Similarly, Fung, *Galatians*, p. 312.

himself and his opponents in the Galatian letter closing.

As in the contrast with respect to boasting, so here with respect to persecution the key issue separating Paul from his adversaries is the cross of Christ. This is made clear in the charge of 6.12 that those advocating circumcision do so 'only in order that they may not be persecuted for the cross of Christ'. The intimate connection between persecution, circumcision and the cross can be seen most clearly in 5.11: 'But if I am still preaching circumcision, why am I still being persecuted? In that case the offense of the cross has been abolished.' The options are obvious: preach the cross and be persecuted; or, preach circumcision and be free from persecution. In order not to rob the cross of its power, Paul obediently chooses the former option and, as result of this decision, bears in his body the marks of Jesus (6.17). The Galatian opponents selfishly chose the latter option, and so sought to avoid persecution—but they did so at the cost of denying the salvific significance of the cross.

Before proceeding further, we need here recognize some of the significant connections that exist between these first two motivational contrasts of the Galatian letter closing and the rest of the letter. For Paul's challenge concerning the self-serving motives of his opponents echoes his attack on them throughout the letter (1.7-9; [2.12]; 3.1; 4.17, 21; 5.7, 10, 12). Furthermore, Paul's emphatic assertion that he boasts in nothing except the cross of Christ (6.14) recalls his passionate claim in 1.10 that he is not seeking the favor of men—something his opponents were apparently accusing him of. Paul, in fact, cleverly turns the tables on his opponents by accusing them of the same charge, of 'wanting to make a good showing in the flesh' (6.12) and of 'boasting' in the Galatians' flesh (6.14). And this charge recalls Paul's earlier words of 4.17: '[Those people] earnestly court you but for no good. What they desire is to exclude you [from us] so that you earnestly court them' (see also 4.18; 5.13; 6.3). Likewise, the subject of persecution for the cross of Christ that is the subject of discussion in the second motivational contrast of the letter closing (6.12, 17) is also a topic addressed earlier in the letter at 4.29 and 5.11 (see also 1.13, 23). Thus the first two motivational contrasts in the closing clearly echo some of the key issues developed in the rest of the Galatian letter.

External Contrast: Circumcision versus Uncircumcision. The third contrast between Paul and his opponents that is set out in the letter closing of Galatians exposes the specific issue over which their respective motivational differences come to expression: circumcision. The opponents were urging the Galatians to become circumcised: 'these ones are compelling you to be circumcised' (v. 12); 'they want you to be circumcised' (v. 13). By persuading Gentile Christians in Galatia to be circumcised, the agitators hoped to safeguard themselves and their fellow Jewish Christians from reprisals at the hands of militant Jewish Zealots for being linked with uncircumcised Gentiles. Paul, however, argues against circumcision, claiming that 'neither circumcision nor uncircumcision means anything' (v. 14). Although there is nothing wrong with circumcision *per se*, this rite done as a religious ceremony belongs to the old age where the distinction between Jew and Gentile was of paramount importance. But such distinctions are no longer significant in the new age, the age of 'new creation', which was inaugurated by Christ's death on the cross.

Here, once again, the cross of Christ becomes the watershed between Paul and his opponents. For the advocacy of circumcision involves the denial of the cross; while the advocacy of the cross involves the denial of circumcision. Paul has argued this point elsewhere in the Galatian letter. In 2.21, for example, we read: 'For if righteousness is through the law, then Christ died for nothing!' In other words, if salvation were possible through the law with its requirement of circumcision, then Christ's death on the cross would have been useless. Similarly, Paul states in 5.2: 'If you let yourself be circumcised, Christ will be of no use to you.' To maintain the necessity of circumcision, even as a supplemental act of faith to appease militant Jewish Zealots, is to deny the completeness of Christ's salvific work on the cross (see 1.4) and the new age that that event has brought about.

This third contrast established in the Galatian letter closing—that having to do with the issue of circumcision—plays, of course, a large role in the rest of the Galatian letter. In his extended self-defense of 1.10–2.14, Paul refers to circumcision in connection with his co-worker Titus (2.3), in his statements regarding his meeting with the leading apostles at Jerusalem (2.7-9), and in his account of his confrontation with Peter (2.12). In particular, there is a full discussion of the incompatibility of circumcision and the cross in 5.2-12 (esp. vv. 2, 3, 6, 11 [12])—with, significantly, there being a striking parallel between 5.6 (οὔτε περιτομή τι ἰσχύει οὔτε ἀκροβυστία) and 6.15 (οὔτε γὰρ περιτομή τί ἐστι οὔτε ἀκροβυστία). Thus we see again how Paul uses his Galatian letter closing to recapitulate a key theme developed throughout the rest of the Galatian letter.

(4) *Theological Contrast: 'World' versus 'New Creation'.* The final contrast that Paul establishes in the letter closing of Galatians between himself and his opponents highlights the broader theological perspective separating the two parties. For whereas the Galatian agitators live under the power and control of the old age characterized by the term 'world' (v. 14, κόσμος [2×]), Paul lives under the new age characterized by the expression 'new creation' (v. 15, καινὴ κτίσις).[1]

What does the term 'world' mean? In the context of the Galatian letter closing itself, 'world' refers to a realm where boasting in the flesh is of value, where the avoidance of persecution for the cross is a legitimate enterprise, and where the distinction between circumcision and uncircumcision is of paramount importance. More broadly in the context of the Galatian letter as a whole, 'world' refers to 'the present evil age' (1.4) where the 'weak and beggarly elemental spirits' (4.9; see also 4.3) have authority, where life is lived in bondage under the law (see esp. 3.23; 4.21; 5.1) and under the control of the flesh (5.13-17), where distinctions are rigidly maintained between 'Jew and Gentile, slave and free, male and female' (3.28-29), and where the Jewish observation of 'days, months, seasons and years' (4.10) continues to be normative for the Christian life.[2]

The antithesis to the 'world', to which the Galatian agitators are enslaved, is the 'new creation', with which Paul identifies himself. The origin of the expression καινὴ κτίσις continues to be a source of debate.[3] This need not, however, hinder our understanding of this cryptic

1.   See Cousar (*Galatians*, p. 154), who, in discussing the meaning of 'new creation', states, 'Paul clearly intends a contrast with "the world" (κόσμος), mentioned twice in verse 14'.

2.   For a more extensive definition of 'world' in Galatians, see P.S. Minear, *To Die and To Live: Christ's Resurrection and Christian Vocation* (New York: Seabury, 1977), pp. 66-88, esp. pp. 71-73.

3.   The debate centers on whether the phrase 'new creation' (along with the rest of v. 15) originated with Paul, or whether he is citing traditional material. The former option is advocated by A. Oepke, 'κρύπτω', *TDNT*, III, pp. 989-990; Lightfoot, *Galatians*, p. 224; Burton, *Galatians*, pp. 356-57; P. Stuhlmacher, 'Erwägungen zum ontologischen Charakter der καινὴ κτίσις', *EvT* 27 (1967), pp. 1-35. A number of scholars who support the latter option argue that Paul is borrowing from rabbinical sources: so, e.g., G.F. Moore, *Judaism in the First Centuries of the Christian Era* (3 vols.; Cambridge, MA: Harvard University Press, 1927), I, p. 533; W.D. Davies, *Paul and Rabbinic Judaism* (London: SPCK, 1955), pp. 119-21; see the evaluation of this view by B. Chilton, 'Galatians 6.15: A Call to Freedom before God', *ExpTim* 89

phrase, for even if Paul were citing a traditional maxim, it is likely that he does so nuancing it in his own manner.

In the context of 6.11-18, particularly in contrast with 'world', καινὴ κτίσις refers not simply to the renewal of an individual person but to the presence of a radically new world—a 'new creation'.[1] This new creation is a world where one boasts not in himself but only in the cross of Jesus, where persecution is not selfishly avoided but willingly accepted, where distinctions such as circumcision and uncircumcision cease to be important. This new creation is a world that stands in antithesis to the world advocated by Paul's opponents—the 'present evil age' (1.4), against which the apostle has been arguing throughout the letter. The concept of new creation, therefore, is of paramount importance for understanding Paul's theology in Galatians. It would not be an exaggeration, in fact, to say that 6.15 and the 'new creation' theme 'epitomizes the major thesis of the letter'.[2]

As with the previous three contrasts, so here, too, the fundamental issue separating Paul and his opponents is the cross. For the cross of Christ is the decisive event in salvation history that marks an end of the old 'world' and ushers in the 'new creation'.[3] Paul, in fact, found that experientially the crucifixion of Christ brought about two further crucifixions: that of the world to the believer and of the believer to the

---

(1978), pp. 311-13. Others appeal to the claim of Georgius Syncellus (Byzantine historian, died c. 810) that the words of Paul appeared in the now lost *Apocalypse of Moses*, and so maintain more generally that Paul is citing 'a proverbial maxim in certain circles of thought' (Longenecker, *Galatians*, pp. 295-96).

1. The contrast between κόσμος and καινὴ κτίσις supports the translation 'new creation' rather than 'new creature'. See R.B. Hays (*Echoes of Scripture in the Letters of Paul* [New Haven: Yale University Press, 1989], pp. 156-59), who claims that there are echoes here of Isa. 65.17-25 which speaks of the new eschatological creation that God will bring about: 'Behold, I will create new heavens and a new earth. The former things will not be remembered, nor will they come to mind' (65.17; see also 66.22).

2. Cousar, 'Galatians 6.11-18', p. 14. See also Betz (*Galatians*, p. 319): 'This concept [καινὴ κτίσις] sums up Paul's soteriology.' Similarly, Longenecker (*Galatians*, p. 296): 'Paul uses it [v. 15] to climax all of his arguments and exhortations in 1.6–5.12 with respect to the judaizing threat'.

3. See Fung, *Galatians*, p. 308: '[Christ's death on the cross] has inaugurated and brought about a new creation: his cross marks an absolute break between the new and old world'. Similarly, Bring (*Galatians*, p. 285): 'The cross of Christ was the boundary between the rule of the old and that of the new'.

world. So he says that it is 'the cross of our Lord Jesus Christ by which[1] the world has been crucified to me, and I to the world' (v. 14). The cross of Christ brought Paul into a radically new situation with a corresponding shift of allegiance. In contrast to his opponents who continue to live in the old world under its enslaving forces, Paul now lives in the freedom of the new creation under the lordship of Jesus Christ.[2]

In all four of the contrasts that Paul sets out in his Galatian letter closing, the cross of Christ is the watershed between the apostle and his opponents. And this focus on the cross in 6.11-18 is but a reflection of the crucial role that Christ's crucifixion plays throughout the Galatian letter. Such an emphasis appears already in the Galatian letter opening, which draws attention to the fact that the cross of Christ lies at the heart of Paul's conflict with his Galatian opponents. For Paul expands his typical opening salutation in order to stress that Christ 'gave himself for our sins to deliver us from the present evil age' (1.4)—a clear allusion to Christ's death on the cross.

Also notable is Paul's declaration in 2.19, 'I have been crucified with Christ.' This statement refers both to Christ's death on the cross, which provides redemption from the curse of the law, and to Paul's spiritual participation in that death, by which he shares in that redemption. The cross of Christ is further stressed in the two subsequent verses where Paul refers to Christ as one who 'gave himself for me' (2.20) and who 'died' (2.21). There is, therefore, a strong emphasis on the cross of

1. The relative pronoun in the prepositional phrase δι' οὗ is either masculine or neuter. If masculine, it may refer either to 'our Lord Jesus Christ' or 'the cross'; if neuter, it may refer to the whole preceding clause. On the one hand, the prominence of the cross in the immediate context (vv. 12, 14) and the use of the verb 'to crucify' in the same phrase suggest that 'the cross' is the intended antecedent; on the other hand, the closest antecedent is 'our Lord Jesus Christ'. The issue of whether the relative pronoun refers to the cross of Christ or the person of Christ is, however, really a moot point, since 'for Paul "Christ" is always the crucified redeemer Christ' (Betz, *Galatians*, p. 318).

2. The christological title 'Lord' in the phrase 'the cross of our Lord Jesus Christ' (v. 14) is probably significant. κύριος appears five other times in the letter: twice in the opening and closing grace benedictions (1.3; 6.18) where it is part of stereotyped formulae; once to describe James as 'the brother of the Lord' (1.19); once to refer to the 'owner' of an estate in an analogy (4.1); and once as part of a confidence formula (5.10). The use of κύριος in 6.14 suggests that 'the cross of our Lord Jesus Christ' involves a change of lordship: the new creation is the realm where Jesus Christ is 'Lord'.

Christ in a section (2.15-21) that occupies a strategic position in the argument of the Galatian letter.[1]

The centrality of the cross is highlighted once again in 3.1: 'O foolish Galatians! Who has bewitched you before whose eyes Jesus Christ was clearly portrayed as having been crucified!' In his original preaching to the Galatians Paul had so clearly proclaimed Christ crucified that he cannot understand how they could fail to appreciate the significance of the cross for the issue at hand. In the same vein he refers to the cross again in 3.13, portraying there Christ as the cursed one who 'hanged on a tree' and so 'redeemed us from the curse of the law'.

Likewise, the cross and Christ's death are surely implied in 4.5 in speaking of God sending his son 'to redeem those who were under the law'.[2] More explicit is 5.11 where Paul speaks of 'the stumbling block of the cross'. Preaching circumcision, indeed, might free Paul from persecution, but it would nullify the saving significance of Christ crucified. A final reference to the cross in the body of the letter is found in 5.24, which states that 'those who belong to Christ Jesus have crucified the flesh with its passions and desires.'

It is clear, therefore, that the central role of the cross in the letter closing of Galatians echoes in a pivotal manner the way in which the cross has been at work in Paul's argument throughout the whole of the Galatian letter. Paul has constructed this letter closing in such a fashion that it sharpens to a razor-point the theological issue at stake in the letter as a whole. Ultimately the Achilles heel of the 'other gospel' that was being advocated by his Galatian opponents is its incompatibility with the cross of Christ.

The Galatian letter closing may also contain one further, albeit indirect, contrast between Paul and his opponents. We have noted earlier that the unique form of the peace benediction in v. 16 relates to the concerns of the letter as a whole in two ways: (1) the conditional nature of the blessing (it applies only to 'those who walk by this rule') reflects the strained relationship between Paul and his Galatian converts that is so

---

1.   Betz identifies 2.15-21 as the 'propositio' (*Galatians*, pp. 113-14). See also Longenecker, who titles 2.15-21 as 'The Proposition of Galatians' and refers to this passage as 'a précis of Paul's theological argument to the Galatians' (*Galatians*, p. 80).

2.   See C.H. Cosgrove (*The Cross and the Spirit* [Macon, GA: Mercer University Press, 1988], p. 180), who notes that the crucifixion 'is certainly implied theologically' in 4.5.

evident throughout the letter; and (2) the phrase 'the Israel of God' (if, as seems likely, it is Paul's description of his Gentile converts) reflects the question addressed throughout the letter of who really are the children of Abraham (see esp. 3.6-9, 14, 16, 26-29; 4.21-23).[1] It is also possible that the phrase 'the Israel of God' was originally a self-designation of Paul's Galatian opponents, which Paul takes over and applies in such a way that yet another contrast is formed between himself and his opponents.[2]

If this be so, then it may be postulated that the Galatian opponents used the phrase 'the Israel of God' to identify themselves and their 'gospel' as the true, fulfilled Judaism vis-à-vis the official Judaism of their national compatriots. The offer they held out to the Galatians, then, was that they as Gentile converts could also become fully 'the Israel of God' by submitting to circumcision and observing other Jewish laws. Paul, however, takes over their self-designation and applies it to his readers. And by referring to his Gentile converts in Galatia as those who already are 'the Israel of God', Paul highlights the spurious nature of their offer. As Richard Longenecker notes:

> Paul here climaxes his whole response to the judaizing threat in something
> of an *ad hominem* manner, implying in quite telling fashion that what the
> Judaizers were claiming to offer his converts they already have 'in Christ'
> by faith: that they are truly children of Abraham together with all Jews who
> believe, and so properly can be called 'the Israel of God'.[3]

The Galatian letter closing, therefore, stands as a powerful testimony to the literary talents of Paul. For within the confines of a few short verses, Paul has masterfully expanded and adapted the closing epistolary conventions of his day in such a way that five sharp contrasts (four explicit and one implicit) are set out between himself and his Galatian opponents. These contrasts involving the themes of persecution, boasting, circumcision, and new creation—as well as the implicit theme of 'the Israel of God'—serve to recapitulate the key themes developed throughout the Galatian letter.

More importantly, however, these closing contrasts allow us to cut

---

1. See pp. 97-98.
2. This proposal, first suggested by Betz (*Galatians*, p. 323), is developed further by Longenecker (*Galatians*, pp. 298-99), who notes that the phrase 'the Israel of God' does not appear elsewhere in Paul's letters nor in the extant writings of Second Temple or Rabbinic Judaism.
3. Longenecker, *Galatians*, p. 299.

through the confusing (at times) rhetoric of Galatians and to see clearly what Paul believed to be the central issue at stake in the Galatian controversy: the cross of Christ. For foundational to Paul's argument throughout Galatians and at the heart of all he says in the closing section of that letter lies the crucifixion of Christ. Instead of 'righteousness', or 'faith' or the 'Spirit'—which are all important in the Galatian letter, but not mentioned even once in its closing[1]—the watershed between Paul and his Galatian opponents is the cross of Christ.

In light of the significant ways in which the letter closing of Galatians both recapitulates and illumines the central themes developed in the rest of the letter, the assertion of Charles Cosgrove that 'the postscript [Gal. 6.11-18] itself affords no immediate entrée into the inner logic of the epistle'[2] is, to say the least, surprising. Rather, it need be insisted that 6.11-18 has great hermeneutical significance for understanding the central themes of Galatians and for identifying the key theological issue at stake in Paul's conflict with his Galatian opponents. In fact, Betz's claim, based on his rhetorical analysis, that Gal. 6.11-18 contains the 'interpretive clues' for understanding the letter and so should be used as the 'hermeneutical key' to unlock Paul's intentions,[3] appears now, from an epistolary perspective, to be far more accurate than even he himself realized.

2. *1 Thessalonians*

a. *Extent of the Letter Closing*
There is debate among scholars whether the letter closing of 1 Thessalonians begins with the peace benediction at 5.23 or the request for prayer at 5.25. Those who accept the latter position see 5.23-24 functioning as a closing prayer to the second half of the letter (4.1–5.22) just as the prayer of 3.11-13 closes the first half of the letter (1.2–3.10),

---

1.   This fact seriously undermines Betz's claim that Paul in Galatians 'presents his defense of the gospel as a defense of the Spirit' (*Galatians*, p. 29), or Fung's assertion on the basis of the Galatian letter that 'the doctrine of justification by faith is of central importance in Paul's understanding and presentation of the gospel' (*Galatians*, p. 320; see also his larger discussion on pp. 315-20).

2.   Cosgrove, *The Cross and the Spirit*, p. 38. See also his rejection of the letter closing's importance on pp. 30-31.

3.   Betz, *Galatians*, p. 313.

and so conclude that 5.23-24 must belong to the letter body and not the letter closing.[1]

Despite this claimed parallel, however, between the two prayer wishes of 3.11-13 and 5.23-24,[2] there are compelling reasons for including the peace benediction of 5.23-24 in the letter closing of 1 Thessalonians. First, it need be noted that both the peace wish of Semitic letters and the health wish of Greco-Roman letters (to which the peace benediction is analogous) clearly belong to their respective letter closings and not to their letter bodies. Second, by including the peace benediction here in the letter closing, Paul creates an *inclusio* with the letter opening: the salutation 'grace to you and peace' that appears at the opening of 1 Thessalonians is echoed in chiastic fashion at its close, first by the peace benediction and then by the grace benediction. Thus Howard Marshall's assertion that 'there are no clear transitions or breaks at the end of the letter'[3] is misleading. For the peace benediction in Paul's letters typically serves as a literary heading that marks the beginning of a letter closing.[4] Consequently, the letter closing of 1 Thessalonians is better seen as 5.23-28.[5]

---

1. E.g., Milligan, *Thessalonians*, pp. 79-81; Rigaux, *Thessalonians*, pp. 602-606; H. Schürmann and H.A. Egenholf, *The Two Epistles to the Thessalonians* (London: Sheed and Ward, 1981), pp. 76-77; Bruce, *Thessalonians*, pp. 133-36; Marshall, *Thessalonians*, pp. 145, 164-66; T. Holtz, *Der erste Brief an die Thessalonicher* (Neukirchen: Neukirchener Verlag, 1986), pp. 270-75.

2. See discussion above (pp. 101-104) concerning the formal distinction between the closing peace benedictions and the so-called 'other' benedictions found within the body of Paul's letters.

3. Marshall, *Thessalonians*, p. 145.

4. See above, 'The Function of the Peace Benediction', p. 100.

5. So the majority of commentators: e.g., Frame, *Thessalonians*, pp. 209-218; Morris, *Thessalonians*, pp. 179-87; Best, *Thessalonians*, pp. 242-47; Doty, *Letters*, p. 43; Roetzel, *Letters of Paul*, pp. 40, 53; see also his 'I Thess. 5.12-28: A Case Study', pp. 367-83; Boers, 'Form Critical Study of Paul's Letters', p. 140; W. Marxsen, *Der erste Brief an die Thessalonicher* (Zürich: Theologisher Verlag, 1979), p. 72; Jervis, *Purpose of Romans*, pp. 134, 140-41; Wanamaker, *Thessalonians*, pp. 48-50, 205-209. On the basis of a rhetorical analysis of the letter, so also G.A. Kennedy, *New Testament Interpretation through Rhetorical Criticism* (Chapel Hill: University of North Carolina Press, 1984), pp. 142-44; F.W. Hughes, 'The Rhetoric of 1 Thessalonians' (unpublished paper, 1986); Jewett, *Thessalonian Correspondence*, pp. 63-78.

b. *Structural Analysis of the Letter Closing*
The letter closing of 1 Thessalonians contains all four of the epistolary conventions typically found in the final sections of Paul's letters. As in Romans and 2 Thessalonians, the closing of this letter opens with a peace benediction (v. 23). Here, however, the peace benediction has a greatly expanded form that is set out in a chiastic pattern: ἀγιάσαι... ὁλοτελεῖς//ὁλόκληρον...τηρηθείη. Paul prays that the God of peace will both 'sanctify wholly' and 'completely keep' the Thessalonians blameless at the coming of the Lord Jesus Christ. The peace benediction concludes with a word of encouragement (v. 24) in which Paul promises his readers that God who calls them is faithful and so will ensure that the contents of the prayer wish are fulfilled in their lives. This is followed by a brief hortatory section (v. 25) that begins with the vocative ἀδελφοί, a standard introductory formula of this particular closing convention. Paul exhorts the Thessalonians to pray for him and his co-workers. Next comes a greeting formula (v. 26) in which Paul requests his readers to greet all the brothers with a holy kiss. In a second hortatory section (v. 27), probably written in his own hand,[1] Paul commands the Thessalonians to have his letter read to all the members of the church. The letter closing then comes to a definitive end, in typical Pauline fashion, with a grace benediction (v. 28).

The letter closing of 1 Thessalonians, therefore, contains the following outline of epistolary conventions:

v. 23   Peace Benediction
v. 24   Word of Encouragement
v. 25   Hortatory Section
v. 26   Kiss Greeting
v. 27   Hortatory Section (Autograph)
v. 28   Grace Benediction

c. *Thematic Analysis of the Letter Closing*
A comparison of the peace benediction at 1 Thess. 5.23 with the peace benedictions found in Paul's other letter closings reveals that here the form of this epistolary convention is strikingly unique. For instead of the simple and relatively fixed formula 'May the God of peace be with you' (see Rom. 15.33; 2 Cor. 13.11; Phil. 4.9b), 1 Thess. 5.23 reads in greatly expanded fashion: 'May the God of peace himself sanctify you wholly; and may your spirit, soul and body be kept whole and blameless at the

1.   See above, pp. 124-25.

coming of our Lord Jesus Christ'. The distinctiveness of this wish is further heightened by the unusual addition of a word of encouragement that concludes the benediction: 'Faithful is the one who is calling you, and he will do it'.[1]

That this form of the peace benediction is not fortuitous but rather deliberate—and so hermeneutically significant—can be seen from a careful comparison of 1 Thess. 5.23-24 with the rest of the letter. For the expanded peace benediction and its concluding word of encouragement echo three major themes of 1 Thessalonians: the call to sanctified living, the certainty of Christ's return, and the comfort for persecuted Christians.[2]

Call to Sanctified Living. One important connection between the closing peace benediction of 1 Thessalonians and the rest of the letter exists in the theme of sanctification. The importance of living a life of holiness is expressed in the peace benediction by means of the two optative verbs: ἁγιάσαι ('may he sanctify') and ἀμέμπτως τηρηθείη ('may it [your spirit, soul and body] be kept blameless'). That sanctification involves a person's entire life is stressed by the two adjectives that form an alliteration, ὁλοτελεῖς ('wholly') and ὁλίκληρον ('complete'), and perhaps also by the threefold reference to πνεῦμα, ψυχή and σῶμα.[3]

Although the call to living a holy life comes distinctly to the fore in

1. The only other place where Paul adds a word of encouragement to conclude a peace benediction is 2 Thess. 3.16b.

2. The recapitulating function of the peace benediction in 1 Thess. 5.23-24 has been noted by at least four commentators, though they fail to develop the significance of this fact in any substantial way. Jewett ('Form and Function of Homiletic Benediction', p. 24) notes that 1 Thess. 5.23 'serves in fact to summarize and climax the entire epistle'. Wiles (*Paul's Intercessory Prayers*, p. 68) comments that both prayers for peace (3.11-13; 5.23-24) 'summarize and place the spotlight on the central message of the letter'. Langevin ('L'intervention de Dieu', p. 90) concludes: 'Cette bénédiction fait écho à plusieurs thèmes ou préoccupations majeures de la lettre. Elle en fournit même une certaine synthèse' ('This benediction echoes several themes or major preoccupations of the letter. It even provides a certain synthesis of it' [trans. mine]). Wanamaker (*Thessalonians*, p. 207), following the lead of Jewett, notes that v. 23 'sums up the dominant theme of the whole letter, parenesis for Christian living' (see also his comments on pp. 50, 205).

3. The connection between the tripartite reference and the theme of sanctification is noted by a few commentators. For example, Bruce (*Thessalonians*, p. 130) comments: 'The three [spirit, soul, body] together give further emphasis to the completeness of sanctification for which the writers [*sic*] pray'.

the second half of the letter (4.1–5.22), the same concern can also be found in the first half (1.2–3.13). Paul opens 1 Thessalonians by commending the Thessalonians for their 'work of faith and labor of love' (1.3), that is, for the outward and visible signs of a sanctified life that testify to their salvation in Jesus Christ. In fact, their 'faith in God', manifested in their holy lives, has served as a powerful example to all the believers in Macedonia and Achaia (1.7-9).

This opening note of thanksgiving leads into an extended discussion of Paul's ministry at Thessalonica. Paul defends his apostolic work among them by appealing to the 'holy, righteous and blameless' (ἀμέμπτως) lives of both himself and his missionary companions (2.10). This holiness exhibited in the apostles' ministry becomes in turn the ground on which Paul challenges the Thessalonians 'to lead a life worthy of God' (2.12). The concern for sanctified living also comes out in the prayer that climaxes the first half of the letter: 'May the Lord...establish your hearts unblameable in holiness (ἀμέμπτους ἐν ἁγιωσύνῃ) before God our Father at the coming of our Lord Jesus with all his saints (ἁγίων)' (3.13).

The second section of the letter, with its paraenetic focus, highlights to an even greater degree the theme of sanctification. The Thessalonians are called on to conduct themselves in a manner pleasing to God (4.1). This manner of conduct is explicitly identified as 'your sanctification (ὁ ἁγιασμὸς ὑμῶν)' (4.3). Believers must abstain from sexual immorality and know how to control their bodies 'in holiness (ἐν ἁγιασμῷ) and honor' (4.4). The motivation for such ethical concerns is that 'God has not called us to uncleanness but in holiness (ἐν ἁγιασμῷ)' (4.7), and so he 'gives his Holy (ἅγιον) Spirit to us' (4.8). Sanctified lives are further characterized by brotherly love, peaceful living, and hard work—all of which win the respect of non-Christians (4.9-12).

The theme of sanctification even occurs in the midst of a lengthy discussion about the return of Christ (4.13–5.11). For Paul reminds his Thessalonian converts that, though the day of the Lord is a day of judgment that will come like a thief in the night, they need not fear that day nor be caught unaware, since they are 'sons of light and sons of the day' in contrast to those 'of the night or of darkness' (5.5; also see 5.4, 7, 8). The metaphors of light and day versus darkness and night, common to the literature of the OT and Second Temple Judaism, are used here, as in Paul's other letters,[1] to refer to holy living, to the righteous

1. See Rom. 1.21; 2.19; 13.11-13; 1 Cor. 4.5; 2 Cor. 4.6; 6.14; Eph. 4.18; 5.8-

lives of the Thessalonians. Thus the return of Christ, which is also a key theme in the letter, is intimately connected with Paul's preoccupation throughout 1 Thessalonians with holy living.

Likewise, concern with sanctification is evident in the various exhortations of 5.12-22. For if the Thessalonians want to be 'sanctified wholly' and 'be kept completely blameless at the coming of our Lord Jesus Christ', they need to ensure that they respect their leaders (vv. 12-13a), are at peace with each other (v. 13b), encourage the fainthearted (v. 14b), help the weak (v. 14c), express patience to all (v. 14d), pursue what is good (v. 15), and so on, to reiterate just a few of the listed activities that are characteristic of a holy life. Paul makes frequent use in these closing exhortations of the adjective πᾶς (vv. 14, 15 [2×], 16, 18, 21, 22), thereby stressing the comprehensive nature of a sanctified life— a point also emphasized, as noted above, in the peace benediction.[1]

It is clear, therefore, that the emphasis on sanctification expressed in the peace benediction of 1 Thess. 5.23-24 echoes, both in content and in direct verbal links, the statements and exhortations given throughout the rest of 1 Thessalonians. Paul, it appears, has carefully adapted and expanded a traditional closing epistolary convention so that it recapitulates a key theme of his letter and so serves to drive home to his readers one last time the importance of living a holy life. Thus the closing peace benediction of 1 Thessalonians functions as a hermenuetical spotlight, drawing our attention to what Paul considers to be one of the major themes of that letter.

Certainty of Christ's Return. A second important link between the closing peace benediction of 1 Thessalonians and the rest of the letter lies in the theme of Christ's return. Paul's closing prayer is that his readers will be kept completely blameless 'at the coming of our Lord Jesus Christ'. This reference to Christ's parousia is all the more striking in light of the fact that it does not occur in any other Pauline peace benediction.

11; 6.12; Col. 1.13. The connection between the metaphor of day/night and light/darkness with the concept of sanctification or holy living is especially clear in Rom. 13.12-13: 'The night is far gone, the day is at hand. Let us then cast off the works of darkness and put on the armor of light; let us conduct ourselves becomingly as in the day, not in reveling and drunkenness, not in debauchery and licentiousness, not in quarreling and jealousy'.

1. This is evident in the use of ὁλοτελεῖς and ὁλόκληρον, as well as in the threefold reference to πνεῦμα, ψυχή and σῶμα.

The readers have been well prepared throughout the body of 1 Thessalonians to read of Christ's return at its closing. Paul begins the first half of his letter by praising the Thessalonians, not only for their 'work of faith and labor of love' (1.3a), but also for their 'steadfastness of hope in our Lord Jesus Christ' (1.3b). In the context of the letter as a whole, this can only refer to their abiding confidence in Christ and his ultimate return.[1] In fact, others in Macedonia and Achaia have heard how they have turned from idols to serve God and 'to wait for his Son from heaven' (1.10). Paul therefore anticipates that the Thessalonian believers will be his 'crown of boasting before our Lord Jesus at his coming' (2.19). To ensure that result, Paul closes the first section of his letter by praying that Christ will establish their hearts unblameable in holiness before God 'at the coming of our Lord Jesus with his saints' (3.13).

The return of Christ is a theme that is developed even more explicitly in the second half of 1 Thessalonians. The Thessalonian believers were apparently concerned about the fate of their fellow Christians who had passed away before Christ's return: Would the deceased not participate in that great eschatological event, or be at some disadvantage to those believers who were still living? Paul responds to such concerns in 4.13-18 by assuring his readers that all believers—those who have passed away as well as those who remain alive—will participate equally in the glorious day of Christ's second coming.

That the subject of Christ's return constituted a major issue within the Thessalonian church can be seen in the fact that Paul proceeds in 5.1-11 to talk at some length about the 'times and seasons' related to the day of the Lord. Because his readers are 'sons of light and sons of the day', they await Christ's return not with unprepared fear and ignorance but with sober readiness and hope. Thus the long section of 4.13–5.11 is permeated with references, both explicit and implicit, to the topic of Christ's parousia.

Such preoccupation with Christ's return, which is a particularly evident theme in 4.13–5.11 but present in the rest of the letter as well, makes it difficult to believe that the unparalleled reference to 'the coming of our Lord Jesus Christ' in the peace benediction of 1 Thessalonians is fortuitous. Rather, it seems apparent that Paul has deliberately adapted and expanded his typical closing peace benediction so that it echoes a

---

1.   See Wiles (*Paul's Intercessory Prayers*, p. 179): 'Clearly the hope referred to here [1.3] was the Thessalonians' fervid expectation of the parousia'.

main theme of this particular letter. And this recapitulating function, in turn, aids our understanding of Paul's purpose in writing and the situation of his readers, thereby highlighting their struggles and Paul's responses vis-à-vis important questions concerning Christ's return.

Comfort for Persecuted Christians. A third important connection between the closing peace benediction and the rest of the letter can be found in the theme of comfort for persecuted Christians. It is clear already at the opening of the letter (1.6, 'you received the word in much affliction') that the Thessalonians had experienced persecution from the moment of their conversion. In this regard, Gentile Christians at Thessalonica were no different than their fellow Jewish Christians in Judea, 'for you suffered the same things from your own countrymen as they did from the Jews' (2.14). That this persecution posed a serious threat to the Thessalonian church is clear, not just from Paul's use of the adjective 'much' (πολύς) to describe their persecution (1.6), but even more so from his sending of Timothy to ensure that 'no one be moved by these afflictions' (3.3; see 3.1-5; 5.16-18; also 2 Thess. 1.4-7; 2.15). Thus a major concern of Paul in 1 Thessalonians is to provide comfort and encouragement for believers in their struggle (note the summary statements of 4.18 and 5.11, 'Comfort one another' [παρακαλεῖτε ἀλλήλους]).

This note of comfort in the face of persecution is also found in the closing peace benediction of the letter. The intensive pronoun αὐτός, which adds emphasis both by its placement at the head of the sentence and by its grammatical function, stresses that it is God 'himself' who will carry out the wish expressed in the prayer. The Thessalonians' ability to resist persecution and be kept completely blameless at the coming of the Lord Jesus Christ does not rest in their own talent or strength but in God's.[1]

In the peace benediction Paul further comforts his afflicted readers by means of a concluding word of encouragement: 'Faithful is the one who is calling you, and he will do it' (5.24). As with the intensive pronoun αὐτός in the previous verse, so also here the adjective πιστός stands in the first position for emphasis. 'Faithful' is the God whom Paul calls on to keep the Thessalonians holy and blameless at the return of Christ. So

---

1. Wiles (*Paul's Intercessory Prayers*, p. 66) comments, 'In the words αὐτὸς δέ he [Paul] seems to point away from the weakness of the converts' own unaided efforts and to place them under the supreme power of God'.

despite their present persecution, believers at Thessalonica need not worry about the ultimate outcome, for this faithful God 'will do it'.[1] Furthermore, they should remember that God also 'is calling (καλῶν) you'. The present tense of the participle is significant. God has not called them once in the past and subsequently abandoned them to their own devices. Rather, as Paul puts it elsewhere, 'he who began a good work in you will bring it to completion at the day of Jesus Christ' (Phil. 1.6).

The description of God in the peace benediction as one who 'is calling you' recalls earlier statements about God's initiative in the conversion of the Thessalonians. In the thanksgiving section (1.2-10), which addresses the subject of how the Thessalonians have turned from idols to serve a living and true God despite persecution, Paul states that the ultimate cause[2] of their conversion rests in their being 'called' (τὴν ἐκλογὴν ὑμῶν) by God (1.4). This divine initiative is more clearly spelled out in 2.12, which identifies God as the one 'who is calling you (τοῦ καλοῦντος)[3] into his own kingdom and glory'. Similarly, Paul grounds his commands concerning sanctified living on the fact that 'God has not called (ἐκάλεσεν) us to uncleanness, but in holiness' (4.7). And although the verb καλέω is not used, God's involvement in the lives of the Thessalonians is clearly central to Paul's reminder to them that 'God has not destined us for wrath but for the obtaining of salvation through our Lord Jesus Christ' (5.9).

The addition of the pronoun αὐτός in v. 23 and the word of encouragement in v. 24, therefore, result in a peace benediction that echoes an important theme found in the rest of the letter, i.e., that salvation is the result of God's initiative and that this divine calling ensures the full completion of salvation at the day of Christ's return. This provides a powerful message of comfort to the Thessalonians who were facing strong opposition because of their faith. And again, it can be seen how

---

1. The verbal idea of God 'doing' or fulfilling the wish of the peace benediction is emphasized in two ways: (1) the addition of καί suggests that God not only calls but 'also' acts; and (2) the omission of any direct object in the phrase has the effect of highlighting the verb. See Milligan, *Thessalonians*, p. 79; Morris, *Thessalonians*, p. 183.

2. The two participles μνημονεύοντες (1.3) and εἰδότες (1.4) introduce clauses that give the grounds or reasons for Paul's thanksgiving. For a detailed discussion of the structure of thanksgiving sections, see Schubert, *Form and Function of Pauline Thanksgivings*, pp. 10-39; O'Brien, *Introductory Thanksgivings*, pp. 6-15; Jervis, *Purpose of Romans*, pp. 86-109.

3. The present tense of the participle here is also significant.

Paul has masterfully adapted the closing peace benediction of
1 Thessalonians so that this epistolary convention now recalls earlier
statements of the letter and better addresses the specific concerns of his
readers.

The recapitulating function of the peace benediction in 1 Thessalonians
suggests a new solution to the vexing problem of the threefold reference
to 'spirit, soul and body' in 5.23. This is the only passage in the NT that
speaks of a tripartite makeup of human nature. A number of diverse
explanations have been forwarded, none of which has proven convincing
to the majority of exegetes.[1] But understanding the closing peace
benediction as echoing the major concerns of 1 Thessalonians as a whole
suggests that the tripartite reference also refers back to some key issue
previously addressed in the letter. A strong candidate for this antecedent
concern is the Thessalonians' fears about the fate of their fellow
believers who have 'fallen asleep' prior to Christ's return (4.13-18). By
closing the letter with a prayer that God may keep their spirit, soul and
body 'whole' (ὁλόκληρον) at the second coming of Christ, Paul responds
one last time to such fears by assuring his readers that a believer's *whole*
person will be involved in the day of Christ's return. Thus those who die

---

1. The various proposals may be briefly outlined as follows: (1) E. von Dobschütz
(*Die Thessalonicherbriefe* [Göttingen: Vandenhoeck & Ruprecht, 1909, 1974]),
believing that Paul is describing the nature of a Christian as distinct from humankind
in general, takes πνεῦμα to refer to the divine Spirit that enters into a believer
alongside the human 'soul' and 'body'; (2) C. Masson ('Sur I Thessaloniciens V,
23: Notes d'anthropologie paulinienne', *RTP* 33 [1945], pp. 97-102) understands
πνεῦμα to refer to the human being as a whole person (see Gal. 6.18; Phil. 4.23) and
that 'soul' and 'body' then explicate this; (3) P.A. van Stempvoort ('Eine stilistische
Lösung einer alten Schwierigkeit in I Thess. v. 23', *NTS* 7 [1960/61], pp. 262-65)
takes πνεῦμα as equivalent to a personal pronoun 'you' and divides up the verse so
that ὁλόκληρον ὑμῶν τὸ πνεῦμα belongs to the first half of the sentence in
parallel to ὑμᾶς ὁλοτελεῖς: 'May the God of peace himself sanctify you wholly and
your spirit completely. May both soul and body be kept blameless at the coming of
our Lord Jesus'; (4) R. Jewett (*Paul's Anthropological Terms* [Leiden: Brill, 1971],
pp. 175-83) proposes that Paul is here taking over the language of enthusiasts in
Thessalonica who adopted a Gnostic type of understanding of man in which the
divinely-given spirit was contrasted with the human body and soul; (5) M. Dibelius
(*An die Thessalonicher I, II; an die Philipper* [Tübingen: Mohr, 1937], p. 229)
believes that Paul has taken over a traditional formula (*Epist. Apost.* 24) and so any
distinctions in it would not necessarily be his own; (6) Marshall (*Thessalonians*,
p. 163) proposes reading the text as referring to three aspects, but not three parts, of a
person's being.

before the parousia of Christ will not miss that glorious eschatological event nor will they be *in any way* at a disadvantage.

The unique form of the grace benediction in 1 Thess. 5.23-24 stems, as has been demonstrated, from Paul's deliberate adaptation and expansion, with the result that this closing convention functions by way of pointing back to the major themes of the letter. This suggests that other distinctive features in the remaining closing conventions of the letter, although seemingly innocent, may also prove to be significant. And this, in fact, appears to be case. For some of the other epistolary conventions in 1 Thess. 5.23-28 seem to highlight as well certain features previously alluded to in the body of that letter.

The existence of some sort of division in the Thessalonian congregation is hinted at by the mere presence of the kiss greeting in v. 26. For in Paul's other letters, the exhortation to greet one another with a holy kiss always occurs in contexts where some degree of conflict exists within the local church.[1] This hint of internal tension becomes more probable in light of the distinctive form of this kiss greeting. For whereas all other occurrences of this command exhibit the fixed form 'Greet *one another* (ἀλλήλους) with a holy kiss,' Paul in v. 26 has 'Greet *all the brothers* (τοὺς ἀδελφοὺς πάντας) with a holy kiss.'[2] Several commentators have taken the shift from 'one another' to 'all the brothers' to be significant, agreeing, basically, with Marshall: 'In view of the fact that there was some tendency to division in the church, this stress on the fact that *all* belong to the one fellowship is probably intentional.'[3] Further evidence of an internal conflict can be seen in the second hortatory section at v. 27, where there is (1) the use of verb ἐνορκίζω expressing

1. See Rom. 16.16a; 1 Cor. 16.20b; 2 Cor. 13.12a, as well as the discussion above of the kiss greeting on pp. 111-117.

2. The distinctiveness of the shift to the phrase 'all the brothers' is further highlighted by the fact that all the references to the kiss greeting outside of Paul also uniformly use 'one another'; see 1 Pet. 5.14; Justin Martyr, *Apology* 1.61.65; *Constitutions of the Holy Apostles* 8.9; *The Divine Liturgy of James* 2 (the relevant texts of the last two cited documents are reproduced in Hendriksen, *Thessalonians*, pp. 143-44).

3. Marshall, *Thessalonians*, p. 165. So also Frame, *Thessalonians*, pp. 215-16; Bruce, *Thessalonians*, p. 134; Hendriksen, *Thessalonians*, p. 142; Whiteley, *Thessalonians*, p. 86. Best (*Thessalonians*, p. 245), however, claims that '*all* need not be emphatic' and 'it can hardly be taken as suggesting that some division within the church needs to be healed'.

strong adjuration regarding the public reading of the letter, and (2) the repeated reference to '*all* the brothers'.

Some scholars have denied any internal conflict among the Thessalonian believers, primarily on the assumption that Timothy's report was completely positive and on the basis of their inability to find evidence for such inner tension in the letter's body.[1] A careful reading of the letter body of 1 Thessalonians, however, does reveal that the church experienced a problem of division—a problem that I believe Paul echoes in the letter's closing.[2] Admittedly, the dissension does not appear to have been widespread, but limited to difficulties that arose between the church's leaders and certain 'idlers' (ἄτακτοι).[3] Paul specifically exhorts that peace should characterize relationships within the church: 'Be at peace among yourselves' (5.13b).[4] Significantly, this exhortation

1. So, e.g., Neil, *Thessalonians*, p. xv; Hendriksen, *Thessalonians*, pp. 11-12; J.M. Reese, *1 and 2 Thessalonians* (Wilmington, DE: Michael Glazier, 1979), p. xiii.

2. There are scholars who have correctly recognized the existence of internal problems among the Thessalonian believers, but who wrongly use this fact to support rather speculative hypotheses. Adolf von Harnack, for example, proposed that a conflict existed between two congregations at Thessalonica, one Gentile and the other Jewish, and that the two letters of 1 and 2 Thessalonians were written to each church respectively (see A. von Harnack, 'Das Problem des zweiten Thessalonicherbriefes', *Sitzungsbericht der Preussischen Akademie der Wissenschaft zu Berlin, philosophisch-historischen Classe* 31 [1910], pp. 560-78; this view was adopted by K. Lake, *The Earlier Epistles of St. Paul: Their Motive and Origin* [London: Rivingtons, 1911]). Earle Ellis argues that a division existed between the leaders and the laity of the Thessalonian church, with 2 Thessalonians written to the former group and 1 Thessalonians to the latter (see E.E. Ellis, 'Paul and His Co-Workers', *NTS* 17 [1970–71], pp. 437-52; reprinted in *idem, Prophecy and Hermeneutic in Early Christianity: New Testament Essays* [Grand Rapids: Eerdmans, 1978], pp. 3-22).

3. C. Spicq observes that the term ἄτακτοι was commonly used in military contexts to describe the insubordination of a soldier and so argues that ἄτακτοι should be translated by the word 'réfractaires', which in English is 'obstinate' or 'insubordinate' (see Spicq, 'Les Thessaloniciens "inquietes" etaient ils des paresseux?' *ST* 10 [1956], pp. 1-13; *idem, Notes de Lexicographie Neo-testamentaire* [3 vols.; Göttingen: Vandenhoeck & Ruprecht, 1978], I, pp. 157-59). While this translation would capture the resistance of the ἄτακτοι to the church leaders, 2 Thess. 3.6-15 clearly identifies the ἄτακτοι as those who do not work (see also 1 Thess 4.11-12) so that the translation 'idlers' appears to be more appropriate.

4. Many commentators want to take this as simply a traditional statement (paraenesis) that does not reflect any specific situation in the Thessalonian church. It is noteworthy, however, that Paul does not speak here of peace with other people in general but peace 'among yourselves' (ἐν ἑαυτοῖς). Furthermore, the same

is preceded by the call to respect church leaders whose task it is to 'admonish' (5.12-13a). Furthermore, it is followed by an exhortation to 'admonish' the idlers (5.14a). The close connection of these exhortations, coupled with the verbal link of the word 'admonish' in 5.12-13a and 5.14, suggests that the conflict in the Thessalonian congregation centered on the idlers who were failing to respect and obey the church's leaders.[1]

Paul had earlier addressed the problem of the idlers in 4.11-12 where their failure to work with their hands, as commanded, was causing tensions in the church (note the exhortation in 4.10 to increase in brotherly love) and threatening the public reputation of the church. The idlers were not only refusing to obey their own church leaders, but they also seem to have been refusing to obey Paul. For a few months later the problem had apparently become worse (2 Thess. 3.6-15).[2]

There is sufficient evidence, therefore, for postulating the existence of internal tensions within the Thessalonian congregation, with those tensions originating from the failure of the idlers to respect and obey the church's leaders. The significance of this for my thesis is that Paul addresses the problem of division not only explicitly in the body of 1 Thessalonians, but also, as we have seen above, implicitly in that letter's closing. For just as Paul adapted the peace benediction of 1 Thessalonians to echo three major themes of that letter, so also he adapted the kiss greeting and his autograph hortatory section of the letter closing to address the internal tensions in the Thessalonian church and to encourage reconciliation and obedience. So here in 1 Thess. 5.23-28, as we found earlier with respect to Gal. 6.11-18, the recapitulating function of Paul's letter closing aids our understanding of that particular letter's key issues as well as our apprehension of the historical situation of its recipients.

exhortation occurs in letters where divisions were clearly present in the local church: e.g., 2 Cor. 13.11; Rom. 12.18.

1. See Marxsen, *Thessalonicher*, pp. 62, 71-72; Marshall, *Thessalonians*, p. 149. So also Frame ('οἱ ἄτακτοι [1 Thess. 5.14]', in *Essays in Modern Theology: A Testimonial to C.A. Brigss* [New York: Scribner's, 1911], pp. 191-206), who rightly links the problem of division to tensions between the leaders and the idlers, but wrongly speculates that this conflict was due to the leaders' tactless treatment of the idlers.

2. Even if 2 Thessalonians were written first, 2 Thess. 3.6-15 would still provide evidence for the existence of tensions in the Thessalonian church stemming from the problem of the idlers.

3. *2 Thessalonians*

a. *Extent of the Letter Closing*
Disagreement among scholars also exists as to where the letter closing of
2 Thessalonians begins. Does it start with the peace benediction of 3.16?
Or does it begin with the autograph greeting of 3.17? A number of
commentators have accepted the latter view, believing that the prayer
wish of 3.16 is not related to the entire letter but only to the immediately
preceding section, being therefore parallel in function to the other prayer
wishes of the letter (2.16-17; 3.5).[1] But this understanding, as noted in the
discussion of 1 Thess. 5.23-24, fails to recognize that a peace benediction
in Paul's letters typically serves as a literary heading that marks the
beginning of a letter closing.[2] Furthermore, the peace benediction of
2 Thess. 3.16 is, as we will see, linked to the whole of the letter and not
just to the preceding section. Thus the fact that this peace benediction
echoes material from the entire letter, coupled with the fact that peace
benedictions typically mark the beginning of letter closings in Paul's
other letters, strongly suggest that the letter closing of 2 Thessalonians
should be seen as beginning at 3.16.[3]

b. *Structural Analysis of the Letter Closing*
2 Thessalonians has a relatively brief letter closing. Yet it contains three
of the four epistolary conventions typically found in the Pauline letter
closings. The closing of 2 Thessalonians begins with a slightly altered and
expanded peace benediction in which Paul prays that 'the Lord of peace
himself' will give believers at Thessalonica peace 'at all times and in all
ways' (v. 16a). This wish for peace concludes with a word of encouragement that 'the Lord be with you all' (v. 16b). Then Paul briefly greets
them in his own hand and explains that a closing autograph section is a

---

1. So, e.g., Milligan, *Thessalonians*, pp. 117-18; Whiteley, *Thessalonians*,
pp. 111-12; Bruce, *Thessalonians*, pp. 211-13; Marshall, *Thessalonians*, pp. 230-31;
Trilling, *Thessalonicher*, pp. 156-60.
2. See above, pp. 174-75.
3. So, e.g., Rigaux, *Thessaloniciens*, pp. 717-18; Morris, *Thessalonians*,
pp. 260-62; Best, *Thessalonians*, pp. 345-48; J.C. Hurd, 'Thessalonians, Second
Letter to the', *IDBSup*, pp. 900-901; Jervis, *Purpose of Romans*, pp. 134, 141-42;
Wanamaker, *Thessalonians*, pp. 51, 291-93. On the basis of a rhetorical analysis of
the letter, so also Hughes, *Early Christian Rhetoric*, pp. 51-73, esp. 66-67; Jewett,
Thessalonian Correspondence, pp. 81-87.

characteristic sign of all his letters (v. 17). Finally, the letter comes to a definitive close with a secondary wish that 'the grace of the Lord Jesus Christ be with you all' (v. 18).

The letter closing of 2 Thessalonians, therefore, may be outlined as follows:

v. 16a	Peace Benediction
v. 16b	Word of Encouragement
v. 17	Autograph Greeting & Explanatory Comment
v. 18	Grace Benediction

A comparison of the letter closing of 2 Thessalonians with the closings of Paul's other letters reveals that each of the epistolary conventions found in this particular final section is, in one or more ways, formally unique. The peace benediction, instead of following the relatively fixed formula 'May the God of peace be with you,' reads 'May the Lord of peace himself give you peace at all times and in all ways; the Lord be with you all.' Five distinctive features of this peace benediction can be observed: (1) the addition of the third person pronoun αὐτός ('the Lord "himself"');[1] (2) the shift in the divine source of the wish from θεός ('God') to κύριος ('Lord'); (3) the addition of δῴη τὴν εἰρήνην ('give peace'), which serves to emphasize the content of the wish; (4) the addition of the double, prepositional phrase διὰ παντὸς ἐν παντὶ τρόπῳ ('at all times and in all ways'); and (5) the addition of a concluding word of encouragement, whose form follows somewhat generally that found in a typical peace benediction: ὁ κύριος μετὰ πάντων ὑμῶν ('The Lord be with you all').[2]

The form of the autograph greeting formula is also distinctive because of its unparalleled explanatory clause that follows the formula: ὅ ἐστιν σημεῖον ἐν πάσῃ ἐπιστολῇ· οὕτως γράφω ('which is the sign in every letter; thus I write'). Finally, even the grace benediction, which exhibits throughout Paul's letters a striking consistency in form, has been expanded somewhat by the addition of the adjective πάντων ('all').

---

1. The addition of αὐτός in peace benedictions occurs elsewhere only in 1 Thess. 5.23. It also occurs in two of the so-called 'other' benedictions found in the body of Paul's letters (1 Thess. 3.11; 2 Thess. 2.16).

2. The only other occurrence of a word of encouragement functioning as a conclusion to a peace benediction is 1 Thess. 5.24.

c. *Thematic Analysis of the Letter Closing*
These adaptations of and additions to the closing conventions found in
2 Thessalonians do not appear to be due simply to stylistic variation or
to chance. Rather, they seem to stem from Paul's attempts to link more
directly the letter closing of 2 Thessalonians to the two major issues
addressed in the body of that letter: the conflict with the idlers, and the
concern over Christ's return.

Conflict with the Idlers. The connection between the letter closing of
2 Thessalonians and the church's conflict with the idlers at Thessalonica
can be seen in the unparalleled double reference to 'peace' in the peace
benediction of 3.16. For the wish that the 'Lord of peace' may give
'peace' relates directly to the tensions and divisions caused by the idlers
(3.6-15). Thus not only is Christ the 'Lord of peace' but he also 'gives
peace' to his believers, thereby removing any conflict that may exist
within the church.

The church's conflict with the idlers is also reflected in the autograph
greeting and the accompanying explanatory comment of 3.17. For
although the autograph may serve to distinguish this letter from other
inauthentic letters claiming to be from Paul (see 2.2), the unlikelihood of
pseudonymous Pauline letters existing at such an early date suggests that
the function of the autograph more likely lies elsewhere, namely, to
underscore the authority of this particular letter to any of the idlers or
others who might be causing tensions in the church.[1] Paul recognizes in
3.14 ('If any one refuses to obey what we say in this letter...') the probability that some in the church will not obey the exhortations contained
in his letter.[2] Consequently, he closes the document in his own hand,
thereby emphasizing the authority of the letter and the need for the
idlers to obey its injunctions.

Finally, conflict with the idlers is also hinted at in the letter closing in
the repeated use of the adjective πᾶς ('all') in 3.16 and 3.18. Four times

1.   Marshall (*Thessalonians*, p. 232) says that Paul's purpose in the autograph is
'to stress the authenticity of this particular letter to any of the idlers or opponents of
Paul's teaching who might try to discredit it...it seems more probable that Paul's
purpose is to emphasize the authority and authenticity of this letter rather than to deny
the authenticity of other alleged letters of his'. See also Frame, *Thessalonians*, p. 311;
Wanamaker, *Thessalonians*, p. 293.

2.   In logical conditions, such as is found in 3.14, the speaker assumes the truth
of the protasis (BDF §372).

this adjective occurs in these two verses (once also in another context in
3.17)—which is a rather striking phenomenon. Paul, it seems, wants to
lay stress on the fact that his wishes for peace and grace include *all* the
members of the church, including those who are the cause of internal
trouble and the object of his rebukes.[1]

Concern over Christ's Return. The letter closing of 2 Thessalonians also
relates, however, to the theme of Christ's return, a subject foreshadowed
in the thanksgiving section (1.3-12) and addressed at length in the letter
body (2.1-17). The wish that the 'Lord of peace himself give you peace'
has in view, therefore, not only the internal tensions due to the problem
of the idlers (3.6-15), but also the anxiety and fears within the
Thessalonian church that stemmed from the claim that the day of the
Lord had already come (2.1-12). Similarly, the addition of the phrase 'at
all times in all ways' to the peace benediction 'refers more naturally to
the discussion of the times and seasons that dominated earlier sections of
the letter (1.5-10; 2.1-12; 2.13–3.5)'.[2] The unparalleled substitution of
'the Lord' for 'God' in the peace benediction, coupled with the additional reference to 'the Lord' in the word of encouragement (3.16b),
also focus the reader's attention on Christ and, in the context of this
letter, more specifically on his expected return.

It comes as something of a surprise that the letter closing of
2 Thessalonians does not address the issues of persecution and sanctification, which were two key concerns of 1 Thessalonians. This suggests
that Paul considered the internal problems of conflict with the idlers and
anxiety over Christ's return to be greater dangers to the church than the
external threat of persecution—a threat they appeared to be handling
fairly well (2 Thess. 1.4).

2 Thess. 3.16-18, it is true, does not recapitulate the main themes of
2 Thessalonians in as explicit a fashion as does either the letter closing of
Galatians or that of 1 Thessalonians. Nevertheless, the epistolary conventions in this brief closing must be seen to have been adapted and
shaped by Paul so that they better reflect the key issues developed in
the rest of the letter. The letter closing of 2 Thessalonians, therefore, aids

1.   See Morris (*Thessalonians*, p. 262 n. 27), who states in his discussion of
3.18: 'The addition of "all" is significant, and is in view of the specific disturbances
noted earlier'.
2.   Jewett, *Thessalonian Correspondence*, p. 81. See also Jewett, 'Form and
Function', p. 25.

our interpretation of that particular letter by drawing attention to the two major causes of unrest within the Thessalonian church, namely, conflict with the idlers and concern over Christ's return.

4. *Philippians*

a. *Extent of the Letter Closing*

The majority of commentators, by far, believe that the letter closing of Philippians is limited to the final greetings and grace benediction found in 4.21-23.[1] This view, however, fails to recognize the closing epistolary conventions that are to be found earlier in the letter. For 4.8-9a contains a closing hortatory section that is introduced in typical fashion by the stereotyped phrase τὸ λοιπόν, ἀδελφοί ('Finally, brothers'). This is followed in 4.9b by a peace benediction—an epistolary convention that always belongs in Paul's other letters to the letter closing, not the letter body. Furthermore, it need be noted that, instead of the particle δέ, the introductory element in the peace benediction is καί, thereby linking the wish for peace with the preceding exhortations.[2] As well, it should be observed that the hortatory section and peace benediction are then followed by a greatly expanded joy expression (4.10-20), which is also an epistolary convention sometimes found in the closings of Paul's other letters (Rom. 16.19a; 1 Cor. 16.17). There is compelling epistolary evidence, therefore, to support the view that the letter closing of Philippians consists of 4.8-23.[3]

1. So, e.g., Lightfoot, *Philippians*, p. 71; Müller, *Philippians and Philemon*, pp. 154-56; W. Hendriksen, *Philippians* (Grand Rapids: Baker, 1962), pp. 211-13; J.L. Houlden, *Paul's Letters from Prison* (Philadelphia: Westminster, 1970), pp. 115-16; G. Barth, *Der Brief an die Philipper* (Zürich: Theologischer Verlag, 1979), pp. 79-80; Russell, 'Pauline Letter Structure', pp. 305-306; Hawthorne, *Philippians*, pp. 212-16; Bruce, *Philippians*, pp. 157-59; M. Silva, *Philippians* (Chicago: Moody, 1988), pp. 241-42; O'Brien, *Philippians*, pp. 551-55.

2. A similar shift from δέ to καί in a peace benediction occurs in 2 Cor. 13.11b and Gal. 6.16. For further discussion of the significance of this shift, see discussion of 'The Introductory Element' above on pp. 88-90.

3. So F.B. Craddock, *Philippians* (Atlanta: John Knox, 1985), pp. 72-82 (although he does not treat 4.8-23 as a unit entitled 'closing', he does say regarding 4.8-9 that 'this passage is a conclusion' and regarding 4.10-20 that this section is a 'postscript'); Jervis, *Purpose of Romans*, p. 135. Gamble (*Textual History*, pp. 145-46; see also pp. 88, 94) rightly includes the peace benediction in the letter closing but fails to recognize the connection between this wish for peace and the preceding exhortation indicated by the introductory element καί. Gamble thus identifies the

b. *Structural Analysis of the Letter Closing*
The letter closing of Philippians is significantly longer than most other closings of Paul's letters, largely due to the lengthy joy expression of 4.10-20. As in both 1 Corinthians and 2 Corinthians, the letter closing of Philippians does not begin with a peace benediction but with a hortatory section (4.8-9a)—here introduced by the stereotyped phrase τὸ λοιπόν, ἀδελφοί, which is a characteristic feature of such a closing convention. The hortatory section of 4.8-9a makes use of several figures of speech (anaphora, asyndeton, polysyndeton and homoioteleuton) in a rather rhetorical fashion,[1] thereby setting this closing material somewhat apart from the preceding text as well as giving it a certain emphasis.[2] The highly stylized character of this hortatory section is apparent from the following grammatical outline:

v. 8　τὸ λοιπόν, ἀδελφοί,
　　　　ὅσα ἐστὶν ἀληθῆ,
　　　　ὅσα σεμνά,
　　　　ὅσα δίκαια,
　　　　ὅσα ἀγνά,
　　　　ὅσα προσφιλῆ
　　　　ὅσα εὔφημα,
　　　　　　εἴ τις ἀρετὴ καὶ
　　　　　　εἴ τις ἔπαινος,
　　　　　　　　ταῦτα λογίζεσθε·
v. 9a　ἃ καὶ ἐμάθετε
　　　　καὶ παρελάβετε
　　　　καὶ ἠκούσατε
　　　　καὶ εἴδετε ἐν ἐμοί,
　　　　　　ταῦτα πράσσετε

Here Paul exhorts his readers to think of those excellent and praiseworthy things that are true, honorable, just, pure, lovely, and gracious (v. 8) and to do those things that they have been taught, given, heard and seen in Paul (v. 9a).

letter closing as 4.10-23. Roetzel (*Letters of Paul*, p. 40) also includes the peace benediction of 4.9 in the letter closing, but views the subsequent material in 4.10-20 as the body of another Pauline letter (so also several others who reject the literary unity of the letter: e.g., F.W. Beare, *The Epistle to the Philippians* [London: A. & C. Black, 1959], pp. 148-58).
　1.　See Hawthorne, *Philippians*, pp. 185-86.
　2.　BDF §460.3: 'asyndeton, by breaking up the series and introducing the items staccato fashion, produces a vivid and impassioned effect'.

This stylized, rhetorical exhortation is followed by a peace benediction (v. 9b) introduced with καί. The shift here from the expected δέ to καί is significant, for it links the wish for peace with the preceding hortatory section and also makes it conditional on compliance with Paul's exhortation.

The third epistolary convention found in the Philippian letter closing is the lengthy joy expression (vv. 10-20), which, as noted earlier, was quite likely written in Paul's own hand.[1] The stereotyped joy formula itself (v. 10, ἐχάρην δὲ ἐν κυρίῳ μεγάλως ὅτι...) is followed by three explanatory sub-units: οὐχ ὅτι...(vv. 11-13); πλὴν καλῶς ἐποιήσατε... (vv. 14-16); and οὐχ ὅτι... (vv. 17-18).[2] Some commentators have characterized this passage rather negatively as a 'thankless thanks' ('danklösen Dank').[3] The majority of scholars, however, recognize the masterful manner in which Paul structures his statements so that, on the one hand, he thanks the Philippians for their financial assistance but, on the other hand, tactfully discourages the sending of further funds— which would be in conflict with his expressed practice (1 Cor. 9.1-18; 2 Cor. 11.7-10; 1 Thess. 2.5-9; 2 Thess. 3.7-12) and would open him up to charges of greed or selfishness.[4] The lengthy expression of joy for their monetary gift closes with a word of encouragement that God will

1. See above, pp. 123-24.

2. See Jervis, *Purpose of Romans*, pp. 144-46.

3. So Dibelius, *Philipper*; *idem*, *Fresh Approach to the New Testament*, p. 154; E. Lohmeyer, *Der Brief an die Philipper* (Göttingen: Vandenhoek & Ruprecht, 1964) pp. 178, 183; J. Gnilka, *Der Philipperbrief* (Freiburg: Herder, 1980), p. 173. Since Vincent (*Philippians*, p. 146) attributes the phrase 'thankless thanks' to K. Holsten, this characterization of 4.10-20 was known already in the late nineteenth century. Note as well the paraphrase of 4.10-20 by Silva (*Philippians*, p. 231), who, however, does not agree with such a negative evaluation of this passage.

4. E.g., Lightfoot (*Philippians*, pp. 70-71) comments: 'With a graceful intermingling of manly independence and courteous delicacy he acknowledges this token of their love.' For other positive evaluations of Paul's discussion in 4.10-20, see Vincent, *Philippians*, p. 152; Beare, *Philippians*, p. 157; Hawthorne, *Philippians*, p. 195; Bruce, *Philippians*, p. 148. Note also Gerald Peterman ('"Thankless Thanks": The Epistolary Social Convention in Philippians 4.10-20', *TynBul* 42 [1991], pp. 261-70), who argues that 'verbal gratitude, as a social convention, was withheld from those who were socially intimate; that gratitude in the form of repayment was of primary significance; and that when verbal gratitude was offered it took the form of an expression of debt' (p. 262), thereby leading to the conclusion that 'Paul's response to the Philippian's gift is in keeping with the thankless thanks practised in the first century Graeco–Roman world' (p. 270).

supply the Philippians' every need (v. 19) and a doxology that expresses Paul's and his readers' praise to God (v. 20).

The letter closing of Philippians winds down to an end with two additional epistolary conventions. First, final greetings from both Paul and others with him, especially those of Caesar's household, are passed on to all the saints in Philippi (vv. 21-22). Then, in typical fashion, a grace benediction serves to bring the letter to a definitive close (v. 23).

Thus the letter closing of Philippians exhibits the following outline:

vv. 8-9a	Hortatory Section	
v. 9b	Peace Benediction	
vv. 10-20	Joy Expression (Autograph)	
	v. 10	Joy Formula
	vv. 11-13	Explanation 1
	vv. 14-16	Explanation 2
	vv. 17-18	Explanation 3
	v. 19	Word of Encouragement
	v. 20	Doxology
vv. 21-22	Greetings	
v. 23	Grace Benediction	

c. *Thematic Analysis of the Letter Closing*

A comparison of the closing conventions found in Philippians with those appearing in Paul's other letters reveals the formal similarities that exist between the peace benediction (v. 9b), the greetings (vv. 21-22), and the grace benediction (v. 23) vis-à-vis those comparable epistolary conventions found in other Pauline letter closings. It does not appear that Paul has adapted these three closing conventions in Philippians in any significant manner. With regard to the two remaining epistolary conventions of the Philippian letter closing, however, it need be noted that they are unique in both form and content. And the distinctive character of the hortatory section (vv. 8-9a) and the joy expression (vv. 10-20) is significant for our purposes here, for a number of connections appear between material in both of these closing conventions and material found in the rest of the letter.

Proper Moral Conduct. The closing exhortations of 4.8-9a recall in a general way the letter's focus on proper moral conduct. For the six 'excellent' and 'praiseworthy' virtues listed in the first half of the closing hortatory section (4.8) all refer to ethical qualities and so reinforce Paul's opening challenge to the Philippians in the thanksgiving section that they be 'pure and blameless' (1.10) and 'filled with the fruit of righteousness' (1.11). Similarly, in the body of the letter, Paul exhorts his readers to be 'blameless and innocent, children of God without blemish in the midst of a crooked and perverse generation, among whom you shine as lights in the world' (2.15; see also 1.27; 4.2). The virtues listed in the closing hortatory section stand in sharp contrast to the vices of those responsible for destroying the unity and fellowship of the Philippian church: envy (1.15), rivalry (1.15), selfishness (1.17, 2.3, 21), insincerity (1.17, 18), conceit (2.3), and a preoccupation with earthly things (3.19).

Imitation Theme. Paul reinforces his emphasis on proper moral conduct that appears in the closing hortatory section by making use of the theme of imitation—which is, it should be observed, another important subject developed within the letter body. For after challenging his readers to think about the listed virtues (4.8), Paul then commands them to do the things that they have learned, received, heard and seen in his own life (4.9a, ἐν ἐμοί). So Paul clearly presents himself here in the letter's closing, as he did earlier in its body, as a model for the Philippians to imitate.[1]

This theme of imitation or modeling echoes Paul's earlier words of 3.17, 'Be fellow imitators of me, brothers, and mark those who thus live according to our example.' To encourage his readers to live a proper moral life, Paul holds up his own life and the lives of other faithful Christians as models for them to follow as they seek to live within a pagan world whose values differed radically from those who live as followers of Christ.

Another clear link between the theme of imitation in the closing exhortation and this same theme as expressed in the body of the letter can be seen in 1.30. For Paul's challenge in 4.9a to do what 'you have heard and seen in me' (ἠκούσατε καὶ εἴδετε ἐν ἐμοί) parallels in a striking way his earlier reminder to the Philippians that they are involved in the same suffering which 'you have seen in me and now have heard in me' (1.30, εἴδετε ἐν ἐμοὶ καὶ νῦν ἀκούετε ἐν ἐμοί). Paul uses his own experience of suffering for the sake of the gospel as an example to

---

1. A number of commentators have recognized that 4.9a ought to be seen as part of the imitation theme used earlier in the letter; see W. Michaelis, 'μιμέομαι', *TDNT*, IV, p. 668; W.P. de Boer, *The Imitation of Paul: An Exegetical Study* (Kampen: J.H. Kok, 1962), p. 187; Martin, *Philippians*, p. 173; Bruce, *Philippians*, p. 146; Silva, *Philippians*, p. 230; O'Brien, *Philippians*, pp. 507, 511.

encourage his readers who were also experiencing persecution for their faith. Similarly in 2.17-18, Paul's ability to rejoice even in the face of intense suffering serves as a model for the Philippians to follow.

The theme of imitation in the Philippian letter closing also recalls the important section of 2.1-11 where Paul uses Christ's life as a powerful example for the Philippians to emulate (2.5). In sharp contrast to the self-seeking and proud attitude that was causing division in the church, there stands the self-sacrificial and humble attitude of Christ, who gave up his rights of equal status with God in order to serve and save others. Likewise, Paul uses the sincere concern of Timothy (2.19-24) and the sacrificial actions of Epaphroditus (2.25-30) as positive examples to be imitated, in contrast to those false leaders in the church who 'look after their own interests, not those of Jesus Christ' (2.20-21).

Reaffirmation of Paul's Authoritative Status. One further noteworthy feature about the final hortatory section of 4.8-9a is the way Paul uses this closing convention to reaffirm, albeit in a subtle manner, his position of leadership and authority. For even though it is not explicitly stated, the close connection between 4.8 and 4.9a naturally leads to the conclusion that the six excellent and praiseworthy virtues are, in fact, those things that the Philippians have heard and seen in Paul's life. The closing hortatory section, therefore, reaffirms the authority of Paul and of his teachings in contrast to his opponents and their conflicting ideas that he has been addressing throughout the letter (1.15-18, 28; 2.1-4, 21; 3.2-11, 18-19). For just as the virtues in 4.8 (implied as belonging to Paul) ought to be seen in contrast to the vices of those causing trouble and division in the church, so also the example of Paul in 4.9a has in view, not only the exemplary moral life of the apostle, but also the contrast between himself and his opponents in Philippi. This can be seen, for example, in 3.17-19, which contrasts imitating Paul and other faithful leaders (3.17) with imitating certain false teachers or earthly-minded leaders (3.18-19). Paul's challenge to imitate him means, then, not simply, 'Do the things that I do', but also, 'Recognize my authority; follow what I say, not what my opponents say; be obedient to me'.[1]

The exhortations of the Philippian letter closing, therefore, focus on three interrelated topics: proper moral conduct, the theme of imitation, and the reaffirmation of the authoritative status of Paul in the Philippian

---

1. So Michaelis, 'μιμέομαι', p. 668; Hawthorne, *Philippians*, p. 161. For a contrary view, however, see de Boer, *Imitation of Paul*, pp. 184-87.

church in contrast to that of his opponents. In this way, the closing hortatory section of Philippians reflects a number of the central concerns previously addressed in the letter.

Likewise, the lengthy joy expression of the Philippian letter closing echoes a number of key themes found in the rest of the letter, particularly in the thanksgiving section (1.3-11). These themes center on the subjects of joy, fellowship, correct mental attitude, suffering, and humility.

Joy/Rejoicing. The first link between the joy expression of the Philippian letter closing and the rest of the letter can be seen in the theme of joy or rejoicing. The joy expression opens with the stereotyped formula: 'I rejoice (ἐχάρην) in the Lord greatly' (4.10). Paul's expression of joy for the Philippians' financial gift recalls the emphasis on joy evident already in the thanksgiving section where the phrase 'with joy' (1.4) has been added in a striking manner to the rather fixed form of this epistolary convention. It also echoes the jubilant note of joy (χαρά) and rejoicing (χαίρω) that rings out in this short letter no less than sixteen times (1.4, 18 [2×], 25; 2.2, 17 [2×], 18 [2×], 28, 29; 3.1; 4.1, 4 [2×], 10), far more than in any of Paul's other letters. The joy that Paul has for the Philippians' financial generosity (4.10-20) also reflects his earlier words of thanksgiving 'for all your remembrance of me' (1.3), which is a clear anticipatory reference to their monetary gift.[1]

Fellowship. A second important connection between the joy expression in the Philippian letter closing and earlier material in the letter has to do with the theme of fellowship or partnership (κοινωνέω).[2] This theme is prominent in the joy expression, for Paul praises the Philippians for 'having fellowship' (συγκοινωνήσαντες) with him in his trouble (4.14)

---

1.   Note particularly the extended discussion of O'Brien (*Introductory Thanksgivings*, pp. 41-46; also *Philippians*, pp. 59-61) in which he convincingly argues that the phrase ἐπὶ πάσῃ τῇ μνείᾳ ὑμῶν ought to be understood as a cause or ground of Paul's thanksgivings (and so translated 'for all your remembrance of me'), rather than as a temporal expression denoting the frequency with which Paul prayed (which would be translated 'on every remembrance of you'). So also Schubert, *Form and Function of the Pauline Thanksgivings*, p. 74; R. Jewett, 'The Epistolary Thanksgiving and the Integrity of Philippians', *NovT* 12 (1970), p. 53; Martin, *Philippians*, p. 47; Jervis, *Purpose of Romans*, p. 99. Note, however, the objections of Hawthorne, *Philippians*, pp. 16-17.

2.   See P T. O'Brien, 'The Fellowship Theme in Philippians', *RTR* 37 (1978), pp. 9-18.

and for 'entering into partnership' (ἐκοινώνησεν) with him from the very beginning of his preaching ministry (4.15). These references to fellowship echo the words in the thanksgiving section where Paul gives thanks to God for the Philippians' 'partnership (κοινωνίᾳ) in the gospel from the first day until now' (1.5) and for the fact that they are 'fellow partakers (συγκοινωνούς) with me of grace' (1.7). This theme of fellowship, which is so evident in the closing, also echoes passages in the body of the letter. For example, the concept of 'fellowship (κοινωνία) with the Spirit' (2.1) serves as the grounds for Paul's appeal that unity and humility ought to characterize relationships within the Philippian church. Or again, the Philippians' fellowship in Paul's suffering (4.14, συγκοινωνήσαντες) recalls Paul's fellowship in Christ's suffering (3.10, κοινωνίαν παθημάτων αὐτοῦ).

Correct Mental Attitude. A third link between the joy expression of the Philippian letter closing and the rest of the letter is the theme of a correct mental attitude, which is expressed by the use of the verb φρονέω. The importance of this theme in Philippians is suggested by the fact that φρονέω occurs a total of ten times in this brief letter, whereas it occurs only eleven times more in all of the remaining Pauline letters. The word occurs twice in the closing joy expression (4.10) in describing the Philippians' attitude to Paul expressed in their financial gift. Earlier the theme appears in the thanksgiving section where it refers to Paul's attitude to his Philippian readers (1.7). It also plays an important role in the body of the letter: first, in the discussion of the proper attitude of believers (2.2 [2×]) who should imitate the attitude of Christ (2.5); second, in the contrast between the right attitude of Paul and other like-minded believers with the wrong attitude of those causing trouble in the church (3.15 [2×], 19); and finally, in the problem of a hostile attitude that exists between two leading women of the congregation (4.2).

Suffering. In addition to the themes of joy, fellowship, and a correct mental attitude, there are a couple of less important, yet noteworthy, themes found in the closing joy expression of Philippians that also appear earlier in the letter. One of these is the theme of suffering or persecution for the gospel.[1] This theme appears in the closing joy expression in 4.14 where Paul praises his readers for sharing in 'my

---

1. See Jewett, 'Epistolary Thanksgivings', pp. 49-51; Russell, 'Pauline Letter Structure', p. 299.

trouble' (μου τῇ θλίψει)—almost certainly a reference to Paul's imprisonment and sufferings. Earlier in the letter this topic is mentioned briefly in the thanksgiving section (1.7) and then developed quite extensively in the first section of the letter body (1.12-30). Paul states that his imprisonment (1.13, 14, 17) has paradoxically served to advance, rather than hinder, the spread of the gospel. Furthermore, his suffering for the sake of Christ serves as a model for similar suffering currently being experienced by the Philippians (1.29-30). In fact, such suffering should be seen as sharing in the sufferings of Christ (3.10). Two further references to Paul's sufferings can be found in 2.17 and 3.8.

Humility. A final link between the joy expression of the Philippian letter closing and the rest of that letter has to do with the subject of humility.[1] This theme is primarily expressed by the use of the verb ταπεινόω, which is an uncommon word in Paul's letters generally but is found three times in the Philippian letter. In the closing joy expression Paul thanks his readers for their gift, but states that such generosity, while appreciated, is not required because he knows how to 'humble himself' (4.12, ταπεινοῦσθαι ἑαυτόν). The use of ταπεινόω here echoes the self-emptying theme of ch. 2 and, in particular, the humility of Christ (2.8, ἐταπείνωσεν).[2] In contrast to his opponents at Philippi who proudly revel in their 'confidence in the flesh' (3.4), Paul humbly rejects any boastful claims that he might make (3.4-11), making it clear that he does not consider himself to have obtained the final goal of salvation or to be already perfect (3.12-16). Instead, Paul humbly awaits the return of Christ 'who will change our lowly (ταπεινώσεως) body to be like his glorious body' (3.21).

A careful study of the letter closing of Philippians, therefore, reveals a series of striking continuities of subject matter and similarities of theme between this final section and the rest of the letter. The hortatory section (4.8-9a) recalls the letter's general concern for proper moral conduct and, more specifically, the theme of imitation. Similarly, the closing joy expression (4.10-20) echoes at least five important themes of the letter:

---

1. See T.E. Pollard, 'The Integrity of Philippians', *NTS* (1966–67), pp. 57-66, who calls attention to the 'kenosis' motif as a unifying strand in the Philippians letter. See also Jewett, 'Epistolary Thanksgiving', p. 52.

2. Hawthorne (*Philippians*, p. 199) states in regard to 4.12, 'There is also in this choice of ταπεινοῦσθαι an echo of the self-humbling of Christ already so poignantly described by the apostle (2.8) and with which he proudly associates himself'.

joy, fellowship, a correct mental attitude, suffering, and humility. Admittedly, the recapitulating function of the letter closing of Philippians is not as immediately apparent as it is in Galatians or 1 Thessalonians. Nevertheless, the cumulative effect of the many links that can be discovered between the letter closing and the rest of the letter is significant and amply supports the conclusion that Phil. 4.8-23 is no incidental appendix but is intimately related to the letter as a whole. The letter closing of Philippians, therefore, provides further evidence of Paul's practice of constructing the final epistolary sections of his letters in such a way that they echo the major themes and issues of their respective letters.

Furthermore, it need be noted that a recognition of the recapitulating function of the Philippian letter closing is important for both the issue of the letter's purposes and the question of its literary unity. In regard to the former, the letter closing of Philippians serves as an important aid for determining what are the central concerns of Paul in the letter as a whole: (1) to express his joy for the Philippians' financial generosity; (2) to reaffirm his fellowship with them and, more particularly, his authoritative status among them, thereby stemming the growing influence of his opponents; (3) to ensure that their lives are characterized by the kind of proper moral conduct and attitude that is in keeping with the example set by Paul and other church leaders; and (4) to encourage them in the suffering that they were experiencing for the sake of the gospel. These major themes of the letter body, many of which were foreshadowed in the thanksgiving section, are all summarized in the letter's closing.[1]

With regard to the issue of the letter's unity, the echoing function of the Philippian letter closing undermines the validity of those partition theories that claim to find in canonical Philippians two or three independent letters.[2] The fact that the letter closing recalls issues found

---

1. Schubert (*Form and Function*, pp. 74-77) was the first to recognize the close relationship in theme and vocabulary between Phil. 4.10-20 and the thanksgiving section of 1.3-11. See also R.C. Swift, 'The Theme and Structure of Philippians', *BSac* 141 (1984), pp. 249-50; Jervis, *Purpose of Romans*, pp. 144-47. In addition to the thematic and verbal connections between 4.10-20 and 1.3-11 listed above, two further links could be identified: (1) καρπός in 4.17 and 1.11 (see also 1.22), a word occurring only six times in all of Paul's other letters; and (2) ὁ θεός μου in 4.19 and 1.3, a rare expression in Paul's letters (Rom. 1.8; 1 Cor. 1.4 [?]; Phlm. 4).

2. For a discussion of the literary integrity of Philippians and the proposed theories of compilation, see the various introductions to the NT as well as the introductions found in the standard commentaries on Philippians. In addition, see M. Jones, 'The Integrity of the Epistle to the Philippians', *Expositor*, Series 8 (1914), pp. 457-

in all the major sections of Philippians provides strong evidence for the literary unity of this letter. Philippians, in fact, exhibits a more careful organization and greater cohesiveness than many commentators have commonly recognized.

5. *1 Corinthians*

a. *Extent of the Letter Closing*
There is a considerable degree of confusion among scholars as to the extent of the letter closing in 1 Corinthians, with a number of diverse starting points being proposed.[1] The epistolary evidence, however, makes it clear that the letter closing begins in 16.13. For the material prior to this point (16.12) belongs to the περὶ δέ units that constitute the body of the letter. But the material after this point contains closing exhortations (16.13-16) and a joy expression (16.17-18), which are both epistolary conventions that typically belong to the final sections of Paul's letters. Thus the letter closing of 1 Corinthians consists of 16.13-24.[2]

73; J. Müller-Bardorff, 'Zur Frage der literarischen Einheit des Philipperbriefes', *Wissenschaftliche Zeitschrift der Universität Jena* 7 (1957–58), pp. 591-604; B.D. Rahtjen, 'The Three Letters of Paul to the Philippians', *NTS* 6 (1959–60), pp. 167-73; V. Furnish, 'The Place and Purpose of Phil. III', *NTS* 10 (1962–63), pp. 80-88; G. Bornkamm, 'Der Philipperbrief als Paulinische Briefsammlung', in *Neotestamentica et Patristica: Eine Freundesgabe für O. Cullmann* (Leiden: Brill, 1962), pp. 192-202; Pollard, 'Integrity of Philippians', pp. 57-66; Jewett, 'Epistolary Thanksgiving', pp. 40-53; W.J. Dalton, 'The Integrity of Philippians', *Bib* 60 (1979), pp. 97-102; D. Cook, 'Stephanus Le Moyne and the Dissection of Philippians', *JTS* 32 (1981), pp. 138-42; C.J. Peifer, 'Three Letters in One', *BT* 23 (1985), pp. 363-68; Jervis, *Purpose of Romans*, pp. 65-68.

1. At least four different proposals as to the extent of the letter closing of 1 Corinthians have been made: (1) 16.1-24; so L. Morris, *The First Epistle of Paul to the Corinthians* (Grand Rapids: Eerdmans, 1958), pp. 236-49; (2) 16.5-24; so C.K. Barrett, *The First Epistle to the Corinthians* (New York: Harper & Row, 1968), pp. 388-99; Bruce, *1 and 2 Corinthians*, pp. 159-62; (3) 16.13-24; so H.A.W. Meyer, *Epistles to the Corinthians* (trans. D.D. Bannerman; London: Funk & Wagnalls, 1890), pp. 400-406; W.G.H. Simon, *The First Epistle to the Corinthians* (London: SCM Press, 1959), pp. 155-57; Fee, *Corinthians*, pp. 825-40; Jervis, *Purpose of Romans*, pp. 134, 142-43; (4) 16.19-24; so Robertson and Plummer, *Corinthians*, pp. 397-402; F.W. Grosheide, *The First Epistle to the Corinthians* (Grand Rapids: Eerdmans, 1953), pp. 405-406; H.-J. Klauk, *Korintherbrief* (Würzburg: Echter Verlag, 1984), pp. 126-27; Belleville, 'Continuity or Discontinuity', pp. 35-36.

2. Note also the parallel between the letter closings of the two extant Corinthian

b. *Structural Analysis of the Letter Closing*

The letter closing of 1 Corinthians contains most of the epistolary conventions commonly found in the final sections of Paul's letters. It lacks
only the peace benediction—whose absence, admittedly, is somewhat
surprising.[1] The letter closing opens with a hortatory section (vv. 13-16)
that can be divided into two parts: first, a series of five seriatim imperatives (vv. 13-14); and second, a παρακαλέω unit highlighting the
leadership position of Stephanas and his household (vv. 15-16). Then
there follows a joy expression (vv. 17-18) in which Paul expresses his
happiness at the arrival of Stephanas, Fortunatus and Achaicus, but also
exhorts his Corinthian readers to recognize the leadership of such men.

The third section of the letter closing contains final greetings (vv. 19-
21). Paul begins by passing on to the Corinthians greetings from three
different groups of people who are with him: first, all the churches of
Asia (v. 19a); second, Aquila and Prisca, along with their whole household (v. 19b); and finally, all the brothers (v. 20a). Paul next exhorts his
readers to greet one another with a holy kiss (v. 20b), and then takes
over from his secretary to greet them in his own hand (v. 21).

Before bringing the letter to a definitive close with a grace benediction, Paul gives an additional and rather sharp exhortation—a pattern
also found in the letter closing of 1 Thessalonians. This warning against
anyone who refuses to submit to Paul's apostolic teaching (v. 22) appears
to be a traditional curse formula that has been borrowed from the
liturgy of the early church, as is also the eschatological prayer μαράνα
θά ('Our Lord, come!').[2] After indicating the end of the letter by the
grace benediction (v. 23), Paul appends a postscript that assures the
Corinthians of his continued love for them (v. 24). The letter closing of
1 Corinthians, therefore, possesses the following outline:

letters: both begin with a series of five brief exhortations, all given in the present tense
(1 Cor. 16.13-14; 2 Cor. 13.11a).

1.   In light of the tensions that existed between Paul and many in the Corinthian
church, the presence of a peace benediction in the letter closing of 1 Corinthians
would have been most appropriate. Its absence should caution us against speaking of
any fixed number of closing conventions that had to be used by Paul in any given
letter.

2.   The traditional character of this verse is suggested by its non-Pauline
language. For elsewhere Paul uses the verb ἀγαπάω to express 'love' (but see Tit.
3.15). Also, in the similar formula found in Gal. 1.8, Paul has ἀνάθεμα ἔστω rather
than ἤτω ἀνάθεμα as found here. Finally, μαράνα θά is a *hapax legomenon* in
Paul's letters as well as in the rest of the NT.

vv. 13-16	Hortatory Section	
	vv. 13-14	Five seriatim imperatives
	vv. 15-16	παρακαλέω unit
vv. 17-18	Joy Expression	
vv. 19-21	Greetings	
	vv. 19-20a	Greetings
	v. 20b	Kiss Greeting
	v. 21	Autograph Greeting
v. 22	Hortatory Section	
	v. 22a	Curse formula
	v. 22b	Eschatological prayer formula
v. 23	Grace Benediction	
v. 24	Postscript: Word of Assurance	

c. *Thematic Analysis of the Letter Closing*

A comparison of 1 Cor. 16.13-24 with the final sections of Paul's other letters reveals a number of unique features of this particular letter closing. One distinctive feature of the letter closing of 1 Corinthians is its emphasis on the theme of love. The exhortation to 'let everything you do be done in love' (v. 14) is emphasized by virtue of its concluding position among the five seriatim imperatives as well as its distinctive form.[1] The theme of love in the letter closing also manifests itself in Paul's sharp warning that 'if someone does not love the Lord, let him be cursed' (v. 22). Finally, the focus on love reappears in the unparalleled postscriptive word of assurance: 'My love is with all of you in Christ Jesus' (v. 24).

The joy expression (vv. 17-18) in the letter closing of 1 Corinthians also possesses a somewhat unique form. For unlike the joy expressions in the closing of Philippians (4.10-20) and Romans (16.19b), which convey Paul's happiness to the churches for their actions (Philippians: their sending of financial gifts; Romans: their obedience), here the stereotyped formula conveys Paul's joy for the actions of certain members from the congregation (their arrival). Thus the joy expression, coupled with the preceding παρακαλέω section, function as commendations of Stephanas and the other leaders, as well as challenges to the Corinthians to submit to their leadership.

These rather unique features of the letter closing in 1 Corinthians (i.e.,

---

1. The last exhortation of v. 14 is formally set off from the preceding four imperatives of v. 13 in two ways: first, it is longer than the preceding exhortations; second, it is a third-person, singular command in contrast to the second-person, plural imperatives given in the previous verse.

Neglected Endings

stress on love, commendation of Stephanas and submission to his leadership) reflect the strained relations that existed between Paul and the Corinthian church.[1] For a careful reading of the letter's epistolary conventions, as well as its contents, reveals the fact of a growing conflict between Paul and his Corinthian converts. To be sure, the church at Corinth also experienced internal divisions. These internal tensions, however, ought to be seen as part of the larger conflict that some in the congregation had with Paul and those loyal to him and his teachings. Thus Paul faces two broad challenges in this letter: first, to reassert his authority in a situation where it had been severely eroded; second, to convince his readers to change their behavior and the errant theology underlying such behavior.[2]

The conflict between Paul and his Corinthian converts comes to the fore early in 1 Corinthians, even in the letter opening. For Paul begins the letter by stressing the divine origin of his apostolic position: 'Paul, called to be an apostle of Christ Jesus by the will of God' (1.2). Since the phrase 'by the will of God' is not normally included in the rather stereotyped description of himself that is typically given in his other letter openings,[3] its presence here reflects the tension that exists between Paul and the Corinthians.[4] Furthermore, when comparing the thanksgiving section of 1 Corinthians (1.4-9) with those of Paul's other letters, a number of matters—particularly with respect to omissions—stand out as suggesting strained relations between the writer and his readers.[5] First, the thanksgiving section omits any reference to Paul's constant remembrance or intercession for the church addressed. Second, it fails to mention any cause for thanks originating in the Corinthian church itself; instead, the reason for thanksgiving is exclusively rooted in God's grace given to them. Finally, it lacks the purpose clause with which Paul normally brings a thanksgiving section to a close and which

1. For a helpful reconstruction of the historical situation at Corinth and of the growing conflict that existed between Paul and his Corinthian converts, see Fee, *Corinthians*, pp. 5-15.

2. Fee, *Corinthians*, p. 7.

3. See 1 Thess. 1.1; 2 Thess 1.1; Phil. 1.1; Phlm. 1.

4. Note a similar elaboration in the letter opening of Galatians, another letter where the issue centers on the apostolic authority of Paul.

5. See Belleville, 'Continuity or Discontinuity', pp. 19-20; Jervis, *Purpose of Romans*, pp. 97-98. O'Brien (*Introductory Thanksgivings*, p. 134) notes that 'Paul was somewhat guarded in his statements in this introductory thanksgiving so that it does not have the warmth or intimacy found in the Philippian counterpart'.

reports what Paul prays for regarding his readers.

The tension between Paul and his converts, as foreshadowed in the letter opening and thanksgiving section of 1 Corinthians, becomes more explicit in the body of the letter. The first major unit of the letter body (chs. 1–4), where issues of greatest importance would be expected to appear,[1] constitutes Paul's defense of his own mission and authoritative status among the Corinthians, thereby ensuring that the counsel given in the remainder of the letter will be accepted and obeyed.[2] And throughout 1 Corinthians basic conflicts between Paul and his converts continue to be evident. In 1.10-12 and 3.2-9, for example, there are indications that some in the church were attempting to play Paul off against other leaders, such as Apollos. In fact, certain Corinthians had been sitting in judgment of the apostle (4.3), preferring Apollos over Paul (4.6). So Paul admonishes them, both by this letter but also by sending Timothy to remind them of *his* ways (4.14-17). Furthermore, Paul threatens to come to them with a rod and to rebuke the arrogant among them (4.18-21). Later in chapter nine he again gives a lengthy defense of himself 'to those who are judging me' (9.3). And later still, after sarcastically asking if the word of God originated only with them, he challenges the Corinthians to recognize that 'what I am writing to you is a command of the Lord' (14.37). Yet further evidence of tensions between Paul and his Corinthian converts can be seen in the apostle's barrage (10×) of pointedly elementary questions, 'Do you not know that...' (οὐκ οἴδατε ὅτι; see 3.16; 5.6; 6.2, 3, 9, 15, 16, 19; 9.13, 24) and his repeated use of sarcasm or irony (e.g., 4.8, 10; 11.22; 14.36) when describing the Corinthians.

The language of 1 Corinthians does not suggest a picture of a man who wants simply to inform his readers about their problematic practices or errant theological views. Rather, as Gordon Fee notes: 'Paul is on the attack, contending with them, arguing with them, trying to convince

1. J.C. Hurd (*The Origin of 1 Corinthians* [Macon, GA: Mercer University Press, 1983 (1965)] p. 96) comments, 'Certainly one would expect Paul to have taken up first the matters which were most important to him, so that the first chapters of 1 Corinthians should be the key to the interpretation of the whole letter'.

2. The apologetic nature of chs. 1–4 is highlighted and developed by N.A. Dahl, 'Paul and the Church at Corinth According to 1 Corinthians 1.10–4.21', in *Christian History and Interpretation: Studies Presented to John Knox* (ed. W.R. Farmer, C.F.D. Moule and R.R. Niebuhr; Cambridge: Cambridge University Press, 1967), pp. 313-35.

them that he is right and they are wrong.'[1] Thus both the epistolary conventions and the express statements of the letter reveal that a substantial degree of tension existed between Paul and his Corinthian converts. And such a view of things is confirmed by the materials contained in 2 Corinthians, most obviously by the reference to the 'painful' visit in 2.1 and the open hostility evident in chs. 10–13.

I have spent some time highlighting the tensions that existed between Paul and many of the believers at Corinth simply because such conflicts are crucial to an understanding of the letter closing of 1 Cor. 16.13-24. In fact, all of the distinctive features of this letter closing can be explained in light of these conflicts. For example, as noted above, the παρακαλέω section (vv. 15-16) along with the joy expression (vv. 17-18) function as commendations of Stephanas, apparently a leader in the Corinthian church who had been loyal to Paul. The apostle is concerned that the Corinthians submit to the authority of Stephanas and to the other leaders also loyal to Paul: 'I urge you to be subject to such men and to every fellow worker and laborer' (v. 16); 'Therefore recognize such men' (v. 17). So Paul structures his closing exhortation and joy expression in such a manner that they support a leadership at Corinth (Stephanas and others like him, who are loyal to Paul) that will enforce his teachings.

The closing greetings of 1 Corinthians must also be seen in light of tensions within the church and conflicts between Paul's converts and himself. For by sending greetings from 'the churches of Asia' (v. 19a), 'Aquila and Prisca' (v. 19b) and 'all the brothers' (v. 20), Paul accomplishes three things. First, he subtly increases his own authority and the weight of his letter by aligning himself with a former leading family in the Corinthian church (Aquila and Prisca) and with the churches from the whole province of Asia.[2] Second, he stresses that these converts at Corinth are not a group unto themselves but belong to a much larger family of believers to whom they are accountable. Here, in fact, Paul's words echo an issue (i.e., that Corinthian believers belong to the wider church) that had been raised earlier in the letter opening (1.2, 'To the church of God in Corinth...called to be saints together with all those who in every place call on the name of our Lord Jesus Christ, both their Lord and ours') and that he developed throughout the entire letter body

1. Fee, *Corinthians*, p. 10.
2. This is the only occurrence in Paul's letters where he sends greetings from all the churches of a province.

(4.17; 7.7; 10.32; 11.16; 14.33, 36; 16.1). Finally, by making reference in the closing greetings to 'the churches of Asia', 'Aquila and Prisca', and 'all the brothers', Paul exerts further pressure on the Corinthians to submit to his apostolic authority and to obey his letter. For Paul implies that a large number of churches and Christians are aware of the problems in Corinth and join him in awaiting a resolution of these matters.

Conflicts between Paul and the Corinthian church likewise explain the presence of the kiss greeting (v. 20b). For this closing convention, which regularly appears in letters addressed to tension-filled churches, serves as Paul's challenge to his Corinthian converts to restore peace and harmony both within the church and with him. The tensions between Paul and the Corinthians also suggest that the primary purpose of the autograph greeting (v. 21) was not to testify to the Pauline authorship of the letter,[1] but rather to emphasize the authority of the letter and the need for its contents to be obeyed—as the autographs of Gal. 6.11 and 2 Thess. 3.17 also function.[2] Somewhat similarly, the curse formula in the following verse (v. 22, 'If someone does not love the Lord, let him be accursed!') also stresses the authority of Paul's letter. For a rejection of Paul and his message is tantamount to a rejection of the Lord and the placement of oneself under judgment.

Finally, strained relations between Paul and his converts must also be seen as a factor in explaining the strong emphasis in the letter closing of 1 Corinthians on the theme of love. The command to 'let everything you do be done in love' (v. 14) is Paul's challenge to the Corinthians to let love control everything they do, particularly their relations with each other and with him. As for himself, Paul is eager to apply that command to his own relations with them, as evidenced in the postscriptive word of assurance: 'My love is with you *all* in Christ Jesus' (v. 24). By emphasizing in the letter closing the importance of mutual love, Paul hopes to strengthen the bond between himself and all the Corinthians.

This study of 1 Cor. 16.13-24 indicates that it would be too much to claim that this letter closing has a recapitulating function. Nevertheless, the evidence does show that the closing conventions of this letter reflect

---

1. So virtually all commentators: e.g., Robertson and Plummer, *Corinthians*, pp. 399-400; Grosheide, *Corinthians*, pp. 405-406; Morris, *Corinthians*, p. 247; Barrett, *First Corinthians*, p. 396; Bruce, *Corinthians*, p. 161.

2. See Fee (*Corinthians*, p. 837), who is one of few who rightly notes that Paul's reason for giving the greeting in his own hand 'is related to the questioning of his authority by some in this church'.

the tensions that existed between Paul and certain of his Corinthian converts—tensions that are evident throughout the rest of the letter. It need be recognized that in the letter closing of 1 Corinthians Paul has adapted and shaped the closing epistolary conventions of his day so that the final section better addresses his primary concern of reasserting his authority within the Corinthian church, thereby making it possible to change his converts' improper conduct and errant theology. The letter closing of 1 Corinthians, therefore, plays an important role in helping us better understand the historical context in which the letter was sent and received. More specifically, it sharpens our awareness of the conflicts that existed between Paul and his Corinthian readers.

6. 2 Corinthians

a. *Extent of the Letter Closing*
The transition from the body of 2 Corinthians to its closing seems to be clearly indicated by the phrase λοιπόν, ἀδελφοί of 13.11. For this expression typically serves in Paul's letters to introduce a closing hortatory section. Paul ends 2 Corinthians, it appears, in the same manner as he ended 1 Corinthians, namely, by beginning the closing with a hortatory section containing five seriatim imperatives, all given in the present tense (see 1 Cor. 16.13-14). The closing of 2 Corinthians, therefore, is best seen as consisting of 13.11-13.

Gordon Bahr, however, argues for a greatly expanded closing of 2 Corinthians that begins at 10.1.[1] Bahr maintains that Paul took over from his secretary after 9.15, and that the whole of chs. 10–13 ought to be viewed as a summary subscription written in the apostle's own hand. This proposal basically repeats the argument of William Bates, who claimed that chs. 10–13 are an autograph 'recapitulation' of the previous material in chs. 1–9.[2] A number of scholars, in fact, have adopted this view as a solution to the literary problems surrounding 2 Corinthians.[3]

1.   See Bahr, 'Subscriptions', pp. 37-38.
2.   See Bates, 'Integrity of II Corinthians', pp. 56-59. Bahr does not appear to be aware of Bates' article.
3.   In addition to Bates and Bahr, so also Meyer, *Korinther*, p. 183; Deissmann, *Light from Ancient East*, pp. 153, 167 n. 7; Holtzmann, *Das Neue Testament*, II, p. 717; Dibelius, *Fresh Approach to the NT*, p. 157; P. Feine and J. Behm, *Einleitung in das Neue Testament* (Heidelberg: Quelle & Meyer, 1963), p. 215; Richards, *Secretary*, pp. 180-81, 190.

That chs. 10–13 constitute an autograph closing of 2 Corinthians is a legitimate proposal and should not be immediately dismissed as impossible.[1] But as suggestive as this view is, it lacks the kind of explicit support in the text needed to warrant the inclusion of material belonging to chs. 10–13 in the letter closing. It seems best, therefore, to limit the closing of 2 Corinthians to 13.11-13.

b. *Structural Analysis of the Letter Closing*
The letter closing of 2 Corinthians contains all four of the epistolary conventions regularly found in the closings of Paul's other letters. The final section of 2 Corinthians begins with a hortatory section (v. 11a) introduced in typical fashion with the adverb λοιπόν ('finally') and the vocative ἀδελφοί ('brothers'). Paul lists in seriatim fashion five imperatives that all deal in one way or another with the problem of division in the Corinthian church. Next there follows a peace benediction (v. 11b) that is introduced by καί instead of δέ, thereby linking the wish more closely with the exhortations that precede it. After the peace benediction come the final greetings (v. 12) of which there are two: the first is a command to greet others with a holy kiss; the second involves the passing on of greetings to the Corinthians from 'all the saints'. The letter closing ends in expected fashion with a grace benediction (v. 13).

The letter closing of 2 Corinthians, therefore, exhibits the following outline:

v. 11a	Hortatory Section
v. 11b	Peace Benediction
v. 12	Greetings
	v. 12a Kiss greeting
	v. 12b Third-person greeting
v. 13	Grace Benediction

c. *Thematic Analysis of the Letter Closing*
A comparison of the closing conventions of 2 Corinthians with those found in Paul's other letter closings reveals unique formal features in the peace benediction of 13.11b and the grace benediction of 13.13. The peace benediction of 2 Corinthians is the only instance in Paul's use of this closing formula where an extra qualifying genitive ('of love') is added. Thus, instead of the expected 'And the God of peace will be with

---

1. See above, pp. 125-26; also Richards, *Secretary*, pp. 180-81, who cites parallels from Cicero's letters.

you,' 13.11b reads: 'And the God of love and peace will be with you.' Similarly, the grace benediction, which elsewhere in Paul's letters exhibits a strikingly consistent pattern, occurs in 2 Corinthians with two additional wishes ('love' and 'fellowship') and their corresponding divine sources ('of God' and 'of the Holy Spirit'). So in place of the near uniform expression 'The grace of the Lord Jesus Christ be with you,' 13.13 reads: 'The grace of the Lord Jesus Christ and the love of God and the fellowship of the Holy Spirit be with you all.' One further distinctive feature about this particular grace benediction is the addition of πάντων ('all') to the recipient of the wish.

The significance of these expansions in the closing peace and grace benedictions of 2 Corinthians comes to the fore when it is realized that such additions cause the two benedictions to be more directly related to the primary issue addressed in that letter, namely, peace and harmony that ought to exist within the church at Corinth. For even though the two remaining closing conventions of 2 Corinthians—the hortatory section and the greetings—are formally similar to comparable conventions found in Paul's other letters, they also are intimately connected with the theme of unity. In fact, every one of the closing conventions of 2 Corinthians has been written and/or adapted in such a way as to relate directly to the primary issue dealt with in this particular letter.

The connection between the letter closing and the problem of division addressed in the rest of 2 Corinthians, particularly in chs. 10–13, can be seen in the hortatory section: 'Finally, brothers, rejoice, aim for restoration, encourage one another, be of the same mind, live in peace' (13.11a). The use of ἀδελφοί, although a characteristic feature in the Pauline closing hortatory sections, suggests that Paul in this letter closing seeks to re-establish relations with the Corinthians after his harsh words of the previous chapters (the term 'brothers' is not used in chs. 10–13 but only at 1.8 and 8.1).[1]

The first imperative, 'rejoice' (χαίρετε),[2] recalls not only Paul's

---

1.   Furnish (*2 Corinthians*, p. 581): 'It [the vocative "brothers"] functions to accentuate the following admonitions by stressing the writer's solidarity with his readers'.

2.   Several translations and scholars do not adopt the literal meaning of χαίρειν ('to rejoice') but translate it as 'farewell' (so KJV; RSV; NIV; NEB; Plummer, *2 Corinthians*, p. 380; Barrett, *2 Corinthians*, p. 342). In support of the translation 'rejoice', at least three factors can be cited: (1) the fact that χαίρετε is given as part of a series of imperatives suggests that it has an imperatival sense along with the four exhortations that follow; (2) the same verb has just been used two verses earlier in

words of 13.9 where he rejoices in the anticipation that the Corinthians will be strong in their faith in answer to his prayers, but also Paul's joy for them expressed elsewhere in the letter (1.24; 2.3; 6.10; 7.4, 7, 9, 13, 16 [8.2]). The second imperative, 'aim for restoration' (καταρτίζεσθε),[1] echoes in an explicit manner Paul's prayer of 13.9 for the restoration (κατάρτισιν) of the Corinthians. The third imperative, 'encourage one another' (παρακαλεῖσθε),[2] recalls in a more general manner the opening exhortation of 10.1, a key transitional verse in the letter.[3] The fourth and fifth imperatives, 'be of the same mind' and 'live in peace', serve with the three preceding exhortations to reflect as well the problem of disunity and disharmony within the Corinthian church that Paul has been addressing, specifically his concern that there exists among his Corinthian readers 'quarreling, jealousy, anger, selfishness, slander, gossip, conceit and disorder' (12.20). It is not surprising, therefore, that a number of scholars have commented on the summary character or recapitulating function of these closing commands in 2 Corinthians.[4]

13.9 with the meaning of 'rejoice'; and (3) in 1 Thess. 5.16, where the same imperatival form of this verb heads a series of commands, it can only mean 'to rejoice'. So Hughes, *2 Corinthians*, p. 486; Bultmann, *2 Corinthians*, p. 249; Furnish, *2 Corinthians*, p. 581; Martin, *2 Corinthians*, pp. 490, 498.

1. The form καταρτίζεσθε can be either middle or passive. The latter can be translated as 'be restored' (so H. Windisch, *Der zweite Korintherbrief* [Göttingen: Vandenhoeck & Ruprecht, 1924], p. 426; Furnish, *2 Corinthians*, p. 581), while the former can be rendered as 'aim for restoration' (so Martin, *2 Corinthians*, pp. 490-91, 499), 'mend your ways' (so RSV; NEB), 'set one another right' (J. Héring, *The Second Epistle of Saint Paul to the Corinthians* [trans. A.W. Heathcote and P.J. Allcock; London: Epworth, 1967], pp. 102-103), or the rather colloquial 'pull yourselves together' (so Barrett, *2 Corinthians*, p. 342).

2. As with the previous imperative, so also here with παρακαλεῖσθε the form can be either middle or passive. The passive could be translated as 'accept my appeal' (so RSV; NIV; NEB; Plummer, *2 Corinthians*, p. 380; Hughes, *2 Corinthians*, p. 487; 'pay attention to my appeals', Furnish, *2 Corinthians*, p. 582), while the middle can be rendered as 'encourage one another' (so Barrett, *2 Corinthians*, p. 342; Bultmann, *2 Corinthians*, p. 252; Bruce, *1 & 2 Corinthians*, pp. 254-55; Martin, *2 Corinthians*, p. 491).

3. Furnish (*2 Corinthians*, p. 585) states that this third exhortation 'looks back especially to 10.1-6 and 12.19–13.10'.

4. E.g., Menzies (*2 Corinthians*, p. 104): 'He [Paul] gathers up the main points of what he has urged on them'; Plummer (*2 Corinthians*, p. 379): 'There are fairly conspicuous links between these concluding verses and those which immediately precede them'; Fisher (*1 & 2 Corinthians*, p. 445): 'The conclusion of this letter fits the letter itself. There is a final appeal (v. 11) which reflects the troubles in Corinth';

The intimate connection between the letter closing of 2 Corinthians and the rest of that letter can also be seen in the peace benediction: 'And the God of love and peace will be with you' (13.11b). As noted above, this peace benediction is the only instance in Paul's use of this closing formula where the extra qualifying genitive 'of love' is added. This addition ought not to be regarded as merely a fortuitous expansion. For in light of the five preceding imperatives, as well as Paul's earlier exhortations against quarreling, anger, disorder, and a spirit of superiority towards others that existed among the Corinthians (see esp. 12.20), it can hardly be doubted that 'love' has been deliberately added by Paul to the peace benediction so that this closing formula better echoes and reinforces the letter's appeal for love and harmony to characterize relations within this fractious church.

Paul's concern to make the letter closing of 2 Corinthians directly relevant to the specific historical situation of the Corinthian church can also be seen in his final two greetings. For by exhorting his readers to 'Greet one another with a holy kiss' (13.12a), Paul challenges believers at Corinth to greet each other in a manner that publicly testifies to the love and unity that they ought to have with others in their church. The kiss greeting of 2 Corinthians, therefore, serves to echo Paul's concern of the previous verses, as well as that of the whole letter, for unity and peace to prevail in this congregation.[1]

The second greeting in the closing of 2 Corinthians ('All the saints greet you' [13.12b]) is also significant. For by speaking so broadly on behalf of 'all the saints',[2] Paul alludes to his own apostolic authority and, thus, indirectly to the obligation that the Corinthians have to obey his exhortations in the letter. Additionally, the reference to 'all the saints'

Fallon (*2 Corinthians*, p. 115): 'Paul enters into his final exhortations, which sum up his concerns in the preceding chapters and the needs of the community'; Carson (*From Triumphalism to Maturity*, p. 183): '2 Corinthians 13.11 casts a backward glance at the rest of the epistle'; Furnish (*2 Corinthians*, p. 585): 'There are several significant links between v. 11 and the letter of chaps. 10–13'.

1.   *Contra* Best (*2 Corinthians*, p. 136), who claims that 'this [the kiss greeting] is not a deliberate attempt to counter disputations'. Compare Martin (*2 Corinthians*, p. 501), who correctly notes: 'Paul now turns to the theme of greeting, but in doing so he does not leave behind the theme of peace and harmony discussed in 13.11. To salute one with a holy kiss continues the themes of 13.11.'

2.   With the exception of Rom. 16.16b ('All the churches of Christ greet you'), this is the broadest group of people for whom Paul speaks in his third-person greetings.

reminds the Corinthians that they are not an independent group accountable only to themselves, but that they belong to a larger body, namely
the universal church.[1] This, too, would provide external pressure on the
Corinthians to accede to Paul's appeal in his letter for love and unity to
characterize their relations with each other. For Paul makes it clear that
other believers are also aware of the conflict in Corinth and support him
in awaiting its resolution.

The greeting from 'all the saints', therefore, like the kiss greeting
before it, is intimately linked to Paul's appeal in 2 Corinthians for unity.
As Ralph Martin notes in his discussion of the greeting of 13.12b: 'The
important thing to remember here is that Paul is calling for unity. Just as
the holy kiss was an "epistolary greeting" that signified unity, so was
the greeting from other "saints".'[2]

The close connection between the closing of 2 Corinthians and the
rest of the letter can be further seen in the grace benediction: 'The grace
of the Lord Jesus Christ and the love of God and the fellowship of the
Holy Spirit be with you all' (13.13). This closing formula in 2 Corinthians
is distinguished from all other Pauline grace benedictions by virtue of its
two additional wishes ('love' and 'fellowship') and their two corresponding divine sources ('of God' and 'of the Holy Spirit'). These supplementary wishes of 'love' and 'fellowship' fit the thrust of the entire
letter closing of 2 Corinthians, and, in turn, echo the concern of the
entire letter—namely, that peace and harmony must exist within the
Corinthian church. In addition to the grace that they receive from Christ,
believers in Corinth also experience love from God and the unity of
fellowship with other believers from the Holy Spirit.[3] So as in the peace

1. Carson (*From Triumphalism to Maturity*, p. 185) similarly notes, 'The
sentence "All the saints send their greetings"…is therefore more than courtesy: it is
a healthy reminder to all believers from the Corinthians on to see themselves as part,
but only part, of the entire body of Christ'. This idea also plays an important part in
the closing of 1 Corinthians (16.20) as well as in the letter opening (1.2) and the
entire letter body (4.17; 7.7; 10.32; 11.16; 14.33, 36; 16.1). See above, pp. 206-207.

2. Martin, *2 Corinthians*, p. 503.

3. Virtually all scholars are agreed in taking the first two phrases ('the grace of
the Lord Jesus Christ' and 'the love of God') as subjective genitives. There is much
disagreement, however, over whether the third phrase ('the fellowship of the Holy
Spirit') is subjective (the fellowship with other believers brought about by the Holy
Spirit: so, e.g., Plummer, *2 Corinthians*, pp. 383-84; Bruce, *1 & 2 Corinthians*,
p. 255; Martin, *2 Corinthians*, pp. 504-505), objective (the fellowship or participation
of a believer in the person of the Holy Spirit: so, e.g., H. Seesemann, *Der Begriff*

benediction of 13.11b, here also in the grace benediction Paul's concern to make the letter closing more relevant to the major theme of the Corinthian letter has resulted in the deliberate expansion of a closing epistolary convention.[1]

The letter closing of 2 Corinthians, therefore, is entirely appropriate to the concerns raised in the letter as a whole, particularly those of chs. 10–13.[2] For every one of the closing conventions of this letter has been

KOINONIA im Neuen Testament [Giessen: Töpelmann, 1933], pp. 62-72; Windisch, *Korintherbrief*, p. 428; Schweizer, 'πνεῦμα', p. 434; K. Prümm, *Diakonia Pneumatos. Der 2 Korintherbrief als Zugang zur apostolischen Botschaft* [2 vols.; Freiburg: Herder, 1960–67], I, pp. 730-33; Furnish, *2 Corinthians*, p. 584) or both (so M. McDermott, 'The Biblical Doctrine of κοινωνία', *BZ* 19 [1975], pp. 223-24; B. Schneider, 'HE KOINONIA TOU HAGIOU PNEUMATOS (II Cor. 13,13)', in *Studies Honoring Ignatius Charles Brady Friar Minor* (ed. R.S. Almagno and C.L. Harkins; St. Bonaventure, NY: Franciscan Institute, 1976], pp. 422, 436-47). Since the first two phrases use a subjective genitive, and a similar reading of the third phrase fits well with the rest of the closing which emphasizes peace and unity within the Corinthian church, it would seem best to take 'the fellowship of the Holy Spirit' as a subjective genitive (although, as several scholars observe, fellowship with others brought about by the Holy Spirit would have to mean, also, a participation in the Holy Spirit).

1. It is important to note also the addition of πάντων ('all') to the benediction, by which Paul stresses that his closing wish is intended for *all* his readers, including those whom he rebuked earlier in the letter (so Plummer, *Corinthians*, p. 384; Fisher, *1 & 2 Corinthians*, p. 446; Martin, *2 Corinthians*, pp. 496, 506). There is no need to postulate that this expanded grace benediction stems from the hand of a final redactor of 2 Corinthians (so Barrett, *2 Corinthians*, pp. 341, 343) or of the entire Pauline corpus (so E.J. Goodspeed, *Problems of New Testament Translation* [Chicago: University of Chicago Press, 1945], p. 57). Instead, as this thesis has demonstrated, it is entirely in keeping with Paul's practice in his other letter closings for him to have expanded this grace benediction in 2 Corinthians so that it better relates to the major concern of the letter as a whole.

2. The letter closing of 2 Corinthians does not appear to provide a conclusive answer to the important question surrounding the literary integrity of this letter. As indicated in our discussion of 2 Cor. 13.11-13, there are several strong links between the letter closing and the material in chs. 10–13. Nevertheless, the letter closing also has a number of connections with chs. 1–9 that are not found in chs. 10–13. For example, the noun ἀγάπη ('love') in the closing (note the two significant additions of 'love' in the peace and grace benedictions) is found throughout the opening chapters (2.4, 8; 5.14; 6.6; 8.7, 8, 24; see 9.7) but not at all in chs. 10–13 (but see verbal form in 11.11 and 12.15). The same thing is true for another important word in the closing, κοινωνία ('fellowship') and its cognate κοινωνός (1.7; 6.14; 8.4, 23; 9.13). Similarly, the vocative ἀδελφοί with which the letter closing begins does not occur in

written and/or adapted in such a way that it relates directly to Paul's preoccupation in the letter for his Corinthian converts to reject the divisive influence of his opponents and to restore peace and harmony both within the church and with him. 2 Cor. 13.11-13, in fact, provides further evidence of Paul's concern to construct letter closings that recapitulate and reinforce the key theme(s) previously raised in their respective letter bodies.

7. *Romans*

a. *Extent of the Letter Closing*

Determining the extent of the letter closing in Romans involves, of course, a decision concerning the integrity of Romans 16. It is not my intent to engage in a detailed study of this vexing problem, for such an inquiry would take us well beyond my specific interest in Paul's letter closings and how they function in his letters. Furthermore, the issues surrounding the textual unity of ch. 16 have already been examined at length by others.[1] Consequently, the following discussion is meant only to be descriptive and allusive in character.

The problem centers on the authenticity of three sections in the final chapter of Romans: the commendation, greetings, and exhortation of 16.1-23; the grace benediction of 16.24; and the doxology of 16.25-27. The lengthy section of 16.1-23 has proven problematic to numerous scholars for many of the following reasons: (1) the benediction of 15.33 is seen to mark the definitive close of the original Roman letter so that the subsequent material in ch. 16 is taken to belong to a separate letter; (2) the commendation of Phoebe in 16.1-2 is claimed to mark the beginning of a separate letter, since letters of commendation were typically brief, independent letters, and are not commonly found in the closing sections of existing letters;[2] (3) the long list of greetings in 16.3-16 is difficult to reconcile with the fact that Paul had never visited Rome; (4) the reference to Prisca and Aquila in 16.3 as being at Rome

---

chs. 10–13 but only in chs. 1-9 (1.8; 8.1). Given the fact that 2 Cor. 13.11-13 has verbal and thematic links with the *whole* of the letter, it would be precarious to appeal to the letter closing for further support against the literary unity of 2 Corinthians.

1. See esp. Gamble, *Textual History*, as well as others cited in the following discussion.

2. See Deissmann, *Light from Ancient East*, pp. 171, 235; Goodspeed, 'Phoebe's Letter of Introduction', pp. 55-57; McDonald, 'Was Romans XVI a Separate Letter?', pp. 369-72.

conflicts with other NT references that place this couple at Ephesus
(1 Cor. 16.19; see Acts 18.18-19, 26); (5) the reference to Epaenetus in
16.5 as being at Rome does not agree with Paul's description of him as
'the first convert in Asia'; and (6) the harsh rebuke in 16.17-20 seems
unlikely after the diplomatic and balanced tone of Paul in 12.1–15.13.

Such perceived difficulties have led many to accept an 'Ephesian
hypothesis', that is, that Romans 16 is a fragment of a genuine Pauline
letter originally directed to the church at Ephesus.[1] This hypothesis, in
fact, has become for many a certain reality.[2] Günter Klein, for example,
states, 'The Ephesian destination of 16.1-20 can hardly be disputed'.[3]

Yet despite such seeming unanimity, a reasonable response can be
given to each of the objections raised above.[4] (1) The peace benediction
never appears as the final element in Paul's letters but typically occupies
the first position in a closing section. (2) The commendation of a third
party in the closing section has parallels in both Greek and Latin letters
of the day.[5] (3) The long list of greetings is especially appropriate to the
Romans letter, for these greetings contain laudatory phrases that
emphasize positive relations between the person greeted and Paul,
thereby bolstering the apostle's credibility among the believers in Rome
who do not know him personally. (4) The death of Claudius in AD 54,
which ended his edict expelling Jews from Rome, would allow Prisca
and Aquila to return to their home city and church. (5) The reference to

---

1. The 'Ephesian hypothesis' was first proposed by D. Schulz, *TSK* 2 (1829),
pp. 609ff.

2. E.g., T.W. Manson, 'St. Paul's Letter to the Romans—and Others', *BJRL* 31
(1948), pp. 224-45 (reprinted in *The Romans Debate: Revised and Expanded Edition*
[ed. K.P. Donfried; Peabody: Hendrikson, 1991 (1971)], pp. 3-15); J. Kinoshita,
'Romans—Two Writings Combined', *NovT* 13 (1964–65), pp. 258-77; M.J. Suggs,
'"The Word is Near You": Romans 10.6-10 Within the Purpose of the Letter', in
Christian History and Interpretation: Studies Presented to John Knox (ed.
W.R. Farmer *et al.*; Cambridge: Cambridge University Press, 1967), pp. 289-312;
Fitzmyer, 'The Letter to the Romans', pp. 292-93; W. Marxen, *Introduction to the
New Testament* (trans. G. Buswell; Philadelphia: Fortress, 1968), pp. 107-108;
G. Bornkamm, *Paul* (trans. D.M.G. Stalker; New York: Harper & Row, 1971),
pp. 79-80, 247; W. Schmithals, *Der Römerbrief* (Gütersloh: Mohn, 1988), pp. 543-
65; F. Fefoulé, 'A contre-courant: Romains 16,3-16', *RHPR* 70 (1990), pp. 409-20;
C.F. Whelan, 'Amica Pauli: The Role of Pheobe in the Early Church', *JSNT* 49
(1993), pp. 67-85, esp. 72-73.

3. G. Klein, 'Romans, Letter to the', *IDBSup*, p. 752.

4. See esp. Gamble, *Textual History*, pp. 36-55.

5. See examples cited by Gamble, *Textual History*, pp. 84-87.

Epaenetus and his special status in Asia is more natural in a letter to Rome than to Ephesus, where his status would be known. And (6) the exhortation of 16.17-20 can be viewed as an autograph summary of the issues raised in the previous chapters pertaining to the 'weak' and the 'strong' (14.1–15.13), so that there is nothing substantially new or inherently anomalous about this passage.[1]

None of the claimed difficulties with the final chapter of Romans, therefore, is without a legitimate response. So it would seem more prudent to accept the text at face value and side with tradition than to adopt the view of an Ephesian destination for 16.1-23. For even though the textual history of the letter is complex, 'it requires', as James Dunn points out, 'no detailed analysis to argue the greater likelihood of Paul's letter to Rome being copied in an abbreviated form than of Paul himself writing more than one version with chap. 16 appended to the version to Ephesus'.[2] I concur with the recent consensus, therefore, which accepts 16.1-23 as part of the original letter to Rome.[3]

Regarding the integrity of the grace benediction of 16.24, although this closing convention is variously attested in three different positions (16.20b, 16.24, 16.28), scholars are almost unanimous in rejecting 16.24 and 16.28 as being secondary additions and accepting 16.20b as original. Gamble, however, argues that the grace benediction of 16.24 should also 'be judged an original reading'.[4] In addition to those textual witnesses that contain the grace benediction in both 16.20b and 16.24, Gamble appeals to the phenomenon of a double occurrence of a farewell wish in Hellenistic letters where, after closing the letter with a first farewell wish, the author takes over from his secretary to write personally a final greeting or command and then to close this autograph section with a second farewell wish. By analogy, Gamble proposes that Paul wrote

---

1. See Donfried, 'A Short Note on Romans 16', p. 449; Achtemeier, *Romans*, pp. 238-39.

2. Dunn, *Romans*, p. lx.

3 . A.J.M. Wedderburn (*The Reasons for Romans* [Minneapolis: Fortress, 1988], p. 13), for example, observes that 'the pendulum of scholarly opinion now seems to have swung back towards the view that this chapter was part of the letter to Rome.' Donfried (*The Romans Debate*, p. lxx) likewise states: 'An especially significant shift has occurred with regard to the understanding of Romans 16, which is now viewed by the majority as being an integral part of Paul's original letter.'

4. Gamble, *Textual History*, p. 130. For an earlier defense of the genuineness of this verse, see T.B. Zahn, *Introduction to the New Testament* (3 vols.; Edinburgh: T. & T. Clark, 1909), I, pp. 408-410.

16.1-20 in his own hand and closes this autograph section (vv. 1-20a) with the grace benediction of v. 20b, and that then some postscriptive greetings (vv. 21-23) were added by his secretary, Tertius—thereby requiring the closing of this section with another grace benediction in v. 24.[1]

Gamble's proposal for the originality of v. 24 is suggestive and deserves more careful consideration than it has typically received. But despite his appealing reconstruction of how the text tradition might have come to furnish two grace benedictions at the closing of Romans, it does not ultimately prove to be convincing. First and foremost, the textual evidence supporting the double occurrence of a grace benediction in both v. 20b and v. 24 is late and limited to miniscules; no major papyrus or uncial texts can be cited in support. Second, Gamble's explanation that v. 24 was later omitted in most MSS because, with the secondary addition of the doxology in 16.25-27, 'there were too many concluding elements', is not persuasive. For if this were, in fact, the case, would not the grace benediction of v. 20b also be omitted? Third, the claimed parallel between Romans and Hellenistic letters that close with a double farewell wish is not exact. For in the Hellenistic letters, the first farewell wish is always written by the secretary and the second by the author, whereas in Paul's letter to the Romans this order is, according to Gamble's reconstruction, reversed. It seems best, therefore, not to include the grace benediction of v. 24 as part of the original letter closing of Paul's letter to the Romans.

The authenticity of 16.25-27 has been, of course, even more hotly contested, both on textual and on literary grounds. The MSS show at least five different ways of placing this so-called 'wandering doxology': after 14.23, after 15.33, after 16.23, after both 14.23 and 16.23, or omitted altogether. Also the language and style of the doxology have been claimed by many to be unPauline. So 16.25-27 is widely viewed as a secondary addition,[2] perhaps originating with Marcion.[3]

1. Gamble, *Textual History*, p. 132. Gamble's proposal has been adopted by Jervis, *Purpose of Romans*, pp. 138-39.

2. E.g., Gamble, *Textual History*, pp. 122-24; E. Best, *The Letter of Paul to the Romans* (Cambridge: Cambridge University Press, 1967), pp. 177-78; C.E.B. Cranfield, *A Critical and Exegetical Commentary on the Epistle to the Romans* (2 vols.; Edinburgh: T. & T. Clark, 1975, 1979), pp. 808-809; E. Käsemann, *Commentary on Romans* (trans. G.W. Bromiley; Grand Rapids: Eerdmans, 1980), pp. 409, 422-23; J.K. Elliott, 'The Language and Style of the Concluding Doxology to the Epistle to the Romans', *ZNW* 72 (1981), pp. 124-30; P. Lampe, 'Zur

There are, however, some scholars who still defend the authenticity of this passage on the grounds that its language, style, and themes are, in fact, consistent with the rest of the letter.[1] Indeed, my examination of 16.25-27 in Chapter 4 has highlighted the fact of the summary character of this doxology in echoing central concerns that were raised in the letter as a whole, particularly in Romans 15. So while fully recognizing the problems having to do with its authenticity, I have elected to include 16.25-27 in this study of the Roman letter closing, largely because of its potential significance for this thesis. In fact, I believe that my thesis concerning the recapitulating function of the Pauline letter closings has some bearing on attitudes taken towards the authenticity of this disputed passage.

Most commentators believe that the final section of Romans begins at 15.14.[2] The difficulty with this view, however, is that the material in 15.14-32 is of the nature of an 'apostolic parousia'—an epistolary con-

---

Textgeschichte des Römerbriefes', *NovT* 27 (1985), pp. 273-77; Dunn, *Romans*, pp. 912-17; Schmithals, *Der Römerbrief*, pp. 566-70; W. Munro, 'Interpolation in the Epistles: Weighing Probability', *NTS* 36 (1990), pp. 431-43, esp. 441-43.

3. This view was evidently first proposed by D. de Bruyne ('Les deux derniers chapitres de la lettre aux Romains', *RBén* 25 [1908], pp. 423-30) and P. Corssen ('Zur Überlieferungsgeschichte des Römerbriefes', *ZNW* 10 [1909], pp. 1-45, 97-102), both apparently independent of the other. See also A. von Harnack, 'Uber I Kor. 14,32ff. und Röm. 16,25ff. nach der ältesten Überlieferung und der marcionitischen Bibel', *Studien zur Geschichte des Neuen Testaments und der Alten Kirche*. I. *Zur neutestamentlichen Textkritik* (Berlin: de Gruyter, 1931), pp. 180-90; G. Zuntz, *The Text of the Epistles: A Disquisition Upon the Corpus Paulinum* (London: Oxford University Press, 1953), pp. 227-28; Kümmel, *Introduction to the NT*, pp. 316-17; Donfried, 'A Short Note on Romans 16', p. 57.

1. See esp. Hurtado, 'Doxology at End of Romans', pp. 273-77. Also Sanday and Headlam, *Romans*, pp. 432-36; Hort, 'On the End of the Epistle to the Romans', pp. 324-28; G.H. Parke-Taylor, 'A Note on εἰς ὑπακοὴν πίστεως in Romans i.5 and xvi.26', *ExpTim* 55 (1943–44), p. 306; Murray, *Romans*, pp. 262-68; Schelkle, *Romans*, pp. 264-67; H.W. Schmidt, *Der Brief des Paulus an die Römer* (Berlin: Evangelische Verlagsanstalt, 1972), pp. 265-66; P. Minear, *The Obedience of Faith: The Purposes of Paul in the Epistle to the Romans* (London: SCM, 1971), pp. 30-31, 35 n. 18; Bruce, *Romans*, pp. 281-82; D. Moo, *Romans 1–8* (Chicago: Moody, 1991), p. 9; D.B. Garlington, 'The Obedience of Faith in the Letter to the Romans. Part I: The Meaning of ὑπακοὴ πίστεως (Rom 1.5; 16.26)', *WTJ* 52 (1990) , p. 201 n. 1.

2. So, e.g., Black, *Romans*, pp. 174-86; Käsemann, *Romans*, pp. 389-408; Cranfield, *Romans*, pp. 749-814; Dunn, *Romans*, pp. 854-917; Morris, *Romans*, pp. 508-548; Moo, *Romans*, p. 31.

vention that typically belongs to the body of Paul's letters, not the closing (see 1 Cor. 4.14-21; Gal. 4.11-20; Phil. 2.19-24; 1 Thess. 2.17–3.13; but see Phlm. 22). Furthermore, the travel plans of Paul in 15.14-32 parallel a similar discussion in the thanksgiving section (1.10-15), and so serve to bracket the intervening material in the body of the letter. Thus the fact that 15.14-32 parallels material in the thanksgiving section—and not in the letter opening—suggests that this section dealing with Paul's travel plans does not belong to the letter closing.

It is better, therefore, to see the final section of Romans beginning at 15.33 with the peace benediction, an epistolary convention that elsewhere serves to mark the start of Paul's letter closings (see 1 Thess. 5.23; 2 Thess. 3.16). Although there are some unique features about the subsequent material (i.e., a letter of commendation [16.1-2], two lists of greetings [16.3-16; 21-23], and a second peace benediction [16.20a]), all of the epistolary conventions found in Romans 16 properly belong to a typical Pauline letter closing. The letter closing of Romans, therefore, is best seen as 15.33–16.27.

b. *Structural Analysis of the Letter Closing*
Rom. 15.33–16.27 contains all the epistolary conventions typically found in the letter closings of Paul's letters, plus some additional closing forms. As a result, the letter closing of Romans is the longest final section in Paul's extant letters. Following the pattern in 1 and 2 Thessalonians, the letter closing of Romans begins with a peace benediction (15.33). This wish is followed, not as elsewhere with either a hortatory section or greetings, but with a letter of commendation (16.1-2). Paul introduces Phoebe as 'a deaconess of the church at Cenchrea'[1] and commends her to the Roman churches, thereby ensuring that she—along with the letter to the Romans that she was apparently bringing on his behalf—would be warmly received.

After the commendation of Phoebe, there appears an expected series of greetings (16.3-16). What is not expected, however, is the large

---

1.   The term διάκονος has been taken by many scholars to indicate that Phoebe had an official position within the church at Cenchrea. See especially Ellis, 'Paul and His Co-Workers', p. 443; *idem, Pauline Theology: Ministry and Society* (Grand Rapids: Eerdmans, 1989), p. 76, n. 76; P. Richardson, 'From Apostles to Virgins: Romans 16 and the Roles of Women in the Early Church', *TJT* 2 (1986), pp. 232-61; D.C. Arichea, 'Who was Phoebe? Translating διάκονος in Romans 16.1', *BT* 39 (1988), pp. 401-409.

number of people greeted. For in seventeen greetings Paul mentions twenty-six people in the Roman churches by name, describing most of them in very laudatory terms—with, then, a second greeting list appended later in the letter closing (16.21-23). The first greeting list consists almost exclusively of second-person type of greetings (vv. 3-15), and it concludes with a command to greet one another with a holy kiss (v. 16a) and the passing on of greetings to the Romans from all the churches of Christ (v. 16b).

This first greeting list is followed by a hortatory section (16.17-20a) that possibly was written in Paul's own hand.[1] This section is longer and formally more complex than the hortatory sections found in Paul's other letter closings, for within it are a number of epistolary conventions. It opens with a παρακαλέω unit (vv. 17-18) in which Paul exhorts the Roman Christians to take note of and avoid those causing divisions and difficulties in the church, arguing that such persons do not serve the Lord Christ but their own selfish desires. These trouble makers deceive simple-hearted believers through their clever speech and fine-sounding words. The hortatory section, however, is interrupted by a joy expression (v. 19a) in which Paul rejoices in the fact that the obedience of the Roman Christians has become known to all. Then it resumes with a general paraenetic command that believers at Rome 'be wise in regard to what is good and innocent in regard to what is bad' (v. 19b). And it concludes with a modified peace benediction that promises that 'the God of peace will crush Satan under your feet speedily' (v. 20a).

After this hortatory section, the letter closing of Romans begins to wind down with the appearance of a grace benediction (16.20b), which is normally the last item in the final section of Paul's letters. Here, however, the grace benediction is followed by a second greeting list (16.21-23) in which Paul passes on greetings from a number of his co-workers and companions, including his amanuensis. The letter closing finally comes to a definitive end with a long doxology (16.25-27) that picks up several of the key themes developed earlier in the letter.

The letter closing of Romans, therefore, contains the following outline:

---

1. See above, p. 123.

15.33	Peace Benediction		
16.1-2	Letter of Commendation		
16.3-16	First Greeting List		
		vv. 3-15	Second-person greetings
		v. 16a	Kiss greeting
		v. 16b	Third-person greeting
16.17-20a	Hortatory Section (Autograph)		
		vv. 17-18	παρακαλέω unit
		v. 19a	Joy expression
		v. 19b	General paraenetic command
		v. 20a	Peace benediction
16.20b	Grace Benediction		
16.21-23	Second Greeting List (Non-Autograph)		
16.25-27	Doxology		

When the letter closing of Romans is compared to the closings of Paul's other letters, several unique features become immediately apparent. In addition to its length, the Romans letter closing is distinctive because of its inclusion of two peace benedictions (15.33; 16.20a), a letter of commendation (16.1-2), the two greetings lists (16.3-16, 21-23) and a doxology (16.25-27). Other striking features of this letter closing include the excessive length (seventeen greetings mentioning no less than twenty-six people) and laudatory character of the first greeting list (16.3-16), as well as the length and more formally complex composition (presence of joy expression, general parenetic command, and peace benediction in addition to the appeal formula) of the hortatory section (16.17-20a).

c. *Thematic Analysis of the Letter Closing*
The distinctive features of the Romans letter closing are completely understandable in light of the letter's specific epistolary situation. For in Romans, as in his other letters, Paul has shaped his letter closing so that it better relates to the major concerns of the letter as a whole. To be specific, Paul has constructed the letter closing of Romans so as to establish further the authority of his apostleship and gospel over the Roman Christians. As the apostle to the Gentiles, Paul felt not only divinely obligated but also uniquely qualified to share with the believers in Rome his gospel in the conviction that this preaching ministry among them, accomplished through the letter, would result in the strengthening of their faith in the face of Jewish–Gentile tensions within their churches. However, before presenting his gospel in the body of the letter, Paul must first induce these readers whom he has neither converted nor

visited (1.13; 15.22) to accept him and the gospel that he proclaims. Thus, the letter closing of Romans, like the other sections that make up the epistolary framework of this letter, plays a crucial role in establishing Paul as the Roman Christians' divinely appointed apostle whose gospel, as conveyed in the body of the letter, should be accepted.[1]

This concern of Paul is evident already in the letter opening (1.1-7), particularly when this epistolary section is compared to the opening sections in Paul's other letters. For whereas elsewhere Paul always includes the names of his co-workers in his letter openings, in Romans he speaks only of himself. This omission is striking not only because it is an anomaly among the other Pauline letter openings but also because Timothy, his closest associate, was in fact with Paul at the time of writing (Rom. 16.21a) as were several other leading Christians from Achaia (Rom. 16.21b-23). Paul, it appears, is seeking to draw the attention of his largely unknown readers to himself and, as the rest of the letter opening indicates, to his gospel.

The same concern also explains why Paul did not use just one title to describe himself, as in all his other letters, but three: 'a servant of Christ Jesus, called to be an apostle, set apart for the gospel of God' (1.1). Paul's apostolic status and authoritative role in relation to the Roman believers is stressed by both the number of titles used and his choice of epithets.

These three titles are followed by Paul's description of the gospel (1.2-4). He first defines the gospel as 'that which was promised beforehand, through his prophets, in the Holy Scriptures' (v. 2). In this way, the Roman Christians are assured that Paul's gospel does not involve some radically new teaching but is in complete continuity with the message of the OT. Paul further wins the confidence of his readers by incorporating what quite likely is confessional material of the early church (vv. 3-4), thereby proving the orthodoxy of his gospel to the Christians at Rome who do not know him personally.

In the remainder of the letter opening (vv. 5-6), Paul continues to establish the legitimacy of his apostleship and the trustworthiness of his gospel but also takes the extra step of placing the Roman believers

---

1. Following the lead of Jervis (*Purpose of Romans*), this is the thesis that I have developed in greater length in a forthcoming article entitled, 'Preaching the Gospel in Rome: A Study of the Epistolary Framework of Romans', in *Gospel in Paul: Studies on Corinthians, Galatians and Romans for Richard N. Longenecker* (ed. L.A. Jervis and P. Richardson; Sheffield: JSOT Press, 1994).

within the sphere of his commission and message. This connection is evident in Paul's claim that the apostleship that he has received from Christ (v. 5a) is 'for the obedience of faith among all the Gentiles for the sake of his name, among whom you also are, the called of Jesus Christ' (vv. 5b-6). The logic of Paul's argumentation here is clear:[1]

> 1st Premise: 'I have received apostleship from Christ to preach the gospel among all the Gentiles.'
>
> 2nd Premise: 'You believers in Rome belong to that group of people, the Gentiles.'
>
> Conclusion: 'I, therefore, have a divine responsibility to share my gospel with you.'

The letter opening of Romans, therefore, gives every indication of having been carefully constructed by Paul so as to underscore his obligation, as the divinely appointed apostle to the Gentiles, to share his gospel with the Roman Christians.

The same concern is evident in the thanksgiving section of the letter (1.8-15). For whereas all of the other Pauline thanksgiving sections open with an adverb that stresses the temporal aspect of his giving thanks ('I/we give thanks *always*'),[2] here Paul opens with a prepositional phrase that stresses his relationship to Christ ('I give thanks...*through Jesus Christ*'). Another distinctive formal aspect of the thanksgiving in Romans is the relative clause in 1.9 ('whom I serve in my spirit in the gospel of his Son') that also emphasizes Paul's apostolic calling to preach the gospel. The most striking feature of this thanksgiving, however, is the lengthy explanation of Paul's desire to come to Rome (1.10-15)—an explanation that skillfully and purposefully builds to Paul's expressed intention 'to preach the gospel also to you who are in Rome' (v. 15).

The fact that Paul's stated desire to preach the gospel to the believers in Rome (1.15) is immediately followed with a bold statement of his gospel (1.16-17) that introduces the main arguments of the letter strongly suggests that, in the body of the letter, he is, in fact, preaching his gospel to the Roman Christians. Since Paul cannot fulfill his divine obligation to his readers in person, he uses the letter as a substitute for

---

1.   A.B. du Toit ('Persuasion in Romans 1.1-17', *BZ* 13 [1989], p. 194) claims that Paul here is using a rhetorical device called an *enthymeme*—a syllogism with one premise omitted.

2.   See 1 Cor. 1.4; Phil. 1.4; 1 Thess. 1.2; 2 Thess. 1.3; Phlm. 4.

his actual presence and in this way is still able to share with them his gospel.[1]

The apostolic parousia (15.14-32) also serves in a number of ways to underscore the intention of Paul at work in the opening and thanksgiving sections. Although it is not possible to examine all these ways here, I want to at least take note of 15.15-16 where Paul makes the clearest statement in the letter regarding his purpose in writing: 'But on some points I have written to you very boldly by way of reminder, because of the grace given me by God to be a minister of Christ Jesus to the Gentiles in the priestly service of the gospel of God, so that the offering of the Gentiles may be acceptable, sanctified by the Holy Spirit.' Here Paul directly connects what he has written to the Roman Christians in the body of the letter with his apostolic responsibility to preach the gospel to the Gentiles. Paul claims that he has received grace from God to be a minister of Christ Jesus—a claim to authority that echoes his assertion of apostleship in the letter opening (1.5). This authoritative ministry is directed to the Gentiles (τὰ ἔθνη is used twice in v. 16) and involves a service 'of the gospel of God'. Therefore, Paul's action of boldly preaching his gospel in the body of the letter should be viewed by the Roman Christians as a fulfillment of his God-given responsibility to the Gentiles.

The concern of Paul in the opening, thanksgiving and apostolic parousia sections of Romans to establish his apostolic authority over the Roman churches in a way that ensures their acceptance of his gospel as it has been preached to them in the body of the letter suggests that a similar purpose is at work in the closing section of this letter. And that, in fact, is what a careful reading of Rom. 15.33–16.27 reveals.

One of the unique formal features of the Romans letter closing is the presence of two greeting lists (16.3-16, 21-23). The greetings in the first list are highlighted by virtue of the list's position (it comes in the first and therefore the emphatic position) and size (seventeen greetings in the

---

1.   The first to suggest that Paul in the letter of Romans is preaching his gospel apparently was N.A. Dahl (*Studies in Paul* [Minneapolis, MN: Augsburg, 1977], p. 71): 'What Paul does in his letter is what he had for a long time hoped to do in person: he preached the gospel to those in Rome (see 1.15).' This position has been adopted by a number of others: e.g., P. Bowers, 'Fulfilling the Gospel: The Scope of the Pauline Mission', *JETS* 20 (1987), p. 196; Jervis, *Purpose of Romans*, p. 129; N. Elliott, *The Rhetoric of Romans* (Sheffield: JSOT Press, 1990), p. 84; G. Smiga, 'Romans 12.1-2 and 15.30-32 and the Occasion of the Letter to the Romans', *CBQ* 53 (1991), p. 260.

first list compared to four greetings in the second). Another unique
feature of the first greeting list is the presence of second-person
greetings—a type not normally used in Paul's other letter closings.[1]

The most distinctive aspect of the first greeting list, however, is the
strong commendatory manner in which those being greeted are
described—a feature not found in any of the other greetings of Paul.
The laudatory character of the greetings is often accomplished by means
of a term of endearment or praise: 'my beloved' (16.5b; 16.8; 16.9;
16.12b), 'esteemed in Christ' (16.10a), 'chosen in the Lord' (16.13), 'in
Christ (Jesus)' (16.3; 16.7; 16.9; 16.10), and 'in the Lord' (16.8; 16.11;
16.12 [2×]; 16.13). The laudatory aspect of the greetings is frequently
emphasized further by means of a relative clause: 'who risked their
necks for my life' (16.4a), 'to whom not only I but also all the churches
of the Gentiles give thanks' (16.4b), 'who is the first convert of Asia for
Christ' (16.5b), 'who has worked hard among you' (16.6), 'who are outstanding among the apostles' (16.7b), 'who also were in Christ before
me' (16.7c), and 'who has worked hard in the Lord' (16.12b).

The reason why Paul includes such terms of endearment/praise and the
relative clauses with the greetings is obviously not to help the Roman
churches identify the persons being greeted, for such persons would have
been well known to the Christian community. Rather, as their laudatory
content makes clear, Paul added these terms of endearment/praise and
the relative clauses in order to give the greetings a strong commendatory function. Furthermore, these additions emphasize the close relations
that existed between the persons being greeted/praised and Paul.[2]
Consequently, Paul builds up his own standing in the Roman churches
not merely by greeting specific persons in the congregation in a commendatory fashion, but also by associating himself so closely with such
persons that he himself shares in the commendations that they receive.[3]

---

1.   Other than the stereotyped kiss greeting formula, the second-person type of
greeting occurs only once elsewhere in Paul's letter closings (Phil. 4.21a).

2.   Käsemann (*Romans*, p. 412) comments, 'Paul is clearly concerned to
underscore his personal tie with as many as possible'.

3.   Gamble (*Textual History*, p. 92) states: 'It is especially striking how, in the
descriptive phrases, a heavy emphasis is placed on the relationship between the
individuals mentioned and Paul himself. He ties them to himself, and himself to them.
From these features it can be seen that Paul's commendatory greetings to specific
individuals serve to place those individuals in a position of respect vis-à-vis the
community, but also, by linking the Apostle so closely to them, place Paul in the same
position.'

That Paul intended the greetings to commend himself and his gospel more fully to the Roman Christians can also be seen in the order in which he greets specific individuals and in the corresponding nature of the descriptions he gives.[1] The first persons greeted are Prisca and Aquila with whom he claimed a missionary partnership (16.3, 'my fellow workers') and whose prominence among 'all the churches of the Gentiles' (16.4) placed them in an excellent position to testify to Christians at Rome about Paul's apostleship and the successful impact his gospel has had among the Gentiles. The second person greeted is Epaenetus who, as 'the first convert in Asia' (16.5b), is a living witness to the effectiveness and power of Paul's gospel. Similarly, the identification of Andronicus and Junias (or Junia)[2] early in the greeting list as 'those who are outstanding among the apostles' (16.7) also makes them good character references for the legitimacy of Paul's own apostolic status and his gospel.

The final greeting of this first long list is also significant: 'All the churches of Christ greet you' (16.16b). For nowhere else does Paul speak so broadly ('all the churches') in passing on the greetings of others. So here, it seems, Paul presents himself to the Romans as one who has the official backing of all the churches in Achaia, Macedonia, Asia, Galatia, Syria and elsewhere in the eastern part of the empire. Furthermore, their support demonstrates that his gospel has a proven track record among believers throughout the Mediterranean world. Consequently, there is in this greeting an implied challenge to believers in Rome that they join these other churches in recognizing the authority of Paul's apostleship and his gospel.[3]

It should now be clear that the greetings of 16.3-16, rather than creating a problem for the textual integrity of Romans (as many scholars have claimed), are entirely appropriate to the purpose of Paul that is evident throughout the rest of the letter. Paul has constructed his closing greetings in such a way that they further establish his apostolic authority

---

1. See Jervis, *Purpose of Romans*, pp. 151-52.

2. Although Ἰουνιᾶν could be a contraction of the masculine Junianus, there is stronger evidence for taking it as the feminine accusative of Junia and that it refers to a female. See V. Fabrega, 'War Junia(s), der hervorrangende Apostel (Rom. 16,7), eine Frau?', *JAC* 27 (1984), pp. 47-64; P. Lampe, 'Iunia/Iunias: Sklavenherkunft im Kreise der vorpaulinischen Apostel (Röm 16.7)', *ZNW* 76 (1985), pp. 132-34; R. Schulz, 'Romans 16.7: Junia or Junias?', *ExpTim* 98 (1986–87), pp. 108-110.

3. Dunn (*Romans*, II, p. 899) states: 'The greeting thus has a "political" overtone: Paul speaks for all these churches, and they are behind him in his mission.'

228   *Neglected Endings*

over the Roman churches and guarantee their acceptance of his gospel.

Two other distinctive features of the Romans letter closing, namely, the letter of commendation and the hortatory section, should undoubtedly be seen as fitting into this overall purpose of Paul as well. The first—Paul's commendation of Phoebe and her acceptance by the Christians at Rome—involves in some sense their acceptance of Paul, for she is his representative and the likely bearer of his letter to them. So the commendation of Phoebe (16.1-2) implicitly contributes to Paul's goal of establishing his authority over the churches at Rome. Furthermore, if Phoebe was a wealthy member of the upper class, her support of Paul might further impress upon the Roman Christians the success of his gospel.[1]

The second—the hortatory section (16.17-20a)—also contributes to this cause. These verses, of course, are often understood as a rebuke of the Roman Christians by Paul, which interrupts rather awkwardly the greetings of vv. 3-16 and those of vv. 21-23. But such an interpretation is entirely unjustified, for Paul in this section actually speaks rather positively of the believers at Rome as he continues to build his relations with them. In this παρακαλέω unit, in fact, he (1) refers affectionately to his readers as 'brothers', (2) affirms that they have learned proper teaching (v. 17), and (3) places them in an entirely different category from those divisive persons 'who do not serve our Lord Christ but their own selfish desires' (v. 18). Paul then inserts a joy expression that praises the Roman Christians for the fact that 'your obedience is known to all' (v. 19a),[2] which is followed by a general and uncritical command that they be 'wise in regard to what is good and innocent in regard to what is bad' (v. 19b).

The hortatory section concludes with a peace benediction that promises that 'the God of peace will crush Satan under your feet speedily' (v. 20a). Unlike Paul's other peace benedictions that describe what God will do to his readers, the peace benediction here describes what God will do to Satan by means of the believers at Rome. This shift in focus to

---

1. On the financial and social status of Phoebe, see R. Jewett, 'Paul, Phoebe, and the Spanish Mission', in *The Social World of Formative Christianity and Judaism* (ed. J. Neusner, E.S. Frerichs, P. Borgen and R. Horsley; Philadelphia: Fortress, 1988), pp. 148-55; also Whelen, 'Role of Pheobe', pp. 67-85.

2. The order of the three elements that typically constitute a joy expression (main verb, adverb of magnitude, causal clause) is here reversed so that the causal clause comes first, thereby placing the emphasis on the obedience of the Roman Christians.

God's use of the Roman Christians in carrying out the wish should probably also be interpreted as another deliberate attempt on Paul's part to build his relations with Christians at Rome.[1]

Another unique feature of the letter closing of Romans is the presence of a doxology (16.25-27). As noted above, there are several scholars who defend the Pauline authorship of this passage on the grounds that its language, style and themes agree well with the rest of the letter. Additional support for the authenticity of the doxology, however, may lie in its summary character. For we have seen in Paul's other letters that he typically adapts and shapes his inherited closing conventions so that they better reflect the key issues discussed earlier in the letter. It would not, therefore, be beyond Paul's ability or practice to take a conventional doxology and to expand it in such a manner as to echo the central purpose(s) of his Romans letter.

The doxology is, in fact, especially striking for the way in which it recapitulates the concern of Paul evident in the epistolary framework of the letter. The reference to '*my* gospel' recalls well Paul's concern in the letter opening, thanksgiving, letter body and apostolic parousia to share his gospel with the Roman believers. The doxology claims that Paul's gospel will be used by God 'to strengthen' (στηρίξαι) the believers in Rome—the same point that was made in the thanksgiving section (1.11, 'in order that you may be strengthened' [στηριχθῆναι]). The doxology further highlights the continuity of Paul's gospel with the message of the OT—a matter also stressed in the letter opening (1.2-4). More specifically, the phrase 'through the prophetic writings' (16.26, διὰ γραφῶν προφητικῶν) is a deliberate allusion to the opening words of the letter, 'through his prophets in the holy writings' (1.2, διὰ τῶν προφητῶν αὐτοῦ ἐν γραφαῖς ἁγίαις). The goal or purpose of making the mystery of the gospel known is 'to bring about the obedience of faith for all the Gentiles' (16.26, εἰς ὑπακοὴν πίστεως εἰς πάντα τὰ ἔθνη). This phrase from the doxology provides yet another direct verbal link with the letter opening: 'to bring about the obedience of faith for all the Gentiles' (1.5, εἰς ὑπακοὴν πίστεως ἐν πᾶσιν τοῖς ἔθνεσιν). It also recalls Paul's point in the apostolic parousia that Christ is working through him 'to bring about the obedience of the Gentiles (15.18, εἰς ὑπακοὴν ἐθνῶν). The strong recapitulating character of the doxology serves as yet a further means by which Paul seeks to establish the authority and acceptability of his gospel among the Roman believers.

1. So Jervis, *Purpose of Romans*, p. 154.

The letter closing of Romans, therefore, provides compelling evidence that this final epistolary unit has been deliberately constructed to support Paul's overall purpose in the writing of this letter. For just as Paul carefully adapts the epistolary conventions in the opening, thanksgiving and apostolic parousia of the Romans letter in order to win the acceptance of his apostleship and gospel by the Roman churches, so also the closing has been constructed to accomplish the same goal. This is most clearly seen in the lengthy greeting list of 16.3-16, but it is also evident in the letter of commendation, the hortatory section, and, if authentic, the doxology. The letter closing of Romans, in fact, plays an important role in reinforcing the overriding purpose of Paul that is at work in the letter as a whole, namely, to preach the gospel to the believers in Rome. Consequently, the letter closing serves as a hermeneutical guide for modern exegetes, leading us through the maze of proposed theories as to the purpose of Romans to the real intention of Paul in this letter.

8. *Philemon*

a. *Extent of the Letter Closing*
The letter to Philemon is perhaps the most difficult of Paul's letters for determining with certainty the extent of the closing section. This difficulty is reflected in the diverse claims made by scholars over what material in the letter properly belongs to the closing. Some limit the letter closing to the greetings and peace benediction (vv. 23-25).[1] Others, believing that the apostolic parousia of v. 22 (Paul's request to have a room prepared for his future arrival) does not relate to the main issue addressed in the letter body, include this verse in the closing section as well (vv. 22-25).[2] A greater number of scholars, however, also include the preceding confidence formula of v. 21 in the letter closing (vv. 21-25).[3] Yet Chan-Hie Kim, who treats Philemon as a Greek letter of

---

1. So, e.g., W. Hendriksen, *Exposition of Colossians and Philemon* (Grand Rapids: Baker, 1964), pp. 225-27; White, 'Structural Analysis of Philemon', pp. 26-47; J. Gnilka, *Der Philemonbrief* (Freiburg: Herder, 1982), pp. 91-95; Wright, *Colossians and Philemon*, pp. 191-92.

2. So, e.g., Müller, *Philippians and Philemon*, pp. 191-93; H.M. Carson, *The Epistles of Paul to the Colossians and Philemon* (Grand Rapids: Eerdmans, 1960), p. 112.

3. So, e.g. Lohse, *Philemon*, pp. 187, 206-208; G. Johnston, *Ephesians, Philippians, Colossians and Philemon* (London: Nelson, 1967), pp. 78-79; G. Bouwman, *De brieven van Paulus aan de Kolossenzen en aan Filemon*

recommendation, believes the closing consists of vv. 18-25,[1] while F. Forrester Church, who examines Philemon from the rhetorical category of deliberative speech, argues that the peroration or closing summary of the argument begins at v. 17.[2]

It should be noted at the outset of the discussion here that a hortatory section introduced by the vocative ἀδελφέ ('brother'), such as is found in v. 20, is an epistolary convention that typically appears in Paul's other letter closings. Furthermore, an autograph formula, such as occurs in v. 19 ('I, Paul, write this with my own hand'), always belongs elsewhere in Paul's letters to the closing.[3] This suggests that the letter closing of Philemon begins with the autograph statement of v. 19, just as in Galatians where Paul takes over from his secretary to begin the closing of that letter (Gal. 6.11-18).

Further support for beginning the Philemon letter closing at v. 19 comes from the fact that the letter body reaches a certain climax in vv. 17-18, where Paul moves beyond the thinly disguised request of the previous verses and explicitly challenges Philemon to receive Onesimus as he would receive the apostle himself. As Norman Petersen notes, 'He [Paul] had brought Onesimus' story to a close when he offered to repay Onesimus' debt in v. 18'.[4] That Paul in this verse is reaching the end of the body section of the letter is also suggested by the presence of οὖν

(Amsterdam: Roermond, 1972), p. 158 (ignore the typographical error in his initial statement of divisions 8-21, 22-25 [p. 158]); R.P. Martin, *Colossians and Philemon* (Grand Rapids: Eerdmans, 1973), pp. 168-70; P. Stuhlmacher, *Der Brief an Philemon* (Zürich: Benziger, 1975), pp. 51-56; Roetzel, *Letters of Paul*, p. 31; P.T. O'Brien, *Colossians, Philemon* (Waco, TX: Word Books, 1982), pp. 304-308; M.J. Harris, *Colossians & Philemon* (Grand Rapids: Eerdmans, 1991), pp. 277-82.

1. See Kim, *Letter of Recommendation*, p. 124, where he argues that the body of the request is contained in vv. 8-17.

2. F.F. Church, 'Rhetorical Structure and Design in Paul's Letter to Philemon', *HTR* 71 (1978), pp. 17-33. Although this is not explicitly stated, Church limits the peroration to the section 17-22, leaving 23-25 to function as an epistolary closing. Church's rhetorical outline is also followed by R.R. Melick, *Philippians, Colossians, Philemon* (Nashville: Broadman, 1991), pp. 340-41, and C.J. Martin, 'The Rhetorical Function of Commercial Language in Paul's Letter to Philemon (Verse 18)', in *Persuasive Artistry: Studies in New Testament Rhetoric in Honor of George Kennedy* (ed. D.F. Watson; Sheffield: JSOT Press, 1991), pp. 322-25.

3. It would, of course, not be impossible for Paul to use a typical closing convention in the body of the letter.

4. N.R. Petersen, *Rediscovering Paul: Philemon and the Sociology of Paul's Narrative World* (Philadelphia: Fortress, 1985), p. 75.

('therefore') in v. 17. Thus, even though such a claim is not completely free from difficulty,[1] there is strong epistolary evidence to substantiate the proposal that the letter closing of Philemon consists of vv. 19-25.[2]

b. *Structural Analysis of the Letter Closing*

After making use of a secretary in the writing of the letter opening and body, Paul takes over at the beginning of the letter closing[3] at v. 19 to write a personal promise of payment: 'I, Paul, write this with my own hand. I will repay it.' This autograph statement becomes a legal promissory note or official IOU[4] in which Paul commits himself to compensating Philemon for any losses he may have incurred because of Onesimus' actions. The latter half of v. 19 is a parenthetical comment by Paul where he uses the rhetorical device of declaring that he will not mention something, thereby in fact doing just the opposite: 'I do not want to mention to you that you, in fact, owe me your very self'.

The letter closing of Philemon then continues with a hortatory section

---

1. Many commentators understand v. 19a as a parenthesis that interrupts the thought expressed in vv. 18 and 19b, rather than a new section that marks the beginning of the letter closing. See Lohse, *Philemon*, p. 204; J. Zmijewski, 'Beobachtungen zur Struktur des Philemonbriefes', *BibLeb* 15 (1974), pp. 290-91; O'Brien, *Philemon*, p. 300. It is also possible, however, to take v. 19b as a parenthetical comment added to the introductory statement of Paul's autograph promise of payment: so F.F. Bruce, *The Epistles to the Colossians, to Philemon, and to the Ephesians* (Grand Rapids: Eerdmans, 1984), pp. 216, 220; see also the translations in RSV, JB, and NIV.

2. This proposal was adopted by G.J. Bahr ('Paul and Letter Writing in the First Century', *CBQ* 28 [1966], pp. 467-68), who argued that vv. 19-25 is a summary subscription written in Paul's own hand. In a subsequent article ('Subscriptions', pp. 33-34), however, Bahr expanded the subscription somewhat, claiming that it began at v. 17.

3. Some scholars view Paul as having written the whole letter by himself (Lightfoot, *Colossians and Philemon*, p. 342; Roller, *Das Formular*, p. 592; Müller, *Philemon*, p. 188). There is overwhelming evidence, however, that the formula 'in my own hand' marks the beginning of an autograph section (see above pp. 21-22). There is much less certainty on whether Paul writes just the promise of payment in his own hand or the rest of the letter closing, although parallels with Greco-Roman letters suggest that the latter is more likely.

4. The verb ἀποτίνω is frequently found in the papyri (e.g., BGU 759.23; P. Oxy. 275.27) as a legal or official term meaning 'to make compensation', 'to pay the damages'. See BAGD, p. 101; Deissmann, *Light from Ancient East*, p. 332; Lohse, *Philemon*, p. 204; O'Brien, *Philemon*, p. 300.

(v. 20) that is introduced in typical fashion by the vocative ἀδελφέ ('brother') and also in not so typical fashion by the intensifying particle ναί ('yes'). The first half of the hortatory section contains a volitive optative that involves a play on Onesimus's name:[1] 'May I profit (ὀναίμην) from you in the Lord' (v. 20a). The second half expresses a simple command that recalls Paul's words earlier in the letter: 'Refresh my heart in Christ' (v. 20b; see vv. 7, 12).

The hortatory section is followed by two stereotyped formulae. First, there is a confidence formula (v. 21) in which Paul expresses his certainty that Philemon will not only be obedient to his request but even do more than asked. Second, there is an apostolic parousia (v. 22) in which Paul requests that a guest room be prepared for him in view of his anticipated release from prison and his future visit to Philemon.

The letter draws to a close with greetings (vv. 23-24) and a grace benediction (v. 25). Paul first passes on greetings from 'Epaphras, my fellow prisoner in Christ Jesus', who was a Colossian (Col. 4.12) and no doubt well known to Philemon. Paul also shares greetings from his 'fellow workers': Mark, Aristarchus, Demas, and Luke. The letter to Philemon then ends in typical Pauline fashion with a grace benediction.

The letter closing of Philemon, therefore, exhibits the following outline:

v. 19a	Autograph Formula
v. 19b	Parenthetical Comment
v. 20	Hortatory Section
v. 21	Confidence Formula
v. 22	Apostolic Parousia
vv. 23-24	Greetings
v. 25	Grace Benediction

---

1. A number of recent commentators have questioned the word play on Onesimus' name in v. 20a because the expression ὀναίμην was so frequently used in other literature of the day (so BDF §488; Lohse, *Philemon*, p. 205; Martin, *Philemon*, p. 167; O'Brien, *Philemon*, p. 302). The fact that this expression was well known, however, in no way precludes the possibility that Paul is using it as a deliberate pun. Rather, the fact that this word is used nowhere else in Paul's writings, that Paul creates a deliberate word play on Onesimus's name in v. 11, and that the whole letter exhibits a highly skillful argumentation, all suggest that the pun in v. 20a was intended (so Lightfoot, *Philemon*, p. 345; M.R. Vincent, *A Critical and Exegetical Commentary on the Epistles to the Philippians and to Philemon* [Edinburgh: T. & T. Clark, 1897], p. 191; Bruce, *Philemon*, p. 221; Wright, *Philemon*, p. 189; Church, 'Rhetorical Structure', p. 30).

c. *Thematic Analysis of the Letter Closing*

The final section of Philemon contains a number of distinctive closing conventions vis-à-vis the final sections of Paul's other letters: a parenthetical comment, a confidence formula and an apostolic parousia.[1] Additionally, there are a number of unique features found within the expected closing conventions: a promise of reimbursement in the autograph formula, the pun on Onesimus's name and a request to 'refresh my heart' in the hortatory section, the rather high number of people mentioned in the final greeting, and a plural recipient of the grace benediction (as also in the apostolic parousia). All these distinctive elements of the Philemon letter closing, it appears, have important connections to the primary purpose of the letter as a whole. For a careful reading of Phlm. 19-25 reveals that this closing section recalls in various ways the key issue dealt with in the rest of the letter.

The autograph formula of v. 19a, with its promise of payment echoes in an official or legally binding manner Paul's promise of the previous verse (v. 18) to reimburse Philemon for any debts he may have as a result of Onesimus's actions. The parenthetical comment of v. 19b, while not repeating anything in the body of the letter, nevertheless directly relates to the primary request found there. For by deliberately reminding Philemon that 'you, in fact, owe me your own self,' Paul creates further pressure on him to acquiesce to the request made in the body of the letter.

The hortatory section also echoes the main theme of the letter. For the pun on Onesimus's name in v. 20a recalls in a general way the primary issue being addressed in the letter (i.e., Paul's appeal for Onesimus) and in a more specific manner the word play of v. 11 ('Formerly he was useless to you, but now he is indeed useful to you and to me'). Similarly, Paul's challenge in v. 20b that Philemon 'refresh my heart in Christ' (ἀνάπαυσόν μου τὰ σπλάγχνα ἐν Χριστῷ) clearly echoes his earlier description of Philemon in v. 7b as one through whom 'the hearts of the saints have been refreshed' (τὰ σπλάγχνα τῶν ἁγίων ἀναπέπαυται διὰ σοῦ), as well as his description of Onesimus in v. 12b as 'this one is my heart' (τοῦτ' ἔστιν τὰ ἐμὰ σπλάγχνα). So also Paul's address of

---

1.   The apostolic parousia and confidence formula are epistolary conventions that elsewhere in Paul's letters always belong to the body of the letter, not the closing. The presence of these epistolary conventions in the closing of Philemon, therefore, is distinctive.

Philemon in v. 20 as 'brother' (ἀδελφέ),[1] although a regular feature of a Pauline closing hortatory section, nevertheless recalls the apostle's previous appeal in v. 16 that Philemon welcome Onesimus back no longer as slave but as a 'beloved brother' (ἀδελφὸν ἀγαπητόν). The confidence formula of v. 21 and the apostolic parousia of v. 22 also echo and reinforce the main theme of the letter. For Paul uses the confidence formula to recall earlier material in the letter by claiming that Philemon will do even more than 'the things that I am saying'. Paul also uses the confidence formula to exert further pressure on Philemon to agree to his request by praising him in advance for his expected obedience. As Stanley Olson notes, 'In Phlm 21 the confidence of compliance functions to reinforce the appeal of the whole letter'.[2] And in a similar fashion, the apostolic parousia recalls and reinforces Paul's earlier request in the letter. For the announcement of his impending arrival serves as an indirect threat in which Paul promises to come and check personally whether his petition has been obeyed.[3]

Paul exerts further indirect pressure on Philemon by including others (v. 2, Apphia, Archippus, the house church) in his conversation with the slave owner. For although Paul has couched the thanksgiving and body of the letter in the singular, in the closing (see the apostolic parousia [v. 22] and grace benediction [v. 25]) he uses the plural, following the pattern found in the opening of the letter. So also the mention of five people in the final greeting (vv. 23-24, Epaphras, Mark, Aristarchus, Demas, and Luke) is significant. For the issue of Onesimus's return is not a private matter limited to Paul and Philemon alone. Instead, it appears

1. Note also Paul's use of the vocative ἀδελφέ to describe Philemon in v. 7.
2. Olson, 'Pauline Expressions of Confidence', p. 288. The following statements of Olson concerning the function of a confidence formula in general are also significant for the use of this epistolary convention by Paul in Phlm. 21: 'An expression of confidence in compliance is clearly part of the persuasive effort, rather than a necessarily sincere statement of the writer's attitude. He intends to undergird his request by this expression' (p. 286); 'The function [of a confidence formula] is to undergird the letter's requests or admonitions by creating a sense of obligation through praise' (p. 289).
3. So Lightfoot, *Philemon*, p. 345; Funk, 'Apostolic Parousia', pp. 249-68, esp. 259; Lohse, *Philemon*, pp. 206-207; Martin, *Philemon*, pp. 168-69. A few commentators, however, deny any element of warning in this verse and want to treat it as a simple and genuine request for lodging (and thus, for some, also further evidence for the Ephesian provenance of this letter): see Bruce, *Philemon*, p. 222; Wright, *Philemon*, p. 190.

that Paul has deliberately made it a public matter so as to exert further pressure on Philemon and those with him to agree to the request of his letter. As Petersen notes, 'With this wider public cognizant of the local problem, the pressure on both Philemon and his church is magnified'.[1]

The letter closing of Philemon, therefore, exhibits a strong recapitulating function.[2] Paul has carefully adapted his regular closing conventions and added a couple of other epistolary formulae in order that the letter closing better echoes and reinforces the appeal made in the body of the letter. Just as Paul carefully foreshadows and sets the stage for his request in the thanksgiving (vv. 4-8), so he summarizes and clinches his request in the closing (vv. 19-25). In fact, Paul has constructed the letter closing in such a skillful manner that it becomes virtually impossible for Philemon not to agree to his petition on behalf of the slave Onesimus.

---

1. Petersen, *Rediscovering Paul*, p. 100 (also p. 87, n. 85). See also U. Wickert, 'Der Philemonbrief—Privatbrief oder apostolisches Schreiben?', *ZNW* 52 (1961), pp. 230-38.

2. Although there are serious difficulties with Bahr's views of Paul's letter closings in general, he was at least correct in speaking of the letter closing of Philemon as a 'summary subscription' (see 'Paul and Letter Writing', pp. 467-68; 'Subscriptions in Pauline Letters', pp. 35-36). Note also Richards (*Secretary*, pp. 178-79), who, despite claiming that 'the category of summary subscription is inappropriate for the letters of Paul', nevertheless concedes that in Philemon 'what follows [i.e., vv. 19-25] could be loosely termed a summary subscription'.

Conclusion

The closing sections of Paul's letters have been almost completely ignored in biblical studies. Scholars have, somewhat naturally, focused their attention on the seemingly 'weightier' sections of Paul's letters—the thanksgivings and the bodies. In addition to this, there is the assumption that letter closings, along with the openings, are primarily conventional in nature and serve only to establish or maintain contact between Paul and his readers. Furthermore, many believe that some of the diverse stereotyped formulae found in Paul's letter closings (e.g., grace benediction, peace benediction, kiss greeting, doxology) have been borrowed by the apostle from the liturgical practices of the early Christian church, and so the presence of such conventions in the closing is assumed to be unrelated to the rest of the letter.

A detailed analysis of Paul's letters closings, however, quickly dispels any notion that these final sections are mere literary abstractions that contain little significance for understanding the rest of their respective letters. For Paul's letter closings consist of several epistolary conventions, all of which exhibit a high degree of formal and structural consistency, thereby testifying to the care with which these final sections have been constructed. The literary quality of Paul's closings and the skill with which these final sections have been written becomes even more clear from a comparison of his closings with those of ancient Hellenistic and Semitic letters. For although Paul clearly was influenced by the epistolary practices of his day, he did not at all feel bound or limited to existing writing practices. In fact, Paul's extensive adaptations and creative additions to the rather hackneyed epistolary conventions so common in ancient letters result in closings that are truly unparalleled among extant letters of his day.

The most significant feature of Paul's letter closings, however, is the way in which they echo major concerns and themes dealt with in their respective letter bodies. This summarizing function is most obvious in the letter closing of Galatians. For Paul here has expanded and adapted the closing conventions in such a way that five sharp contrasts—all centered on the issue of the cross of Christ—are set out between himself and his Galatian opponents. And these contrasts involving the themes of persecution, boasting, circumcision, new creation and 'the Israel of God', as well as the watershed issue of the cross, serve to recapitulate the key themes that Paul has addressed throughout the Galatian letter.

In a similar fashion, the letter closing of 1 Thessalonians summarizes the key themes and concerns of that letter. For Paul has expanded greatly the typical formula of the peace benediction in such a way as to recall the themes of sanctification, Christ's return and comfort for persecuted Christians that are developed at length throughout the letter body. Paul also adapted the other closing conventions of this letter so that they relate more directly to the problem of tensions within the Thessalonian church stemming from the failure of the 'idlers' to respect and obey the church's leaders—an issue also addressed in the body of the letter.

It is true that the remaining letter closings of Paul do not exhibit the same high degree of recapitulation as found in the closings of Galatians and 1 Thessalonians. Nevertheless, it must be recognized that all the remaining letter closings of Paul have been carefully written and adapted in such a way that they better reflect the key issues developed in their respective letter bodies. Thus, for example, the closing conventions of 2 Thessalonians point back to the two major issues of that letter, namely, conflict with the idlers and anxiety over Christ's return. So also the closings of 1 and 2 Corinthians have both been written so as to reflect better Paul's concern in these letters over opposition to his leadership, as well as the division and hostility experienced within the Corinthian church resulting from this opposition. Or again, the letter closing of Romans reinforces in significant ways Paul's overriding concern in that letter to share his gospel with the believers in Rome. Every one of Paul's letter closings, in fact, relates in one way or another to the key issue(s) taken up in their respective letter bodies.

The summarizing or recapitulating function evident in Paul's letter closings is of hermeneutical significance. For as demonstrated in this study, the letter closing aids, in varying ways and degrees, our understanding of Paul's purpose, arguments and exhortations—as well as our understanding of his readers and their historical situation(s). The closings serve as an hermeneutical spotlight, highlighting the central concerns of the apostle in his letters and illumining our understanding of these key themes and issues. The letter closings of Paul, therefore, can no longer be ignored. Instead, they must play an important role in any examination and interpretation of Paul's letters.

BIBLIOGRAPHY

Aalen, S., 'Glory, Honour', *NIDNTT*, II, pp. 44-48.

Achtemeier, P.J., *Romans* (Atlanta: John Knox, 1985).

—'*Omne verbum sonat*: The New Testament and the Oral Environment of Late Western Antiquity', *JBL* 109 (1990), pp. 3-27.

Albert, P., *Le genre épistolaire chez les anciens* (Paris: Hachette, 1869).

Alexander, L., 'Hellenistic Letter-Forms and the Structure of Philippians', *JSNT* 37 (1989), pp. 87-101.

Alexander, P.S., 'Remarks on Aramaic Epistolography in the Persian Period', *JSS* 23 (1978), pp. 155-70.

—'Epistolary Literature', in *Jewish Writings of the Second Temple Period* (ed. M.E. Stone; Assen: Van Gorcum, 1984), pp. 579-96.

Archer, R.L, 'The Epistolary Form in the New Testament', *ExpTim* 68 (1951–52), pp. 296-98.

Arichea, D.C., 'Who was Phoebe? Translating διάκονος in Romans 16.1', *BT* 39 (1988), pp. 401-409.

Aune, D.E., *The New Testament in Its Literary Environment* (Philadelphia: Westminster, 1987).

Aus, R., 'Paul's Travel Plans to Spain and the "Full Number of the Gentiles" of Rom. xi 25', *NovT* 21 (1979), pp. 232-61.

Bahnsen, G.L, 'Autographs, Amanuenses and Restricted Inspiration', *EvQ* 45 (1973), pp. 100-110.

Bahr, G.J., 'Paul and Letter Writing in the First Century', *CBQ* 28 (1966), pp. 465-77.

—'The Subscriptions in the Pauline Letters', *JBL* 87 (1968), pp. 27-41.

Bailey, J.L. and L.D. Vander Broek, *Literary Forms in the New Testament* (Louisville, KY: Westminster/John Knox, 1992).

Balogh, J., 'Voces paginarum: Beiträge zur Geschichte des lauten Lesens und Schreibens', *Philologus* 82 (1927), pp. 84-109, 202-240.

Bandstra, A.J, 'Paul, the Letter Writer', *CTJ* 3 (1968), pp. 176-80.

Barrett, C.K, *The Epistle to the Romans* (New York: Harper & Row, 1957).

—*The First Epistle to the Corinthians* (New York: Harper & Row, 1968).

—*The Second Epistle to the Corinthians* (New York: Harper & Row, 1973).

Barth, G., *Der Brief an die Philipper* (Zürich: Theologischer Verlag, 1979).

Bates, W.H., 'The Integrity of II Corinthians', *NTS* 12 (1965), pp. 56-69.

Beare, F.W., *The Epistle to the Philippians* (London: A. & C. Black, 1959).

Beer, G., 'Zur israelitisch-jüdischen Briefliteratur', in *Alttestamentliche Studien Rudolf Kittel zum 60. Geburtstag dargebracht* (ed. A. Alt *et al.*; Leipzig: Hinrichs, 1913), pp. 20-41.

Belleville, L.L., 'Continuity or Discontinuity: A Fresh Look at 1 Corinthians in the

Light of First-Century Epistolary Forms and Conventions', *EvQ* 59 (1987), pp. 15-37.

Benko, S., 'The Kiss', in *Pagan Rome and the Early Christians* (Bloomington: Indiana University Press, 1984), pp. 79-102.

Benoit, P., J.T. Milik and R. de Vaux (eds.), *Discoveries in the Judaean Desert*. II. *Les Grottes de Murabba'at* (Oxford: Clarendon, 1961).

Berger, K., 'Apostelbrief und apostolische Rede: Zum Formular frühchristlicher Briefe', *ZNW* 65 (1974), pp. 191-207.

Best, E., *The Letter of Paul to the Romans* (Cambridge: Cambridge University Press, 1967).

—*A Commentary on the First and Second Epistles to the Thessalonians* (London: A. & C. Black, 1972).

—*Second Corinthians* (Atlanta: John Knox, 1987).

Betz, H.D., 'The Literary Composition and Function of Paul's Letter to the Galatians', *NTS* 21 (1975), pp. 353-59.

—*Galatians* (Philadelphia: Fortress Press, 1979).

Betz, O., 'στίγμα', *TDNT*, VII, pp. 657-64.

Beyer, H.W., 'Der Brief an die Galater', in *Die kleineren Briefe des Apostels Paulus* (Göttingen: Vandenhoeck & Ruprecht, 1949).

Bickermann, E., 'Ein jüdischer Festbrief vom Jahr 124 v. Chr. (II Macc. 1.1-9)', *ZNW* 32 (1933), pp. 233-54.

Bjerkelund, C.J., *Parakalô: Form, Funktion und Sinn der parakalô-Sätze in den paulinischen Briefen* (Oslo: Universitetsforlaget, 1967).

Black, M., *An Aramaic Approach to the Gospels and Acts* (Oxford: Clarendon, 1946).

—'The Maranatha Invocation and Jude 14, 15 (I Enoch 1:9)', in *Christ and Spirit in the New Testament* (ed. B. Lindars and S.S. Smalley; Cambridge: Cambridge University Press, 1973), pp. 189-96.

Bligh, J., *Galatians: A Discussion of Paul's Epistle* (London: St. Paul's Publications, 1969).

Boer, W.P. de, *The Imitation of Paul: An Exegetical Study* (Kampen: J.H. Kok, 1962).

Boers, H., 'A Form-Critical Study of Paul's Letters: 1 Thessalonians as a Case Study', *NTS* 22 (1976), pp. 140-58.

Boman, T., 'Die dreifache Würde des Völkerapostels', *ST* 29 (1975), pp. 63-69.

Boobyer, G.H., *'Thanksgiving' and the 'Glory of God' in Paul* (Leipzig: Noske, 1929).

Bornkamm, G., 'Das Anathema in der urchristlichen Abendmahlsliturgie', *TLZ* (1950), pp. 227-30.

—'Der Philipperbrief als Paulinische Briefsammlung', in *Neotestamentica et Patristica: Eine Freudesgabe für Oscar Cullmann* (Leiden: Brill, 1962), pp. 192-202.

—*Early Christian Experience* (New York: Harper & Row, 1969).

—*Paul* (trans. D.M.G. Stalker; New York: Harper & Row, 1971).

Borse, U., 'Die Wundermale und der Todesbescheid', *BZ* 14 (1970), pp. 88-111.

Bouwman, G., *De brieven van Paulus aan de Kolossenzen en aan Filemon* (Amsterdam: Roermond, 1972).

Bowers, P., 'Fulfilling the Gospel: The Scope of the Pauline Mission', *JETS* 20 (1987), pp. 185-98.

Bradley, D.G., 'The *Topos* as a Form in the Pauline Paraenesis', *JBL* 72 (1953), pp. 238-46.

Bresciani, E., and M. Kamil, *Le lettere aramaiche di Hermopoli* (Rome: Atti dell' Accademia Nazionale dei Lincei, 1966).

Bring, R., *Commentary on Galatians* (trans. E. Wahlstrom; Philadelphia: Muhlenberg, 1961).

Brinsmead, B.H., *Galatians—Dialogical Response to Opponents* (Chico, CA: Scholars, 1982).

Brock, B.L., and R.L. Scott (eds.), *Methods of Rhetorical Criticism: A Twentieth-Century Perspective* (Detroit: Wayne State University Press, 1980).

Brooke, D., *Private Letters Pagan and Christian: An Anthology of Greek and Roman Letters from the Fifth Century before Christ to the Fifth Century of Our Era* (New York: Dutton, 1930).

Bruce, F.F., *1 and 2 Corinthians* (Grand Rapids: Eerdmans, 1971).

—*The Epistle to the Galatians* (Grand Rapids: Eerdmans, 1982).

—*1 & 2 Thessalonians* (Waco, TX: Word Books, 1982).

—*The Epistles to the Colossians, to Philemon, and to the Ephesians* (Grand Rapids: Eerdmans, 1984).

—*Philippians* (Peabody: Hendrikson, 1989).

Bruston, C., 'Trois lettres des Juifs de Palestine', *ZAW* 10 (1890), pp. 110-117.

Bruyne, D. de, 'Les deux derniers chapitres de la lettre aux Romains', *RBén* 25 (1908), pp. 423-30.

—'La finale marcionite de la lettre aux Romains retrouvée', *RBén* 28 (1911), pp. 133-42.

Buell, M.D., *The Autographs of Saint Paul* (New York: Eaton and Main, 1912).

Bultmann, R., *The Second Letter to the Corinthians* (trans. R.A. Harrisville; Minneapolis: Augsburg, 1976, 1985 [Eng.]).

—*Theology of the New Testament* (trans. K. Grobel; 2 vols.; London: SCM, 1952, 1955).

Burton, E.D., *A Critical and Exegetical Commentary on the Epistle to the Galatians* (Edinburgh: T. & T. Clark, 1921).

Buss, M., 'Principles for Morphological Criticism: with special reference to Letter Form', in *Orientation by Disorientation: Studies in Literary Criticism* (ed. W.A. Beardslee and R.A. Spencer; Pittsburgh: Pickwick Press, 1980), pp. 71-86.

Campbell, J.Y., 'κοινωνία and Its Cognates in the New Testament', *JBL* 51 (1932), pp. 352-80.

Carson, D.A., *From Triumphalism to Maturity: An Exposition of 2 Corinthians 10–13* (Grand Rapids: Baker, 1984).

Carson, H.M., *The Epistles of Paul to the Colossians and Philemon* (Grand Rapids: Eerdmans, 1960).

Cazelles, I.H., 'Formules de politesse en hébreu ancien', *Groupe linguistique d'études chamito-sémitiques, Comptes rendu* 7 (1954–57), pp. 25-26.

Chamberlain, W.D., *An Exegetical Grammar of the Greek New Testament* (New York: Macmillan, 1941).

Champion, L.G., *Benedictions and Doxologies in the Epistles of Paul* (Oxford: Kemp Hall, 1934).

Charlesworth, J.H., 'A Prolegomenon to a New Study of the Jewish Background of the Hymns and Prayers in the New Testament', *JJS* 33 (1982), pp. 265-85.

Chilton, B., 'Galatians 6.15: A Call to Freedom before God', *ExpTim* 89 (1978), pp. 311-13.

Church, F.F., 'Rhetorical Structure and Design in Paul's Letter to Philemon', *HTR* 71 (1978), pp. 17-33.

Clarke, W.K.L., 'St. Paul's "Large Letters"', *ExpTim* 24 (1912–13), p. 285.

Clemens, J.S., 'St. Paul's Handwriting', *ExpTim* 24 (1912–13), p. 380.

Cole, R.A., *Epistle of Paul to the Galatians* (Grand Rapids: Eerdmans, 1965).

Collins, R.F., *Studies on the First Letter to the Thessalonians* (Leuven: Leuven University Press, 1984).

Collins, R.F. (ed.)., *The Thessalonian Correspondence* (Leuven: Leuven University Press, 1990).

Constable, G., *Letters and Letter-Collections* (Turnhout: Brepols, 1976).

Conzelmann, H., *1 Corinthians* (trans. J.W. Leitch; Philadelphia: Fortress, 1975).

Cook, D., 'Stephanus Le Moyne and the Dissection of Philippians', *JTS* 32 (1981), pp. 138-42.

Cook, E., 'The latest on MMT: Strugnell vs. Qimron', *BARev* 20 (1993), pp. 68-69.

Corssen, P., 'Zur Überlieferungsgeschichte des Römerbriefes', *ZNW* 10 (1909), pp. 1-45, 97-102.

Cosgrove, C.H., *The Cross and the Spirit* (Macon, GA: Mercer University Press, 1988).

Cotton, H., *Documentary Letters of Recommendation in Latin from the Roman Empire* (Königstein: Hain, 1981).

—'Greek and Latin Epistolary Formulae: Some Light on Cicero's Letter Writing', *AJP* 105 (1984), pp. 409-425.

Cousar, C.B., *Galatians* (Atlanta: John Knox, 1982).

—'Galatians 6.11-18: Interpretive Clues to the Letter' (unpublished paper at *SBL* Annual Meeting [1989]).

Cowley, A., *Aramaic Papyri of the Fifth Century BC* (Oxford: Clarendon, 1923).

Craddock, F.B., *Philippians* (Atlanta: John Knox, 1985).

Cranfied, C.E.B., *A Critical and Exegetical Commentary on the Epistle to the Romans* (2 vols.; Edinburgh: T. & T. Clark, 1975, 1979).

Cross, F.M. Jr., 'La Lettre de Simeon Ben Kosba', *RB* 63 (1956), pp. 45-48.

Cullmann, O., *Early Christian Worship* (London: SCM, 1953).

Cumming, G.J., 'Service-endings in the Epistles', *NTS* 22 (1976), pp. 110-113.

Dahl, N.A., 'Der Name Israel, I: Zur Auslegung von Gal. 6,16', *Judaica* 6 (1950), pp. 161-70.

—'Paul and the Church at Corinth According to 1 Corinthians 1.10–4:21', in *Christian History and Interpretation: Studies Presented to John Knox* (eds. W.R. Farmer, C.F.D. Moule, and R.R. Niebuhr; Cambridge: Cambridge University Press, 1967), pp. 313-35.

—'Letter', *IDBSup*, pp. 538-41.

—*Studies in Paul* (Minneapolis, MN: Augsberg, 1977).

Dalton, W.J., 'The Integrity of Philippians', *Bib* 60 (1979), pp. 97-102.

Davies, W.D., 'Paul and the People of Israel', *NTS* 24 (1977), pp. 4-39.

—*Paul and Rabbinic Judaism* (London: SPCK, 1955).

Deichgräber, R., *Gotteshymnus und Christushymnus in der frühen Christenheit* (Göttingen: Vandenhoeck & Ruprecht, 1967).

Deissmann, A., *Bible Studies* (trans. A. Grieve; Edinburgh: T. & T. Clark, 1901).

—*Light from the Ancient East* (trans. L.R.M. Strachan; London: Hodder & Stoughton, 1910).

—*Paul: A Study in Social and Religious History* (trans. L.R.M. Strachan; London: Hodder & Stoughton, 1912).

Delling, G., *Worship in the New Testament* (London: Darton, Longman & Todd, 1962).

Denniston, J.D., *The Greek Particles* (Oxford: Clarendon, 1934).

De Passe-Livet, J., 'L'existence chrétienne: participation à la vie trinitaire, 2 Cor 13, 11-13', *AsSeign* 31 (1973), pp. 10-13.

Dewailly, L.M., 'Mystère et silence dans Rom 16:25', *NTS* 14 (1967–68), pp. 111-18.

Dibelius, M., 'Zur Formgeschichte des Neuen Testament (ausserhalb der Evangelien)', *TRu* 3 (1931), pp. 207-42.

—*From Tradition to Gospel* (trans. B L. Wolfe; New York: Charles Scribner's Sons, 1935).

—*A Fresh Approach to the New Testament and Early Christian Literature* (trans. D.S. Noel and G. Abbott; New York: Charles Scribner's Sons, 1936).

—*An die Thessalonicher I, II; an die Philipper* (Tübingen: Mohr, 1937).

—*An die Kolossar, Epheser; an Philemon* (rev. H. Greeven; Tübingen: Mohr, 1953).

Dieter, G., *The Opponents of Paul in Second Corinthians* (Philadelphia: Fortress, 1986).

Dinkler, E., 'Jesu Wort vom Kreuztrage', in *Neutestamentliche Studien für R. Bultmann* (BZNW 21 [1954]), pp. 110-29.

—*Signum Crucis: Aufsätze zum Neuen Testament und zur christlichen Archäologie* (Tübingen: Mohr–Siebeck, 1967).

Dion, P.E., 'La lettre Araméenne passe-partout et ses sous-espèces', *RB* 80–81 (1973–74), pp. 183-95.

—'A Tentative Classification of Aramaic Letter Types', in *SBL Seminar Papers* 11 (Missoula, MT: Scholars, 1977), pp. 415-41.

—'Les types épistolaires hébréo-araméens jusqu'au temps de Bar-Kokhbah', *RB* 86 (1979), pp. 544-79.

—'The Aramaic "Family Letter" and Related Epistolary Forms in other Oriental Languages and in Hellenistic Greek', *Semeia* 22 (1981), pp. 59-76.

Dix, G., *The Shape of the Liturgy* (Glasgow: Glasgow University Press, 1945).

Dobschütz, E. von, *Die Thessalonicherbriefe* (Göttingen: Vandenhoeck & Ruprecht, 1974 [1909]).

—'Zwei- und dreiliedrige Formeln. Ein Beitrag zur Vorgeschichte der Trinitätsformel', *JBL* 50 (1931), pp. 117-47.

Dölger, F.J., *Sphragis: eine altchristliche Taufbezeichnung in ihren Beziehungen zur profanen und religiosen Kultur des Altertums* (Paderborn: Ferdinand Schoningh, 1911).

Donfried, K.P., 'A Short Note on Romans 16', *JBL* 89 (1970), pp. 441-49.

Donfried, K.P. (ed.), *The Romans Debate: Revised and Expanded Edition* (Peabody: Hendrickson, 1991 [1977]).

Doty, W.G., 'The Epistle in Late Hellenism and Early Christianity: Developments, Influences, and Literary Form' (unpublished PhD dissertation, Madison, NJ, Drew University, 1966).

—*Letters in Primitive Christianity* (Philadelphia: Fortress, 1973).

Driver, G.R., *Aramaic Documents of the Fifth Century BC* (Oxford: Clarendon, 1965).

Duncan, G.S., *The Epistle of Paul to the Galatians* (London: Hodder & Stoughton, 1934).

Dunn, J.D.G., *Romans* (2 vols.; Dallas: Word Books, 1988).

Dunphy, W., 'Maranatha: Development in Early Christology', *ITQ* 37 (1970), pp. 294-308.

Dupont, J., 'Pour l'histoire de la doxologie finale de l'épître aux Romains', *RBén* 58 (1948), pp. 3-22.

Ellicott, C.J., *Epistle to the Galatians* (Andover, MA: Draper, 1880).

Elliott, J.K., 'The Language and Style of the Concluding Doxology to the Epistle to the Romans', *ZNW* 72 (1981), pp. 124-30

Elliott, N., *The Rhetoric of Romans* (Sheffield: JSOT Press, 1990).

Ellis, E.E., 'Paul and His Co-Workers', *NTS* 17 (1970-71), pp. 437-52.

—*Prophecy and Hermeneutic in Early Christianity: New Testament Essays* (Grand Rapids: Eerdmans, 1978).

—*Pauline Theology: Ministry and Society* (Grand Rapids: Eerdmans, 1989).

Erbes, K., 'Zeit und Ziel der Grüsse Röm 16,3-25 und der Mitteilungen 2 Tim 4,9-21', *ZNW* 10 (1909), pp. 128-47, 195-218.

Exler, F.X.J., *The Form of the Ancient Greek Letter. A Study in Greek Epistolography* (Washington: Catholic University of America, 1923).

Fabrega, V., 'War Junia(s), der hervorrangende Apostel (Rom. 16,7), eine Frau?', *JAC* 27 (1984), pp. 47-64.

Fallon, F.T., *2 Corinthians* (Wilmington, DE: Michael Glazier, 1980).

Fee, G.D., *The First Epistle to the Corinthians* (Grand Rapids: Eerdmans, 1987).

Fefoulé, F., 'A contre-courant: Romains 16,3-16', *RHPR* 70 (1990), pp. 409-420.

Feine, P., and J. Behm, *Einleitung in das Neue Testament* (Heidelberg: Quelle & Meyer, 1963).

Festugiere, A.-M., 'La trichotomie de 1 Thess v, 23 et la philosophie grecque', *RSR* 20 (1930), pp. 385-415.

Filson, F.V., *'Yesterday': A Study of Hebrews in the Light of Chapter 13* (Naperville, IL: Allenson, 1967).

Fischer, J.A., 'Pauline Literary Forms and Thought Patterns', *CBQ* 39 (1977), pp. 209-223.

Fisher, F., *Commentary on 1 & 2 Corinthians* (Waco, TX: Word Books, 1975).

Fitzmyer, J.A., 'The Padua Aramaic Papyrus Letters', *JNES* 21 (1962), pp. 15-24.

—'The Letter to the Romans', in *The Jerome Biblical Commentary* (ed. R.E. Brown, J.A. Fitzmyer and R.E. Murphy; 2 vols.; Englewood Cliffs, NJ: Prentice–Hall, 1969), pp. 291-331.

—*Essays on the Semitic Background of the New Testament* (London: Chapman, 1971).

—'Some Notes on Aramaic Epistolography', *JBL* 93 (1974), pp. 201-225.

—*A Wandering Aramean: Collected Aramaic Essays* (Missoula, MT: Scholars, 1979).

—'Aramaic Epistolography', *Semeia* 22 (1981), pp. 25-57.

Fitzmyer, J.A., and D.J. Harrington, *A Manual of Palestinian Aramaic Texts* (Rome: Biblical Institute Press, 1978).

Frame, J.E., 'οἱ ἄτακτοι (1 Thess. 5.14)', in *Essays in Modern Theology: A Testimonial to C.A. Briggs* (New York: Charles Scribner's Sons, 1911), pp. 191-206.

—*A Critical and Exegetical Commentary on the Epistle of St Paul to the Thessalonians* (Edinburgh: T. & T. Clark, 1912).

Francis, F.O.,'The Form and Function of the Opening and Closing Paragraphs of James and I John', *ZNW* 61 (1970), pp. 110-26.

Fung, R.Y.K., *Epistle to the Galatians* (Grand Rapids: Eerdmans, 1988).

Funk, R.W., *Language, Hermeneutic, and Word of God* (New York: Harper & Row, 1966).

—'The Apostolic *Parousia*: Form and Significance', in *Christian History and Interpretation: Studies Presented to John Knox* (ed. W.R. Farmer *et al.*; Cambridge: Cambridge University Press, 1967), pp. 249-68.

—'The Form and Function of the Pauline Letter', *SBL Seminar Papers* (Missoula, MT: Scholars, 1970).

Furnish, V.P., 'The Place and Purpose of Phil. III', *NTS* 10 (1962–63), pp. 80-88.

—*II Corinthians* (Garden City, NY: Doubleday, 1984).

Gamble, H. Jr, *The Textual History of the Letter to the Romans* (Grand Rapids: Eerdmans, 1977).

Garland, D.E., 'The Composition and Unity of Philippians: Some Neglected Literary Factors', *NovT* 21 (1974–75), pp. 141-73.

Garlington, D.B., 'The Obedience of Faith in the Letter to the Romans. Part I: The Meaning of ὑπακοὴ πίστεως (Rom. 1.5; 16.26)', *WTJ* 52 (1990), pp. 201-224.

—*'The Obedience of Faith'. A Pauline Phrase in Historical Context* (Tübingen: Mohr–Siebeck, 1991).

George, A.R., *Communion with God in the New Testament* (London: Epworth, 1953).

Gerhard, G.A., *Untersuchungen zur Geschichte des griechischen Briefes*. Pt. 1: *Die Anfangsformel* (Tübingen: Mohr, 1903).

Gibbs, J.M., 'Canon Cumings "Service-Endings in the Epistles": A Rejoinder', *NTS* 24 (1977–78), pp. 545-47.

Gielen, M., 'Zur Interpretation der paulinischen Formel ἡ κατ' οἶκον ἐκκλησία', *ZNW* 77 (1986), pp. 109-125.

Gilliard, F.D., 'More Silent Reading in Antiquity: *Non Omne Verbum Sonabat*', *JBL* 112 (1993), pp. 689-94.

Gnilka, J., *Der Philipperbrief* (Freiburg: Herder, 1980.)

—*Der Philemonbrief* (Freiburg: Herder, 1982).

Goodspeed, E.J., *Problems of New Testament Translation* (Chicago: University of Chicago Press, 1945).

—'Phoebe's Letter of Introduction', *HTR* 44 (1951), pp. 55-57.

Gough, L F., 'Epistolary Literature of the New Testament', *AThB* 6 (1973), pp. 28-40.

Greenwood, D., 'Rhetorical Criticism and Formgeschichte: Some Methodological Considerations', *JBL* 89 (1970), pp. 418-26.

Grosheide, F.W., *The First Epistle to the Corinthians* (Grand Rapids: Eerdmans, 1953).

Guthrie, D., *Galatians* (Grand Rapids: Eerdmans, 1969).

Güttgemanns, E., *Der leidende Apostel und sein Herr: Studien zur paulinischen Christologie* (Göttingen: Vandenhoeck & Ruprecht, 1966).

Hall, R.G., 'The Rhetorical Outline for Galatians: A Reconsideration', *JBL* 106 (1987), pp. 277-87.

Halm, C. (ed.), *Rhetores Latini Minores* (Leipzig: Teubner, 1863).

Hansen, G.W., *Abraham in Galatians* (Sheffield: JSOT Press, 1989).

Hanson, A.T., *The Paradox of the Cross in the Thought of St. Paul* (Sheffield: JSOT Press, 1987).

Harder, G., *Paulus und das Gebet* (Gütersloh: Bertelsmann, 1936.)

Harnack, A. von, 'Das Problem des zweiten Thessalonicherbriefes', *Sitzungsbericht der Preussischen Akademie der Wissenschaft zu Berlin, philosophisch-historischen Classe* 31 (1910), pp. 560-78.

—'Über I Kor. 14,32ff und Röm. 16,25ff nach der ältesten Überlieferung und der marcionitischen Bibel', *Studien zur Geschichte des Neuen Testaments und der Alten Kirche*, I, *Zur neutestamentlichen Textkritik* (Berlin: de Gruyter, 1931), pp. 180-90.

Harris, J.R., 'A Study in Letter Writing', *Expositor* 8 (1898), pp. 161-80.

Harris, M.J., '2 Corinthians', in *The Expositor's Bible Commentary*. Vol. 10 (ed. F.E. Gaebelein; Grand Rapids: Zondervan, 1976), pp. 301-406.

—*Colossians & Philemon* (Grand Rapids: Eerdmans, 1991).

Hauck, F., 'κοινωνία, *TDNT*, III, pp. 797-809.

Hawthorne, G.F., *Philippians* (Waco, TX: Word Books, 1983).

Hays, R.B., *Echoes of Scripture in the Letters of Paul* (New Haven: Yale University Press, 1989).

Hendriksen, W., *I–II Thessalonians* (Grand Rapids: Baker, 1955).

—*Philippians* (Grand Rapids: Baker, 1962).

—*Exposition of Colossians and Philemon* (Grand Rapids: Baker, 1964).

Hengel, M., *Judaism and Hellenism* (trans. J. Bowden; 2 vols.; Philadelphia: Fortress, 1974).

Hercher, R., 'Zu dem griechischen Epistolographen', *Hermes* 4 (1870).

Héring, J., *The Second Epistle of Saint Paul to the Corinthians* (trans. A.W. Heathcote and P.J. Allcock; London: Epworth, 1967).

Hirsch, E., 'Zwei Fragen zu Gal 6', *ZNW* 29 (1930), pp. 192-97.

Hofmann, K. M., *Philema Hagion* (Gütersloh: Bertelsmann, 1938).

Holland, G.S., *The Tradition that You Received from Us: 2 Thessalonians in the Pauline Tradition* (Tübingen: Mohr–Siebeck, 1988).

Holtz, T., *Der erste Brief an die Thessalonicher* (Neukirchen: Neukirchener Verlag, 1986).

Holtzmann, O., *Das Neue Testament nach der Stuttgarter griechischer Text übersetzt und erklärt* (2 vols.; Giessen: Töpelmann, 1926).

—'Zu Emanuel Hirsch, Zwei Fragen zu Gal 6', *ZNW* 30 (1931), pp. 82-83.

Hort, F.J.A., 'On the End of the Epistle to the Romans', in *Biblical Essays* (ed. J.B. Lightfoot; London: Macmillan, 1893), pp. 321-51. (Originally published in *Journal of Philology* 3 [1871], pp. 51-80).

Houlden, J.L., *Paul's Letters from Prison* (Philadelphia: Westminster, 1970).

Hout, M. van den, 'Studies in Early Greek Letter-Writing', *Mnemosyne: Bibliotheca Classica Batava* 4 (1949), pp. 19-41, 138-53.

Huit, C., 'Les Épistolographes Grecs', *Revue des Études Grecques* 2 (1889), pp. 149-63.

Hughes, F.W., 'The Rhetoric of 1 Thessalonians' (unpublished paper, 1986).

—*Early Christian Rhetoric and 2 Thessalonians* (Sheffield: JSOT Press, 1989).

Hurd, J.C. Jr, *The Origin of 1 Corinthians* (Macon, GA: Mercer University Press, 1983 [1965]).

—'Concerning the Structure of 1 Thessalonians' (unpublished paper at *SBL* Annual Meeting, 1972).

—'Thessalonians, Second Letter to the', *IDBSup*, pp. 900-901.

—'Concerning the Authenticity of 2 Thessalonians' (unpublished paper at *SBL* Annual Meeting, 1983).

Hurtado, L.W., 'The Doxology at the End of Romans', in *New Testament Textual*

Criticism: Its Significance for Exegesis: Essays in Honor of Bruce M. Metzger (ed. E.J. Epp and G.D. Fee; Oxford: Clarendon, 1981), pp. 185-99.

Jackson, J.J., and M. Kessler (eds.), *Rhetorical Criticism. Essays in Honor of James Muilenberg* (Pittsburgh: Pickwick, 1974).

Jeremias, J., *Jerusalem zur Zeit Jesu* (2 vols.; Göttingen: Vandenhoeck & Ruprecht, 1958).

Jervis, L.A., *The Purpose of Romans: A Comparative Letter Structure Investigation* (Sheffield: JSOT Press, 1991).

Jewett, R., 'The Form and Function of the Homiletic Benediction', *ATR* 51 (1969), pp. 13-34.

—'The Epistolary Thanksgiving and the Integrity of Philippians', *NovT* 12 (1970), pp. 40-53.

—'The Agitators and the Galatian Congregation', *NTS* 17 (1971), pp. 198-212.

—*Paul's Anthropological Terms* (Leiden: Brill, 1971).

—'Romans as an Ambassadorial Letter', *Int* 36 (1982), pp. 5-20.

—'Following the Argument of Romans', *WW* 6 (1986), pp. 382-89.

—*The Thessalonian Correspondence: Pauline Rhetoric and Millenarian Piety* (Philadelphia: Fortress, 1986).

—'Paul, Phoebe, and the Spanish Mission', in *The Social World of Formative Christianity and Judaism* (ed. J. Neusner, E.S. Frerichs, P. Borgen and R. Horsley; Philadelphia: Fortress, 1988), pp. 142-61.

Johanson, B., *To All the Brethren: A Text-Linguistic and Rhetorical Approach to I Thessalonians* (Stockholm: Almquist & Wiksell, 1987).

Johnston, G., *Ephesians, Philippians, Colossians and Philemon* (London: Nelson, 1967).

Jones, M., 'The Integrity of the Epistle to the Philippians', *Expositor*, Series 8 (1914), pp. 457-73.

Jordan, H., *Geschichte der altchristlichen Literatur* (Leipzig: Quelle & Meyer, 1911).

Kamlah, E., 'Traditionsgeschichtliche Untersuchungen zur Schlussdoxologie des Römerbriefes' (unpublished dissertation, Tübingen University, 1955).

Käsemann, E., *Commentary on Romans* (trans. G.W. Bromiley; Grand Rapids: Eerdmans, 1980).

Kaye, B.N., '"To the Romans and Others" Revisited', *NovT* 18 (1976), pp. 37-77.

Kelly, J.N.D., *A Commentary on the Pastoral Epistles* (Grand Rapids: Eerdmans, 1963).

Kennedy, G.A., *Classical Rhetoric and Its Christian and Secular Tradition from Ancient to Modern Times* (Chapel Hill: University of North Carolina Press, 1980).

—*New Testament Interpretation through Rhetorical Criticism* (Chapel Hill: University of North Carolina Press, 1984).

Kerns, V., 'Letter Writing—St. Paul's Way', *Bible Today* 68 (1973), pp. 1326-28.

Keyes, C.W., 'The Greek Letter of Introduction', *AJP* 56 (1935), pp. 28-44.

Kim, C.-H., *The Familiar Letter of Recommendation* (Missoula, MT: Scholars, 1972).

Kinoshita, J., 'Romans—Two Writings Combined', *NovT* 13 (1964–65), pp. 258-77.

Kistemaker, S.J., *I Corinthians* (Grand Rapids: Baker, 1993).

Kittel, G., 'δόξα', *TDNT*, II, pp. 233-53.

Klassen, W., 'Galatians 6.17', *ExpTim* 81 (1969–70), p. 378.

—'The Sacred Kiss in the New Testament', *NTS* 39 (1993), pp. 122-35.

Klauck, H.-J., *Korintherbrief* (Würzburg: Echter Verlag, 1984).

Klein, G., 'Romans, Letter to the', *IDBSup*, pp. 752-54.

Knox, B.M.W., 'Silent Reading in Antiquity', *GRBS* 9 (1968), pp. 421-35.

Koffmahn, E., *Die Doppelurkunden aus der Wüste Juda* (Leiden: Brill, 1968).

Koskenniemi, H., *Studien zur Idee und Phraseologie des griechischen Briefes bis 400 n. Chr.* (Helsinki: Akateeminen Kirjakauppa, 1956).

Kraeling, C.H., *The Synagogue* (New Haven: Yale University Press, 1956).

Kramer, W., *Christ, Lord, Son of God* (Naperville, IL: Allenson, 1966).

Kreider, E., 'Let the Faithful Greet Each Other: The Kiss of Peace', *Conrad Grebel Review* (Waterloo, Ontario) 5 (1987), pp. 28-49.

Kuhn, K.G., 'μαράναθα', *TDNT*, IV, pp. 466-72.

Kümmel, W.G, *Introduction to the New Testament* (Nashville: Abingdon, 1973).

Kutscher, E.Y., 'New Aramaic Texts', *JAOS* 74 (1954), pp. 233-48.

—'The Language of the Hebrew and Aramaic Letters of Bar-Koseva and his Contemporaries', *Leš* 25 (1960–61), pp. 117-33.

Lake, K., *The Earlier Epistles of St. Paul: Their Motive and Origin* (London: Rivingtons, 1911).

Lampe, P., 'Iunia/Iunias: Sklavenherkunft im Kreise der vorpaulinischen Apostel (Röm 16.7)', *ZNW* 76 (1985), pp. 132-34.

—'Zur Textgeschichte des Römerbriefes', *NovT* 27 (1985), pp. 273-77.

Langevin, P.-É., *Jésus Seigneur et l'eschatologie: exégèse de textes prepauliniens* (Paris: Desclee, 1967).

—'L'intervention de Dieu, selon 1 Thes 5,23-24. Déjà le salut par grâce', *ScEs* 41 (1989), pp. 71-92. Article also published in R.F. Collins (ed.), *The Thessalonian Correspondence* (Leuven: Leuven University, 1990), pp. 236-56.

Lausberg, H., *Handbuch der literarischen Rhetorik* (2 vols.; Munich: Hueber, 1960).

Lehmann, M.R., 'Studies in the Murabba'at and Nahal Hever Documents', *RevQ* 4 (1963–64), pp. 53-81.

Lietzmann, H., *An die Römer* (Tübingen: Mohr, 4th edn, 1933 [1906]).

—'Zwei Notizen zu Paulus', *Kleine Schriften, II, Studien zum Neuen Testament* (ed. K. Aland; Berlin [1910], 1958), pp. 284-91.

—*An die Galater* (Tübingen: Mohr–Siebeck, 1971).

—*The Mass and the Lord's Supper* (trans. D.H.G. Reeve; Leiden: Brill, 1979 [1926]).

Lifshitz, B., 'Papyrus grecs du désert de Juda', *Aeg* 42 (1962), pp. 240-58.

Lightfoot, J.B., *St. Paul's Epistles to the Colossians and to Philemon* (London: Macmillan, 1875).

—*St. Paul's Epistle to the Galatians* (New York: Macmillan, 1890).

—*Notes on the Epistles of St. Paul* (London: Macmillan, 1895).

Lindemann, A.,'Zum Abfassungszweck des Zweiten Thesalonicherbriefes', *ZNW* 68 (1977), pp. 35-47.

Lipsius, R.A., *Briefe an die Galater, Römer, Philipper* (Freiburg: Mohr, 1891).

Lohmeyer, E., *Der Brief an die Philipper* (Göttingen: Vandenhoek & Ruprecht, 1964).

Lohse, E., *Colossians and Philemon* (trans. W.R. Poehlmann and R.J. Karris; Philadelphia: Fortress, 1971).

Longenecker, R.N., 'Ancient Amanuenses and the Pauline Epistles', in *New Dimensions in New Testament Study* (ed. R.N. Longenecker and M.C. Tenney; Grand Rapids: Zondervan, 1974), pp. 281-97.

—'On the Form, Function and Authority of the New Testament Letters', in *Scripture and Truth* (ed. D.A. Carson and J.D. Woodbridge; Grand Rapids: Zondervan, 1983), pp. 101-114.

—*Galatians* (Dallas: Word Books, 1990).

Lönnermark, L.G., 'Till frågan om Romarbrevets integritet', *SEÅ* 33 (1969), pp. 141-48.

Löw, I., 'Der Kuss', *MGWJ* 65 91921), pp. 253-76, 323-49.

Lyons, G., *Pauline Autobiography: Toward a New Understanding* (Atlanta: Scholars Press, 1985).

McCaig, A., 'Thoughts on the Tripartite Theory of Human Nature', *EvQ* 3 (1931), pp. 121-38.

McDermott, M., 'The Biblical Doctrine of κοινωνία', *BZ* 19 (1975), pp. 64-77, 219-33.

McDonald, J.I.H., 'Was Romans XVI a Separate Letter?' *NTS* 16 (1969–70), pp. 369-72.

McGuire, M.R.P, 'Letters and Letter Carriers in Christian Antiquity', *Classical World* 53 (1960), pp. 150-57.

Mack, B.L., *Rhetoric and the New Testament* (Minneapolis: Fortress, 1990).

Malherbe, A.J., *Ancient Epistolary Theorists* (Atlanta: Scholars, 1988). (Originally published as an article under the same title, in *Ohio Journal of Religious Studies* 5 [1977], pp. 3-77.)

Malherbe, A.J. (ed.), *The Cynic Epistles* (Missoula, MT: Scholars, 1977).

Manson, T.W., 'St. Paul's Letter to the Romans—and Others', *BJRL* 31 (1948), pp. 224-45 (reprinted in *The Romans Debate: Revised and Expanded Edition* [ed. K.P. Donfried; repr.; Peabody: Hendrickson, 1991 (1977)], pp. 3-15).

Manus, C.U., 'Amanuensis Hypothesis: A Key to the Understanding of Paul's Epistles in the New Testament', *Biblebhashyam* 10 (1984), pp. 160-74.

Marshall, I.H., *Last Supper and Lord's Supper* (Exeter: Paternoster Press, 1980).

—*1 and 2 Thessalonians* (Grand Rapids: Eerdmans, 1983).

Martin, C.J., 'The Rhetorical Function of Commercial Language in Paul's Letter to Philemon (Verse 18)', in *Persuasive Artistry: Studies in New Testament Rhetoric in Honor of George Kennedy* (ed. D.F. Watson; Sheffield: JSOT Press, 1991), pp. 321-37.

Martin, J., *Antike Rhetorik: Technik und Methode* (Munich: Beck, 1974).

Martin, R.P., *The Epistle of Paul to the Philippians* (Grand Rapids: Eerdmans, 1959).

—*Colossians and Philemon* (Grand Rapids: Eerdmans, 1973).

—*New Testament Foundations* (2 vols.; Grand Rapids: Eerdmans, 1978).

—*Philippians* (Grand Rapids: Eerdmans, 1980).

—*2 Corinthians* (Waco, TX: Word Books, 1986).

Martin, V., *Essai sur les lettres de St. Basil le grand* (Rennes, 1865).

Marty, J., 'Contribution à l'étude de fragments épistolaires antiques, conservés principalement dans la Bible hébraïque: Les formules de salutation', in *Mélanges syriens offerts à Monsieur René Dussaud* (2 vols.; Paris: Geuthner, 1939), II, pp. 845-55.

Martyn, J.L., 'Apocalyptic Antinomies in Paul's Letter to the Galatians', *NTS* 31 (1985), pp. 410-24.

Marxsen, W., *Introduction to the New Testament* (trans. G. Buswell; Philadelphia: Fortress, 1968).

—*Der erste Brief an die Thessalonicher* (Zürich: Theologisher Verlag, 1979).

Masson, C., 'Sur I Thessaloniciens V, 23: Note d'anthropologie paulinienne', *RTP* 33 (1945), pp. 97-102.

Matera, F.J., 'The Culmination of Paul's Argument to the Galatians: Gal. 5.1–6.17', *JSNT* 32 (1988), pp. 79-91.

Mayer, H.T., 'Paul's Advent Doxologies', *CurTM* 9 (1982), pp. 331-43.

Meecham, H.G., *Light from Ancient Letters* (London: George Allen & Unwin, 1923).

Melick, R.R., *Philippians, Colossians, Philemon* (Nashville: Broadman, 1991).

Menzies, A., *The Second Epistle of the Apostle Paul to the Corinthians* (London: Macmillan, 1912).

Meyer, H.A.W., *Kritisch-exegetischer Handbuch über den zweiten Brief an die Korinther* (Göttingen: Vandenhoeck & Ruprecht, 1840).

—*Kritisch-exegetischer Handbuch über den Brief an die Galater* (Göttingen: Vandenhoeck & Ruprecht, 1841).

—*Epistles to the Corinthians* (trans. D.D. Bannerman; London: Funk & Wagnalls, 1890).

Michaelis, W., 'μιμέομαι', *TDNT*, IV, pp. 659-74.

Milik, J.T., 'Une Lettre de Simeon Bar Kokheba', *RB* 60 (1953), pp. 276-94.

—'Le travail d'édition des manuscrits du Désert de Juda', in *Volume du Congrès Internationale pour l'Etude de l'Ancien Testament* (ed. J.A. Emerton *et al.*; VTSup, 4; Leiden: Brill, 1957)., pp. 17-26.

Milligan, G., *St. Paul's Epistles to the Thessalonians* (London: Macmillan, 1908).

—*Selections from the Greek Papyri* (Cambridge: Cambridge University Press, 1912).

Milling, D.H., 'The Origin and Character of the NT Doxology' (PhD dissertation, Cambridge University, 1972).

Minear, P.S., *The Obedience of Faith: The Purposes of Paul in the Epistles to the Romans* (London: SCM, 1971).

—*To Die and To Live: Christ's Resurrection and Christian Vocation* (New York: Seabury, 1977).

—'The Crucified World: The Enigma of Gal. 6.14', in *Theologia Crucis, Signum Crucis: Festschrift für Erich Dinkler* (eds. C. Andresen and G. Klein; Tübingen: Mohr–Siebeck, 1979), pp. 395-407.

Mitchell, M.M., *Paul and the Rhetoric of Reconciliation: An Exegetical Investigation of the Language and Composition of 1 Corinthians* (Tübingen: Mohr–Siebeck, 1992).

—'New Testament Envoys in the Context of Greco-Roman Diplomatic and Epistolary Conventions: The Example of Timothy and Titus', *SBL* 111 (1992), pp. 641-62.

Mitteis, L., *Römisches Privatrecht bis auf die Zeit Diokletians* (2 vols.; Leipzig: Duncker & Humblot, 1908).

Moffatt, J., *Introduction to the Literature of the New Testament* (New York: Charles Scribner's Sons, 1918).

Moo, D., *Romans 1–8* (Chicago: Moody, 1991).

Moore, G.F., *Judaism in the First Centuries of the Christian Era* (3 vols.; Cambridge, MA: Harvard University Press, 1946).

Morris, L., *The First Epistle of Paul to the Corinthians* (Grand Rapids: Eerdmans, 1958).

—*The First and Second Epistles to the Thessalonians* (Grand Rapids: Eerdmans, 1959).

—*The Epistle to the Romans* (Grand Rapids: Eerdmans, 1988).

Morton, A.Q., and J. McLeman, *Paul: The Man and the Myth* (New York: Harper & Row, 1966).

Moule, C.F.D., 'A Reconsideration of the Context of "Maranatha"', *NTS* 8 (1959–60), pp. 307-310.

—*Worship in the New Testament* (London: Lutterworth, 1961).

—*The Epistle of Paul the Apostle to the Colossians and to Philemon* (Cambridge: Cambridge University Press, 1962).

Moulton, J.H., 'The Marks of Jesus', *ExpTim* 21 (1909–10), pp. 283-84.

Muilenburg, J., 'Form Criticism and Beyond', *JBL* 88 (1969), pp. 1-18.

Müller, J.J., *The Epistles of Paul to the Philippians and to Philemon* (Grand Rapids: Eerdmans, 1955).

Muller, P., 'Grundlinien paulinischer Theologie (Rom 15,14-33)', *KD* 35 (1989), pp. 212-35.

Müller-Bardorff, J., 'Zur Frage der literarischen Einheit des Philipperbriefes', *Wissenchaftliche Zeitschrift der Universität Jena* 7 (1957–58), pp. 591-604.

Mullins, T.Y., 'Greeting as a New Testament Form', *JBL* 88 (1968), pp. 418-26.

—'Formulas in New Testament Epistles', *JBL* 91 (1972), pp. 380-90.

—'Visit Talk in New Testament Letters', *CBQ* 35 (1973), pp. 350-58.

—'Benediction as a New Testament Form', *AUSS* 15 (1977), pp. 59-64.

Munro, W., 'Interpolation in the Epistles: Weighing Probability', *NTS* 36 (1990), pp. 431-43.

Murray, J., *The Epistle to the Romans* (Grand Rapids: Eerdmans, 1968).

Mussner, F., *Der Galaterbrief* (Freiberg: Herder, 1974).

Neil, W., *The Epistle of Paul to the Thessalonians* (London: Hodder & Stoughton, 1950).

Neumann, K.J., *The Authenticity of the Pauline Epistles in the Light of Stylostatistical Analysis* (Atlanta: Scholars, 1990).

Nijenhuis, J., 'This Greeting in My Own Hand—Paul', *Bible Today* 19 (1981), pp. 255-58.

Oates, J.F., R.S. Bagnall and W.H. Willis, *Checklist of Editions of Greek Papyri and Ostraca* (Bulletin of the American Society of Papyrologists, Suppl. 1; Missoula, MT: Scholars, 2nd edn, 1978).

O'Brien, P.T., *Introductory Thanksgivings in the Letters of Paul* (Leiden: Brill, 1977).

—'The Fellowship Theme in Philippians', *RTR* 37 (1978), pp. 9-18.

—*Colossians, Philemon* (Waco, TX: Word Books, 1982).

—*The Epistle to the Philippians* (Grand Rapids: Eerdmans, 1991).

Oepke, A., 'κρύπτω', *TDNT*, III, pp. 957-1000.

Olson, S.N., 'Confidence Expressions in Paul: Epistolary Conventions and the Purpose of 2 Corinthians' (PhD dissertation, Yale University, 1976).

—'Epistolary Uses of Expressions of Self-Confidence', *JBL* 103 (1984), pp. 585-97.

—'Pauline Expressions of Confidence in His Addressees', *CBQ* 47 (1985), pp. 282-95.

Olsson B., *Papyrusbriefe aus der Frühesten Römerzeit* (Uppsala: Almqvist & Wiksells, 1925).

O'Neill, J.C., *The Recovery of Paul's Letter to the Galatians* (London: SPCK, 1972).

Pack, R.A., *The Greek and Latin Literary Texts from Greco-Roman Egypt* (Ann Arbor: University of Michigan Press, 1965).

Panikulam, G., *Koinonia in the New Testament* (Rome: Pontifical Biblical Institute, 1979).

Pardee, D., 'An Overview of Ancient Hebrew Epistolography', *JBL* 97 (1978), pp. 321-46.

—*Handbook of Ancient Hebrew Letters* (Missoula, MT: Scholars, 1982).

Parke-Taylor, G.H., 'A Note on εἰς ὑπακοὴν πίστεως in Romans i.5 and xvi.26', *ExpTim* 55 (1943–44), p. 306.

Parkin, V., 'Some Comments on the Pauline Prescripts', *IBS* 8 (1986), pp. 92-99.

Parry, R.St.J., *The Epistle of Paul the Apostle to the Romans* (Cambridge: Cambridge University Press, 1912).

Pease, E.M., 'The Greeting in the Letters of Cicero', in *Studies in Honor of Basil L. Gildersleeve* (Baltimore: The Johns Hopkins University Press, 1902), pp. 395-404.

Peifer, C.J., 'Three Letters in One', *BT* 23 (1985), pp. 363-68.

Perella, N.J., *The Kiss: Sacred and Profane* (Berkeley: University of California Press, 1969).

Perelmuter, H.G., 'Can the Letters of Paul be Read in the Jewish Responsa Mode?' (unpublished paper at SBL/AAR Annual Meeting [1991]).

Perry, A.M., 'Epistolary Form in Paul', *Crozier Quarterly* 26 (1944), pp. 48-53.

Peterman, G.W., '"Thankless Thanks": The Epistolary Social Convention in Philippians 4.10-20', *TynBul* 42 (1991), pp. 261-70.

Petersen, N.R., *Rediscovering Paul: Philemon and the Sociology of Paul's Narrative World* (Philadelphia: Fortress, 1985).

Peterson, R.J., *The Structure and Purpose of Second Thesslonians* (PhD dissertation, Harvard University, 1967).

Picirilli, R.E., *1, 2 Corinthians* (Nashville: Randall House, 1987).

Plummer, A., *Second Epistle of St. Paul to the Corinthians* (New York: Charles Scribner's Sons, 1915).

Pobee, J.S., *Persecution and Martyrdom in the Theology of Paul* (Sheffield: JSOT Press, 1985).

Pollard, T.E., 'The Integrity of Philippians', *NTS* 13 (1966–67), pp. 57-66.

Pool, D. de Sola, *The Kaddish* (New York: Bloch, 1929).

Preaux, C., 'Quelques caractères des lettres privées grecques d'Egypte', *Chronique d'Egypte* 7 (1928), pp. 144-55.

Preisigke, F., *Wörterbuch der griechischen Papyrusurkunden* (ed. E. Kiessling; Berlin: Grete Preisigke, 1925), I.

Prior, M., *Paul the Letter-Writer and the Second Letter to Timothy* (Sheffield: JSOT Press, 1989).

Probst, H., *Paulus und der Brief: Die Rhetorik des antiken Briefes als Form der paulinischen Korintherkorrespondenz (1 Kor 8–10)* (Tübingen: Mohr–Siebeck, 1991).

Prümm, K., *Diakonia Pneumatos: Der 2 Korintherbrief als Zugang zur apostolischen Botschaft* (2 vols.; Freiburg: Herder, 1960–67).

Qimron, E., and J. Strugnell., 'An Unpublished Halakhic Letter from Qumran', in *Biblical Archaeology Today. Proceedings of the International Congress on Biblical Archaeology, April 1984, Jerusalem* (Jerusalem: Israel Exploration Society, 1985), pp. 400-407.

Rabinowitz, I., 'A Hebrew Letter of the Second Century from Beth Mashko', *BASOR* 131 (1953), pp. 21-24.

Rahtjen, B.D., 'The Three Letters of Paul to the Philippians', *NTS* 6 (1959–60), pp. 167-73.

Reese, J.M., *1 and 2 Thessalonians* (Wilmington, DE: Michael Glazier, 1979).

Rengstorf, K.H., 'σημεῖον', *TDNT*, VII, pp. 200-261.

Richards, E.R., *The Secretary in the Letters of Paul* (Tübingen: Mohr–Siebeck, 1991).

Richardson, C.C., *Early Christian Fathers* (Philadelphia: Westminster, 1953).

Richardson, P., *Israel in the Apostolic Church* (Cambridge: Cambridge University Press, 1969).

—'From Apostles to Virgins: Romans 16 and the Roles of Women in the Early Church', *TJT* 2 (1986), pp. 232-61.

Rigaux, B., *Saint Paul: Les Épîtres aux Thessaloniciens* (Paris: Gabalda, 1956).

—*Letters of St. Paul* (trans. C. Ynoick; New York: Herder & Herder, 1968).

Robbins, V.K. and J.H. Patton, 'Rhetorical and Biblical Criticism', *Quarterly Journal of Speech* 66 (1980), pp. 327-50.

Roberts, W., *The History of Letter-Writing from the Earliest Period to the Fifth Century* (London: Pickering, 1853).

Robertson, A., and A. Plummer, *A Critical and Exegetical Commentary on the First Epistle of St. Paul to the Corinthians* (New York: Charles Scribner's Sons, 1911).

Roberston, A.T., *A Grammar of the Greek New Testament in the Light of Historical Research* (New York: Hodder & Stoughton, 1919).

Robinson, D.W.B., 'Distinction between Jewish and Gentile Believers in Galatians', *AusBR* 13 (1965), pp. 29-44.

Robinson, J.A.T., 'Traces of a Liturgical Sequence in 1 Cor. 16.20-24', *JTS* 4 (1953), pp. 38-41.

—*Wrestling with Romans* (London: SCM, 1979).

Roetzel, C.J., 'I Thess. 5.12-28: A Case Study', *SBL Seminar Papers*, 2 (ed. L.C. McGaughy; Missoula, MT: Scholars, 1972), pp. 367-83.

—*The Letters of Paul: Conversations in Context* (Atlanta: John Knox, 1975.)

Roller, O., *Das Formular der Paulinischen Briefe: Ein Beitrag zur Lehre vom antiken Briefe* (Stuttgart: Kohlhammer, 1933).

Russell, R., 'Pauline Letter Structure in Philippians', *JETS* 25 (1982), pp. 295-306.

Sanday, W., and A.C. Headlam, *A Critical and Exegetical Commentary on the Epistle of the Romans* (New York: Charles Scribner's Sons, 1897).

Sasse, H., 'αἰών', *TDNT*, I, pp. 197-208.

Schelkle, K.H., *The Epistle to the Romans* (Freiburg: Herder & Herder, 1964).

Schlier, H., 'ἀμήν', *TDNT*, I, pp. 335-38.

—*Der Brief an die Galater* (Göttingen: Vandenhoeck & Ruprecht, 1951).

Schmidt, H.W., *Der Brief des Paulus an die Römer* (Berlin: Evangelische Verlagsanstalt, 1972).

Schmidt, J.E.C., 'Vermuthungen über die beiden Briefe an die Thessalonicher', in *Bibliothek für Kritik und Exegese des Neuen Testaments und ältesten Christengeschichte* 2.3 (Hadamar: Gelehrtenbuchhandlung, 1801), pp. 380-86.

Schmidt, N., 'Maranatha: 1 Cor. xvi.22', *JBL* 13 (1894), pp. 50-60.

Schmithals, W., *Der Römerbrief* (Gütersloh: Mohn, 1988).

Schneider, B., 'HE KOINONIA TOU HAGIOU PNEUMATOS (II Cor. 13,13)', in *Studies Honoring Ignatius Charles Brady, Friar Minor* (ed. R.S. Almagno and C.L. Harkins; St. Bonaventure, NY: Franciscan Institute, 1976), pp. 421-47.

Schneider, N., *Die rhetorische Eigenart der paulinischen Antithese* (Tübingen: Mohr–Siebeck, 1970).

Schnider, F., and W. Stenger, *Studien zum Neutestamentlichen Briefformular* (Leiden: Brill, 1987).

Schrenk, G., 'Was bedeutet "Israel Gottes?"', *Judaica* 5 (1949), pp. 81-94.

—'Der Segenwunsch nach der Kampfepistel', *Judaica* 6 (1950), pp. 170-90.

Schubert, P., *Form and Function of the Pauline Thanksgivings* (Berlin: Töpelmann, 1939).

—'The Form and Function of the Pauline Letters', *JR* 19 (1939), pp. 367-89.

Schulz, D., *TSK* 2 (1829), pp. 609ff.

Schulz, R., 'Romans 16.7: Junia or Junias?' *ExpTim* 98 (1986–87), pp. 108-110.

Schulz, S., 'Maranatha and Kyrios Jesus', *ZNW* 53 (1962), pp. 125-44.

Schürer, E., *The History of the Jewish People in the Age of Christ* (ed. G. Vermes, *et al.*; 4 vols.; Edinburgh: T. & T. Clark, 1979).

Schürmann, H., and H.A. Egenhelf, *The Two Epistles to the Thessalonians* (London: Sheed and Ward, 1981).

Schweizer, E., 'πνεῦμα', *TDNT*, VI, pp. 332-455.

—'Zur Trichotomie von 1 Thess 5,23 und der Unterscheidung des *pneumatikon* vom *psuxichon* in 1 Kor 2.14, 15, 44; Jak 3.15; Jud 19', *TZ* 9 (1953), pp. 76-77.

Scott, E.F., *Paul's Epistle to the Romans* (London: SCM Press, 1947).

Seeburg, R., *Aus Religion und Geschichte* (Leipzig: Deichert, 1906).

Seesemann, H., *Der Begriff KOINONIA im Neuen Testament* (Giessen: Töpelmann, 1933).

Silva, M., *Philippians* (Chicago: Moody, 1988).

Simon, W.G.H., *The First Epistle to the Corinthians* (London: SCM Press, 1959).

Slusser, M., 'Reading Silently in Antiquity', *JBL* 111 (1992), p. 499.

Smiga, G. 'Romans 12.1-2 and 15.30-32 and the Occasion of the Letter to the Romans', *CBQ* 53 (1991), pp. 257-73.

Smit, J., 'The Letter of Paul to the Galatians: A Deliberative Speech', *NTS* 35 (1989), pp. 1-26.

Spicq, C., 'Les Thesaloniciens "inquiètes" étaient ils des paresseux?' *ST* 10 (1956), pp. 1-13.

—*Notes de Lexicographie Néo-testamentaire* (3 vols.; Göttingen: Vandenhoeck & Ruprecht, 1978).

Srawley, J.H., *The Early History of the Liturgy* (Cambridge: Cambridge University Press, 1947).

Stählin, G., 'φιλήμα ἅγιον', *TDNT*, IX, pp. 138-41.

—'φιλέω', *TDNT*, IX, pp. 113-46.

Stecker, A., *Form und Formeln in den paulinischen Hauptbriefen und in den Pastoralbriefen* (PhD dissertation, Munster, 1968).

Steen, H.A., 'Les Clichés épistolaries dans les lettres sur Papyrus Grecques', *Classica et Mediaevalia*, 1, 2 (1938), pp. 119-76.

Stempvoort, P.A. van, 'Eine stilistische Lösung einer alten Schwierigkeit in I Thess. v. 23', *NTS* 7 (1960–61), pp. 262-65.

Stirewalt, M.L., 'Paul's Evaluation of Letter-Writing', in *Search the Scriptures* (ed. J.M. Myers *et al.*; Leiden: Brill, 1969), pp. 179-96.

—'A Classifed Index of Terms used in reference to Letter-Writing in Greek Literature' (unpublished article, 1975).

—'The Form and Function of the Greek Letter-Essay', in *The Romans Debate: Revised and Expanded Edition* (ed. K.P. Donfried; Peabody: Hendrickson, 1991 [1977]), pp. 147-71.

256   *Neglected Endings*

—'A Survey of the Uses of Letter-Writing in Hellenistic and Jewish Communities through the New Testament Period' (unpublished article).

Stowers, S.K., *The Diatribe and Paul's Letter to the Romans* (Chico, CA: Scholars, 1981).

—*Letter Writing in Greco-Roman Antiquity* (Philadelphia: Westminster, 1986).

Stuhlmacher, P., 'Erwägungen zum ontologischen Charakter der καινὴ κτίσις', *EvT* 27 (1967), pp. 1-35.

—*Der Brief an Philemon* (Zürich: Benziger, 1975).

Stuiber, A., 'Doxology', *RAC* 4 (1959), p. 215.

Suggs, M.J., '"The Word is Near You": Romans 10.6-10 Within the Purpose of the Letter', in *Christian History and Interpretation: Studies Presented to John Knox* (ed. W.R. Farmer *et al.*; Cambridge: Cambridge University Press, 1967), pp. 289-312.

Suhl, A., *Der Brief an Philemon* (Zürich: Theologischer Verlag, 1987).

Swift, R.C., 'The Theme and Structure of Philippians', *BSac* 141 (1984), pp. 234-54.

Sykutris, J., 'Epistolographie', in *Realencyclopädie der klassischen Altertumswissenschaft*, Supplement 5 (ed. A. Pauly, G. Wissowa and W. Kroll [1931]), pp. 186-220.

Taatz, I., *Frühjüdische Brief: Die paulinischen Briefe im Rahmen der offiziellen religiösem Briefe des Frühjudentums* (Göttingen: Vandenhoeck & Ruprecht, 1991).

Tcherikover, V.A., A. Fuks and M. Stern, *Corpus Papyrorum Judaicarum* (3 vols.; Cambridge, MA: Harvard University Press, 1957–64).

Thraede, K., 'Ursprünge und Formen des "Heiligen Kusses" im frühen Christentum', *JAC* 11/12 (1968–69), pp. 124-80.

—*Grundzüge griechisch-römischer Brieftopik* (Munich: Beck, 1970).

Thrall, M.E., *Greek Particles in the New Testament* (Leiden: Brill, 1962).

Toit, A.B. du, 'Persuasion in Romans 1.1-17', *BZ* 13 (1989), pp. 192-209.

Torrey, C.C., 'The Letters prefixed to II Macc.', *JAOS* 60 (1940), pp. 120-50.

Trilling, W., *Untersuchungen zum zweiten Thessalonicherbrief* (Leipzig: St. Benno, 1972).

—*Der zweite Brief an die Thessalonicher* (Neukirchen: Neukirchener Verlag, 1980).

Turner, E.G., *Greek Papyri. An Introduction* (Princeton: Princeton University Press, 1968).

—*Greek Manuscripts of the Ancient World* (Princeton: Princeton University Press, 1971).

Turner, N., *A Grammar of the New Testament* (3 vols.; Edinburgh: T. & T. Clark, 1963).

—*Grammatical Insights into the New Testament* (Edinburgh: T. & T. Clark, 1965).

Unnik, W.C. van, '"Dominus Vobiscum": The Background of a Liturgical Formula', in *New Testament Essays in Memory of T.W. Manson* (ed. A.J. Higgins; Manchester: Manchester University Press, 1959), pp. 270-305.

Van Elderen, B., 'The Verb in the Epistolary Invocation', *CTJ* 2 (1967) pp. 46-48.

Vielhauer, P., *Geschichte der urchristlichen Literatur* (Berlin: de Gruyter, 1975).

Vincent, M.R., *A Critical and Exegetical Commentary on the Epistles to the Philippians and to Philemon* (Edinburgh: T. & T. Clark, 1897).

Volterra, E., 'Intorno a AP. 131 in. 17–18', *Mélanges Eugene Tisserant*, vol. 1: *Ecriture sainte—Ancien Orient* (Città del Vaticano: Biblioteca apostolica vaticana, 1964), pp. 443-48.

Walkenhorst, K.-H., 'The Concluding Doxology of the Letter to the Romans and its Theology' [in Japanese], *Katorikku Kenkyu* [Tokyo] 27 (1988), pp. 99-132.

Wanamaker, C.A., *The Epistles to the Thessalonians* (Grand Rapids: Eerdmans, 1990).

Watson, D.F., *Invention, Arrangement, and Style: Rhetorical Criticism of Jude and 2 Peter* (Atlanta: Scholars, 1988).

Wedderburn, A.J.M., *The Reasons for Romans* (Minneapolis: Fortress, 1988).

Weima, J.A.D., 'Gal. 6.11-18: A Hermeneutical Key to the Galatian Letter', *CTJ* 28 (1993), pp. 90-107.

—'Preaching the Gospel in Rome: A Study of the Epistolary Framework of Romans', in *Gospel in Paul: Studies on Corinthians, Galatians and Romans for Richard N. Longenecker* (ed. L.A. Jervis and P. Richardson; Sheffield: JSOT Press, 1994).

Welles, C.B., *Royal Correspondence in the Hellenistic Period* (New Haven: Yale University Press, 1934).

Wendland, H.D., *Die Briefe an die Korinther* (Göttingen: Vandenhoeck & Ruprecht, 1964).

Wendland, P., 'Die urchristlichen Literaturformen', in *HNT* 1: Teil 3, pp. 191-357.

Westermann, A., *De epistularum scriptoribus Graecis I–VIII. Progr.* (Lipsiae: Staritz, 1851–1854).

Whelan, C.F., 'Amica Pauli: The Role of Phoebe in the Early Church', *JSNT* 49 (1993), pp. 67-85.

White, J.L., 'The Structural Analysis of Philemon: A Point of Departure in the Formal Analysis of the Pauline Letter', in *SBL Seminar Papers*, 1 (Missoula, MT: Scholars, 1971), pp. 1-47.

—'Introductory Formulae in the Body of the Pauline Letter', *JBL* 90 (1971), pp. 91-97.

—*The Body of the Greek Letter* (Missoula, MT: Scholars, 1972).

—*The Form and Structure of the Official Petition* (Missoula, MT: Scholars, 1972).

—'Epistolary Formulas and Clichés in Greek Papyrus Letters', in *SBL Seminar Papers*, 2 (Missoula, MT: Scholars, 1978), pp. 289-319.

—'The Ancient Epistolography Group in Retrospect', *Semeia* 22 (1981), pp. 1-14.

—'The Greek Documentary Letter Tradition: Third Century BCE to Third Century CE', *Semeia* 22 (1981), pp. 89-106.

—'Studies in Ancient Letter Writing', *Semeia* 22 (1981).

—'Saint Paul and the Apostolic Letter Tradition', *CBQ* 45 (1983), pp. 433-44.

—'New Testament Epistolary Literature in the Framework of Ancient Epistolography', *Aufstieg und Niedergang der römischen Welt*, II, 25.2 (Berlin: de Gruyter, 1984), pp. 1730-56.

—*Light from Ancient Letters* (Philadelphia: Fortress, 1986).

—'Ancient Greek Letters', in *Greco-Roman Literature and the New Testament* (ed. D.E. Aune; Atlanta: Scholars, 1988), pp. 85-105.

White, J.L., and K. Kensinger, 'Categories of Greek Papyrus Letters', in *SBL Seminar Papers* (ed. G. MacRae; Missoula, MT: Scholars, 1976), pp. 79-92.

Whitehead, J.D., 'Handbook of Early Aramaic Letters: Preliminary Presentation' (unpublished work copied by SBL for 1975 Annual Meeting).

Whiteley, D.E.H., *Thessalonians in the Revised Standard Version, With Introduction and Commentary* (Oxford: Oxford University Press, 1969).

Wickert, U., 'Der Philemonbrief—Privatbrief oder apostolisches Schreiben?', *ZNW* 52 (1961), pp. 230-38.

Wilckens, U., 'Zu den syrischen Göttern', in *Festgabe für Adolf Deissmann zum 60. Geburtstag* (Tübingen: Mohr, 1927), pp. 1-19.

Wilder, A., *Early Christian Rhetoric: The Language of the Bible* (Cambridge, MA: Harvard University Press, 1971).

Wiles, G.P., *Paul's Intercessory Prayers* (Cambridge, MA: Cambridge University Press, 1974).

Williams, A.L., *The Epistle of Paul the Apostle to the Galatians* (Cambridge: Cambridge University Press, 1910).

Windisch, H., *Der zweite Korintherbrief* (Göttingen: Vandenhoeck & Ruprecht, 1924).

—'ἀσπάζομαι', *TDNT*, I, pp. 496-502.

Winter, J.G., 'In the Service of Rome: Letters from the Michigan Collection of Papyri', *Classical Philology* 22 (1927), pp. 237-56.

—*Life and Letters in the Papyri* (Ann Arbor: University of Michigan Press, 1933).

Wrede, W., *Die Echtheit des zweiten Thessalonicherbriefes* (Leipzig: Hinrichs, 1903).

Wright, N.T., *Colossians and Philemon* (Grand Rapids: Eerdmans, 1986).

Wuellner, W., 'Greek Rhetoric and Pauline Argumentation', in *Early Christian Literature and the Classical Intellectual Tradition in Honorem Robert M. Grant* (ed. W.R. Schoedel and R.L. Wilken; Paris: Editions Beauchesne, 1979), pp. 177-88.

—'Where is Rhetorical Criticism Taking Us?', *CBQ* 49 (1987), pp. 448-63.

Wünsche, A., *Der Kuss in Bibel, Talmud, und Midrasch* (Breslau: Marcus, 1911).

Yadin, Y., 'Expedition D', *IEJ* 11 (1961), pp. 36-52.

—'More Light on the Letters of Bar Cocheba', *BA* 24 (1961), pp. 86-95.

—'The Excavation of Masada—1963/64, Preliminary Report', *IEJ* 15 (1965), pp. 105-114.

—*Bar-Kokhba* (New York: Random House, 1971).

Zahn, T.B., *Introduction to the New Testament* (3 vols.; Edinburgh: T. & T. Clark, 1909).

Ziemann, F., *De Epistularum Graecarum Formulis Sollemnibus Quaestiones Selectae* (Berlin: Haas, 1912).

Zmijewski, J., 'Beobachtungen zur Struktur des Philemonbriefes', *BibLeb* 15 (1974), pp. 277-94.

Zuntz, G., *The Text of the Epistles: A Disquisition Upon the Corpus Paulinum* (London: Oxford University Press, 1953).

INDEXES

INDEX OF REFERENCES

INDEX OF AUTHORS